CORRELATION OF FORCES

Julian Lider

This book provides a comprehensive analysis of the Marxist-Leninist, and in particular Soviet, concept of the correlation of world forces. With the traditional concept of the global balance of power, commonly used in the West, this has become one of the basic terms in contemporary political and military analyses and also in diplomatic discussion.

The concept of the correlation of world forces has deep roots in Marxist-Leninist theory and these roots are analysed in the first part of the book. This is followed by an analysis of the political dimension of the correlation, including all forms of social struggle, both in the domestic and international setting.

The second part of the book examines the basic category of the correlation of world forces and compares it with the concept of the world balance of power. The study concludes with a detailed analysis of the correlation of military forces, and its role as a component of the correlation of world forces.

CORRELATION OF FORCES

Correlation of Forces

An Analysis of Marxist-Leninist Concepts

JULIAN LIDER

St. Martin's Press   New York

First published in the United States of America in 1986.

Library of Congress Cataloging-in-Publication Data

Lider, Julian.
    Correlation of Forces.

    Bibliography: p.
    Includes indexes.
    1. Power (Social sciences)   2. International relations.
    3. Politics and war.   I. Title.
    JC330.L53   1986   303.3'3   85—27841

ISBN 0—312-17004—1

Printed in Great Britain by Blackmore Press, Shaftesbury, Dorset

Contents

PART III   CORRELATION OF WORLD FORCES

PART IV   MILITARY DIMENSION

Acknowledgements

I am indebted to Margaretha Dufwa, Ingrid Gustafson and Lars Rönnberg who carefully prepared the manuscript for publication. Thanks go to Atis Lejins who helped gather material for my research.

To Janka

1 Introduction

Concept

The Soviet concept of the *correlation of world forces* or the world correlation of forces *(sootnoshenie sil v mire)* has become one of the basic terms in contemporary political and military analyses as well as in diplomatic intercourse, together with the traditional concept of the global balance of power which is commonly used in the West.

In Marxist-Leninist theory, the concept of the correlation of world forces has, in actual fact and sometimes even *expressis verbis*, acquired the status of a category, which in this theory includes the general features, aspects and relationships of a field of social activities. The career made by the concept of the correlation of world forces has given the incentive for an intensification of the Marxist-Leninist analysis of three concepts: the correlation of *socio-economic* forces, the correlation of *political* forces and the correlation of *military* forces.

Since the category of the correlation of world forces is used to mean a correlation of all the socio-economic, political and military forces of the two antagonistic world-wide camps, the content of this category may be regarded as a synthesis of the three above-mentioned concepts.

The concept of the correlation of *socio-economic* forces may be used to analyse processes in which social groups interact as components of national societies. In Marxist-Leninist theory the basic social groups are classes; the interaction between them primarily occurs in, and affects, the socio-economic interests of the classes in question. It is

1

reflected in the establishment of, and changes in, the class structure of society.

The concept of the correlation of *political* forces is based on two assumptions about the protagonists and their activities. In the first place, politics, in the sense of the activities undertaken by a social group (or a social institution) to promote its basic interests in the domestic or the international sphere, is the highest form of the inter-action of social groups. It includes and subordinates all other forms of interaction. In the domestic sphere, the principal goal — and at the same time the method — of securing all the group's interests, including the economic ones, is the seizure (or the maintenance) of state autho-rity. In the international sphere the main goal is to gain more influence on other states — again in order to secure the basic interests of the governing group (class) and to strengthen the political and strategic power of the state. The efforts to spread the ruling ideology of the country also play an essential role. All the fronts on which a social group or class fights for its interests — economic, ideological, and if need be, military — are subordinated to the aims and strategy of the political struggle.

As regards the protagonists in the domestic sphere, the correlation of political forces is used in the analysis of the interaction of *political entities*, whether these be classes organised politically under the leader-ship of political parties, some of which may use the state apparatus to achieve their political goals or, in practice, political coalitions under the heading of the so-called antagonistic classes. In the international sphere, the political entities in question are usually nation-states or alliances of states.

The use of the third concept — that of the correlation of *military* forces — in science and political intercourse springs from the fact that *armed violence* is the mainstay of the sociopolitical rule and state power, and it is the means of last resort in the interaction of the social forces and institutions in a society, when they aim at radical changes or oppose such changes.

It is also the means of last resort in interstate relations, and this use of armed violence has always been in the focus of political intercourse and scientific analysis. The correlation of military forces is that between *military organisations* — armed forces, or more broadly, between the military forces of states, coalition of states and classes — provided that they possess armies.

One may comment that the distinction between the three above-mentioned concepts is an arbitrary one. In Marxist-Leninist theory all political actions are social ones, and all military actions have political aims. However, the distinction between the three kinds of correlation connected with the distinction in the spheres of interaction of the competing forces may help in the analysis of the immense variety of social (and particularly socio-economic), political and military events, various kinds of conflicts and of methods used in resolving them, in both the domestic and the international spheres.

The correlation of social forces, in all the above-mentioned variations, seems to fulfil the criteria of the socio-political category as this is defined in Marxist-Leninist theory (cf. Chapter 3). It is regarded by the Marxist-Leninists as reflecting and expressing the main motive force of the entire social development — i.e., the class struggle — and as the main factor in the political struggle in the domestic and the international spheres. Moreover, it constitutes one of the determining factors in war, i.e., in the extreme form of the domestic class and interstate struggle. Thus it seems that the concept of the correlation of forces may be regarded as an intermediate category between the categories which are characteristic of individual sciences and those which are most broadly philosophical: it may be applicable to social development, to domestic and international politics and to military affairs.

It may be suggested that the correlation of social forces is a feature of the Marxist-Leninist *paradigm* of the social system, in both the national and the international communities, which differs from all non-Marxist models of the social systems (cf. Chapter 3).

In the Marxist-Leninist research the definition of the category of the correlation of social forces was implied rather than expressed. It was only occasionally discussed, yet it was always an issue inherent in the theory of social development. The renewal of research work has been connected with the interest in the correlation of world forces, which became first an instrument of political struggle and then required a theoretical justification. This renewed interest has been extended to all dimensions and all variations of the correlation of social forces. Soviet writers have been going through the abundant literature on ideological, sociological and international relations in order to reconstruct and systematise and make generalisations concerning the correlation of forces.

The wish to demonstrate the multi-dimensional character of the correlation of world forces as contrasted with the traditional — and in the Marxist-Leninist view one-sided — concept of balance of power also motivated the multi-directional research.

Organisation of this study

This study is devoted to the Marxist-Leninist category of the correlation of social forces in its variations. Unlike the theory of the balance of power, which is an aggregate term for several theories with different approaches, scopes and definitions of the subject, there exists *one* definite Soviet version of the Marxist-Leninist approach which is approved by the leadership and used in the establishment and the implementation of foreign and domestic policies. The different wordings in various declarations, discussions and comments apply to developments and changes within a single approach. They may also represent various tendencies in the Soviet leadership as regards foreign and domestic policies. However, there seems to be a common basic interpretation of the category in question. This is the concept investigated in this study.

In spite of the ever-extending range of the issues analysed, and in spite of their growing importance in the Soviet theory and practice, the subject as a whole has not yet been analysed in a systematic way. There exists only a loose aggregate of disparate descriptions of single issues, of which the commonest are general descriptions of the correlation of world forces.

Three approaches to the organisation of the analysis are conceivable and in my studies of these problems I have tried to use each of them in turn.

The first approach would be to *focus* on the concept (category) of the *correlation of world forces.* The socio-economic, political and military dimensions of this, in both the domestic and the international contexts, would be treated as aspects of the synthetic category and discussed more or less thoroughly according to the position which they have acquired in Marxist-Leninist theory. (This was my first attempt, as reflected in a brief essay which was published in two versions.)[1]

However, such an approach may hinder a more thorough investigation of all the above-mentioned dimensions (or partial correlations) and, moreover, the domestic framework may be wholly eclipsed by the international perspective which is basic to the correlation of world forces.

The second approach may be described as *logical-analytical.* This starts with an analysis of the correlation of forces in the socio-economic basis of society. Then it deals with the correlation of forces in the highest form of class struggle — the political one — and deals first with its domestic and second with its international framework. Then the focus shifts to the correlation of military forces which concerns the decisive form of the political struggle carried on in the determining phases of history. Finally, the analysis arrives at the basic aim of the study, the correlation of world forces, which is a synthesis of all the dimensions of social struggle on the world scale, including all the fighting forces and all the methods of struggle.

This approach might best correspond to the historical place of the particular 'correlations' in the Marxist-Leninist theory. Marx and Engels focused on the socio-economic basis of capitalist society and the struggle proceeding in this, and — perhaps more implicitly — on the correlation of forces in it. Lenin concentrated on the political front of the class struggle and, in the period preceding the October Revolution and during it, he considered the military forces to be an important — perhaps the most important — factor. In Stalin's time the problems of the correlation of forces in the international sphere grew in importance and finally the concept of the correlation of *world* forces was developed. (This was my second attempt which resulted in an essay on the correlation of world forces as a synthesis of three 'dimensional' correlations.)[2]

This approach also seems to cause some doubts. The correlation of socio-economic forces (also called class social forces), in which classes clash with one another in the basic economic and class structures of society, plays an independent role only in transitional periods of history. It refers to the correlation of the forces of antagonistic classes in the period of the emergence of a class society and then in the periods of transition from a given socio-economic formation to the following one.

In these periods, the classes are *in statu nascendi* as classes; the correlation of their economic power determines the methods which they use in struggling for a place in the emerging formation and the prospect for this struggle. However, relations of economic power soon change into political relations. The place of the class in the authority structure, which is part of the political superstructure of the new society, becomes decisive: only by the use of political power can the class which controls the economy safeguard its interests in a permanent and stable way. And only by struggling against this political power can the economically oppressed class rise and finally escape from its inferior economic position.

It may be asked whether in our time, when the world-wide socio-economic formations coexist and compete, this kind of correlation of social forces has not acquired a new international meaning. The area of socio-economic relations has become an important part of international relations and, to some extent, it is independent and affects the entirety of them. In Soviet writings on international affairs, this correlation is mentioned *a casu ad casum.*

However, no analysis of this concept has been made, and, if mentioned, it is considered to be only one aspect of the correlation of world forces. The direct relations between 'international' classes in the economic sphere are viewed as a part of the global relations between them and, in this respect, the relations between capitalist and socialist states — which also directly reflect inter-class relations — are considered much more important. Moreover, the economic relations in the international sphere assume a political character and must be regarded as a part of the correlation of political forces in the broad sense.

In consequence, a third approach has been chosen in the present study. Following the analysis of the theoretical premises of the correlation of social forces and its general characteristics (Chapters 2 and 3), the political dimension in the broad sense, which includes all forms of social struggle, is analysed in both the domestic and the international settings (Chapters 4 and 5). The next part is devoted to a description of the concept (category) of the correlation of world forces and a comparison of this with the concepts of the global balance of power (Chapters 6—7).

There follows an analysis of the correlation of military forces which focuses on its role as a component of the correlation of world forces (Chapters 8—12). The study concludes with some general comments on the correlation of world forces and the correlation of military forces.

Such an organisation of the study seems to be more pragmatic. It has two focuses which correspond to the *actual* fundamental interest of Marxist-Leninist theory and Soviet policy. The first corresponds to the Soviet political and academic interest, in which the correlation of world forces is the key concept; it is complemented by the analyses of the domestic and international correlations, which in theory precede and are premises to the 'world correlation'. The prevention of war, the military policy of the great powers, arms control and *détente*, the future of particular regions and individual states, the possibility and prospect of resolving interstate and domestic conflicts — these and similar issues are always considered in connection with the correlation of world forces and are said to depend on it.

The correlation of military forces constitutes the second centre of attention in this study; this seems to correspond to the interest of the Soviet politicians, military leaders and researchers. It has its specific analytical and practical problems and difficulties. Military action is always undertaken for certain political purposes but its specific features are so different from all non-military social activities and it may have such far-reaching consequences for all mankind that it merits separate treatment.

Notes

1   'The Correlation of World Forces', *Journal of Peace Research*, 1980:2: *Military Force*, 1981, Ch. 10.

2   'Styrkeförhållandena i varlden. En syntes av sociala, politiska och militära dimensioner', in *Fred och Säkerhet. Debatt och Analys 1982—83*, Förlaget Akademiliteratur, Stockholm 1983.

PART I
THEORETICAL PREMISES

2 Theoretical premises

Agenda

In Marxist-Leninist theory, sociological (or socio-political) categories are defined as fundamental concepts which reflect the general and essential features, aspects and relationships in a field of social activities or in social development as a whole.[1]

It may be suggested that, in Marxist-Leninist theory, the correlation of social forces is in actual fact a paradigmatic category which reflects the basic features of social system, its basic structure and the relationships between the main components of the system. It reflects the view (1) that the social system has a *two-party* structure; (2) that the basic components are the opposites which combat each other and thereby express the main contradiction of the system in the given epoch; (3) that the *coexistence and interaction* of the opposites determine the basic processes within the system, the development of it and its future transformation; (4) that such coexistence constitutes the system and entails *cooperation and conflict.* The cooperation makes possible a relatively stable functioning of the system for some time; the conflict impels the system towards a transformation into another system. The correlation of the opposites is *dynamic;* it changes as the system develops and the change greatly affects the development. To sum up, the category in its full interpretation expresses the essence of the Marxist-Leninist paradigm of social system as regards both the national and the international communities.

The category of the correlation of social forces is rooted in the philosophy of dialectical materialism and in the Marxist-Leninist theory of social development. The former views all developments as proceeding through the struggle of opposites which compose a transitory whole. The latter regards society as having emerged from social conflict, as constituting a framework for both cooperation and conflict of its components and as developing by conflict-resolutions that resemble a series of leaps. An interconnected idea is that social forces in the course of the class struggle tend to become polarised: the interacting social forces are gradually transformed into two antagonistic camps. This proposition also concerns international relations.

For purposes of analysis these theoretical premises will be divided into three: philosophical, sociological and systemic.

Philosophical premises

The development of the material world and of society is said to proceed through the struggle of internal contradictions. The contradiction between the 'old' and the 'new' in any phenomenon, which coexist but permanently conflict with each other, is the basic contradiction. A gradual quantitative increase in the strength of the 'new' and a corresponding gradual weakening of the 'old' lead at some point to essential qualitative changes in the correlation of their forces and, through the clashes between these, to radical changes in the essence of the phenomenon in question. Less radical changes periodically occur. They mark the beginnings of new phases in the development of the phenomenon which however preserves its principal features. The final and most radical change consists in a revolutionary replacement (called 'negation') of the old essence of the phenomenon by a new essence, which means a transformation of this phenomenon into another one. In turn, the 'new' gradually becomes 'old' and weak and it is doomed to give way to yet another new phenomenon ('negation of the negation').

Since this struggle is a perpetual one, the dynamic and constantly changing correlation of forces of the 'old' and the 'new' plays the determining role not only in the final outcome of the struggle but also in the shape of it at any given moment; the correlation determines the forms and methods of the struggle.

This is most visible at the moment of the final 'negation' when the 'new' is becoming decisively stronger than the 'old'. It is the change in the correlation of forces which makes it possible to accomplish 'negation'; it determines the way in which the revolutionary changes will be carried out — what form of violence will be used, for instance; and it also determines how much of the 'old' can be preserved in the 'new'.

In short, *development through conflict,* through the struggle of contradictory elements, is the essence of Marxist-Leninist dialectics. Development is the highest type of movement and action and the highest type of changes in matter and human conscience. It proceeds by and through the transition from an old quality to a new quality.

> Development does not mean just any change but a specifically qualitative change connected with a transformation in the internal structure of an object, which constitutes a complex of elements, ties and dependences combined in a functional way.[2]

Development is not the sum of smooth quantitative increases but is rather a sequence *(cheredovanie)* of evolutionary quantitative changes and revolutionary qualitative leaps from one condition to another.

The interpretation and application of the philosophical concepts of the struggle of contradictory or opposite forces — particularly of the interaction of the 'old' and the 'new', then of the 'quantitative' and 'qualitative' changes, and, finally, of 'negation', which are expressed in the so-called dialectical laws — depend on the kind of phenomena and processes which they concern. Let us see how they appear in the interaction of social groups.

Sociological premises

Emerged from conflict

In Marxist-Leninist theory, the state has emerged from the conflict of social groups, from their drive to build some structure or framework, for two reasons: (1) for the maintenance of the process of production; (2) for setting the struggle of the conflicting social groups in some organisational structure.

In such a structure (or system) one of the antagonistic parties expects to preserve and enhance its dominating position in the production process and protect, even enlarge all the privileges connected with it, and the other party aims to overthrow the governing social group and to replace it as a ruler of society.

The state appeared at a point in man's social development where antagonisms between social groups — classes in the process of formation — which occupied different positions in the production process could no longer be reconciled without a governing organ which would regulate the everyday life of society. The purpose of the state was therefore to establish some sort of order by legalising and perpetuating the domination of one class and by precluding any violent opposition from the governed class or classes. The governing class became capable of defending its interests both inside and outside the country. In sum, the state apparatus became an instrument for resolving class conflicts according to the interests of the governing class and for preventing conflicts from exploding into a violent revolution which might transform the existing social order of production and the entire socio-economic and political system.

At the same time, the emerging state and its armed forces defended the society's interests — in the first line those of the rulers — against other states and thereby they exercised nation-generating and nation-integrating functions.[3]

Class struggle

Since conflicts preceded the emergence of society, and society is a system in which conflicts are perpetual, the laws of dialectics — i.e., of development through conflict — are clearly visible and applicable in social development and in analyses of this.

The pursuit of the interests of *conflicting* social groups is the motive force of the development. It manifests itself in the economic, political and ideological forms of class struggle and, if necessary, in the use of armed violence.

The basic social groups in question — the main protagonists in social development — are *classes,* i.e. groups of men united by their common role in the process of production and distribution of material values, e.g., landowners, peasants, factory owners, industrial workers, etc. This common role stems from the identity in the people's relation to property of the means of production.[4] In each socio-economic structure (or formation, as it is called in Marxist-Leninist theory) there are two basic classes: one of them owns the means of production which are basic in this formation while the other consists of workers. The capitalists and the working class are the two basic classes in so-called capitalist society. Since they both cooperate and struggle against each other in pursuit of their economic and political interests, their interaction is that of antagonists. This is the determining feature of the social *system* which in Marxist-Leninist literature is called an *antagonistic class structure (formation).* Society develops through cooperation and the struggle of antagonistic classes, of which one is the carrier of the 'new' element — i.e., of the progressive future of society — while the other represents the 'old' or reactionary force which, though still governing, is doomed to defeat.

This view of social structure differs from the numerous non-Marxist theories of the stratification of society, according to which society consists of a great number of different social layers (strata), both horizontal and vertical. There are no dominant social relations but a great number of different roles, which people fill (several different roles at the same time, since they belong to different groups dependent on the way of classification). These represent very different interests and thus relations, and lead to various forms of competition, rivalry and struggle, which are universal. In various theories, the groups are determined by various factors: by their property, prestige or proximity to the sources of power,[5] or by combination of all of them; they may include people with identical income and sources of income, i.e., they are classified according to the relations of distribution. However, none of them follows the criterion used in Marxist-Leninist theory, i.e., the relation of people to property in the means of production which involves the way of the distribution of the social product.

Thus the laws of dialectics are directly applicable to the analysis and assessment of social forces in action and consequently in social development. Social laws differ from the laws of nature in that they are manifest in social activity — they do not exist outside society. These are laws-tendencies, which determine the main course of development and do not exclude chance events and deviations. Dependent on external conditions, for instance on more or less favourable natural environment, geographical situation, international situation, intrasocietal correlation of forces, national traditions and others, men can cover the general path of development in various ways.

The general sociological laws operate throughout the history of human society; among them are the law of the primacy of social being and the secondary nature of social consciousness and the law of the correspondence of production relations to the nature and development level of the productive forces. Other laws relate only to antagonistic class societies, such as the laws of class struggle or the law of the replacement of socio-economic formations in a revolutionary way; social revolution is rooted in the contradictions between the new productive forces and the obsolete production relations, which are reflected in the respective class contradictions. Some laws operate only in one formation, such as the law of producing and appropriating surplus value, which is the main economic law of capitalism. The law of balanced development of all aspects of social life operates only in the communist formation, that is, under socialism and communism.[6]

These laws operate *through* the struggle of social forces, through the action of classes as well as other social groups, or even individuals. Research into any society must be related to the specific socio-economic basis on which its entire social life and the activities of social groups and individuals are built. The entire social development may therefore be viewed as an interaction of *objective* factors — the laws of social development and the socio-economic basis in which the interests of social groups are anchored — and the *subjective* factors — constituting the activities of the people and their pursuit of class interests.

13

Since, however, contemporary societies take the form of nation states, the national interests of the people must also be taken into account. The complex relationship between class and national interests will be discussed below.

In the Marxist-Leninist view, the *correlation of the strengths of opposing social forces,* which are primarily social classes, determines the basic aspects of social development and the methods used by the adversaries, finally, the outcome of their struggle. Therefore a correct assessment of the correlation at a given moment, with regard to both the material and non-material components, is indispensable to any historical analysis of any social event or process.

All social development is the result of the class struggle behind which there is a clash of different social interests, most importantly economic, writes Shakhnazarov. To understand the nature of the basic existing political, ideological and other social institutions in a given society or an international system, which participate in this struggle and in social development, and to construct a theory about the probable course of this development, one must first of all form an idea of the correlation of class forces there. Analysis of the correlation of forces can explain why a particular order exists in the international arena and in which direction it is most likely to change.[7]

Polarisation

The theory of the development of society through stages and the transition from one stage to the next, occurring through the clash of opposite class forces, includes the proposition that social development tends to combine various social forces in *two* struggling camps and to reduce all social conflicts to a zero-sum struggle between them. (In the international development this concept of bipolarity takes the form of the 'two-camp world'.)

According to a Soviet writer, the growing polarisation of social forces not only in the capitalist countries but in the entire world is one of the main specific features of our time.[4]

The Marxist thesis on the struggle of opposites concerned polarisation in a capitalist society; but now the main attention in the sociopolitical analyses seems to be paid to the 'struggle of opposites' in the international system.

> To make a dialectico-materialistic analysis of the epoch, one must consider it a unity and struggle of opposites. The struggle of opposites on a world scale manifests itself primarily as a competition between the two opposite social systems, which exist simultaneously but which constitute qualitatively different stages of the

society's progress: its past and future. The two social formations are developing in opposite directions.[8]

Both these antagonistic forces may have multi-layered structures but these are subordinated to the 'centres' — to the working class and its party in the anti-monopoly camp in domestic society, and to the Soviet Union in the socialist camp — which lead and direct the struggle.

The developments in the Third World in the first years after most of the areas there gained statehood seemed to refute the proposition that international relations were becoming increasingly polarised. Several countries were in a state of constant internal flux and often changed their external affiliations. However, Soviet scholars say, gradually, the *internal polarisation* in some of these underdeveloped countries led to a decision about future development: either to an attempt to build socialism there or to move towards capitalism. This led towards a polarisation of these countries in the international arena also. They began to support similar socio-economic regimes in other countries of the Third World and to combat countries with opposing systems. Objectively, although rarely formally, they drew nearer to either the Eastern or the Western bloc.

Although Marxist-Leninist writers note that, parallel to the 'capitalism/socialism' polarisation, a multi-polar structure is emerging in the capitalist world, (cf. Chapter 6), they find that this does not diminish the *basic* tendency to polarisation in the world.

Social violence

In Marxist-Leninist theory, the class struggle which characterises any antagonistic class society — i.e., any society consisting of two basic antagonistic classes and others which are considered to be 'intermediate' between them — takes the form of the use of social violence. 'Violence' or 'social violence' is defined as the use by social groups of various forms of *coercion* for the attainment, or defence, of their rights, privileges, values, and so on;[9] in other words, violence is applied in pursuit of social groups' interests. Violence is also defined as a specific means used by a class, state or political group, in pursuit of its aims, primarily in order to break the will and power of the adversary.[10] In a broad concept, violence also includes the *threat* of coercion, which is one of the indirect forms of its use.

Kinds of violence may be classified according to either a direct/indirect dichotomy or its subject content (fields of social activity). In the former one distinguishes between the direct use of force, as in political repression, war, or armed insurrection and indirect (covert) violence in the form of psychological pressure, political blackmail, econo-

15

mic repressive measures, the threat of the use of force, and so on.[11] In the latter kind of classification violence is divided into political, economic, diplomatic, ideological, administrative and military forms;[12] in this division each kind of violence may be used in the respective kind of social activity, which is at the same time a front of class struggle. In most instances, a combination of various kinds of violence is used.

Violence may also be divided into armed and non-armed violence; military forms of coercion have their specifics radically different from all forms of non-military violence.

It has been stressed that class domination is a kind of coercion in itself and that in actual fact it constitutes violence in a permanent form. The producers — workers and peasants — are deprived of a great part of their products in a 'legal' way, in the form of the owners' profits, of taxes and so on; the deprivation is effected under laws *imposed* by the owners. The obedience to these laws is imposed by the existence of means of armed violence, — police and armed forces — which are at the disposal of the ruling classes.

'Reactionary coercion is', writes P. Golub, 'a constantly operating factor in any society based on private property and class oppression, a factor that assumes economic, political, ideological and, during the most strained moments of the class struggle, armed forms. In this society the function of the state, to quote Engels, is to maintain "by force the conditions of existence and domination of the ruling class against the subject class".'[13]

As regards the social character and purpose of violence, the basic distinction is made between *revolutionary* and *counter-revolutionary* violence, which are progressive and reactionary, respectively. This is a direct reflection of the division of society into exploiting and exploited classes struggling against each other.

Two Marxist propositions about the motives for social violence reflect the roles of the two sides in the social struggle: on the one hand, the exploiting classes always use social violence in various forms in order to defend their rule and increase their exploitation; on the other hand, violence is indispensable to the social and national struggle for liberation. The existence of exploitation *generates* violence — but the struggle to end exploitation also *necessitates* violence. Although revolutionary violence is an *answer* to the exploiters' violence it is the only means of social progress; the collision of these two vehicles of violence underlies progress. If the former is inevitable, so also is the latter.[14]

While these ideas constitute, in brief, the classical exposition of the subject, the contemporary development may suggest some changes in it — if not in its ideological premises, then in concrete doctrines and practices. It seems that the development of the doctrine and practice of using revolutionary violence as a means of promoting social progress through socialist revolutions is characterised by three tendencies; these, however, are not fully compatible.

The first tendency is to stress the importance of revolutionary violence in the socialist transformation of the countries of the Third World. The revolution in Cuba was regarded as an example of the successful use of revolutionary violence despite an unfavourable regional correlation of forces; the overthrow of Allende in Chile in 1973 demonstrated the difficulties of establishing a socialist regime without using armed violence. In both cases the importance of using revolutionary violence was considered to have been confirmed. Revolutionary parties, it was said, should prefer the violent seizure of power to electoral politics and the limited aims pursued by the coalitions in which they participate. If such alliances succeed in attaining tactical goals, revolutionary parties should proceed to seize power by mass action and a proletarian dictatorship.[15]

Moreover, it is justified that any indigenous revolutionary movement be supported by the Soviet Union — directly, or indirectly through proxies — in revolutionary civil wars and in the defence of the power seized against an imperialist counter-revolution. 'Where such /revolutionary/ forces are engaged in a struggle, they have the right to depend on our solidarity and support.'[16] In the words of the then Minister of Defence in the USSR, Dmitri Ustinov:

> Loyal to its international duty, the Soviet Union has always rendered and continues to render fraternal aid to the peoples struggling for their independence and for their revolutionary gains... It is precisely with this noble mission that limited contingents of our armed forces were sent to the Democratic Republic of Afghanistan.[17]

(As we see, the justification of the armed support of revolutionary movement has been extended to cover the use of it in defence of the power seized against an attempted counter-revolution.)

The second tendency is to tone down the use of revolutionary violence in the *developed capitalist societies* of today — if not in theory (by changing the classical propositions) then at least in practice. It is difficult, indeed, to construct scenarios of social revolutions in these countries, not least because the Communist parties there are opposed to giving the theoretical assumptions any practical form.

Finally, as regards the *socialist countries,* in spite of the unchanging philosophical and sociological premises, radical changes in the doctrine of the use of armed violence may also be noted there. The classical theory envisages no need to use revolutionary violence in a socialist country after the initial period of suppressing the remnants of the overthrown classes. However, the events in Hungary, Czechoslovakia and Poland prompted Soviet politicians and theorists to make changes in doctrine, if not in the sociological premises. More than before, it has been stressed that after the victory of socialist revolution, violence remains indispensable. It continues in other forms, to combat the resistance of the overthrown classes which is manifested in very acute forms, such as civil war, counter-revolutionary conspiracies, sabotage, subversion, etc.[18] All these actions can be, and as a rule are, supported from outside. Socialist society is *by definition* a society without class conflicts that would necessitate the use of political violence and, where necessary, of armed violence. However, in the 1970s and 1980s, a recurring theme in political discussions has been the danger of an imperialist action against socialist system *both from within and without* particular socialist societies. In the Marxist-Leninist view, this necessitates a vigorous counteraction which means some form or other of social violence against the bearers of hostile ideologies: 'Our implacable opposition to the enemies of socialism is not confined to the defence of our concrete achievements: it presupposes a vigorous attack on subversion, ideological excursions and all hostile phenomena...'[19] To bring about such a profound change in actual policies some theoretical adjustments would also be needed. Thus it is maintained that while the conflicts in socialist society have remained essentially non-antagonistic,

> from the methodological standpoint, it would be an over-simplification to think that all contradictions in a society following the socialist road are always and under any circumstances bound to be non-antagonistic. Historical experience shows that in certain conditions — when major shortcomings have long been accumulating in economic and cultural construction, in social administration, etc. — non-antagonistic contradictions could acquire features of antagonistic ones. This cannot be ruled out for the simple reason that so long as capitalism exists, antagonistic and non-antagonistic contradictions are tied in with each other. The non-antagonistic nature of the contradictions arising in the advance along the socialist road is not a self-fulfilling imperative. Apparently it will be objectively impossible for non-antagonistic contradictions to degenerate into antagonistic ones only when socialism reaches a definite stage of maturity, at which the whole complex of social relations is completely restructured on collectivist lines intrinsic to socialism — that is, with the building of developed socialism.[20]

Commenting on this, we may say that although in the beginning of this analysis major shortcomings in the economic and cultural construction processes, as well as in social administration, are specified as the causes of the re-emergence of antagonistic contradictions (disguised by the expression 'non-antagonistic contradictions acquiring the features of

18

antagonistic ones'), in the final section the existence of social strata not included in 'collectivistic' structure is said to constitute the social root of antagonistic contradictions. This means that, in the stage before socialistic society becomes a 'mature' one, it is still not a completely classless one.

Thus, in spite of some qualifications two principles of the class theory have remained unchanged: (1) there are no antagonistic classes in socialist society, and all antagonistic contradictions arise from accumulated errors in the socialist structure and the impact of both the remnants of the non-socialist strata and the 'outside' capitalism; (2) eventually, in developed socialism, even those contradictions will disappear.

In a final comment on the theory of the role of violence as one of the principal sociological premises of the category of the correlation of social forces one may suggest that the actual policy of the Soviet Union does not strictly follow theoretical propositions concerning 'just', 'justified' or 'necessary' social violence. Soviet armed support or political support of a progressive movement, or even the mere approval of it, is often subordinated to the tactics of diplomatic intercourse and calculations of the correlation of world forces and of regional correlations. The relationship of the movement in question to the Soviet Union — friendly, neutral or hostile — also plays an essential role.

Systemic approach

Concept

The Soviet concept of social development and international relations is based on the systemic approach. 'One of the instruments in the Marxist-Leninist methodological arsenal is the systemic approach'.[21] Both society and the international community constitute *social systems* of which the components interrelate and interact in a specific way. Social structure is defined as the internal organisation of society seen as an entity, which includes the way in which its components (subsystems) interact.[23] The structure of the international system is similarly defined. A system is determined by the nature of its components and in turn it affects the components. However, some components may change while the system remains basically unchanged. Relations of coordination, subordination, determination and compatibility *(sovmestimost)* of the components help to preserve the system; basic conflicts between the components bring about systemic changes.

In the Marxist-Leninist concept, society is a system of a special kind: namely, a permanently changing and developing system. During certain periods society remains relatively stable (otherwise it would not constitute a system), but even then it is in a state of constant gradual change. Periodically the accumulation of gradual changes leads to a radical leap-like development — i.e., to a revolutionary transformation of the system as a whole. The difference between the functioning of a system connected with gradual change and the radical development — indeed, the transformation of it — is thus essential. The functioning of a system — the routine everyday interaction of its components — is conservative in its nature; it slows down transformations and, in a sense, it conflicts with development. However, inevitable changes occurring in this every-day process of interaction create the conditions for development.

This contradiction between the gradually changing content of the components of the system and the relatively stable form of their inter-connection and interaction is said to lead to periodical radical trans-formations of the system as a whole. In the Marxist-Leninist view, the approach to domestic society and the international community as systems requires a theory that expresses the principle of the inter-connection between the elements of the system, establishes their hier-archy and explains the mechanism of changes in them and of the deve-lopment of the system. This cannot be done by means of the general systems theory which implies, in the Soviet view, that all phenomena, whether of the animate or the inanimate world, ultimately represent similar types of organisation in which qualitative characteristics may be expressed in quantitative terms.

One of the basic deficiencies of all variants of bourgeois system theories (for a more comprehensive criticism see pages 46—8), especially those based on the general systems theory, it is said, is that they cannot explain changes in social systems, whether intrasocietal or international; they cannot point out a basic factor that motivates the changes and they cannot discover the mechanism of the changes. Indeed, all such theories assume that the capitalist system will endlessly continue.

Marxist-Leninist system theory is said to give a comprehensive picture of domestic and world phenomena in their unity and inter-dependence and explain changes and developments in both the domes-tic and the international systems. The system analysis provided by Marxism-Leninism derives from the principles of materialistic dialectics; it is related to materialistic dialectics as a special (or partial) theory is related to the general theory.[24] While the dialectical method investi-gates general laws of development, the Marxist-Leninist system analysis is confined to individual systems and processes and, in particular, to the domestic and international systems. As regards the principles of materialism underlying this analysis, in Marxism-Leninism top priority is given to the social factor; the class struggle is regarded as the motive force behind social development.

This system theory serves definite purposes: to facilitate the revolu-tionary process by providing scientific analysis of the current situation and an effective prognosis for its development.

As regards developments on the domestic level, the purposes are:
(1) to evaluate the correlation of forces in a given society and the tendencies towards changes in this;
(2) to evaluate the impact of the world situation and the regional situation on the prospects for this development;
(3) to determine the time when decisive class struggles will take place;
(4) to develop the strategy of class struggle.

As regards developments on the world level, the purposes are:
(1) to evaluate the general relation of world forces and the tendencies towards changes in this;
(2) to determine the prospects for the socialist world;
(3) to evaluate the resources of capitalism and diagnose the capitalist crisis;
(4) to determine when and/or where in the world revolutionary process a decisive step towards the elimination of capitalism would be possible;[25]
(5) to contribute to the strategy of the world revolutionary movement.

Society as a system

Every society is characterised by a definite type of economic structure i.e., the sum-total of the production relations.[26] This is called the *basis* of the given society. The relations of production depend on the level of development of the forces of production (the objects and means of labour) and are determined by the form of ownership of them. The productive forces together with the relations of production corresponding to them constitute the mode of production.

> In the social production which men carry on they enter into definite relations that are indispensable and independent of their will; these relations of production correspond to a definite stage of the development of their material powers of production. The sum total of these relations of production constitutes the economic structure of society — the real foundation, on which rise legal and political superstructures and to which correspond definite forms of social consciousness.[27]

Every society has also its specific *superstructure*. The composition of the superstructure is variously described in different Marxist-Leninist writings but the resultant structure may look as follows: superstructure consists of (1) political relations between various classes, (2) the state with all its instruments of compulsion in the form of the army, police, courts and prisons as well as other institutions as churches, schools, and so on; (3) ideology of the various classes and social groups expressed in various forms: political, legal, moral, aesthetic, religious and philosophic. The superstructure stems from the economic basis: it reflects the struggle which proceeds in the basis and serves this struggle. The state and other institutions which are dominated by the governing class, serve to perpetuate, strengthen and develop the economic system on whose basis they have appeared. So also do the governing political, legal, moral and other ideas and norms. For instance, legal rules always formalise and reproduce the form of ownership existing in a given society, and serve their preservation. The programmes and ideologies of the exploited classes aim at overthrowing the existing political system and creating conditions for a radical change of the economic basis.

The socio-economic basis together with the whole superstructure form a system called the social or socio-economic *formation*. This develops through a gradual growth of the material means of production and corresponding changes in the relations of production and in the superstructure; periodically the changes become qualitative ones and assume a leap-like pattern. A revolution creates the conditions for the transition from one formation to another one.

> At a certain stage of their development the material forces of production in society come into conflict with the existing relations of production, or — what is but a legal expression for the same thing — with the property relations within which they had been at work before. From forms of development of the forces of production these relations turn into their fetters. Then comes the period of social revolution. With the change of the economic foundation the entire immense superstructure is more or less transformed.[28]

Revolutionary transitions from one formation to another constitute deep qualitative shifts in social development, new levels in the historical progress of humanity. Thus the sequence of socio-economic formations reflects the gradual evolution of human society.

In the development of the social system, the correlation of social forces decisively affects the course of events. The development does not proceed automatically and unconsciously; it depends on how social forces act: on their policy — both that planned and that accomplished, i.e., on their political doctrine and its accomplishment, political strategy. Since according to Marxism-Leninism, both the value of the political forces and their action depend on the socio-economic basis, a thorough analysis of the *mechanism of the determination* (seemingly, still lacking) would be highly useful for understanding the dynamics of the correlation of forces.

It is stated only generally that the economic basis determines the content of the superstructure and its make-up, that the changes occurring in the economic system are reflected in the superstructure, that the politics of a state depend in the first place on the economic interests of its ruling class, etc.[30] On the other hand, equally generally it is stated that the superstructure is by no means a passive appendix to the basis, that it promotes the development of the basis, consolidating the economic system, regulating its functioning and eliminating the outmoded elements of it. Though it is not directly linked with production, the superstructure affects it via the economic basis.[31]

Some theoretical changes may here be pointed out, however. In orthodox Marxism the socio-economic basis directly produced the superstructure. Now it is said that the impact of the basis on the superstructure, particularly on policy, is indirect and varies according to the concrete historical situation. Economic interests, economic situation of the governing class constitute only the 'deepest roots' of politics, both domestic and foreign. They determine them merely in principle, in the final account, always indirectly and in various ways. One should reject primitive economic determinism.[32] (Cf. Chapter 4.)

Moreover, the superstructure has developed in such a way that it begins ever more actively to affect the economic basis. This process, say Soviet analysts, may be visible even in the developed industrial and monopolistic countries where monopolies and the state — their instrument — try to gain full control of the economic and financial processes, to introduce socio-economic reforms and avert economic crises. However, the process is much more visible in socialist societies.

In the classical Marxist concept the state, after a socialist revolution, would gradually wither away. As regards the external justifications for its existence (since revolution was supposed to occur simultaneously in most or all of the developed industrialised countries), the need to maintain the state apparatus for the purpose of success in the rivalries between states and in the defence of their interests would quickly disappear. With regard to internal affairs, the state would be needed for some time as an instrument for effecting the evolution towards a classless society, but subsequently it would become superfluous. However, in the light of the factual developments, especially in the Soviet Union, this model dwindled to an abstract scheme.

The main tendencies in the evolution of the Soviet state may be summarised as follows:[33]

(1) The Soviet state *constantly extends its internal functions.* This is caused by the fact that the whole socialist superstructure serves the constructive aims of building the new society. 'Socialism, which necessarily presupposes control of production on the scale and in the interests of the whole of society, and implies that social spontaneity is replaced by conscious, planned building up of a new social relation, by

its very nature explains and conditions the enhanced activity of the socialist superstructure.'[34] Thus the Soviet state increasingly promotes economic, cultural and educational activities. It continues to exercise its function of paralysing the counter-revolutionary plots that are alleged to be inspired by external forces. And — although this is not admitted — it maintains its function of counteracting the manifestations of national and social dissatisfaction that continue to occur. The official version is that the external sources of all anti-socialistic activities have replaced their disappearing internal basis although, as mentioned before, antagonistic contradictions may re-emerge as a result of shortcomings in state activities and the revival of the private economic sector.

(2) The Soviet socialist state *constantly extends its external functions.* Such a process, which apparently is opposed to the classical model, may be explained by factors external to the development of socialist society — the increasing rivalry of the two antagonistic systems. It is stressed that one of the basic functions of the Soviet state is to create favourable external conditions for the building of communism. This means ensuring the appropriate level of national defence, developing all-round cooperation with countries of the socialist community, pursuing a policy of peaceful coexistence with states having different social systems, conducting a consistent struggle for peace, and supporting the developing countries and peoples fighting against colonialism and neo-colonialism.[35] The Soviet state plays an extremely important role in the world-wide equation of progressive versus reactionary forces, i.e., in the correlation of world forces, which greatly contributes to the exercise of the above-mentioned external functions.

(3) The Soviet state *constantly attempts to influence the development of social and national struggles*, especially in the Third World.

(4) The Soviet state's activity is indispensable in resolving, together with other states, the *basic global problems* facing humanity: the problem of the prevention of world war; that of achieving a just division of resources corresponding to the size of the population; that of underdevelopment; and the ecological problem (pollution of the environment).[36]

The textbook on the basics of Marxist-Leninist theory reads: '... the present need to preserve, strengthen and develop the state is dictated by internal and external conditions in which Soviet society exists'.[37]

To sum up, the global expansion — or, in Soviet parlance, 'transformation' — of the functions of the state which was previously justified by the allegations of a capitalist encirclement, is now explained basically by the requirements of the socialist construction and by the rivalry of the two systems and the reactionary and bellicose policies of the imperialists. This is often presented as a strengthening of the directing role of the Communist Party. However, the expansion is a fact, even

24

if this word is not used.[38]

There is also another motive for this extension, which is now noted by Soviet and other Marxist-Leninist writers. This is said to be connected with the increasing functional specialisation of society. In the abstract model for the construction of a classless society, the latter was considered to be characterised by the disappearance of the functional specialisation which had always been reflected in the class division of society; this also included the difference between the working class and the peasants — i.e., the so-called non-antagonistic classes. In the orthodox theory, the disappearance of functional specialisation was considered to be an essential indication of the superfluous character of the state. In fact, however, functional specialisation continues and even increases and it is said not only to necessitate the preservation of the state but also to require that the state should expand in order to govern the highly complicated and increasingly sophisticated organisation of society.

In consequence of this and other developments, the superstructure gradually becomes ever less determined by the basis, while the basis gradually becomes ever more dependent on the leading and directing activities of the state, and of the Party as its leading force.

(It may be asked whether the process whereby the Party and state apparatus become independent of the socio-economic basis and thereby advance their own bureaucratic interests generates a tendency not only to legitimise the rule by revising the theory but also to strengthen it by expanding the apparatus for coercion. It may also be asked whether under these conditions the concept of the correlation of societal forces — the forces of two social adversaries — has ceased to be of any use in the analysis of socialist society.)

On the other hand, however, the scientific and technical revolution introduced much that was new into the functions of the superstructure. It has complicated social administration which has the continuous task of developing a socialist superstructure adequate to the socio-economic basis. It has raised the significance of timely development of a strategic line for a long period ahead, and has called for a deepening of the scientific principles of the management of society. The socialist state must adapt to this new situation the forms and methods of administration and management, must meet the current needs of the economy and fundamental research and must attach special attention to tackling the key task of ensuring steady growth of the economy's efficiency.[39]

Soviet writers attempt to belittle the extent of changes in the concept of the functions of the state and to deny that they have a revisionary nature. They try to present them as representing a continuation and development of the classical ideas or, at least, not a radical alteration of these. They never concede that some predictions by the fathers of Marxism may be wrong; the classical scheme, including the disappearance of the state, is said still to be right, but it can be realised only in the distant future. The main method of justifying the present changes, however, is to relate them not to the original classics, Marx and Engels, but to Lenin who radically changed the communist vision painted by the fathers of Marxism. The revision is presented as merely filling in details in Marx's uncomplicated picture of the future society and *fulfilling the legacy of Lenin who advocated a strong state* which, independently of its form, would always be a variant of the proletarian dictatorship.

Soviet writers also repeat Stalin's statement (without referring to its author) that the state, before it withers away, must first be continuously strengthened, since only a strong state will be able to liquidate the classes and build up communism. This also applies to the nation-wide state, into which, in the Soviet Union, the state of the dictatorship of the proletariat has grown. Under developed, mature socialism this is a state of the whole people representing the interests of all classes: the workers, the peasants and the people's intelligentsia.[40] However, they continue, while gaining more and more strength, even a nation-wide state must preserve its class character and even a nation-wide Communist Party must remain the instrument of the working class, which is the leading force in society. The very concept of class here means something quite different from what it means in a capitalist society, where it emerges from the contradictions in socio-economic relations. The socialist society consists of classes, but they are collaborating in a brotherly way since they have common interests. *The class terminology is combined with the picture of a society consisting of non-antagonistic classes.*

This ideal picture has been distorted by the factual development in which, apart from the two basic non-antagonistic classes, the existence of certain strata not following the 'collectivist line' and the reappearance of antagonistic contradictions are admitted. Moreover, in some countries, the peasants, who do not belong to the socialist-sector of the economy, are said to be one of the basic sources of the re-emerging antagonistic contradictions. This may only confirm the doubts about the complete disappearance of the question of correlation of intra-societal adversary forces as related to socialist society.

Without admitting any changes in the classical theory, however, Soviet scholars make, although indirectly, essential changes by presenting a 'new interpretation' of the traditional propositions. Thus, as regards the thesis on the withering away of the state under socialism, Zarodov writes that is necessary to distinguish (1) the beginning of the withering away of the *state proper,* understood as an instrument of coercion and the domination of one class over the others, and (2) the withering away of the socialist state. The socialist state is a 'semi-state', i.e., it is no longer a state in the strict sense of the term, since its main function is not coercion, but organisational, economic and cultural activity; it is set up not to perpetuate the domination of one class but ultimately to eliminate classes in general. This state will also wither away, but only when it ceases to be necessary from both an internal and external point of view, for instance when it is no longer necessary to defend the country. This is a long-drawn-out, historical process, however.[41]

The active role of the superstructure in forming the shape of society in a transitional period from one formation to another one, which was not emphasised in the first post-revolutionary years in the Soviet republic, now seems to be firmly stated. The transfer of political power from one class to another class — i.e., a radical transformation of the determining part of the superstructure — is a condition of a change of the form of property of the basic means of production, i.e., of the decisive element of the basis. The new superstructure takes an active part in the formation of the new basis.

This new proposition is not only illustrated by the socialist construction in the Soviet Union and other socialist countries, but also by the developments in the newly free countries of the Third World. These countries will build new social relations, free from exploitation, only provided the working people retain political power and use it not only for defending their rule but also for establishing new economic relations and developing all other elements of the superstructure such as their own law, ideology and culture; the strengthening of the state apparatus is here the *condition sine qua non.*[42]

The international system

The international system is considered in Soviet writings to exist on three levels.[43] This is connected with its being in actual fact an interaction of two systems belonging to different socio-economic formations and with the entry of the class struggle into the international arena.

On the most general level of international relations are the relations *between class forces and class policies* on the world-wide scale — i.e., inter-class relations in the international arena. These are pursued indirectly through class states (or coalitions of states) and also directly through alliances and organisations of class character such as international associations of trade unions and capitalist associations of various kinds. In our epoch, these relations are primarily determined by the struggle of the two antagonistic social systems, and by socialist and national-liberation revolutions.

On the second level is the complex of *international economic, political, ideological, cultural, legal and military relations between various organised forces* in particular countries, in which states constitute the main kind of protagonists.

On the third and narrowest level are the *intergovernmental* or *inter-state* political relations.

The three levels form a hierarchical unity; the system of the inter-state relations (or simply the interstate relations) forms however, the core of the international system.

Interstate relations as a system have a complex structure. The system includes states, coalitions of states and international state organisations (government organisations) which are characterised by specific regu-larities in their functioning and development. The global level, regional level and bilateral interstate level constitute the descending hierarchy of the scope of the relations.

The system of interstate relations is relatively independent of other international phenomena and, as mentioned, it is not identical with the entire system of international relations. The latter, which constitutes a broader concept, includes a sophisticated complex of economic, social, ideological, cultural, military, scientific and other links and processes. It exists and develops objectively, not only apart from the foreign policy of particular states but even sometimes against it. It affects the foreign policy of particular states both directly and indirectly, through the system of interstate relations as a whole.[44]

However, not all Soviet writers distinguish between the components of the international system in the above-mentioned way. The well-known theorist of international relations, N.N. Inozemtsev, defines international relations as the entirety of the economic, political, ideo-logical, legal, diplomatic, military and other links and relationships between states and systems of states, between the basic classes and the main social, economic and political forces, organisations and social movements which operate in the international arena — i.e., 'between nations in the broadest sense of the term'. At the same time he states that 'only states can be the subjects of these relationships'.[45] (This statement may be merely inconsistent; it also betrays the lack of clearly defined differences between the two concepts — that of interstate relations and that of international relations.)

President of the Soviet Political Science Association, Georgi Shakhnazarov, defines international relations as 'the totality of inte-grational contacts which shape human community'; here any kind of interaction — economic, ideological, scientific or cultural — but also the use of armed violence, is seen as a contact.[46]

In a collective study on international politics, which represents a compromise approach, a distinction is made between a broad and a narrow interpretation of international relations. In the broad sense, there exists a system of economic, social, political, ideological, techno-scientific, cultural, moral, socio-psychological, military-strategic and other relations between states, nations, social, religious and other intrasocietal organisations, groups of states and international organisations having an interstate or social character. In the narrow sense international relations form a system of inter-governmental political relations, including organisations of states. Since states constitute the foundation of the international system, and economic, ideological, techno-scientific and other activities are undertaken through the state mechanism and thus become political ones, political relations are the principal kind of international relations.[47]

International system: structure and changes

For all these reasons, the nature of interstate relations has attracted increasing attention. The system of states is seen as a structure in which the role of each element or component is to a considerable extent determined by the whole — i.e., by the system. The foreign policy of a particular state — the subjective factor — cannot be analysed separately from the whole, from the system. The *interaction* of the character of the system and the mechanisms of systemic relationships with the process of establishing and implementing the foreign policy of particular states must be in the focus of every analysis of international relations and foreign policy.

Various *domestic factors* also influence the behaviour of a state on the international arena, in the opinion of Soviet analysts. The following factors exert the most direct influence: (1) the political system; (2) the economic and techno-scientific potentials; (3) the military potential; (4) geography, natural resources, ecology; and (5) population. The character of the economic system greatly affects foreign policy but in an indirect way.[48]

However, although the foreign policy of particular capitalist states remains essentially a *class policy* and is mainly determined by the class structure of the state in question and the interests of the governing class, the *form* of this policy is mainly determined by the power of that state and by the global structure, features and regularities of the international system. The structural relations in the system at any juncture and the specific features of its functioning set limits to the decisions of a particular state and restrict its 'options'.

Capitalist states do not simply react to the actions of other states: they act in the framework of the global structure of interstate relations. 'The complex of interstate relations considered in their entirety, as a system, exerts an essential influence on the foreign policy of a capitalist state and largely determines its foreign policy.'[49] Therefore, independently of the specific features of the foreign policy of particular states as determined by their specific interests and goals, the degree of activity and effectiveness of this policy 'is always objectively determined (and

29

limited) by the established relations in the system of interstate relations'.[50] Over relatively long periods this influence remains relatively stable. As regards the socialist states the dependence of their international behaviour on the characteristics of the interstate system has not been analysed but from the general character of the propositions concerning the impact of the system it may be concluded.

The emphasis on the impact of international relations as a system on the behaviour of its components — states and coalitions of states — and the acceptance that the impact of the domestic economic system on foreign policy has become an indirect one *mean a doctrinal change.* The orthodox over-emphasis on the determining influence of the economic system on the entire superstructure and on the foreign policy of the state is no more in vogue.

Nevertheless remnants of the classical propositions are still valid since in the final account, it is said, the character of the domestic system determines the international behaviour of the state. Moreover, domestic changes which lead to a radical transformation of the character of the state may, *eo ipso,* affect the shape of the international system. According to the general proposition of the Marxist-Leninist system theory, the main cause of *basic* transformations in any system consists in the contradiction between, on the one hand, the *existing form* — i.e., the way in which the components of the system are interlinked and on the other hand, the *changing components* of the system. A corollary idea is that changes in the system follow changes in the components. Applied to the interstate system it means that transformations in this system are caused by internal changes in the states. Such changes produce a profound impact, if the state which undergoes a transformation is one of the pillars of the 'central balance'. The October Revolution in Russia is mentioned as an historical example of such a change.

Impact of economy

Although the international community of states and nations has no common socio-economic basis, and in this respect does not resemble domestic society with its 'basic-superstructure' composition, the socio-economic factor plays a large and, in some respects, determining role in shaping and developing the international system. Some dependences are formulated by the Soviet writers in a very general way, others are closely linked to the current foreign and domestic policies of states which have different socio-economic systems.[51]

In the first place, the character of international relations is said to depend on the level of the productive forces and the relations of productions in the given epoch that is on the mode of production which predominates in this epoch called the *socio-economic formation.* The latter determines which classes are the basic protagonists both in particular countries and in the international system — i.e., which kind of class conflict characterises the epoch.

> International relations 'form the outward aspect of the process which determines world development and at the heart of which lie the productive forces and production relations of the socio-economic formations and the corresponding classes, nations (nationalities) and states.[52]

The present-day international relations are of a special kind: they constitute a system of relations belonging to the period of *transition* from capitalism to socialism, which was characterised by a transitory coexistence of *two formations*, the capitalist and the socialist. Thus the class struggle, which has a socio-economic basis, is carried on simultaneously in the individual capitalist countries and on the *international* scale.

> The struggle of different social forces within the national framework seems to be summed up and 'weighed' in international relations, revealing the gains and 'true worth' of a subject in the historical process.[53]

These general assertions culminate in a statement that 'world politics is a concentrated expression of world economy'. It is based on the aggregate of the economy of the world as a whole, of particular states, coalitions of states, economic associations and social systems. The economic situation and economic interests of classes, states and economic systems determine the roots of world politics, its aims and methods used.[54]

Second, the laws of development characteristic of the capitalist system — for instance, the law of the uneven economic and political development of capitalist countries — continue to operate. This law has a big impact on international relations, since the existing distribution of markets and spheres of influence of the capitalist powers periodically conflicts with the new alignment of economic forces and periodically must be readjusted. This dependence generates constant tensions and an inter-imperialist struggle for economic and political positions.

Third, the international economic exchange which is an important part of international relations, is interdependent with the international political relations. 'It is well known', writes Shakhnazarov, 'that one of the main achievements of Marxism has been the discovery of inter-dependence of the economic base (the relations of production) of society, and its political superstructure (the political, legal, moral, aesthetic, philosophical and religious views and beliefs). This interdependence is equally important in international affairs'.

The direction of economic relations has its own motive power — and sometimes expresses economic necessity; economic requirements quite often influence foreign policy so much that it is appropriate to talk of the 'economisation' of international political relations.[55] Thus economic relations may be regarded as a socio-economic basis *sui generis* of the international system.

Fourth, the foreign policy of each country is primarily determined by the economic, political, ideological and other interest of that country's (or society's) ruling class. Foreign policy, in the opinion of Andrei Gromyko, expresses the interests of the ruling classes of states, and the class struggle of the opposing socio-economic systems constitutes the essence of world policy.[56]

Certainly, Marxism-Leninism does not view international relations as the mechanical projection of internal social relations into the international sphere. Nevertheless, in the final account, the nature of the socio-economic system of a given country or coalition of states determines the direction of their policies. Thus in the present-day world, the so-called imperialist countries try to export their internal socio-economic conflicts in order to ensure high profits and avoid social troubles at home. The United States is said to be trying to recarve the markets and raw-material sources to its own advantage, to gain political and economic control of its allies and to exert pressure on the socialist countries. This imperialist policy, in conjunction with the military build-up generates tensions and wars.

In contrast, the projection of socialist domestic social relations into the international arena creates a new kind of cooperative relations and mutual support in the socialist world, which promotes peace in the international system as a whole.

Finally, all these dependences of international relations on the socio-economic system (in fact, on the coexistence of two formations, socialism and capitalism) are expressed — and culminate — in the extremely important socio-economic causation of the international conflicts and wars. Apart from the direct causes, these conflicts and wars have their deepest roots in socio-economic conflicts of interest which are domestic or international, or a mixture of both.

Changed view of world revolution

However, only an accumulation of radical revolutionary socio-economic and political transformations within particular states — such as in this view are coming to a head in various areas — may lead to a final transformation of the interstate system as a whole.

Domestic struggle, say Marxist-Leninists, leads inevitably to a decisive clash, a revolutionary transformation of society. This is genally effected by the use of armed violence, although theoretically it may be accomplished by peaceful means. The transformation may take one of three forms: (1) a revolutionary sudden leap with a total replacement of the old system by a new one; (2) a series of leaps: first a national-liberation or democratic revolution, then a socialist revolution and (3) following a national-liberation or democratic revolution a gradual change towards socialism, like those occurring in countries of the Third World with a 'socialist orientation'.

International developments are now seen in another light. Although interstate wars may occur and probably often will occur, they will not decisively affect the basic character of the contemporary world system which consists of two opposing camps and a multitude of non-aligned countries. The conflict between the two basic international adversaries probably will not develop into a decisive combat which will finally answer the questions 'Who whom?' and will produce a revolutionary new international system.

This was one of the main assumptions in the traditional Marxist-Leninist theory, in which war between the two antagonistic systems was considered inevitable, because it was expected that the capitalist world would try, sooner or later, to destroy the socialist system. This classical proposition has now been renounced. In Soviet view, the present correlation of world forces favourable to socialism has rendered any such capitalist endeavour unrealistic; this can but constrain the imperialist powers from an open attack on the socialist system.

In the present Marxist-Leninist view, the world system of capitalism will change gradually, as a result of domestic struggle and internal revolutions, which will break out in a long succession of capitalist countries. The basic conflict of our epoch, between capitalism and socialism, will therefore be resolved *not in the sphere of international relations,* but *on national basis,* by virtue of the internal class struggle unfolding in accordance with the objective laws of social development. The Marxist-Leninists state that the socialist countries draw a clear line between the spheres of class struggle and interstate relations and oppose any attempts to erase this line. As distinct from this line, the imperialist countries by interfering in the domestic affairs of the socialist countries, try to transfer the class struggle to the sphere of interstate relations and to substitute one for the other. The Marxist-Leninist approach has resulted in the Soviet theory of peaceful coexistence, which (1) condemns interstate wars, (2) condemns open military interventions by the United States and other capitalist states in the Third World, (3) justifies more or less direct military interventions by the socialist states, even in the form chosen in Afghanistan called 'the support of a lawfully established government against imperialist counter-revolutionary attacks', and (4) justifies domestic revolutionary violence — e.g., in the form of national and/or social revolutions.

The justification of the direct or indirect military support given by socialist countries to internal liberation movements in general purports to be based on the laws of social development, which are irresistibly impelling the world towards socialism and which require such action by the already victorious socialist governments.

Certainly, class struggle between capitalism and socialism is said to constitute the basic content of international relations. A well-known researcher writes: 'During the age of transition from capitalism to socialism the struggle between the working class and the bourgeoisie has assumed the form of an interstate struggle between socialist and capitalist states which is constantly being waged in interconnected spheres: economic, political and ideological.'[5][7] The entire world, he continues, has become an arena for the struggle between the two social systems; it is an axis around which the whole international life and much of the domestic life of states of all types revolve; all the political processes and events in the world are related to the main conflict of the age and many of them arise from it. The crucial tasks are the liberation of nations from imperialist oppression, the build-up of socialism and communism in several states and the transition of mankind from capitalism to socialism. The latter task constitutes the basic aim of the entire international development.

However, this purpose will be achieved without a war between the two camps. The avoidance of wars between states should facilitate the expansion of communism by preserving the field for the class struggle in capitalist societies, for social revolutions and for wars waged by oppressed nations and dependent states against their oppressors. It is implied that this development will gradually lead to the disappearance of capitalism throughout the world. Such a development, apparently, would deprive the international system of its own development and dynamism.

The orthodox scheme of the leap-like development of a system, which culminates in a final clash of the polarised opposing forces, and the victory of the new over the old, has been abandoned. The main contradiction in the system ('the basic contradiction of the epoch') is said to constitute the basis of all conflicts in international relations; the proceeding polarisation is often pointed out. Yet a radical change in the system would come in a quite different way: through internal changes in the components. Moreover, it is stressed that the equilibrium in a national society is transitory, while the class struggle is continuous and must lead to a revolution. As regards the international system, the need to strengthen the status quo is constantly emphasised.

In the view of some Soviet writers, this difference between the development of the two systems expresses a deeper and more essential difference. While the domestic system is governed by laws of social development which inevitably impel it towards higher forms of social organisation, the international system is also regulated by diplomatic intercourse and political agreements.

Let us look at the Soviet reasoning on the avoidance of a direct clash between the two opposing camps. Soviet writers suggest that the bourgeois propaganda includes in the concept of the status quo two different issues: (1) the stability of the existing international relations — i.e., the political equilibrium; and (2) the unchangeability of the capitalist social system. However, the former issue concerns mutual relations between states and is regulated by normal diplomatic means. The latter issue concerns social development and is regulated by complex laws of social development and not by activities of politicians and diplomats. Changes in the social and political life of society are an inevitable process. They do not depend on agreements between states.[58] Accordingly, peaceful coexistence means the *avoidance of changing the status quo* between states *by violence.*

Two comments may be made. First, either this proposition means a radical change in Marxist-Leninist theory, which asserts that the international system will inevitably undergo a transition into a socialist one, which cannot be realised without breaking the resistance of capitalism, or it must be viewed as a set of *tactical* political principles for a very long transitory period and without a forecast concerning the way in which the decisive transformation would be accomplished. A contradiction arises between an unclear strategy for attaining the final aim — the transformation of the international system — and the tactics for an indefinite time, which means the preservation, and even the defence, of the status quo. One may wonder whether the basic aim for an indefinite and long period in the history of international relations can be called a tactical aim.

Second, the shift from the foreign framework to the domestic one in the expectation of changes which will finally convert the world from capitalism to socialism has not advanced the prospect of such a change in the foreseeable future. While there are possibilities of new socialist revolutions in developing countries, which are in a state of constant social flux, in developed industrialised countries, with their relatively high standard of living and reluctance (even as regards the Communists there) to provide concrete programmes for a socialist revolution, the prospect of such revolutions seems dim.

But in the Marxist-Leninist view, what is needed to determine the final outcome of the rivalry between socialism and capitalism is just revolutions in the developed countries. In a Soviet textbook for political education, prepared by a group of leading theorists in political science, it has been stated that the *final* victory of the socialist revolution on a world scale depends on the liquidation of the capitalist system in the industrially advanced states of North America and Western Europe and also Japan and Australia because these states constitute 'the citadel of modern capitalism accounting for its main economic, political and military forces'.[59] On the other hand, a victory in these countries would be decisive because the position of the working class there is crucial in the world revolutionary movement. Numerically the proletarians of these countries account for nearly 40 per cent of the working class in the world. They are highly organised and are experienced in class struggle.

Since in the foreseeable future socialist revolutions in the advanced capitalist countries seem unlikely, and since, on the other hand, they constitute the condition of the final victory of socialism on a world scale, the revision of the orthodox theses that only a decisive clash between capitalism and socialism will decide questions 'Who whom?' appears to be a tactical one and subordinated to the theory of peaceful coexistence.

Differences between domestic society and the international system

As we have seen, the Marxist-Leninist systemic approach assumes far-reaching systemic differences between domestic society and the international system.

Society, say the Marxist-Leninists, is a two-party system which comprises the socio-economic basis and the complex superstructure. As distinct from this, international relations do not constitute a superstructure on the basis of an aggregate economic basis common to all countries. The political and the economic interstate relations are relatively separate fields of interaction: they constitute a complex product of, on the one hand, an interaction between international and domestic policies of particular states and, on the other hand, a relatively independent process of self-development. Conflicts between particular protagonists in international relations depend on several variables. In many instances they are not mainly economic, but develop quite differently at different levels.

In international relations, the interaction of political, economic, ideological, military, legal and other relations is very complex. It is non-automatic and develops in a non-linear way. Political relations constitute the core of international relations and take primacy over all others.

Differences in the structures of the two kinds of systems and in the forces operating in them entail differences in the means and methods applied and in the prospects of the outcome of the struggle within the systems.

As regards the methods applied, the following differences seem to be implied.

(1) There is more asymmetry in the means used in the domestic struggle than those used in interstate rivalries. Whereas in domestic affairs, the means used by the basic adversaries are quite different (see

below), in international affairs the state apparatus of particular states, and of the two opposing camps, are the main instruments used by the two or more parties involved.

(2) Domestic class struggle directly reflects the economic basis, while international relations are only indirectly connected with it.

(3) Domestic relations constitute an interaction of one kind of opponents — the class adversaries — and they are both cooperative and competitive. International relations are affected by two kinds of factors: by the interaction of competitive and cooperative interstate relations and by the international class struggle.

(4) Interstate rivalry and cooperation are conceivable without war, whereas class struggle within particular countries leads to revolution often followed by civil war.

Lack of a general theory

It may be suggested that while the theory of society as a system operates with generalisations based on examples taken from different historical formations (structures), the theory of international systems is reduced to an analysis of the so-called imperialist system and of the contemporary mixed or bi-polar system. No 'laws' or regularities concerning *all* historical international systems — i.e., generalisations which may constitute a *theory* of international relations — have been formulated. Various formulae concerning the basic propositions and the frequent changes in them show that such a theory is perhaps only *in statu nascendi*. At the same time the increasing emphasis on the systemic approach to international relations may reflect the search for this theory. The need for the theory may be explained, if only partly, by the development of the Soviet Union into a global power.

Changes in interaction between the two kinds of systems

The above-mentioned changes in the Marxist-Leninist approach to the development of the domestic and the international systems also mean that the interaction between them has changed. To the fathers of Marxism, the expected simultaneous revolution in all of the developed countries would mean that the international system would *eo ipso* radically change its character and become a Communist one.

Lenin concluded that the international crisis and international war would lead only to the liquidation of capitalism in the weakest link of the world capitalist system. Stalin believed that this idea was confirmed by the emergence of several new socialist states after the Second World War. Although Marxism-Leninism denied this, it has been obvious that until recently, socialist revolutions as a rule have occurred in the conditions of large-scale international wars, or else were set off by such wars. Since the emergence of the first socialist state, and subsequently of several others, meant profound changes in the nature of the international system, the mutual conditioning of the two kinds of systems seemed to mean that each shake-up in the international system leads to domestic revolutions, which change the international system in turn.

At the same time, however, it was held that only a decisive clash of the two world-wide socio-economic formations — capitalism and socialism — would *ultimately* defeat capitalism.

Both these assumptions have recently changed. In the first place, it is now held that domestic revolutions can occur without great international crises and wars. In the assessment of a Soviet theorist one of the main features of our epoch is that war is no longer a prerequisite for revolution. A revolution can — and preferably it should — be carried through to success in the conditions of peace and peaceful coexistence.[60]

Second, as mentioned above, the final transformation of the international system will result from the 'accumulation' of domestic revolutions in one country after another.

It is only because of the *correlation of world forces*, which is advantageous to socialism *and which keeps changing to its advantage*, that domestic revolutions break out and achieve success without the danger of being repressed by the international bourgeoisie. In turn, these revolutions affect — positively for socialism — the correlation of world forces. Thus the impact is mutual. The features of the international system may be regarded as *permissive* causes of a gradual international change leading to a final transformation of the system into a socialist one. This occurs through revolutionary transformations in the particular countries, which thus constitute the *necessary* and *direct* causes of changes in both the international and domestic systems.

One may add that the pro-socialist correlation of world forces has also another implication. Since the policy of the leading Western powers is much more cautious than that of the Soviet Union and, at the same time, indecisive, the latter is able to support the Communist forces in various countries directly — even by means of an open invasion, as in Afghanistan — and thus impel one country after another along the road to socialism.

It may be said, however, that if, in our times, domestic revolutions are to become the primary link in the interaction between the domestic system and the international system, this will represent a radical departure from the previous scenerio of evolution also in another sense, but not in that approved by Marxist-Leninist theorists.

Lenin asserted — and his proposition is now quoted by the leading Soviet theorists as wholly justified by the subsequent revolutions — that no wars and no external factors can by themselves generate revolutionary changes in particular countries,[61] that internal conditions, a crisis in the 'dogs' together with a crisis in the 'tops' — i.e., the existence of a revolutionary situation — are *necessary* preconditions and prerequisites of any revolution. However, several socialist 'revolutions' in the countries of Eastern Europe in the final phases of the Second World War could hardly be assessed as genuine revolutions, which resulted from conscious actions by revolutionary popular masses. If future revolutions are to be truly domestic ones, this will mean the reversal of the present *actual* relationship between the domestic system and the international system.

Changes in theory

It seems that also modifications in the Marxist-Leninist *concept and classification* of the domestic and international systems are under way. In the orthodox theory, two categories of social formations were recognised: the so-called class society and the classless society. Among the former, the slave-owning, feudal and capitalist formations were the types, and, apart from primitive society, there is only one instance of a class-less society — i.e., the Communist one, which in its first phase is called socialism. It was implied that international systems corresponded to domestic systems: they were uniform in particular formations.

The first change was that in the view taken of classless societies. In the orthodox-Marxist view, a socialist society would be a classless society. The actual conditions in the socialist construction in the Soviet Union forced a revision of this view and the introduction of the concept of 'friendly (brotherly) classes': the working class and the peasants. Apart from the circumstance that remnants of the former exploiting classes also appeared to survive for a long time, the existence of 'friendly classes' prompted Marxist-Leninist writers to call pre-socialist societies 'antagonistic societies' and to stress the antagonistic character of the basic classes in those societies. In this terminology, socialist societies are the 'non-antagonistic' ones.

The second change has been more far-reaching. While previously the very idea of a transitional system between capitalism and socialism has been rejected by Marxist-Leninist scholars,[62] in the recently-published military encyclopaedia it is explained that if it is impossible precisely to classify a given type of social structure as slave-owning, feudal, bourgeois or socialist, then 'it should be called a *transitory type* or a state or society in the process of development towards one type or another'. For instance, states of transitory type emerge during the collapse of colonialism. As regards their political and economic systems, such states cannot yet be classified as belonging to any of the main types.[63]

In most recent publications, the status of the transitory system has been raised almost to the level of a transitory formation. There are said to exist 'transitory inter-formational stages of social development'[64] which are analysed as separate stages. They are described as including features of both the previous and the following formations in all systemic elements: in the means of production, the relations of production, the class structure and the politico-legal superstructure, in ideology and the forms of social consciousness.[65] The inter-formational stages begin with the emergence of a conflict between the means of production and the relations of production in a formation and end with the resolution of this conflict. Two authorities may emerge in this transitional period: one represents the previous class structure and the other the revolutionary forces and the new structure. While formations are characterised by evolutionary development — partial changes occurring under the influence of changed conditions and the requirements of social progress, primarily those of material production — the inter-formational stages are characterised by a specific (revolutionary) type of development.

A novelty in the description of these issues given by some Marxist-Leninist writers is their very cautious approach to making generalisations in the field of social development. The concept of a socio-economic formation as well as of social revolution constitute, they write, an 'extreme abstraction'. In regard to revolution, it expresses only the most general, essential and law-like features in the transition from one formation to another — namely, that it proceeds in a revolutionary way. 'No revolution has proceeded — nor could it have proceeded — in a "pure manner" *(v chistom vide)*, writes Seleznev.[66] The revolutionary transition from one antagonistic formation to another is quite different from that from capitalism to socialism. Moreover, a factual revolution in a country takes an individual and unrepeatable form.

In our time, for instance, there is the possibility that the popular masses, headed by the working class, may seize power without changing the legal superstructure; this happened in Chile in December 1970. However, in 1973, a counter-revolution was carried out by the armed forces. In Cuba the revolution was effected in a very different way. These and other historical examples demonstrate that the various anti-imperialist revolutions may follow very different courses, depending, on the one hand, on the degree of involvement of the popular masses and, on the other, on the kind and amount of resistance offered by the bourgeoisie.

(It often has happened in countries where a bourgeois revolution was imminent, say some Soviet analysts, that, becoming aware of the growth of social forces representing a new socio-economic formation, and sometimes even after an attempted revolution by the bourgeoisie, reactionary feudal forces representing the outmoded formation themselves have carried out reforms which paved way to the new formation. Thus the Russian feudal aristocracy abolished serfdom in 1861; the Prussian junkers in the 1850s and 1860s, introduced several reforms paving the way to the emergence of an industrial united Germany; in Japan a progressive part of the feudal class, on taking power in 1868–9, began the process of political centralisation of the country, which facilitated the growth of the bourgeoisie. The development of progressive social forces in the old formation played a large role in all these transformations.)[67]

Since, as we see, Soviet writers began to treat certain classical Marxist doctrines as very broad *generalisations*, within which *specific* cases deserve *specific* interpretation, *some general premises could be left unchanged*. The very concept of a socio-economic formation, as determined by the nature of the relations of production, and the concept of its law-like revolutionary change as representing social development still distinguish the Marxist-Leninist theory from all other approaches. All concepts of social history starting from the techno-material basis — for instance, those concerning a uniform agriculture society in general, or a uniform industrial and post-industrial societies in general — have been rejected as 'technical determinism', in which social life develops primarily under the *direct* impact of technical development.[68] (See below.)

It seems, however, that at least some Marxist-Leninist writers recently have been trying to free themselves from the rigid schemes imposed by orthodox theory. Empirically, they describe the deviations from the classical functions of the state, from the classical course of revolution and from the classical scheme of social development.

With regard to the theory some of these writers[69] maintain that:

(1) The manner of reasoning in theories, concepts and so on should be regarded as an abstraction drawn from a multi-dimensional and multifarious historical process. Theory must be modified if applied to individual historical events.

(2) One should therefore distinguish between two levels of social development: (a) the uniform and formative and (b) the many-sided and situational. The former connotes a search for *general* principles and the prospects of social development. The latter connotes the *avoidance of simplifications* and reduction of events (for instance, social revolution) to a pure scheme, in which there is no place for historical specifics and everything is predetermined by the development of the forces of production. The significance of practical activity is then reduced to zero.

(3) In certain theories, therefore, two concepts have been introduced, one of which concerns the process in its ideal form, developing in accordance with the laws, while the other concerns the actual process of human action, which is subject to various influences, develops in

various forms and sometimes deviates from the ideal form. Thus Seleznev, in his recent and apparently modified interpretation of the Marxist theory of social revolutions, distinguishes between revolution as social *change* and revolution as social *action*. The former is covered by the theory of social revolution as a natural-historical process of transition from a lower socio-economic formation to a higher one. This theory contains classical or orthodox propositions about the contradiction and conflict between the means of production and the relations of production as the determining cause of the revolutionary transition from one formation to another. The research concerning concrete revolutions however, is quite different: it means a concrete historical analysis leading perhaps to the discovery of many variants of revolution which do not fit into the classical scheme. Thus Seleznev describes three variants of the bourgeois revolution none of which are 'classical' — i.e., accord with classical Marxist schemes. Seleznev also asserts, in general, that social revolutions are irreversible, yet he considers that in the variety of concrete revolutionary events, the specific historical environment, including international conditions, may cause a revolution to stagnate or even to decline and die away.[70]

Marxist-Leninist versus non-Marxist approaches to the analysis of social systems

Differences between the Marxist-Leninist and non-Marxist approaches to the analysis of social systems greatly affect their interpretations of the correlation of forces versus the traditional concept of the balance of power (cf. Chapter 7). Since the analysis of the Marxist-Leninist concept is the subject of this study, it seems worthwhile to point out the differences in the systemic premises for these interpretations *as Marxist-Leninist science sees them*. Their view of non-Marxist approaches and the criticism of these approaches may be distorted by their wish to dismiss these as unscientific; when necessary, the distortions will be pointed out. However, the Marxist-Leninists also use criticisms of other opinions and concepts as a means of developing and presenting their own views. Soviet ideology requires that each theory in social science develops through the criticism of so-called bourgeois views and thereby also contributes to the ideological struggle.[71]

In previous sections it was implied that the Marxist-Leninist view of society and the international system differs from non-Marxist views (1) in its concept of the laws governing social systems, (2) in its interpretation of the genesis of these systems and their structure and (3) in the explanation of the mechanism of their development. The criticisms mainly concerned these points.

While society develops according to historical laws, in the view of the Marxist-Leninists, there is no theory of the laws of social development in contemporary Western thought. The dominant view there is that the concept of law suggests a type of determination that is too 'strong' to provide an explanation of social behaviour; such a concept is found even less acceptable with regard to social development. Social laws — even if they exist — cannot be cognized. The tangle of links and relationships between phenomena is such that one cannot discover the determining cause or distinguish a single condition as a cause. Some writers replace social causation by the more general idea of interrelations between social phenomena, interpreted as functional dependence of events. These, according to causal principle, are the results of other events — but here they constitute the function of them. According to Marxists, this approach may be used to explain *single functions* of social systems, but it can by no means explain the *development* of them.

The Marxist-Leninist criticisms go much further, however. Western theories reject the propositions (1) that social events are rooted in the development of the material basis and that they have their definite and determined place in this development, and (2) that links between social phenomena reflect the laws of dialectics and they can be cognized and the knowledge of them can be utilised. This leads to social events being inexplicable in terms of the laws of social development and to social history becoming a chaotic and inexplicable process. Indeed, any possibility that social science may exist is here denied. This, say the critics, brings us to the motives for adopting such a position. The total absence of laws of social development leads to a denial of the inevitability of such a development and, in particular, to a denial of the inevitability of the disappearance of capitalism in the course of a law-like social development.

Objections of the second kind are levelled against attitudes which although accepting the existence of the laws of social change, do not consider them as springing from the material basis of society. Common to the many variants of these views, say the critics, is that various kinds of non-material causal factors have been substituted for material and objective laws.

In one of the main currents of this philosophical stream, which Marxist-Leninist writers describe as objective-idealistic and which is said to derive from the Hegelian tradition, history is the manifestation and expression of the self-development of the 'world spirit'. The laws and regularities of social development which we detect are but a reflection and expression of the laws of development of this world spirit. This means, say the critics, that material reality has no movement of its own. The process of thinking, of the development of ideas, the tendency of the world spirit towards self-perfection and the acquisition of full consciousness create reality, which follows the laws imposed by the spirit, thought or mind. The development of material reality is an external manifestation and reflection of the development of the mind.

According to another view, which the Soviet critics call the subjective-idealistic approach, the human intellect is the 'creator'. Its development underlies social development: the latter depends on the development of human knowledge. The main motive forces of history are the great individuals, since knowledge develops through their intellectual efforts.

In a variant of this, the psychological development is said to underlie social development as a whole. The critics consider that since the development of the social (i.e., collective) psyche is regarded in the criticised approach as a projection of the individual psyche and the latter is governed by its own laws, the motive force of social development is here reduced once again to the individual psyche.

In the argument against both of these currents, Soviet writers repeat the main assumptions of historical materialism which underlie the criticism of all non-Soviet philosophy, sociology, economics and other social sciences: that the lawful development of the system of production (with its basic law of the necessary correspondence of productive relations to the forces of production) determines the lawful development of the political, ideological, legal and moral superstructure — i.e., the whole material and spiritual life of society. Therefore, the laws of the material development determine the course of history. In both the approaches criticised, what is secondary in real social life becomes primary and vice versa; what is, in fact, only superstructure becomes the motivating force, and the real motivating force — the economic basis — is presented as following laws invented and imposed by the spiritual superstructure.

Another non-Marxist approach to social development — the so-called 'technical determinism' — is also criticised. In this, the development of the means of production is presented as the cause of social development. Particularly now when science has become an immediate productive force, the growth of scientific knowledge and the resulting development of new technology exercises a great influence on the structures of production and thereby also, through intermediate stages, on the entire mode of life society.

Soviet scholars see two kinds of 'technical determinist' approaches. The first predicts the development of the world towards a 'post-industrial' society based on high scientific and technical levels. This society would constitute an improved capitalist society, while the contemporary socialist system would be swallowed by it. In the second approach, capitalism and socialism would converge into a system which combined the features of both. It is not clearly said, however, where the two systems will fuse, at what time and what the future combination will be like, and in fact these theories imply that the need for socialism will drop under the impact of the all-powerful alliance of the scientific-technical revolution and capitalist efficiency. It also implies that the United States is the model for such development.[72]

The criticism is that the development of productive forces exercises a revolutionary influence not directly but through the socio-economic structure.[73] The relations of production may correspond to the level of the productive forces and may stimulate their further development, or hinder it. If the latter takes place, the class struggle leads to a revolutionary change in the entire socio-economic system, and there follows a change in the superstructure. Technical innovations pave the way for changes in the social order, but the changes themselves are effected not by machines but by human beings acting as social classes. Classes constitute the social forces which play a leading role in laying down the new socio-economic basis and shaping the corresponding political and ideological superstructure.

The theories in question proceed from the assumption that the present era is not an era of class struggle rooted in the contradictions of the socio-economic basis but one in which scientific and technical progress wholly and completely determines all varieties of social order. Ignoring the actual mechanism of social change, these theories fail to take into account that only a revolutionary change of the *whole* basis, together with its class structure, can free the world from misery and social injustice.

Taking the development of productive forces as the determining factor, one may suggest that social progress may be advanced in the existing social order without a social revolution. This, like other bourgeois theories, serves to perpetuate the capitalist system.

Mechanisms of social change:
(1) Developing system versus equilibrium theories

In criticising the non-Marxist theories of social development, systems theories based on the idea of social equilibrium constitute one of the main objects of analysis. These are said to proceed from the view that society is in a state of equilibrium and follow the line that society and international systems are stable organisms in which all events are determined by their unchanging structure, by the unchanging relationships between the components, and concomitantly by the unchanging patterns of behaviour designed to preserve the system.

As mentioned above, Marxist-Leninist theory considers the procedure of the systemic structural analysis of the social processes to be the basic one:[74] all the internal and international social processes and all the laws and regularities characterising their occurrence and course are said to be rooted in the internal structure of the class society. Such an approach also includes the characteristics of the international system as an important factor influencing all international events. However, Soviet writers insistently contend that the present international system is a *unique* phenomenon. Unlike all previous international systems, it is *heterogeneous;* it is based on the competition of two antagonistic socio-economic and political groupings. A *radical transformation* of it in the future is desirable and inevitable. Likewise, no essential features of this system can be derived from other systems and from abstract and artificial models, and no phenomena and processes in it can be explained by the structure of such models.

Soviet writers criticise various Western systems theories concerning the international system for the following characteristics:[75]

(1) These systems theorists try to apply to the analysis of international relations the concept of a homogeneous stable system, characterised by a structure and regularities that are designed to preserve and maintain its stable identity. This implies that the present international system will preserve its form for ever, which is obviously erroneous.

(2) Non-Marxist systems theorists see the international system not only as a timeless but also a classless construction. The variables proposed by particular analysts lack a concrete socio-political content.[76]

(3) The models of the international systems presented are highly abstract and artificial; they bear very little resemblance to the systems which have existed in some periods of history, and even less to the present system.[77] No analysis of international relations can be based on such models and their hypothetical attributes and regularities.[78]

(4) Systems theorists absolutise the role of power in the structure of system models and the patterns of behaviour which characterise them. In many instances, the resultant models of the contemporary, or future, or desirable, international system are based on the distribution of power; but this is only one of factors affecting international relations.

(5) By disguising the true nature of the international system, these theories seek to justify policies for preserving the unjust socio-economic and political status quo in both the international system itself and the particular antagonistic class societies.

Non-Marxist theories are also basically criticised for methodological premises that are closely related to the philosophical and sociological views of society and the international system. The prevailing approach is said to be that of so-called *structural functionalism.* It assumes that all systems, including antagonistic class societies and the international system, possess structures designed to satisfy standard functional requirements.[79] These functions are the determining characteristics of the systems: they maintain them in a stable shape. The constant patterns of action followed in the fulfilment of these functions are necessary to the continued existence of the system.

In this approach, the critics say, the erroneous ideas that both antagonistic class society and the international system possess stability, is combined with the further erroneous assumption that such stability is strictly connected with inherent functions of the system and the patterns of behaviour of its members (components, elements) serve this stability. In other words, it is held that a system is maintained in a stable shape by the functions which its structure fulfils. This approach is rooted in the philosophy of society as a harmonious organism, the elements of which serve to preserve it — a view which is rejected by Marxist-Leninist analysts.

It is not surprising, they say, that no patterns of domestic as well as international behaviour and no regularities of the causation of conflicts can be discovered by a comparison of the actual class society or international system with some model system built on the patterns of behaviour, links, dependences and factors which are alleged to be *common* to all systems, or at least to a group of them.

They mention, for instance, the concept presented by George Modelski,[80] who points out four basic functions as being common to all international systems: resource allocation, authority, solidarity and culture. In this structural-functionalist perspective, Modelski proposes a spectrum of models of international relations with two models at each end of it: Agraria and Industria. The former, which poorly fulfils its basic functions, is regarded as generating wars, while in Industria, which is viewed as much more homogeneous, integrated and politically conscious — i.e., as a much better functioning system — the resort to war is generally regarded as undesirable. All really-existing systems should be studied and assessed in relation to these extremes.

This concept is criticised not only for its structural-functionalist philosophy but also for its application. The imperialist powers, which are highly industrial and fit the model of 'Industria', are presented as peaceful, while agrarian states and all underdeveloped countries fall into the 'Agraria' category and are accused of causing conflicts and wars. The veritable division of the world is obviously quite different from this concept, as also is the role played by particular groups of countries.[81]

While the criticism of concrete models of international systems is quite understandable from the Soviet angle, the motives for criticism of the main ideas of the theory of structural functionalism deserve a brief comment.

The Marxist-Leninist theory does not, in principle, reject the idea that class society and the international system are during many periods, sometimes long ones, relatively stable, that in these periods they have relatively durable structures and that in the international system all the component states contribute to its functioning on the basis of some —

tacit or open — consensus. Obviously, the very fact that the international system is a system means that the relations between its members are characterised by some repetitive functions. This also accords with the above-mentioned Soviet view that society is a system, since it consists of classes each of which performs functions indispensable to the existence of society. Without the interaction of the antagonistic classes the class society would lose its identity.

Thus the criticism is levelled not against the idea of the stability of the system, which in a sense and within certain limits and periods is also accepted in Soviet theory, but against the equation of the stability of both the class society and the international system with their capacity to survive regardless of the conditions intrinsic to the system — or, indeed, just because of them.

Soviet researchers emphasise that the stability of social systems is only *relative and temporary*. It is based not on harmonious cooperation but on a relative *balance between members having conflicting interests*. It expresses a dynamic correlation between opposing social and political forces, pregnant with revolutions and wars; and sooner or later the conflict between these *must lead to the replacement* of the given system by another one.

Thus while in the structural-functional concept both internal and international wars are 'normal' if they help to maintain the stability, and 'abnormal' if they endanger it, in the Soviet concept they are always natural in the sense that they are rooted in the very essence of the class society and of the international system, with its interaction of conflicting class and national interests.

Once more, the criticism reveals the strong emphasis with which the Soviet concept of social development and its laws is presented as unique in the history of science and its intolerance of any ideas that would not fit the determination of social events by class struggle and their development, through the use of violence, towards a classless society.

Mechanisms of social change:
(2) Development through class struggle versus power theories

The second basic object of the criticism of misleading theories of social change are those which consider that social systems are based on the struggle for power. These are the so-called political realist views, which were elaborated in detail with regard to the international system.[82] Here only the main points of them as seen and criticised by Marxist-Leninists will be taken up.

The political realist assumption that the search for power reflects the drive for dominance which characterises individual man is countered by the proposition that the feelings, emotions and views of the individual (like the views and actions of the leaders of states) are a social and class product; both depend on class interests and only a class-political analysis can explain them. Neither a collective nor an individual 'search for power' can explain social conflicts and social developments.[83]

As always in such a criticism, the erroneous content of the theories is said to be deeply anchored in an erroneous philosophy and its role in the ideological rivalry. Power theories, in all versions and with all corollary concepts, are said to justify the bellicose policy of imperialist states, by disguising the actual causation of wars and diverting attention to non-existent or secondary links and to the dependence of war on the structure of the international system.

In the Marxist-Leninist concept, the world rivalry and confrontation, as well as their course and predicted outcome, follow the laws of social history, i.e., serve the purposes of progressive change. Imperialism is presented as resisting the world revolutionary process by force, which is also in accordance with laws, since imperialism *must* resist progressive changes and defend the status quo. To Marxist-Leninists, it is no wonder that such attempts fail and that imperialist doctrines mention no laws that would reveal the nature and destiny of imperialism.

Power theories which assume that no radical change in the existing structure of the international system is either predictable or desirable, are concerned with the search for the most stable type of this system. Contrary to this, the Marxist-Leninist theory assumes that the international system will and should be transformed and that it must sooner or later be replaced by the system of socialist states. Instead of the more or less stable balance of power envisaged in the political realist version, they see a dynamic correlation of forces between the two antagonistic camps, which is constantly changing in favour of the so-called socialist and progressive forces.

Thus the Marxist-Leninist concept does not negate the significance of power but it sees it as a class phenomenon: in our world, power is an instrument of class struggle between the antagonistic systems rather than a means of pursuit of state interests.

Quite different criticisms are raised against the approach of the power theorists to developments in national societies. While in international relations the search for power and the use of it as a means of solving conflicts, maintaining the balance of power and ensuring the stability of the system, are overemphasised, in domestic relations they are toned down. Power theorists pass in silence over the basic motive force of social life and social development which is the class struggle for state power. They ignore the fact that revolution — which is inevitable — means a transfer of power from one class to another class and a change of the form of property which is conditioned by this transfer: it either accompanies such transfer of power or is its subsequent aim.[84]

What is common in the power approach to both the international system and domestic societies is that the theorists see them as *stable systems* and ignore the laws of social development which operate on behalf of the future transformation of both kinds of social systems into socialism.

Mechanisms of social change:
(3) Development through revolution versus evolution

Marxist-Leninist criticism is also directed against various theories of social change which reduce the mechanism of the development of human society to a gradual evolution. The following features seem to characterise these theories, as the critics see them.

(1) They deal predominantly with domestic change and rarely try to apply the concept of evolutionary development to the international system;

(2) they see progress as consisting of a better adaptation of society to the environment, through growth in size and increasing societal complexity and functional specialisation;

(3) they focus on individuals whose solidarity with other individuals in society is seen as growing, owing to the similarity and cooperation that arise from interdependence;

(4) they focus on economic development (for instance, industrialisation and techno-scientific revolution) and parallel with this, on social development that is confined to better conditions of individual life and increasing social integration.

Marxist-Leninist theory shares with the evolutionary theories the view that society is developing in the direction of increasing complexity, functional specialisation and better adaptation to the environment. However, in almost all other respects it differs from them. It is not individuals but classes that are in focus. The development does not involve greater cohesion but, within a single socio-economic formation, it sharpens the contradictions and the conflicts. Progress is not confined to smooth cumulative changes but proceeds through revolutionary 'leaps' which radically change the entire social structure. And it is the change in the social *structure*, which in the final — Communist — formation, will bring about a classless society, which is *the* basic social change and the principal manifestation of social development.

The contrast between theories which see social development as an evolutionary process and the revolutionary theory of Marxism-Leninism has been reflected in the contrast between the social-democratic and communist ideological assumptions and political programmes, according to the Marxist-Leninist view.[85] Social Democrats have abandoned — in fact rejected — socialist revolution which is (1) transfer of power from the capitalist class to the working class and other working people, and (2) change of the form of property of the basic means of production from private property to property of all society. Social democracy aims at reforming the existing capitalist system, i.e. pursuing policies which aim at improving and perfecting some specific parts of the social mechanism of capitalism without impinging on its basic principles. It says only in a very general way that the quantity of reforms will grow into a new quality of society but does not explain what the 'new quality' will mean — only that it will *not* mean the change of state power and the form of property of the basic means of production. Its only argument for the evolutionary mechanism of social change is that the scientific-technical revolution makes possible quick material progress *within* capitalist society.

K. Zarodov[86] writes:

> In their interpretation, the Marxian theory of the transition to socialism is no more than a product of the nineteenth century useless for modern conditions. When it was created, they declare, capitalism was quite different; today, they say, it has qualitatively altered, and the antagonism between the proletariat and the capitalist class has disappeared while capitalist society, in their view, has become democratic and 'socialist' elements have appeared in it. All that, social reformists say, makes a revolutionary transformation of the capitalist system unnecessary; socialism will gradually grow over out of capitalism.[87]

The Marxist-Leninist criticism is fierce and bitter. The social democrats have taken an anti-revolutionary and anti-socialist position, since socialism cannot be attained by gradual improvements of capitalism.

G. Shakhnazarov states that social democrats 'do not set themselves the deliberate goal of abolishing capitalism and building socialism'.[88]

Marxism-Leninism is not against reforms, say Soviet scholars. In the old society, reforms can help improve working conditions and conditions of life for the oppressed classes; they can enlarge democracy; they may even sometimes weaken the motive centres of the capitalist system and create favourable conditions for revolution. Moreover, *after* a victorious revolution, in the new society reforms concerning economy, and the social structure become a *modus operandi* for the ruling revolutionary class. But reforms do not constitute an alternative road to socialism. Reforms and revolution supplement each other, since the former may lay the ground for the latter. Reforms can never *replace* revolution, they can bring about quantitative changes, while radical qualitative transformations can be effected by revolution only. Quantitative changes prepare for a qualitative jump (law of dialectics), evolution prepares for revolution.[89]

Certainly, revolution should not be identified with the use of force, even less with armed violence. The following is a representative quotation:

> This passage (to socialism — JL) is necessarily performed by force where the revolutionary class and its allies are resisted by the reactionary class, and resisted by force. It may also be a peaceful passage where the relation of forces is so strongly in favour of the revolutionary classes that the outgoing social strata ... are unable to resort to force, to take up arms, and are compelled to reconcile themselves to the inevitability of change. Marxism-Leninism not only admits the possibility of, but also regards as preferable, a peaceful transfer of power to the working class, and therefore also the possibility of carrying out revolutionary reconstruction by non-violent means — any means made available by the historical process, be it universal suffrage, the legislative will of parliament, or a general strike — so long as they lead to the formation of a revolutionary government and thereby set in motion a social revolution.[90]

The criticism of the social democratic 'evolutionary' road to socialism has been supplemented with apologia for the programmes established by the revolutionary Communist parties of the developed capitalist countries (France, Great Britain, Italy and others). The activity of these parties in our time is said to be based on new, more flexible, strategic and tactical principles. The new strategy is that of small steps, of gradually enhancing the scope of democracy and of solving current economic and political problems. In the alliance with other oppressed classes and strata of society the Communist parties use traditional democratic institutions including parliament.

The difference, however, between this strategy and the 'evolutionary' programme of the social democrats is *hardly detectable*. It has been reduced to the general assertion that the Communist parties *expect* a peaceful transition to socialism in some distant future, that such passing will involve sudden revolutionary changes, alteration in the character of ownership of the means of production and exchange and a passing of political power from the capitalist class to the working class. The solution of current economic and sociopolitical issues should be linked with a socialist perspective.[91] The programmes do not include any indication on *how* such a transition to socialism will proceed and they avoid any call for a *struggle* for socialist revolution.

Mechanisms of social change:
(4) Development through the resolution of the basic conflict
versus ubiquity of conflicts without development

Marxism-Leninism differs from various theories of social *conflict* which assert the ubiquity of such conflict. These theories state that each element in society is subject at every moment to change, but do not point out which conflict is the basic one and how to resolve it. Such an assumption means that society is constantly experiencing a multitude of conflicts that are different in form, degree of intensity and extent of the resultant changes; and this obscures the principal question: how do radical structural changes in society occur?[92]

This question is the primary concern of Soviet research, and it reveals one of the determining characteristics of the Soviet concept. Society develops by means of 'leaps' — i.e., revolutionary structural changes effected by violence in the form of social revolutions. These radical changes in the entire socio-economic and political structure are seen as milestones in social development. Such changes can occur only as the result of an aggravation of the basic class conflict which underlies all others, a fact which should not be allowed to become obscured or drowned in the multitude of ubiquitous lesser conflicts.

Conflicts differ in many essential respects: the field of human activity (political, economic, cultural, psychological, ideological, etc.); the social level (interstate, interclass, interpersonal, intrapersonal); the method of resolution (peaceful or by armed violence); and the social setting (capitalist or socialist). So various, indeed, are the kinds of conflict that no regularities common to all can be found.

A general theory of conflict tends to obscure not only the qualitative distinctions between various kinds of conflict but also the distinctions between their causation and role in social life. Different conflicts have different causes, and different correlates, links and dependences with other phenomena. The lumping together of all conflicts without due differentiation obscures the fact that the economic class struggle is the mainspring of all conflicts in social development.

Modern non-Marxist theories of conflict have inherited from orthodox Marxism the idea that society is subject to constant change, but they reject the Marxist dialectics of change and all the basic conclusions drawn from this. By asserting that social conflict and change are ubiquitous they reduce the importance of the polarisation of the basic conflicting social forces. They substitute the conflict and struggle for dominance in society — i.e., for the seizure and maintenance of power, which is *not* rooted in the socio-economic position — for conflict of classes defined with regard to the relations of production.[93]

The failure of these theories to point out the basic class contradiction as the motive force of social development results in the identification of the confrontation of antagonistic classes with many other forms of conflict — between and inside classes, and some outside classes — which are never the impulse for revolutionary change of society. In other words, by dissolving class struggle in a sea of other contradictions, theory of conflict minimises the significance of this struggle. Moreover, it declares most of social contradictions as derivative primarily from human nature thus insuperable, which makes the prospect of revolutionary social change miserable. Some of the conflict theories regard 'conciliation' as the main method characterising capitalist society, contrasted with the alleged 'command method' in socialist society. All these traditional and novel ideas in modern conflict theories carry them even more away from the idea of conflict inherent in Marxist-Leninist social theory.

Certain elements of conflict theory in contemporary Marxist-Leninist writings have also changed. Political conflict — i.e., that occurring in the superstructure — more than ever before affects the forms and methods of economic struggle; polarisation may be noted in the superstructure rather than in the economic substructure; consequently the significance of the correlation of intrasocietal forces as a factor which may determine the resolution of the basic social conflict is increasing. However, it seems that with these modifications, the difference between this approach and the non-Marxist theories of conflict is growing rather than declining.

Similar differences between the Marxist-Leninist approach and non-Marxist theories of social conflict may be observed in the analysis of international relations. The general theory of conflict treats international relations as an arena where many conflicts are waged which are similar as regards their general structure and content, and each of them, to some extent, changes the system. Thus the theory lumps together all international conflicts without taking into account that: (1) they differ as regards their level, intensity, scale and form; (2) they are generated by various contradictions, have various socio-political causes and contents; and (3) contradictions and conflicts between imperialist states, between these states and developing countries and within the Third World should be distinguished from the basic contradiction of the epoch — that between capitalism and socialism — and conflicts generated by it.

The general theory of conflict, as a rule, does not relate the various conflicts to the *development* of the international system, nor does it show that the basic contradiction leads to a polarisation of the world into two opposing camps, nor that it generates the basic conflict, the resolution of which would mean the decisive transformation of the international system. Particular conflicts may be linked directly or indirectly to the basic contradiction, but may also emerge independently of it. In the general theory of conflict, the category of a conflict deprived of any sociopolitical content replaces the category of contradiction. However, the latter, being the source of both cooperation and the conflict of the opposites, makes it easier to understand why the international system is relatively stable in some periods, yet inevitably moves towards a transformation through conflict.

The view which sees the international community as an arena of conflict but does not take account of the basic contradiction and the polarisation of the basic opposing international forces does not reflect the real content and structure of the system, with its class contradictions and tendencies to develop into a class-less system, conclude Marxist-Leninist analysts.

Summary

(1) The non-Marxist theories of social systems may or may not formulate concepts of 'direction' in social change; when they do so they may call it progress. Marxism-Leninism in a categorical and apodictic way interprets social progress, as a revolutionary development from one socio-economic formation to another — and an assertedly higher — one.
(2) Non-Marxist theories usually focus on either the domestic social system or the international system. Marxism-Leninism connects them conceptually and functionally by means of the concept of the class state, which is a protagonist in both systems.
(3) Marxist-Leninist social system theories differ from non-Marxist ones in placing social class rather than individuals or an indefinite 'social group' in the focus of social development.

Notes

1 *Politicheskii slovar,* B.N. Ponomarev, (ed.), Gospolitizdat, Moscow 1958, p. 257; 'Kategorii voennoi nauki' in *Sovetskaya Voennaya Entsiklopeiya,* vol. 4, pp. 121—2; 'Kategorii' in *Filosofskii Entsiklopedicheskii Slovar* , Izd. Sovetskaya Entsiklopediya, Moscow 1983, p. 251; Yurkovets, 1984, p. 260.
2 *Filosofiya i voennaya istoriya,* 1979, Ch. 8: 'Dialekticheskaya kontseptsiya razvitiya i nekotorye problemy voennoi istorii', p., 196.
3 Cf. J. Lider, *Military Force,* 1981, Ch. 2.
4 Lenin's definition of classes reads: 'Classes are large groups of people differing from each other by the place they occupy in a historically determined system of social production, by their

relation (in most cases fixed and formulated in law) to the means of production, by their role in the social organisation of labour, and, consequently by the dimensions of the share of social wealth of which they despose and the mode of acquiring it. Classes are groups of people one of which can appropriate the labour of another owing to the different places they occupy in a definite system of social economy' ('A Great Beginning', *Collected Works,* Progress Publishers, vol. 29, p. 421.)

5   Thus taking as the criterion the proximity of a group to legislative, executive or judicial power in the state, Ralf Dahrendorf distinguishes between four class groups in industrialised capitalist societies: the upper class, the service class, the subordinate class and the class of free intellectuals *(Konflikt und Freiheit. Auf dem Weg zur Dienstklassengesellschaft,* Poper, Munchen 1972, pp. 112, 136). Other non-Marxist authors who understand class as a synonym for status group enumerate, for instance, the following classes: upper class, upper middle class, lower middle class etc. For a detailed criticism of these theories see Nadel, 1982, Part I, Ch. I. Likewise, Galkin who analyses the bourgeois theories of social structure points out that even those theories which acknowledge the existence of large social classes, reject the Marxist criteria related to the property of the means of production and propose unclear criteria such as 'status', 'power', etc. (1982, pp. 96—7).

6   *The Fundamentals of Marxist-Leninist Philosophy,* 1982, Ch. XV; Yurkovets, 1984, Ch. VIII.2.

7   Shakhnazarov, 1984, pp. 16—17.

8   Piotr Fedoseyev, 'The Dialectics of Social Life', *World Marxist Review,* (afterwards quoted as *W.M.R.*). 1981:9, p. 42.

9   Yasyukov, 1973, p. 17.

10 'Vooruzhennoe nasilie' in *Sovetskaya Voennaya Entsiklopediya,* vol. V, pp. 517—18; 'Gewalt' in *Wörterbuch der marxistischen-leninistischen Soziologie,* Westdeutscher Verlag, Opladen 1971, p. 168. In *Voina i Armiya* violence is defined as 'a system of economic, political (including military) and ideological measures of compulsion applied by certain classes and states to others' (1977, p. 59).

11 Denisov, 1975, pp. 6—7.

12 Yasyukov, 1973, pp. 19—23.

13 Golub, 1979, pp. 11—16; Fr. Engels, *Anti-Dühring,* Moscow 1975, p. 171.

14 'Let us note, first of all, that the class struggle itself, which is the law governing the development of antagonistic formations, is in fact none other than violence. On the part of the oppressed classes it is a quite understandable response to the regime of oppression and exploitation. The revolution, being the highest form of class

struggle, only serves to reveal the resistance of the exploited masses, ever present in antagonistic society, to the violence of the ruling classes. Hence revolution does not beget violence but only stimulates new forms of it — revolutionary violence. Secondly, the economic relations of private property, exploitation and political power as objects of revolutionary action are fixed in definite political organisational forms (the state, law) which rely on powerful material forces (the army, police, intelligence service, courts, bureaucratic apparatus). Hence the revolutionary class has to overcome the resistance of the state-organised exploiting classes and is therefore compelled to use force in response to the latter's violence. This is specifically expressed in a direct armed uprising, the arrests of counter-revolutionaries, the expropriation of private property, the dissolution of reactionary state institutions, etc.' (Kharin, 1981, pp. 180—1.)

15 Cf. Konstantin Zarodov, 'Leninskaya strategiya i taktika revolutsionnoi bor'by', *Pravda*, 6 August 1975, pp. 2—3; id. 'Demokratizm velikogo Oktyabr'ya', *Kommunist*, 1977:5, pp. 50—60; id. 'Velikaya sila primera i opyta Oktyabr'ya', *Pravda*, 26 August 1977, pp. 2—3. Krasin, 1985, Essay Four: 'The Majority in a Socialist Revolution', esp. pp. 68—9.
16 Boris N. Ponomarev, 'Neobkhodimost' osvoboditelnogo dvizheniya', *Kommunist*, 1980:1, p. 23.
17 Speech by D. Ustinov, *Pravda*, 14 February 1980, p. 3.
18 Kharin, 1981, p. 181.
19 D. Volkogonov, 'Ideologischeskaya bor'ba v usloviyakh razryadki', *Kommunist Vooruzhennykh Sil* (afterwards quoted as *K.V.S.*), 1977:3, pp. 15, 20—1.
20 Piotr Fedoseyev, 'The Dialectics of Social Life', *W.M.R.*, 1981:9, p. 46.
21 *Protsess formirovaniya i osushchestvleniya vneshnei politiki kapitalisticheskikh gosudarstv*, 1981 (afterwards quoted as *Protsess ...*), p. 248.
22 Marxism-Leninism distinguishes between material systems and abstract systems. Material systems are subdivided into systems in organic nature and living systems; the latter embrace a long spectrum from the most primitive biological systems to such complex ones as ecosystem. Social systems constitute a special class in the category of living material systems. Cf. 'Sistema' in *Filosofskii Entsiklopedicheskii Slovar'*, Izd. Sovetskaya Entsiklopediya, Moscow 1983, pp. 610—11.
23 V.G. Afanas'ev, *Sistemnost' i obshchestvo*, Moscow 1980, p.110.
24 Shakhnazarov, 1978, p. 39.
25 Ibid., p. 40.
26 Cf. *Fundamentals of Political Science*, 1979: 'Social Formations'

in Ch. I; *The Fundamentals of Marxist-Leninist Philosophy*, 1982, Ch. XI: 'The Social-Economic Formation'; Zarodov, 1983, 'Socio-Economic Formations and Historical Ages', in Ch. II; Yurkovets, 1984, Ch. VIII, 'Types of Society and the Laws of Their Succession'.

27 Karl Marx, 'A Contribution to the Critique of Political Economy', quoted in *Basic Writings*, Doubleday, New York 1959, pp. 43—4.
28 Ibid.
29 In *Fundamentals of Political Science* the superstructure embraces political relations, the state and ideology, p. 18; *The Fundamentals of Marxist-Leninist Philosophy* defines superstructure as the sum total of social ideas, institutions and relations arising on a given economic basis (p. 242); Zarodov writes about 'the juridical and political superstructure' (p. 54); Yurkovets defines superstructure as 'ideological relations' consisting of various 'layers': relations of government (political relations and the state), relations of community (legal and moral), philosophical relations, religious relations, aesthetic relations (relations connected with the nature of culture), and others (pp. 158—9).
30 *Fundamentals of Political Science*, 1979, p. 19; *The Fundamentals of Marxist-Leninist Philosophy*, 1982, pp. 245—6.
31 Yurkovets, 1984, p. 161.
32 *Protsess ...*, pp. 23—4.
33 Cf. J. Lider, *Military Force*, 1981, pp. 118—20.
34 *The Fundamentals of Marxist-Leninist Philosophy*, 1982, p. 246.
35 *The Basics of Marxist-Leninist Theory*, 1982, p. 235:
36 *Global Problems of Our Age*, 1984; Shakhnazarov, 1984, Part III: 'Peace and the Vital Needs of Mankind'.
37 *The Basics of Marxist-Leninist Theory*, 1982, p. 236.
38 Zarodov, 1983, pp. 204 ff.
39 Cf. Zarodov, 1983, p. 254; *The Basics of Marxist-Leninist Theory*, 1982, Ch. XIV.
40 Yurkovets, 1984, p. 134; Zarodov, 1983, pp. 253 ff.
41 Zarodov, 1983. pp. 254—5.
42 Yurkovets, 1984, p. 162.
43 *Protsess ...*, pp. 53—7.
44 Ibid., pp. 253—4.
45 Inozemtsev, 1978, p. 11.
46 Shakhnazarov, 1984, pp. 14—15.
47 *Mezhdunarodyne konflikty sovremennosti*, 1983, pp. 141—2.
48 *Protsess ...*, Ch. II.1.
49 Ibid., p. 250.
50 Ibid., p. 249.
51 Gromyko, 1983; Rybkin, 1983; Kapchenko, 1984.
52 Rybkin, 1983, p. 36.

53 Ibid.
54 Shakhnazarov, 1984, p. 7.
55 Ibid., p. 14.
56 Gromyko, 1983, p. 12.
57 Kirshin, 1982; Burlatskii, 1982.
58 Cf. Kapchenko, 1977, 1983; Kortunov, 1977; Sanakoyev, 1975 and many other Soviet studies on the character of international relations.
59 *Fundamentals of Political Science,* 1979, p. 430.
60 Fedoseyev, (Note 8) p. 48.
61 In Inozemtsev, 1978, p. 19.
62 *Voina i Armiya,* 1977, pp. 296-7.
63 'Gosudarstvo' in *Sovetskaya Voennaya Entsiklopediya,* vol. 2, pp. 622—5.
64 Seleznev, 1982, pp. 8 ff.
65 Yu. G. Yershov, 'Spetsifika mezhdunarodnogo perekhodnogo perioda' in *Sotsialnaya dialektika v kategoriyakh istoricheskogo materializma,* Sverdlovsk 1980, pp. 97—105; Yu. A. Krasin, 'Sotsialnaya revolutsiya XX veka: rezultaty, problemy, perspektivy' in *Marksistsko-leninskaya teoriya sotsialnogo razvitiya,* Moscow 1978. The character of a transitory epoch is determined by the revolutionary class which embodies progress (*Filosofiya i voehnaya istoriya,* 1979, p. 235).
66 Seleznev, 1982, p. 17.
67 Ibid.
68 Ibid., pp. 11—12.
69 Ibid., pp. 47—8.
70 Ibid.
71 Shakhnazarov writes that different schools of thought influence each other. 'Even incompatible theories borrow each other's techniques and, more, separate elements of the method of research. Besides, they influence each other by their mutual criticism, which draws attention to their faults and weaker points and stimulates checks and re-checks of drawn conclusions, impelling search of new arguments in their favour. Marxism-Leninism, like any other true science, processes all the valuable elements of the latest social practice and the latest theoretical thought. Some of the observations in futurological research, too, have found a place in the general system of Marxist knowledge' (1982, pp. 57—8).
72 Shakhnazarov, 1982, Chs. 1, 2, especially pp. 12—17, 41.
73 Cf. Shakhnazarov, 'The Decisive Impact of the Social Factor' in 1979, Ch. I, pp. 40—5. Cf. Id., 1982, Ch. 1.
74 Soviet scholars do not deny the importance of the general systems theory (or the general theory of systems theory) and acknowledge

that it should be developed. They point out, however, that it has not so far received a uniform interpretation and cannot be applied to the analysis of social systems (Cf., V.N. Sadovskii, 'Obshchaya teoriya sistem kak metateoriya', *Voprosy Filosofii*, 1972:4).

75 Cf. *Sovremennye burzhuaznye teorii mezhdunarodnykh otnoshenii*, Izd. 'Nauka', Moscow 1976, Ch. III.1. a) 'Teoriya mezhdunarodnykh sistem Mortona Kaplana', pp. 216—31.

76 For instance, in Kaplan's concept, the state of the system at any point in time is determined by the values of five sets of variables; the essential rules, the transformation rules, the actor classification variables, the capability variables, and the information variables. These lack, however, a concrete socio-political content. But such variables as 'the actor classification variables', i.e., the military and political potential are obviously dependent on the type of socio-political systems (ibid.)

77 Kaplan presents six such models, of which only two (the balance of power system, and the loose bipolar system) resemble real systems which existed in the past (ibid.).

78 Thus E.A. Pozdnyakov asserts that one cannot separate the analysis of a given system from its concrete content: form and content constitute one whole and it would be erroneous to 'apply' the former to the latter (*Sistemnyi podkhod i mezhdunarodnye otnosheniya*, Moscow 1976, p. 14).

79 'By the use of the structural-functional analysis bourgeois sociology attempts to consider society as a single comprehensive and stable system, in which stability of the system is equated with its capacity for survival' (*Sovremennye burzhuaznye teorii mezhdunarodnykh otnoshenii*, 1976, p. 41). 'Considering the social functions from the standpoint of "stabilisation" and "equilibrium" it (structural functionalism — JL) fully corresponds to the reactionary bourgeois ideology of conservatism and social stagnation', E.D. Modrzinskaya, 'Sotsiologicheskie aspekty natsionalnogo suvereniteta' in *Sotsiologicheskie problemy mezhdunarodnykh otnoshenii*, Izd. 'Nauka', Moscow 1970, p. 13.

80 Cf. *Sovremennye burzhuaznye teorii mezhdunarodnykh otnoshenii*, 1976, Ch. III.1.g: 'Strukturno-funktsionalnyi podkhod Dzordza Modelskogo', pp. 242—5.

81 For instance, Charles A. McClelland is criticised for his interpretation of international relations as an expanded version of an interaction of two states. This takes the form of a behaviourist demand-response interaction: initial action — response from the other state — response by the state which initiated the interaction. To put it in the perspective of the international system, the activity of any state takes the form of taking from and giving to

the international environment. 'All the giving and taking, when considered together — and for all the national actors — is called the international system.' This approach results in reducing all the complexity of international relations to a single behaviourist model deprived of any socio-political content. McClelland is charged with combining, in a mechanistic way, the structural-functional method with the behaviourist approach, which only compounds the deficiencies of both (Cf. *Sovremennye burzhuaznye teorii mezhdunarodnykh otnoshenii*, 1976, Ch. III.1. 'Model sistemy vzaimodeistvuiushchikh gosudarstv Charlsa Maklellanda', pp. 239—42).

82 Cf. J. Lider, *On the Nature of War*, (1977, 1979), Ch.I and Part I.

83 E.A. Bagramov, 'Burzhuaznaya sotsiologiya ob istochnikakh mezhdunarodnykh konfliktov' in *Sotsiologicheskie problemy mezhdunarodnykh otnoshenii*, 1970; Modrzinskaya, op.cit. (N 47).

84 Shakhnazarov, 1982, p. 114.

85 Shakhnazarov, 1982, Ch. 3; Zarodov, 1983, Ch. I.2,3.

86 Editor-in-chief of the international journal *World Marxist Review (Problems of Peace and Socialism)* (1968—1982), and a leading Soviet publicist and historian of the international working-class movement.

87 Zarodov, 1983, p. 13. Krasin writes that, certainly, the working class may use some of the democratic institutions of the bourgeois society as bridgeheads in the struggle for revolution. It should remember, however, that whatever the opportunities this democracy holds out to the working class, it is an instrument of the bourgeois political domination (1985, pp. 29, 31).

88 1982, p. 118.

89 Shakhnazarov, 1982, Ch. 4: 'Revolution or Reform'. The main proposition is: 'There is only one answer to the question "reform *or* revolution?" and that is: revolution *and* reform' (p. 119).

90 Ibid., p. 115.

91 Cf. Zarodov, 1983, pp. 35—7.

92 Ralph Dahrendorf's model of a constant conflict within each 'imperatively coordinated group' between competing interest groups challenging or defending of the status quo, — leading to possible change in the dominance relations and restructuring of the group — is said to be too abstract and to ignore the issue of revolutionary structural change. Cf. Ralph Dahrendorf, *Soziale Klassen und Klassenkonflikt in der industriellen Gesellschaft*, Stuttgart 1957.

93 Ralph Dahrendorf, 'Towards a Theory of Social Conflict' in *Social Change*, Amitai and Ezra Etzioni, (eds.), Basic Books, New York

1964, p. 107, Cf. id., *Essays in the Theory of Society*, Stanford University Press, Stanford 1968.

94   Shakhnazarov, 1982, pp. 177—78.

3 Correlation of forces — general characteristics

Before discussing the specific forms of the correlation of social forces, let us examine the general characteristics of this emerging category, as it reflects the above-mentioned theoretical premises.

Correlation of social forces — category *in statu nascendi*

Socio-political categories

Like all concepts in the social sciences, categories are not voluntary constructions of the human mind but are reflections of objective reality in the whole of its multi-dimensional, objective and subjective complexity — a reality which develops according to dialectical laws.

Categories reproduce the properties and relationships of reality in global and most concentrated form: they are the result of generalisation, of the intellectual synthesis of the achievements of science and socio-historical practice and are, therefore, the key points of cognition, 'the moments when thought grasps the essence of things'.[1] Thus they can become the organising principles of cognition, of gathering facts and analysing them, of practice and the thought process.

Each science provides its own categories which reflect the general and essential features, phenomena and processes of a certain field of objective reality and their internal links and regularities. The most general are the philosophical categories which concern the existence, activities and development of the nature in its entirety, of human society and human thinking.[2]

Sociopolitical categories differ from categories in the natural sciences, in two respects.

First, they not only constitute an effect of a scientific research into reality and an analysis of how objective laws manifest themselves in it but also represent a special kind of cognition: one which concerns not merely the truth, but also the interests of social forces — i.e., classes. Therefore the results of cognition are determined by the choice of the philosophical world outlook which may be either the philosophy of working class (Marxism-Leninism) or one of the philosophies of the bourgeoisie. In other words, in contrast to the categories in the natural sciences, sociopolitical categories have a class content.

(Non-Marxist social sciences seem increasingly to accept the proposition that cognition is affected by the subjective approach of the scientist.

> Explanatory statements do not arise simply out of congruence with sense data; the most important components of these statements are the assumptions and categories that the investigator brings with him into the analysis. Who you are and how you look at the world would crucially affect what you see... We must be aware of the extent to which our intellectual predispositions follow from those traditions of thought about social reality in which we are embedded, often without realizing the extent to which our attitudes are so constrained.[3]

The Marxist-Leninists maintain, however, that: (1) the assumptions and categories themselves are also an effect of cognition that is affected by 'intellectual predispositions'; (2) the meaning of 'what you are and how you look at the world' depends largely on the interests of the social group — usually the class — which determine the scientist's 'intellectual predispositions'; (3) in the long run, social — usually class — interests decide which social theories gain widespread acceptance.)

Second, sociopolitical categories are related to a concrete socioeconomic formation. They do not exist over and above historical epochs, they change together with the changes in concrete formations and can be comprehended only if they are not considered by themselves, in isolation, as a kind of absolute concept, purged of transient and historically rooted content.[4]

The first consequence of these two peculiarities is that the same phenomena are expressed by different concepts in different philosophies. For instance, in the analysis of the socio-economic basis of society (or what the Marxists call the relations of production) the bourgeois theory operates with the category of the employer — a benefactor who provides jobs — while in the Marxist-Leninist theory the same protagonist is called a capitalist and his main characteristic is that he exploits the workers.

The second consequence is that some categories are incomprehensible outside a concrete formation. For instance, in the Marxist-Leninist view, the bourgeois concept of the balance of power is said to mean the alignment of state powers in a system characterised by each country's drive for power in pursuit of its national interests — in other words, it is related to the capitalist system.

As distinct from this concept, the Soviet category of the correlation of world forces relates to the contemporary epoch which is characterised by the coexistence and rivalry of two quite different coalitions of states: the capitalist and the socialist camps.[5]

The scientific and class-motivated contents of the sociopolitical categories in the Marxist-Leninist analytical apparatus, entail in their view, the following functions:

(1) the categories are used in the analysis of the sociopolitical situation in the world and in particular countries and in the development of the current political strategy as well as the strategy of revolutionary transformation;

(2) as an analytical tool, they facilitate the development of Marxist-Leninist science;

(3) they serve to spread Marxist-Leninist knowledge both among scientists and the public throughout the world;

(4) they are used in the ideological struggle, which is an important front of the political struggle.

Interplay of the objective and the subjective

On both sides, the forces under comparison *consist of objective and subjective components.* A novelty in recent Marxist-Leninist analyses of social action seems to be the emphatic contention that 'the objective' should not be equated with 'the material' and that the dichotomy matter/conscience should not be equated with the dialectical dichotomy of the objective and the subjective factors in the historical process.[6]

On the philosophical level, the basic Marxist proposition is that matter is primary in relation to consciousness in all respects: the genetical, functional and contentional ones; and that individual and social consciousness depend on the material objective conditions in which they are formed and function.

However, with regard to social development, the dependence of social consciousness on the material, i.e., socio-economic conditions is not a direct one. The process of reflecting material conditions in the awareness and activities of a social group is a complex one. The development of the subjective factor does not simply reflect the movement of the objective factor. It may be delayed; it may forestall the changes in the objective; it may run parallel to the objective, but not adequately; it may even reflect the objective in a distorted way. This means that human activity does not have to correspond automatically and directly to the objective conditions. Thus domestic subjective social factors — the interests, views, motives and corresponding actions of a class or other social group — may in various ways be affected by, and may variously reflect, the domestic objective conditions; they are also affected by international processes. In turn, they inevitably influence the objective conditions of social life.

Moreover, the results of human activity are included in the objective conditions themselves. When we consider a socio-economic formation, its contradictions, social relationships and conflicts — that is the objective conditions of social activities and development — we are considering factors which result from the preceding human activity, i.e., partially from the actions of the subjective factor of 'yesterday'. Similarly, speaking of the objective conditions in state activities, we mean not only its economic, financial or military potentialities, the character of the socio-economic and political systems, the level of science and technology, or its geopolitical situation, but also the broadly interpreted cultural level of the population, including the accumulated political experience — the results of past social activities.

Generally, *there is a growth in the role of the subjective factor* in domestic and international life, a general tendency of the growth of its role as society develops.

Among the *universal* causes of this tendency the following deserve mention:

(1) The increase in the population; extension of the physical limits and scale of its activities; the increase in the economic and technological potentialities of society as well as its capacity for communication.

(2) The increasing extent to which the *broad popular masses* are entering political life, the development of their awareness and self-assertiveness, the broadening of the range of forms in which they participate in mass movements and organisations.

(3) The increasing amount of *human knowledge* available, the enhanced human cognitive potentialities, the growing possibilities of *using* the accumulated knowledge in all fields of social activity, including social management and politics — all this may be noted mainly in socialist countries but also in developed capitalist countries.

(4) As society develops and its organisational structure becomes more complex, the subjective factor also grows more sophisticated; new qualitative aspects arise, new subjects of social relations and actions emerge.

(5) In international relations, the role of socio-psychological factors

in the formulation and realisation of foreign policy of states increases. It includes the conscious activity of men, acting through their formal and informal associations — the classes, social groups and institutions which they create in the form of parties, states and bureaucratic apparatuses, and social and other organisations in order to achieve certain external political aims. It also includes the evolution of the ideas and feelings which precede and accompany the foreign policy of states.[7]

There are also *specific* causes of the growth of the subjective factor, which are connected with the peculiarities of the contemporary epoch. For instance, we are witnessing a restructuring of international relations which is largely the result of conscious social action — namely:

(1) The emergence of the system of socialist states, which has accelerated the process of transforming socialism into a decisive force of social progress and has essentially affected international relations.

(2) The turning-point which has been reached in most developing countries which are beginning consciously to build the economic, social and political bases of their progressive future.

(3) The pressure on the imperialist countries to seek new answers to their old but now aggravated problems.

The restructuring of international relations which has begun affects further growth of the subjective factor — the efforts for *détente,* the struggle of the developing countries for equal rights, the peace movement, the non-alignment movement and so on.

These developments have affected the possibility of a conscious exploitation of the laws of social development. Men can act successfully only if their actions take into account the impact of laws governing the given kind of action. Each law imposes certain demands — certain conditions which must be fulfilled if it is to be operating — and only by reckoning with these demands can the desired results be obtained. The unintended violation of the demands of a given law, or a conscious action against it (if one wants to counteract its influence) may yield results opposite to those which should follow. On the other hand, human behaviour decides to a great extent how much scope is granted for the action of the objective laws, and therefore although the behaviour of men is not absolutely voluntary, it influences the outcome of the operation of the laws and the course of events. The better men know the laws, and the greater their potentialities for using them, the more successful can be their actions.

Material and spiritual components of the correlation of social forces

In any correlation of social forces, say Marxist-Leninists, the forces on both sides of the equation consist of material and non-material components. The material components include the material power of the social classes: their economic assets, means of coercion, their access to the mass media and other means of information and ideological influence and so on. The principal non-material components are class consciousness, organisation and a rational and proper combat strategy.

The material factors offer the possibility of successfully carrying out the struggle; at the same time they place limits and constraints on it. The non-material factors determine whether, how and with what results the possibility will be realised.

To put it another way, the actual state and the tendencies of the development in the material basis of the correlation of forces *determine to a considerable extent* the methods, the course and outcome of class struggle or international rivalry — at each moment and in the long run. However, the state of the correlation of material strengths of the opposing social forces *does not prejudice* the course of social development. The impact of the correlation depends on the *cognition* and assessment of it by the protagonists and on how social groups decide to act and *do act* on the basis of this cognition; and also how they exploit the advantages of the correlation and combat the negative aspects.

Here we arrive at another basic component in the assessment of the correlation of social forces. In assessing and comparing the impact of social forces on domestic and international developments, one should see them, perhaps, as *forces in action*, forces whose influence must be coupled with their action. This is seemingly implied in the Soviet reasoning about the correlation of world forces, which is said to include 'the correlation of class forces *and the struggle of classes* both in individual countries and in the international arena, by taking into account the real forces — economic, political, moral and others — which stand behind the classes'.[8]

Thus also a *strategy* which is to a great extent based on the assessment of the existing correlation of forces plays a significant role in exploiting this correlation for the purposes of action. Strategy and the correlation of social forces influence each other. An advantageous correlation allows scope for many options and a choice between them — in other words, it allows greater freedom of action. On the other hand, the proper choice of the strategy and means used permits a successful exploitation of the correlation of forces. Moreover, an appropriate strategy may lead to further advantageous changes in the correlation of forces and may provide scope for an increase in the number of missions which can be successfully performed.

However, the connection between the correlation of forces and the strategy for their use is *more than a mutual impact.* Since social forces are forces in action, the planned, expected or actual strategy, the chances for its realisation and the expected results of its application can — indeed, they must — be included in the assessment of the potential and real impact of the social forces themselves, i.e., in the assessment of the *value* of the correlation of forces. The significance of strategy as an indispensable component of the value of the correlation is most visible when extreme forms of social violence are used — in civil or international wars, in social revolutions, and so on — since strategy at these times plays a decisive role.

The importance of strategy also leads to another aspect of the correlation of social forces. It means that the impact of the correlation of social forces on social action and its results — whether in particular countries or in the international arena — is not only, and perhaps not mainly, the effect of an objectively existing relation of two social strengths. It greatly depends on how it is perceived by the protagonists. It may be suggested that the relation of the strength of social adversaries *is highly affected by the perception* by each opponent of what the actual state of the correlation and the tendencies of its development are. Such a perception is based on two components: on each adversary's own estimate and on the assessment of the correlation presented by the opponent. Both assessments are highly subjective and they may be erroneous. Each party's estimate may be inadequate because of the lack of exact information about several intangible (and perhaps also tangible) values and because of possible defects in the method of measuring them. 'Wishful thinking' may also have an effect. At the same time the opponent presents his own strength with a political purpose in a misinformative way — for instance, in order to frighten the enemy and to encourage his own supporters and allies.

In domestic social struggle, the side which possesses less material strength (for instance, the working masses which face the armed forces, police and those in leading economic positions in the governing social forces) must emphasise intangible values, point out the tendencies in the development of the correlation, present its own cause as just, stress the social weaknesses of the opponent and emphasise the importance of strategies and actions, which may change the correlation of material strengths. This is one of the aims of any revolutionary programme.

In the international arena, the perception of the correlation plays an even greater role. Each side tends to emphasise its strength and describe the developments as being to its advantage.

For instance, the Soviet Union, by presenting the current correlation of world forces as being greatly to its advantage, and as continuously changing in its favour and at the same time attempting to justify its foreign and military policy, apparently aims:

(1) to encourage its allies and maintain its dominance of the socialist camp;

(2) to pave the way for the spread of Communist ideology and the influence of the Soviet state in other countries (in the neutral group, the Third World, Western Europe); and

(3) to persuade other countries of the need to make concessions.

It is true that such propaganda may cut both ways and also have negative consequences: the adversary may exploit this exaggeration in order to justify an increase in his own military effort and, in general, to pursue a more active foreign policy and to mobilise all forces on the pretext of nullifying his opponent's superiority. For instance, in order to counteract Soviet propaganda, the United States tries to convince world opinion that while the USSR aims to achieve strategic superiority the United States, in spite of its much greater economic and techno-scientific potentialities does not; that while the USSR regards military force as the main component of the correlation of world forces, the United States does not; and that while Communism focuses on internal revolutions in so-called capitalist countries, the United States defends the democratic way of life.

Likewise the American government tries to frighten neutral countries by exaggerating the Soviet 'menace'; this may also affect the natural allies of the Soviet Union — the Communist parties in the developed countries. The presentation of the development of the correlation of world forces as inevitably enhancing the strength of Communism and making the collapse of 'imperialism' inevitable may also impel the enemies of the USSR to take preventive action.

In sum, both sides try to convince world opinion, domestic opinion and third parties of the justice of their policy. The assessment of the correlation of forces has become not only a basis for political and military strategy but also — in the form of the tendentious presentation of the correlation — a *means* of strategy.

Complex assessment

The analysis of the correlation of social forces begins with determining the *character* of forces acting in society or/and the international system, proceeds with determining the *alignment or configuration* of these forces, and concludes with the *comparison of the strengths* of the two basic opponents. The latter is most often called 'correlation' but the term 'balance of forces' has also been used.[9]

As we have seen, social forces, whether in domestic society or in the international arena — the comparison of which is the subject of this study — are hardly measurable. Their strength is composed of objective and subjective elements, and it constitutes and expresses a complex of material and non-material assets; moreover, it also includes the degree of organisation and the strategy of action. The composition of the correlation is discussed in detail in the following chapters. It can be assessed basically in terms of the potential, expected or actual impact on the course of events. The way the correlation is presented and its perception are extremely important.

Moreover, the correlation of social forces is highly dynamic. Both sides of the correlation change; they may both grow in strength but, in the Marxist-Leninist view, the correlation generally changes to the advantage of the progressive forces.

When Marxist-Leninists speak of a correlation of intrasocietal or world forces that is advantageous to socialism as a phenomenon characteristic of our times, they have often in mind a *tendency* of development rather than a *fixed and stable* correlation. This pro-socialist tendency is said to express and accord with the laws of social development.

One may ask whether, for all these reasons, the correlation is or is not an objective reality. Is it only a cliché used for tactical reasons and for justifying certain policies and political moves?

A preliminary answer given by Marxist-Leninist writers would be as follows:

(1) In spite of the use of the correlation of social forces for tactical reasons (in their view only by the 'imperialist' side) which entails presenting it incorrectly in order to affect the perception of the adversaries, allies and neutrals — this correlation *does* reflect an objective reality. The forces *have* a definite magnitude and the correlation of them *has* a real value.

(2) It should be noted that other sociological (or socio-political) categories such as politics and the class struggle, although likewise constituting a unity of objective and subjective elements which are difficult to express in exact magnitudes or values, and although also used in the ideological struggle and for purposes of misinformation — are nevertheless indispensable to the analysis of intrasocietal and international rivalries, struggles and bargaining and in developing political and military strategies.

Conclusions

In discussions concerning the interaction of the objective and subjective in the domestic policy and international relations and on the growth of the subjective aspect of social processes, the content of the correlation of social forces appears as a combination of subjective and objective, of material and non-material values. This presentation may be used for extra-scientific reasons:

(1) It enables an emphasis to be placed on one or another component in various periods. For instance, if the material assets — economic or techno-military — possessed by one side, are clearly inferior to those of its adversary, one may focus on the assessment of non-material values connected with the socio-economic and political system.

(2) One may emphasise the subjective factors which are more elusive, and exploit the thesis on the determining role of the subjective factor

in presenting the superiority of the revolutionary side of the social equation.

(3) One may present the asserted superiority of the socialist socio-economic and political systems and of socialist policies as the asserted source of superiority in both the material and the spiritual components of, and objective and subjective aspects in, all forms of the correlation of social forces.

(4) The concept (category) of the correlation of social forces can be used even more easily than other social concepts for purposes of mani-pulation in politico-psychological struggles; the determining impact of the relation of forces on the course and outcome of any event is a rela-tively simple idea reflecting easily detectable factors and dependences in natural processes and in social life.

Correlation of social forces as a systemic feature

Systemic feature of a special kind

The concept (category) of the correlation of social forces as presented in Marxist-Leninist writings seems to be a systemic feature. It repre-sents an essential relationship between the components of a system, both intrasocietal and international, which affects and is characteristic of the interaction between the components.

This is a systemic feature of a special kind, however. It is highly dynamic and has a definite and constant direction of change which affects and even entails changes in the system as a whole. It may deve-lop gradually together with the system itself; it may hasten other changes or impede them; and, finally, it may create the conditions for a rapid transformation of the entire system. Unlike the usual systemic features in non-Marxist theories, the correlation of social forces does not promote the equilibrium and stability of the system in the long run. On the contrary, through its changes and impact on systemic processes it functions as an instrument of systemic change. (see also below.)

In most non-Marxist approaches, a systemic feature constitutes a functional pattern without which the system ceases to be itself — a coherent clearly defined whole. Since such a system tends to stability, the functional patterns represent relationships between elements of the system which enable it to adapt to changing circumstances, to eliminate disturbances — either of internal or external origin — and, if necessary, to contribute to a gradual change in which the basic charac-teristics of the system will be preserved. The balance of power consti-tutes such a systemic feature in the pluralistic concept of society (c.f. Chapter 4) and in the concept of the international balance-of-power system (cf. Chapter 7).

The correlation of social forces is a feature of a system which *should develop* through conflicts. It is a correlation of two basic and opposing forces of the system which are in a state of permanent conflict. It reflects this conflict and it contributes to its resolution, which leads to the transformation of the system as a whole into quite another system. In other theories of systems *bipolar* constructions may emerge as transitory structures, but as a rule the systems consist of *several* basic elements. For instance, in the post-war period in the modified international balance-of-power system, the multi-party international system has taken the form of a bipolar balance, but it is said to be tending again to become multi-polar because of the emergence of new centres of power.

Different philosophies underlie these two different concepts of systems and systemic features (see Chapters 2 and 7). The basic difference is that the correlation of social forces proceeds from the Marxist-Leninist view of society as consisting of antagonistic classes and of the international system as composed of states having different socio-economic and political systems. The correlation differs basically from all variants of non-Marxist views in which other criteria are used for the conceptual division of domestic society and in the international system other criteria are used to distinguish between various types of states (democratic states, for instance, being set against authoritarian ones). Let us examine the application of these Marxist-Leninist ideas in the domestic and the international spheres.

Feature of domestic systems

In the analysis of the correlation of forces as a feature of domestic systems in the pre-socialist class societies, two extreme cases are conceivable. An absolute political and military dictatorship, which has an absolute control of the means of production and the whole economy and unrestrained power over the state apparatus (including, naturally, the monopoly of armed forces and of policy) cannot tolerate any gradual changes in the correlation of intrasocietal forces that would lead to essential changes. A revolutionary change may occur only at a time of acute crisis (for instance, after a lost war) and take the form of an armed uprising.

However, even there and then, the revolution must be prepared for: forces capable of political and military combats must be provided. Admittedly, radical changes in the correlation of intrasocietal forces must occur in an extraordinarily short time, but some preconditions must be created in advance. The population must become aware of the need for violent change; moreover, an embryo of revolutionary forces which can rapidly expand must be organised and trained.

In a democratic system characterised by political pluralism and dispersal (although uneven and unequal) of the means of production, conditions for gradual changes in the correlation of forces seem to be more favourable. The state may be restrained in using the means of compulsion; the opposition may not only use various means of confrontation and gradually increase its political economic and ideological strength but also in some cases build up a covert military organisation. Conditions are conceivable in which the system is changed through a violent but purely *political* action. As regards this kind of action, Soviet politicians and researchers accept it in theory but are sceptical about it as a practical proposition.

In both of these extreme cases the correlation of intrasocietal forces will play the determining role; in the first case, only at the time of revolution and, in the second, in the everyday processes of social struggle, bargaining and gradual development.

Feature of the international system

The character of the correlation of forces as a systemic feature is also clearly visible in the international system. It affects all patterns of relations in all fields of international intercourse to a greater extent than ever before.

Some reasons for such a development are:
(1)   Before the First World War, there existed a constantly changing alignment of power among the leading European states. This could be regarded merely as a partial systemic feature, since it did not include all (or even nearly all) the states, and since the main tendencies in the alignment of power did not mean that all the essential changes in the world were pointing in a definite direction.

Nowadays, the inclusion of nearly all states in the international system and the division of the world into two rival and antagonistic camps which are socially and politically different, has become a permanent feature of the system.
(2)   The rivalry of the two camps *determines* the main course of world events. Moreover, although the correlation of world forces constitutes a highly dynamic value, the main tendencies in its constant changes definitely point towards socialism.

The periodical changes in the correlation of international forces resemble a succession of leaps. They are connected with basic changes *of* and *in* the international system and profoundly affect the course of world events. Thus the extension of the socialist part of the world to constitute an entire system of socialist states has meant not only the transformation of the international system into two socio-economic formations — a transitory system between the capitalist and socialist formations — but also a basic change in the correlation of forces between socialism and capitalism. This has meant a change *of* the international system. The liquidation of the colonialist system was a change of a similar kind, although its consequences were less far-reaching. The establishment of strategic parity between the superpowers in the early 1970s created quite new prospects of preventing wars and counter-revolutionary interventions — i.e., quite new prospects of further changes towards socialism in the world. This, according to Marxist-Leninist writers, may be called a change *in* the international system.

In Marxist-Leninist theory, the correlation of international forces in the present bipolar world has taken the form of the so-called correlation of world forces (cf. Chapter 6). Some Soviet scholars regard it not only as a systemic feature with the status of a category but also as the *key factor* in the development of international relations, the changes of which are lawful and necessarily push the world towards socialism. A few descriptions of this correlation (also called balance) may testify to the significance attached to it.

Thus G. Shakhnazarov[10] asserts that the correlation of forces in the world arena is the key factor in, or the source of, the development of international relations. It constitutes the motor which puts the whole mechanism of international links into motion and gives the motion a particular direction and speed.

> ...neither particular events, nor the sum total of events can be understood without considering the general correlation of forces in the world. This is, as it were, the historical background before which the complex interaction of classes, parties, political movements and states unfolds and which, in the final analysis, determines their outcome.[11]

N. Kapchenko regards the 'balance of forces' as one of the key factors determining the structure of international relations and the nature of their development.

> Balance of forces is a constantly developing, dynamic process, which is manifested not only in a change of the military-economic potentials of states, but also in profound social-class changes, affecting the very nature of international relations in a respective historical period.[12]

Balance of forces in the world is one of the basic categories in the Marxist-Leninist science on international relations, writes V. Zagladin. It is also the decisive factor in making political decisions.[13]

Finally, N. Lebedev[14] asserts that 'the change in the correlation of forces in favour of socialism is an objective and natural law of world development. It is realized through the actions of states, classes, and parties, and through a very complex interaction of diverse social forces, which influence the general situation in the world, and of shaping tendencies and counter-tendencies in world development.'[15]

Notes

1   Spirkin, 1983, p. 62.
2   *Marksistsko-leninskaya filosofiya i metodologicheskie problemy voennoi teorii i praktiki*, 1982, p. 107.
3   John J. Weltman, 1974, 'On the Obsolescence of War', *International Studies Quarterly*, December 1974, p. 403; cf. Janowitz, 1975, p. 11.
4   'Concerning the Dialectics of Categories', 1981, p. 90.
5   In the 1980s some Soviet authors use the term 'alignment of forces', and sometimes also the traditional term 'balance of power' (or 'of forces'). 'Alignment of forces' usually means 'configuration of forces', however, rather than comparison of strengths. Zagladin points out this difference (1985, p. 67); Sheidina writes that the alignment *and* correlations of forces are the key problems in the study of international relations (1984, p. 10). The term 'correlation of world forces' *(sootnoshenie sil v mire)* has been well established, Cf. works of Shakhnazarov (1980, 1982, 1984), utterances of Marshal N. Ogarkov ('the correlation of forces in the international arena has changed irreversibly in favour of the forces of peace and social progress' — November 1984), articles of A. Arbatov, N. Kapchenko and many others. As regards military comparison, some authors use the term 'balance of military power' or 'strategic balance' both in the sense of comparison of forces and equilibrium (parity) of them, others, however, use it only in the latter sense. Thus Arbatov writes: '... strategic balance — that is, a correlation of forces which excludes the superiority or unilateral advantage of any side...' (1984).
6   Kosolapov, 1983, pp. 24—33.
7   *Mezhdunarodnye konflikty sovremennosti*, 1983, pp. 218—19.
8   Cf. Martin, 1975, 1977.
9   Cf. Zagladin, 1985, p. 67.
10 President of the Soviet Political Science Association and Vice-President of the World Political Science Association, author of several books on international affairs.
11 Shakhnazarov, 1984, pp. 16—19.

12 Kapchenko, 1984, p. 104.
13 Zagladin, 1985, p. 66.
14 Rector of the Moscow State Institute of International Relations, author of several books on world history.
15 Lebedev, 1982, p. 141.

PART II
CORRELATION OF
INTRASOCIETAL FORCES

4 Correlation of intrasocietal forces

Agenda

Concept

The theoretical premises of the theory of the correlation of social forces discussed in the previous chapters apply most directly to the analysis of national society.

Marxists differ from non-Marxists in viewing society as (1) emerging from conflict and developing through conflict of its basic components – social classes, i.e., through *class struggle*, (2) being composed of the socio-economic *basis* and political *superstructure* (in the broad sense – i.e., including legal, ideological, cultural and other elements); and (3) being governed by dialectical laws.

These features involve a peculiar mechanism of development in which the correlation of social forces plays a vital role. To distinguish it from the international correlation of forces – which is also 'social' in the broad sense of the term – it may be called the 'intrasocietal correlation of forces'. It means the correlation of the forces of *two basic antagonistic classes* together with their allies.

In Marxist-Leninist theory, the concept of the intrasocietal correlation of forces may be used only in the analysis of the so-called antagonistic class society, since only in such a society do antagonistic classes exist whose correlation of forces determines the methods used in their struggle and its outcome. Therefore the following Marxist-

Leninist discussion will concern only non-socialist societies.

From the correlation of socio-economic forces
to the correlation of political forces

The correlation of intrasocietal forces can be analysed on its lower level: this concerns the correlation of socio-economic forces in which the two basic classes of an antagonistic society confront each other directly in a struggle for their economic interests and their position in the socio-economic basis of society. However, as mentioned above (Chapter 1), this is the basic form of class struggle only in transitory periods between the successive socio-economic formations. It is predominant in periods when the classes emerge *as* classes aware of their interests, preceding a social revolution; the latter makes one of the classes the new ruler of society, the other the exploited class. The oppressor class immediately strengthens the apparatus for the defence and preservation of its power, while the exploited class begins a struggle against the rulers. The struggle gradually comes to include ideological and organisational forms; parties representing the oppressed classes emerge and take up the *political fight* which, together with economic developments, leads to an increasing polarisation of society. The political fight takes various forms and includes efforts to create the political alliances without which it is difficult for the rulers to retain power and impossible for the ruled to seize it. Thus the correlation of political forces becomes the essence, moreover the synthesis, of the correlation of intrasocietal forces.

In the analysis of this concept, two questions seem basic: What should be regarded as the *object* of the intrasocietal struggle? and Who are the *protagonists?* An interconnected problem concerns the employed strategy — the general strategy and the particular methods used in conflicting situations. We shall begin with the interests defended and the aims pursued, since the changing and developing positions of particular classes and social strata are hardly explicable without an interpretation of their respective interests and aims.

Dialectics of social and national interests

Politics

In Marxist-Leninist theory, politics means the activities of organised social groups *vis-à-vis* other social groups; it is generated by the basic interests of the groups and expresses the mutual relations between them. Since all pre-socialist societies, apart from the so-called primitive society, are class-antagonistic societies — that is, consist of classes with contradictory interests — politics means the relations between classes. These relations primarily reflect the relative economic positions of the classes and the basic interests connected with their positions in the socio-economic structure.

Classes fight to protect their interests by various means. One method is the political struggle to seize and retain political power and obtain control of the organs of government. Only state power enables a certain class to establish and maintain a socio-economic and political system that favours its interests. The state apparatus is used as an instrument for resolving class conflicts in accordance with the interests of the governing class and to prevent conflicts from exploding into a violent revolution which might transform the existing social mode of production with its socio-economic basis and political superstructure.

(Admittedly, the state apparatus, being a special political organism which in a sense is separate from society and the struggling classes, and, in the words of Friedrich Engels, 'endowed with a movement of its own', may appear to play a more or less independent role. Since, however, the governing class often directly commands the state apparatus or/and exerts a decisive influence on it by economic or other means, the state apparatus is really an instrument of that class.)[1]

For the ruling class the purpose of the political struggle is to resolve all conflicts of economic and other interests in its favour by using the political power at its disposal; for the governed class, the struggle aims to tear down the existing superstructure and create conditions for the transformation of the entire socio-economic structure. Thus politics may be defined as the activity by which a particular social class aims to seize, maintain and make use of the authoritative institutions of the state.[2]

As mentioned above, the class struggle within a society takes the initial form of economic struggle, and then is 'elevated' to include ideological and organisational rivalries, finally becomes a political struggle. The class consciousness of the workers develops from the awareness of common economic interests in a single factory to the gradual growth of a socialist ideology. This generates an awareness of the need to unite organisationally on the national level and create a political party. The party establishes a comprehensive political programme for the struggle for revolution and socialism.

Political struggle has a double nature, however. It is the *highest* form of social struggle, but it is waged *through* other forms of struggle also. The economic and the ideological struggles and, if necessary, the use of armed violence are means of politics which are subordinated to the pursuit of political aims. Thus the correlation of political forces includes components taken from all other kinds of correlation of intrasocietal forces.

Social and national interests

Political interests may be directly related to the interests of *classes* or other social groups in their competitive interaction, or they may express *national* interests — i.e., the interests of broader social communities, which are usually national societies or nation-states. However, the latter also have a class flavour.

In Marxist-Leninist theory, class and national political interests are closely intertwined — in both the domestic and the international environments. The basic propositions underlying the analysis state that:
(1) the class aspect is the determining one,
(2) the progressive classes represent national interests in the best and most complete way, in both the domestic and the international spheres.

Let us examine these statements and some interpretations and explanations of them.
(1) The basic assumption is that classes determine the *content* of social life. Nations are only a historically necessary and transitory *form* of social development, in particular in capitalist society and in the period of transition from capitalism to world communism. Class interests are therefore primary; national interests, although they may appear to be independent, reflect, in the final analysis, class interests.

In pursuing its class interests, a progressive class also pursues national interests and strives for real independence and real progress of the nation in all respects. In terms of Marxist-Leninist philosophy, the relationship of social and national interests of a progressive class may therefore be regarded as that of the whole and its part, or of the general and the particular.[3]
(2) A political goal is a concept broader than a political interest: it also contains an awareness and an assessment of the interest — an assessment of the chances of its realisation and the expectation of the results of action undertaken to achieve the aim.

The formulation of a political goal and the choice of an appropriate strategy are affected by the domestic correlation of political forces and the dynamics of the class struggle as well as by the international correlation of forces. Therefore it is necessary to take into account the complex of all the interests of all the rival parties and the real conditions and possibilities of safeguarding them.
(3) National interests can be safeguarded — i.e., the development of a nation can be secured — if it enjoys (a) territorial independence and integrity as well as freedom from harassment and oppression by another

nation — which means freedom to develop its economy and its culture; (b) progressive intranational social relations which means the direct intermingling of national and social interests and (c) the possibility of using external sources of development through, among other relations, cooperation and techno-scientific exchange.

(4) The ruling classes of an antagonistic society after a short period when they liquidate the former outmoded system are becoming reactionary. They attempt to freeze the domestic social status quo, thereby hindering the social progress. Likewise in foreign policy, they fight to further their egoistic class interests — to dominate other peoples, to gain territories, new markets, higher profits, and so on. As a rule, these interests cannot be equated with the national interest — indeed, they often conflict with it. Since the state apparatus is in the hands of the ruling oppressive class, the avowed foreign policy interests are, in actual fact, the interests of the ruling class.

(5) The oppressed classes, on the other hand, generally represent social progress. They are also progressive in international relations. They represent the best national interests since they aim to strengthen the nation's independence, develop the means of production and implement social reforms which will create the conditions for national progress on a broad front.

They have a completely different understanding of the national state interest from the bourgeoisie.[4] If this interest is deeply and correctly comprehended, it cannot be achieved at the expense of other nations and what is more, it must include an active concern for the welfare of all the members in the community of nations.

This position is also reflected in the working class's attitude towards the increasing economic, scientific, technological and cultural cooperation between nations and their proceeding interrelation. Capitalist 'internationalisation' and 'integration' of nations is based, say Marxist-Leninists, on the attempt to establish the master-and-servant relationship, which promotes the interests of the more powerful countries, and also to create supra-national monopoly-oligarchic coalitions, which betray the people's national interests and promote their own selfish ends.[5] The socialist states and the communist movements pursue the aim of establishing a truly international cooperation based on equality of nations.

(6) On the international level, the classes constitute national contingents of *international class forces*. The international bourgeois class is unable to base the relations between the national contingents of the bourgeoisie on equality and cooperation, since this class is inherently nationalistic and since the interests of the particular 'contingents' are often in competition. They compete, for instance, for markets. In contrast, the international working class consists of national contingents supporting one another, and the relations between them are based on

85

equality, friendship and solidarity.

(7) To the proletariat the struggle to further national interests is a part of the combat for international class interests. It is waged to further national and international interests *at the same time* and it combines them both. This is a combination of the *general* and the *particular*, i.e., *specifically national* in a class struggle.[6]

In the long run, national interest coincides with international interest, i.e. the duty of the working class to the international workers' movement. In pursuing today's interests, the proletariat should never forget the interests of the future; worrying about the particular, i.e. the national, it should always remember the general, i.e. the international.[7] (The relationships of national interests and the proletarian internationalism are discussed in more detail in Chapter 5, pages 131—7.)

These basic assumptions are here summarised without examples, since they constitute a secondary theme in our study. However, the literature on the subject is abundant and is growing.[8]

General characteristics

Structure

The structure of the correlation of intrasocietal forces and the contents of the two sides of the political equation are an effect of a complex process of interaction between the economic basis and the political superstructure. In theory,[9] the development of the socio-economic basis — i.e., class structure of society — is directly reflected in the relation of political forces, that is in the power and positions of the political parties and organisations representing various classes and social groups. Thus it also influences the *form* of the state authority.

However, for several reasons this influence is not a direct one. In the first place, the political parties and organisations do not exactly reflect the interests and positions of classes and social groups. Their activities depend on their socio-political awareness and are also affected by the policy of other classes and parties. The governing classes try to indoctrinate the working masses and their representatives with the governing ideology.

Second, the intermediate social strata often change their political positions, as also do their political representatives who wander between various political alliances.

Third, the working class absorbs 'émigrés' from other social strata who affect its political awareness and its position in the political struggle (see below).

Fourth, changes in the economic position of a class or a social group are not rectilinear and do not immediately produce a corresponding change in the position of its political representation.

Fifth, the political development has its own regularities and it proceeds to some extent independently of socio-economic changes. Moreover, the ruling political élite actively affects economic relations — for example, through a system of laws and decisions. The governing class uses its political power to prevent disadvantageous economic developments (for instance, crises) and their political consequences (see comments in Chapter 6 on the policy of the 'monopoly-capitalist state').

Finally, economic development itself proceeds in an uneven way. According to one of the basic propositions in Marxist-Leninist theory capitalism develops in an uneven way both in particular societies and in the international arena; this is called the law of the uneven development of capitalism. In the internal sphere the law means that particular fields of the economy — e.g., production — and economy on the whole develop unevenly; in the international context it means that for socio-political, techno-economic and natural-geographical reasons the economy of the capitalist powers develops unevenly and some powers advance beyond the others in a leap-like way. This uneven development is internally expressed by irregular changes in the alignment of political forces. In general, it may be said that the forces of the working class and its allies are growing, but the development is a zigzag one which includes temporary retreats of the working masses.

Generally, since the socio-economic basis is essentially a bipolar one, consisting of two opposing classes, the development of the political forces also tends to combine various socio-political forces in two struggling camps, and the alignment of political forces is becoming bipolar. This allows to assess the correlation of forces of the two adversaries.[10]

To sum up, the determining influence of economics on politics consists in the fact that the political superstructure *as a whole* is the product of definite economic relations, that economic development decisively affects the general direction of the political development and that in the final account both of them exert a 'push' towards a social revolution.

Difficulties of measurement: forces and strategies

Intrasocietal — and, as their synthesis, political — forces are largely intangible — *inter alia,* because they include several subjective components. Then there is also an asymmetry in the kind, value and extent of the means at the disposal of the adversaries. Both the elusive character of the forces and the lack of comparable magnitudes in the means make it hard to choose an appropriate strategy and methods that are applicable in specific conflicts.

In spite of these difficulties, an assessment — if only a rough one — of the correlation of intrasocietal forces must be made since without this no strategy can be established. The latter is the more necessary since it has to be implemented in a definite social setting and must overcome a definite social resistance. In particular, a knowledge of the enemy's forces and strategy is indispensable since this will provide the basis for choosing methods to deal with specific conflicts, discovering the enemy's weak points and attacking at the right time. A general strategy may avoid some of these difficulties as it is based on general political goals and on an assessment of the global development of the intrasocietal situation; nevertheless, it must take into account the expected long-range strategy of the adversary.

There is an interdependence of strategy and forces which implement it. An appropriate strategy strengthens the forces and creates possibilities for successful action. It may therefore be conceived of as an element in each side of the intrasocietal equation. Thus, in a sense, 'forces' may be interpreted as a unity of political, ideological, economic and military strength with an appropriate strategy.

It seems that in the final stage of the class struggle, when it takes the form of revolution and civil war, the political forces of the social adversaries — including their military component — which mobilise all means, act openly and directly clash with the opposing forces, are becoming more measurable. Perhaps only in this phase can one speak of an assessable correlation of intrasocietal forces in a strict sense.

The difficulties in measuring the correlation of intrasocietal (or political) forces and the need to take account of its multi-dimensional character, dynamics and interconnection with action and strategy reflect the weaknesses of all the social sciences. The key concepts in the intrasocietal struggle — 'class forces', 'politics', 'strategy' and 'correlation of intrasocietal (political) forces' — the analysis of which is indispensable to the analysis of the social development, are more or less immeasurable.

One may therefore suggest that the assessment of the correlation of intrasocietal forces is primarily used for recognition of the *tendencies* of the development of the domestic political struggle and for the forecasting, establishment and preparation of the *crucial actions* by which the adversaries in the correlation may realise their long-range plans; it may help to pinpoint the time when the decision concerning a violent action can be taken and implemented.

The proletariat — the leading force on the anti-monopoly side of the social equation

Main protagonists

Which are the forces that constitute the two antagonistic components in a non-socialist society? The Marxist-Leninist proposition about the polarisation that must develop in any antagonistic class society may suggest a simple clear-cut structure consisting of two mutually opposed forces, each of which represents a more or less cohesive whole. In a developed industrial society, however, this proposition is not valid.

Far back in history, the fathers of Marxism, in their analyses of the bourgeois society of the mid-nineteenth century concluded that the correlation of class forces was not a simple one, with only two classes — the bourgeoisie and the proletariat — on the two sides of the intra-societal equation, although these were always presented as the *basic* protagonists. The existence of a peasant class was, for instance, incompatible with such a two-class equation. Engels wrote that

> The isolation of the peasant in a remote village with a rather small population which changes only with the generations, the hard monotonous work, which ties him more to the soil and which remains always the same from father to son, the stability and monotony of all his conditions of life, the restricted circumstances in which the family becomes the most important, most decisive social relationship for him — all this reduces the peasant's horizon to the narrowest bounds which are possible in modern society. The great movements of history pass him by, from time to time sweep him along with them, but he has no inkling of the nature of the motive force of these movements, of their origin and their goal.[11]

The social structure has become much more complex in the age of advanced capitalism which in Marxist-Leninist theory is also called imperialism or monopoly-capitalism. Both the basic antagonistic classes have become stratified: the capitalist class has split into its monopoly stratum and the various strata of the middle and the petty bourgeoisie, the proletariat in various countries has different components. The peasantry now also consists of several elements, ranging from the owners of large farms which, in fact, are monopoly enterprises, through middle-size farmers to small farmers and day labourers who are landless. Several other middle sections of society have emerged; they have ceased to be marginal strata and now represent a considerable percentage of the population.

Under such conditions, it would seem that there is no simple correlation of *two* forces, of two camps, but rather an alignment of many forces the configuration of which changes in different periods and at different points of time, and even in relation to particular questions.

In the Marxist-Leninist view, however, the polarisation of forces continues though their relative strengths keep changing. The ruling group in the advanced capitalist societies is gradually shrinking: it becomes stratified and instead of the bourgeois class as a whole, the 'monopolist bourgeoisie' has become the main item on that side of the intrasocietal equation. In the anti-monopolist camp tendencies towards cohesion may be noted, which arise from the proceeding consolidation of the working class but it is often difficult to build alliances with the middle strata of society. However, the idea of two social antagonistic camps has outlasted all these changes.

Missions of the proletariat

Let us examine the basic aims of the proletariat. In Marxist-Leninist theory the proletariat (the working class) accomplishes two basic missions in social development:
(1) it is in the forefront of the anti-bourgeois struggle (and, in highly developed capitalist societies, the anti-monopoly struggle); and (2) in the final stage of the development of the correlation of intrasocietal forces in its favour, it exploits this correlation for the purpose of revolution. Both missions, accomplished as operations in the class struggle, have been described and analysed in Marxist-Leninist historical and socio-political studies rather than conceptualised; only a few generalisations were made concerning regularities of the strategy-making process as well as methods and principles of action.

The factors which are said to favour successful actions by the proletariat include the following: the gradual accumulation of the experience of class struggle, the systematisation of this and formulation of conclusions about strategy; the development of ideological class awareness (consciousness); the accumulation of capabilities for waging a class struggle and, finally, the elaboration of a set of forms and methods of combat. Among the factors that are vital if the proletariat is to play a dominating role, the Communist Party's leadership is of primary importance. The party must develop a proper strategy and build up an organisation to implement it. Ideological work must be carried out on a permanent basis among the workers to make them fully aware of their role and mission. The struggle against reformist, anarchist, revisionist, social-democrat and other non-Communist ideologies, theories and programmes forms a part of this educational process. The difficult organisational and ideological mission of gaining allies and building effective alliances must also be fulfilled.

The following factors negatively affect activities and the leading role of the working class: the ideological penetration carried out by the bourgeoisie and its parties; the influence of the social-democrat and socialist parties on the workers' movement; the administrative pressure of the government which hinders the organisational growth of the working movement; the difficulties of creating a stable alliance with the middle (intermediate) strata; and the defection of those workers who win privileges and better conditions (the workers' 'aristocracy').

The latter issue has always received much attention. The 'aristocracy' of the workers is said to consist of those whose remuneration is on a level with the incomes of the higher middle sections of society. By their way of life and their psychology the 'aristocracy' constitutes a petty-bourgeois stratum within the working class and it conducts an 'intermediate' policy. Its representatives are among the leaders of reform parties and trade unions and they hold positions in the bourgeois state apparatus. Lenin is reported to have stated that

> their actions are designed to split the revolutionary working movement and to transform the proletarian organization into a political complement (*pridatok*) of the liberal bourgeoisie. As the main social bastion of the bourgeoisie in the working movement, the working aristocracy in a given country sides with the national bourgeoisie against the proletariat.[1][2]

Changed conditions

Some Marxist-Leninist writers observe that, in general, certain conditions for the growth of the revolutionary awareness of the working class have significantly declined. It seems paradoxical that, while in their view material premises of a socialist revolution have greatly increased, since the development and socialisation of production in the United States, Japan, the Federal Republic of Germany and other highly developed countries have reached a high level, a considerable percentage of the workers in capitalist countries have become less conscious of the objective processes which would enhance the prospects of a revolution.[1][3]

However, the Marxist-Leninists say that this development cannot be explained either by the proposition that the working class has lost its revolutionary potential and that the bourgeoisie has been able to integrate the workers into the capitalist system; or by the proposition that the proletariat has abandoned revolutionary methods as a means of implementing socialistic ideas; or by the essential improvement of the material conditions of the working class which is now taking place. They maintain that the objective and subjective premises of a political revolution are developing *unevenly,* since the capitalist countries are developing unevenly and that Marx's proposition that the workers tend to grow poorer in highly developed countries remains valid in our times. However, its manifestations vary in various epochs. In a certain epoch it takes the form of absolutely increasing poverty, in others of relatively, or socially, increasing poverty. *The growth of exploitation is common to all epochs.* Characteristic of our epoch is the growth of social conflict and of unemployment. The discrepancy between the level of the forces of production and the capitalistic relations of production must periodically generate crises, and there is a strong probability that crises will develop into revolutions.[14]

Despite general statements of this kind, Soviet researchers accept that the prospects of immediate revolutionary transformations in the developed countries have worsened. The bourgeoisie, they say, is trying to integrate the working class socially into the capitalistic system, to impose on them bourgeois ideas concerning, *inter alia,* cooperation between the classes. Though these writers state that the proletariat as a whole cannot be integrated in the capitalist system, they admit that the bourgeoisie has succeeded in relation to a part of it. However, in spite of all evidence to the contrary, they conclude that, although the difficulties in bringing about revolutions in the highly developed industrial countries are great, they are only transitory difficulties.[15]

Quite different difficulties are with the revolutionary awareness of the proletariat in several countries of the Third World. (see below.)

Structure of the proletariat

The growing numerical strength of the working class has always been adduced as a reason why it should play a leading role. In the view of those who criticise the idea of the hegemony of the proletariat, however, the proportion of persons in the population who can be described as 'workers' is now declining at an increasing rate. The continuing scientific and technological revolution, they say, leads to a diminution of the working class, which also means a narrowing of the social basis of the anti-monopoly side of the social equation.

The answer of Marxist-Leninist writers is that the concept of the vanishing proletariat is based on an erroneous equation of 'the workers' in general with manual workers. However, with the proceeding scientific-technological revolution, the worker becomes the co-creator and operator of highly productive plants, the leading protagonist in the production process as a whole and not merely on a 'basement level' which is oriented chiefly to manual labour. 'White collar workers' are also workers.[16] Workers are now defined as follows: 'A class of wage workers who are deprived of the means of production and therefore live by selling their labour, are subject to capitalist exploitation and perform purely operational functions in the fields of production, distribution, office work and services'.[17] A way of demonstrating that the numerical strength of the working class has not decreased is also to include in it the strata which formerly were not included. Seleznev, for instance, includes in the working class those employed in the field of 'material services' *(materialnye uslugi)* calling this 'an important group of workers'.[18]

Pro and contra 'the hegemony of the proletariat'

Some critics have also other arguments against the contention that the working class remains in the forefront of the revolutionary struggle.[19] They assert that, with the increasing proportion of 'mental workers', of intellectuals, technologists and other white collar workers in capitalist society, and their increasing socio-political activities and powers, the working class is losing its place in the forefront of the revolutionary movement. Wage-earners, it has been said, aspire to socialism, even if they are not 'led' by the proletariat.

It has also been held that reformist ideology is beginning to prevail over revolutionary sentiments and that the revolutionary potential of the working class is diminishing.

Against these criticisms, two kinds of counter-arguments have been advanced. One is based on an analysis of the situation in the contemporary world workers' movement. It is held that never before has the working class been so well organised and so strong as today and that all the conditions for maintaining its leading role still exist. The second argument is more complex and, indeed, it contradicts the optimistic view expressed above. The working class is said to derive its leading role from the *laws* of social development: the most progressive class *must* lead the struggle against the outmoded socio-economic and political system and forces. However, it is also said that 'the leading role objectively assigned to the working class, and the exercise of this role are not one and the same thing'.[20] The workers are now handicapped in their role by several factors: the reformist sentiments that prevail over the revolutionary ones among the non-proletarian strata, the inadequate awareness of the working class, the revolutionary initiative coming from other, non-proletarian strata. However, these processes should be treated as *deviations from a rule.* The working class has all the potentialities for assuming the leadership but these must be transformed into real capabilities. The laws of social development, mentioned above, will ensure the transformation.

Again, the reasoning concerning the hegemony of the proletariat in the countries of the Third World is somewhat different (cf Chapter 6).

Class alliances

Significance of alliances

For many reasons, the working class will be unable to prepare for, and win, a socialist revolution, if it stands alone and the ruling class can use against it not only the state apparatus and other instruments and forces proper to that class, but also the intermediate sections of society. Therefore, it is held, the working class can win the proletarian revolution only if it succeeds in allying itself with the non-proletarian working masses, which consist basically of the so-called middle sections of cities and villages.[21] In other words, the proletariat must maximally extend the anti-monopoly side of the correlation of intrasocietal forces. In Marxist-Leninist writings the creation and continuous extension of the alliances with the intermediate sections are considered objectively to be feasible, since *all* these groups suffer increasingly from the rule of monopolies and the increasing capitalist exploitation of society.

The approach to potential allies, however, must be differentiated. Alliances should be created not only for the purposes of the everyday struggle against monopolies to achieve democratic reforms and other social gains. The prospect of a socialist revolution should never be allowed to drop out of sight. Not every social stratum, however, joining the anti-monopoly camp desires a socialist revolution and, in the event of such a revolution, is prepared to become a participant or motive force. Only the proletariat and the poorest sections of the peasantry can be regarded as such forces. Therefore at the time of acute crisis which may lead to a revolution, some of the allies may have to be neutralised. It may happen that some of them turn their backs on the revolution and must be opposed.[22] However, if the revolution is successful, a new approach may be taken and an attempt made to win the intermediate sections for the development of the socialist society.

Strategy

The following principles underlying the strategy of developing and directing intrasocietal alliances are described as implied in Marxist-Leninist writings:[23]

(1) The struggle to achieve democratic reforms, and then probably to bring about a democratic revolution may — and, indeed, usually does — precede the transition to a socialist revolution.

Democratic changes are of considerable value. They compel the rulers to exercise their political power in the framework of democratic norms and thus to make concessions and promises, and to accept the prospect of further reforms. The struggle for democracy allows the proletariat to establish alliances with the spectrum of the broad non-proletarian masses, which after common political campaigns are becoming accustomed to fighting together with the working class. Moreover, democracy, political liberties, a participation — however modest — in the management of production and social self-administration should be regarded not only as factors operating for success in the class struggle but also as social gains having a value *per se*.[24]

In the words of a Marxist writer, beginning with the Communist Manifesto, the keynote of the works of Marx, Engels and Lenin is that the working class can approach the socialist revolution, win allies and lead the way to revolution and triumph only if it links every step in its movement and further development to demands for democracy that are expressed with the utmost resolution and consistency. This is borne out by the history of movements that have truly reshaped society in the world. Anti-fascist, anti-imperialist or national-democratic in their nature, reforms always paved the way for a socialist revolution. They speeded the development towards socialism with the aid of demands for democratic reforms implemented in their most radical and consistent forms.[25]

(2) The struggle should not stop with the attainment of democratic changes; the transition to socialism cannot be achieved through a gradual improvement of bourgeois democracy. The roots of oppression lie in the capitalist relations of property and power — i.e., in the capitalist socio-economic basis and political superstructure. To liquidate oppression and exploitation one has to liquidate these bases and superstructure.

(3) Through ideological work and in the course of the common struggle, one should be able to convince the middle strata that a socialist revolution is in their interest. The implementation of democratic reforms in their most radical and consistent form, and a steady radicalisation of further demands by the working masses, may also lead to a gradual radicalisation of the non-proletarian masses.

The revolutionary party of the working class ought to explain to allied groups that various social shortcomings, such as the crisis in the system of education or culture, the unsatisfactory state of public health, the conversion of dwellings into commodities, the disparities in the prices of farm produce and so on, are not individual and separate social problems, which bring one or another segment of the population into conflict with the state. These are *interconnected* part-problems and the results of monopoly policy which can be solved only with the abolition of the state's monopoly system and its class character.

(4)   The working class and its party should be prepared for a difficult process of overcoming the irresolution of the non-proletarian strata, their links with the bourgeois system deriving from their integration in the capitalist system, their lack of belief in socialism, their desire to stop at democratic reforms, their inclination to side with and adapt to the strong. The proletariat should reckon with convulsions, crises and serious setbacks and be prepared to make temporary compromises not only with its adversary but also with its allies.

(5)   Strategy and tactics should be adapted to the particular conditions in individual countries. Account must be taken of the fact that the fundamental law of capitalism — an uneven economic and political development — governs not only the relative dynamics of development of the various capitalist countries as political entities but *also the processes taking place in those countries*.[26] Thus flexibility is needed in the domestic struggle for partial aims: highly organised state-monopoly capitalism can be gradually weakened and finally brought down by circumspect, inventive and flexible struggle for the participation in the work of various government institutions and organisations, for bridgeheads and for every possible position in the superstructure, particularly in its political component.

(6)   Certain dangers should also be taken into account. Under the influence of the allies and their illusions about the possibility of resolving society's basic problems through a renewal and extension of democracy without a change in the relations of property and power, a considerable part of the proletariat may forget the final aim of the struggle — namely, socialism. This may in turn lead to calling a halt at the stage where some democratic reforms have been achieved.

(7)   Finally, one of the basic tactical goals of the alliance with the non-proletarian strata is to increase the global strength of the anti-monopoly forces. With an increasingly advantageous correlation of the intrasocietal forces it becomes possible to make more demands, to pursue further goals, to extend the alliance and weaken the adversary.

Intermediate classes, strata and sections:
general characteristics

In most capitalist countries, apart from the two basic antagonistic classes there also exist other classes, strata and sections: the peasantry (farmers), petty bourgeoisie (owners of small enterprises, shops and workshops) and the intelligentsia — i.e. scientists, men of arts and letters, engineers and other intellectual workers.[27]

These classes, strata or sections, it is said, are not neutral in class struggle but join one side or other in the social equation, depending on the concrete situation; the outcome of the class struggle, especially at a time of acute crisis or revolution largely depends on which side they join. Their role has attracted much attention not only in sociological analyses but also in official documents. Thus the Conference of the Communist and Workers' Parties of Europe in June 1976 appealed to the working class, the peasantry, the middle sections, scientists, cultural workers and other groups in society to devote their energies to the cause of peace.

In the most general and simplified division, 'working people' are said to consist of the proletariat and the non-proletarian strata or sections, which are also called 'intermediate strata', 'middle strata' or 'middle sections' of the population: peasants, traders, students and intellectuals. In other contexts, 'wage labour' is used to mean all 'hired' persons, of whom the working class forms the largest and the most conscious of its aims contingent.[28]

Some Marxist-Leninist scholars include in the middle stratum only the urban middle stratum, omitting the peasants and intellectuals. However, in the predominant view, they comprise all the social groups that objectively do not belong to either the bourgeoisie or the working class but take an intermediate place between them.[29]

Expressing this opinion, a Marxist research group in an article published in the *World Marxist Review* refers to Lenin, who considered that capitalist society included 'three main groups or classes: the exploited, the exploiting and the intermediate classes'.[30]

In an attempt at further differentiation, a group of Marxist-Leninist writers divide the middle urban stratum into two categories: (1) the petty bourgeoisie who, having a little capital, can exploit the labour of others but, because of the modest size of this capital, is obliged to create, by its own labour, a portion of the new value; and (2) other non-proletarian groups who possess no means of production and therefore hire themselves out either to the state (officials, physicians, teachers) or to capitalist enterprises (managers, office and service staffs), or to small petty bourgeois businesses (apprentices, learners, salesmen and saleswomen). New middle groups which are growing in numbers with the scientific and technological revolutions (engineers, technicians and other specialists) also belong to the latter category.

Wage-earners belonging to the urban middle stratum are distinguished from the proletariat not only by their incomes which are usually larger, but above all by their different role in social production: they are further from its material sphere, they are connected mainly with the service sector and are generally engaged to a lesser extent in manual labour.[31]

Marxist-Leninist writers criticise the alleged attempt by bourgeois ideologists to include all the intermediate strata in a single 'middle class'. Moreover, some of these ideologists assert that this 'class' does exist and it has absorbed segments of other classes and has become both the leading force in society and a factor stabilising the capitalist system.

In conclusions to his detailed analysis of the middle classes in capitalist society, S.N. Nadel writes about the changes in their structure consisting in the irreversible decline in the total number of the petty-bourgeois strata of the population in agriculture and a clear shift in favour of the urban middle classes; he also notes intensified proletarianisation of the middle classes as a whole. The proportion of peasants, artisans, small shopkeepers, etc., who are not in a position to exist on the income from their own undertakings, and are therefore forced to work as employees, is steadily increasing. It means, in other words, that there is a trend toward an increase in the proportion of semi-proletarian elements among the intermediate strata and toward an absolute and relative reduction in the numbers of the petty bourgeoisie in the employed population.[32]

Potential allies

In Marxist-Leninist theory, the non-proletarian sections of society — with the exception, naturally, of the monopolist bourgeoisie — are the potential allies of the working class in all issues concerning its struggle for democratic and socialist changes. They are, in other words, potential forces on the anti-monopoly side of the correlation of intrasocietal forces. 'Anti-monopoly movements' — for instance, the peace movement — are also regarded as such items in the social equation. Let us consider these potential allies of the working class.

(1) *Peasants* In the era of classical Marxism, the peasants were regarded as the main potential ally of the working class. They were the most numerous class; since their mode of production kept them isolated from one another, the relations between them were not national but merely local; they could hardly create a political organisation and defend their class interests by themselves.

In our times, a substantial decrease has occurred in the proportion of peasants, although in many countries they still constitute the majority of the working people or form the most numerous group after the working class. This could mean that their role in the political life of society decreases. However, nowadays their condition is changing: they are more educated, they use modern technology and form organisations to defend their rights. Their role in the class struggle is changing: from an anti-feudal, anti-landowner factor into an anti-monopoly one. The process of change began long ago but in recent decades has accelerated.

There are several socio-economic reasons for this change. In the view of a Marxist research group, 'This is a result of the increasing monopoly and capitalist control of agricultural production, of the growing direct and indirect exploitation of the countryside by the town through credits, the supply of technical facilities and fertilisers, the marketing of farm produce, and so on, all of which are in the hands of the big capitalists.'[33]

Agriculture in recent years has become much more intensive. Its growing productivity through the use of the latest machines, fertilisers, pesticides and other equipment supplied to the peasants at monopoly-high prices has resulted in the industrialisation of this branch with the financial side-effect of the peasants' debt growing with every year. In some Western European countries they cannot effectively compete with large capitalist farms, and with the entry into force of the Common Market's agricultural agreements, many of them cannot compete with large specialised capitalist farmers from other countries. The small rural producer is confronted not by an individual large landowner, but by a gigantic (and frequently international) monopoly, by a state of monopoly-capitalism and even a supra-national association of interstate monopolies.

The rapid decline in the number of farmers, as the small landowners suffer ruin and leave the land, is typical of many developed capitalist countries. In the USA, for instance, over 110,000 farmers are ruined every year, Marxist-Leninist writers point out. The only way out of this situation for the small farmers is to pool their efforts in defence of their interests in the fight against the highly productive large capitalist farms and against the wholesalers who have been steadily pressing down their buying prices.

In the view of the Marxist-Leninist analysts, the numerical strength of the peasants, the steady deterioration of their socio-economic situation and the anti-monopoly orientation of the peasant movements make the worker-farmer alliance an important factor for success in the anti-monopoly struggle.

(2) *The middle urban sections* A somewhat similar evolution is occurring among the middle urban sections, consisting of the masses of artisans, owners of semi-handicraft enterprises, small traders and others. These groups are becoming increasingly dependent on orders and marketing outlets through wholesale channels or through a direct dependence on the subsidiaries of large concerns. They suffer from heavy taxation, lack of credits, urban developments, import duties and so on. In effect they seek allies in their efforts to cope with their worsening economic and social position.

(3) *The intelligentsia* This group in society is sometimes called the 'special social stratum'. It is not directly connected with material production and its upper levels form part of the ruling class. It is

heterogeneous and absorbs representatives of other classes. The intelligentsia is in a state of constant flux. It is highly differentiated with regard to ideology: it includes a wide range of views on basic social and political problems — particularly concerning foreign policy: *détente,* disarmament, arms control and so on.[34] Thus the intelligentsia can support various policies and political camps with regard to particular questions.

Since in the highly developed countries (the USA, Japan, West Germany, France, the United Kingdom, Italy) and in several moderately developed countries (Spain, Greece, Portugal, Mexico, Argentina, etc.) the exploited intelligentsia has quickly grown in numbers, it may become the main ally of the working class, some Marxist-Leninist writers believe.[35] They consider, moreover, that, after a successful revolution in these countries, it will be easier to reconstruct the economy since there will be no need to create a new intelligentsia.

However, some Marxist-Leninist researchers point out that the stratified composition of the intelligentsia is such that it can hardly be viewed as a definite social group and this diminishes its role as a potential ally of the proletariat. They refer to the traditional teaching of Marxism in which the intelligentsia was not treated as a separate independent class or stratum since it did not have a definite place in production and served the ruling class in feudal and capitalist societies. In the words of one writer the intelligentsia is a heterogeneous group.[36] Lenin wrote:

> Educated people, and the 'intelligentsia' generally, cannot but revolt against the savage police tyranny of the autocracy, which hunts down thought and knowledge; but the material interests of this intelligentsia bind it to the autocracy and to the bourgeoisie and compel it to be inconsistent, to compromise, to sell its oppositional and revolutionary ardour for an official salary or a share of the profits or dividends.[37]

The position of the contemporary intelligentsia has not changed much, say the Marxist-Leninists. The intelligentsia has no common interests worth mentioning, since it is not a social entity. Its component groups are all in different situations. One component group, which supplies most of the bureaucratic élite, is integrated into the state-monopoly system and seeks to limit (and does limit) democracy as far as possible. Another group, which is much larger, but heterogenous, is in an entirely different position. It is oppressed and impinged on by the state monopoly system and suffers under that system together with the working class, but in many respects it differs from the latter. Lastly, there is a fairly well-defined large and increasing group of white collar workers, whose objective condition and place in the production process are drawing closer to those of the working class, with whose interests it is most closely linked although it has many interests of its own.[38]

However, the conclusion is that large sections of the intelligentsia may be treated as allies in spe since there is some coincidence of interests between it and the working class — namely, the wide gulf between the actual role of these social groups in the process of production and reproduction and their influence on decisions which affect their salaries, social position and, more generally, the meaning of their lives.

However, two obstacles in the way of an alliance with the intelligentsia under conditions of the hegemony of the proletariat remain to be overcome: the intelligentsia, generally, believes in the possibility of improving the bourgeois democracy and because of their educational status, which is higher than that of the workers, and their increasing political activities, they are unwilling to be 'led' by the working class.

(4) *'The new working class'* The continuously growing stratum of office workers, technicians and engineers, and the salary-earners in science, education and culture are sometimes collectively called 'the new working class'.[39] This is a highly diverse stratum with many conflicting interests. Its technocratic 'upper crust' is cooperating with the monopolies and its social and economic situation is steadily improving. Another substratum of it, however, is becoming proletarian and thereby a natural ally of the working class. There is also an intermediate substratum, vacillating between the two extremes. It is connected by all sorts of privileges with the 'upper crust', but because of its relatively uncertain economic position it is a potential ally of the workers. To become a real ally, this group will have to overcome psychological barriers — primarily their attachment to their privileges in society.

(5) *Oppressed nationalities and national minorities.* In many developed countries there exist oppressed nationalities and national minorities who are inclined to side with the workers in their fight for equal rights. For instance, in the democratic liberation movement of the 20-million Negro population in the USA, the social and national elements are inextricably fused, say the Marxist-Leninist writers.[40] The Negroes fight for civil rights and an end to racial discrimination. Riots and uprisings in the 'ghettos' of many American cities provided striking examples of this struggle.

'Anti-monopoly' movements

Democratic movements such as the peace movement, the anti-fascist movement, the movement for equal national rights, student movements and so on are also regarded by Marxist-Leninist researchers and Soviet politicians as potential members of the anti-monopoly camp — i.e., they may be included on the 'worker side' of the correlation of intrasocietal forces.

(1)   The general radicalisation of the peace movement with the active participation of the Communists is seen as bringing the peace movement people closer to the working class.

(2)   The anti-fascist movement today has a very broad social composition: together with the workers who constitute its backbone, it includes many intellectuals, especially students. Its slogans are being more widely adopted by social groups which earlier sometimes offered support and sustenance to fascism — i.e., by the middle urban and rural groups and even by some members of the army and police forces. The fascist coups which previously were carried out 'from below' — or, at least, with considerable support from below — are nowadays possible only 'from above'.

(3)   Student movements bring together students whose economic situation and prospects of employment are worsening. Many of them are unable to complete their education because of the steady growth in the cost of food, transportation and housing; their grants have become fewer and smaller. Students are increasingly faced with socio-economic and sociopolitical barriers when searching for employment and their discontent is increasingly directed at the educational system which, in their view, has a class bias. They realise that the groups which they will join, the engineers, technicians, teachers, physicians and officials are gradually losing their privileged status in society and sinking to the level of the working class, where they will be subject, as the workers are, to increasing exploitation.

Armed forces: enemies or allies?

The armed forces as the instruments of the governing classes have an unequivocal role in the correlation of intrasocietal forces. In times that are fairly free from social unrest their class role is disguised. The national functions which constitute their second basic mission, but which are largely exaggerated and distorted by myths and propaganda disguise their role in the class struggle. The crucial role played by the armed forces in the resolution of social conflicts becomes more apparent at times of acute social crisis when the state power is at stake in the class struggle.

For the same reason, the 'labour side' of the correlation of forces regards the destruction, the neutralisation or the winning over of at least a part of the armed forces to the workers' side as the principal strategic task before and during the revolution. In orthodox Marxism it was held that the destruction of the machinery of coercion and the success of revolution are interrelated. The former is unrealisable without the latter and the latter without the former. In this connection Engels noted that 'the disorganisation of the army and the total breakdown of discipline have hitherto been the indispensable condition and the result of all successful revolutions'.[41]

Subsequently a different view was taken — namely, that a part of armed forces *could be neutralised* and another part *won over* to the side of the revolution. The October Revolution provided the first example of this, and in the final stages of the Second World War in several countries of Eastern Europe the old army was either purged of reactionary elements and reorganised, or a part of it was included in the armed forces of the revolution.

Several Soviet publications are devoted to the struggle of the working class in Czarist Russia and its revolutionary party (meaning here the Bolsheviks) to democratise and radicalise the armed forces and persuade them to participate in the revolution. During and after the February Revolution of 1917, for instance, the Bolsheviks tried to persuade the armed forces to join in the fight against the Czarist forces, and during the preparations for the October Revolution they struggled — *inter alia*, through propaganda and organisational work in the armed forces — to win over as much as possible of the army and navy for the revolt against the bourgeois government.[42]

In our times, say Soviet scholars, the aim to win over the armed forces for the socialist transformation has become in some respects more difficult, in others easier.

On the one hand, in the developed capitalist countries, a fusion proceeds of the monopolies, the military establishment and some state organs in the military-industrial complex, and the army-police machinery of violence has become larger. The ruling classes resist the penetration of socialist influence into the troops, the emergence of class consciousness among the personnel, the attempts by them to organise politically and to protect their interests. These purposes are served by strong discipline, military laws, ideological indoctrination, the influence of the Church and the separation of the armed forces from the people. In some developed industrialised countries all these economic, political and ideological developments and efforts have resulted in a clear tendency towards militarisation of social life.

On the other hand, an opposite trend is developing in the armed forces: the growth of democratic awareness, strengthening of the links of the democratic forces in the army with the popular masses, a widening political differentiation among the rank and file. The process of militarisation also encounters increasing resistance of the masses which struggle for democratic reforms and human rights. Militarism can perish as a result of its own development, of the growth of the internal contradictions which will bring both the population and the million armies to an explosion. The downfall of the military-fascist dictatorships in Greece, Portugal and Spain demonstrates this tendency.

Recently, much attention has been paid to the armies of the developing countries (see below) in which a quite unorthodox phenomenon may be noted: in several countries the armed forces have become almost independent social bodies and, moreover, the only ones which are sufficiently organised to be able to take effective political action. The army has gained the position of a possessor (or one of the possessors) of power, and not merely its instrument. It has become a subject in politics, and not merely one of its means, which gives it a quite new position in the correlation of intrasocietal forces.[43] In some cases it may lead to the establishment of reactionary regimes, which pursue a nationalistic expansive policy, in others to the establishment of power of progressive military regimes. Soviet scholars analyse, however, this new role from an empirical rather than conceptual viewpoint.

All these developments stress the necessity to regard the struggle for the armed forces as one of the most crucial and difficult areas of class struggle, conclude Marxist-Leninists.

Methods

General ideas

(1) The methods used by the main adversaries in the intrasocietal struggle are very different, the difference being connected with the asymmetry of the means which they have at their disposal. The ruling class possesses the state apparatus, including the means of organised coercion — i.e., the penal system, the police and the armed forces — as well as dominating economic positions. It also uses instruments of education and propaganda (including church activities) for the purpose of ideological indoctrination. If the resistance of the working people takes forms which endanger the government, particularly in acute crises, when a social revolution seems possible or imminent, it makes a direct use of its armed forces.

The working class can oppose these measures primarily by organising economic strikes and demonstrations; then they can begin to organise themselves professionally and politically; and finally, they use various forms of political combat. They may also prepare for armed uprisings.

The potential allies of the working class are, in the Marxist-Leninist view, ideologically weak and inexperienced in class struggle and they mainly use separate *ad hoc* means and methods differing from those used by the proletariat. Blockades of land traffic organised by peasants, shop closures by the petty bourgeois, student demonstrations, city riots involving national minorities, and marches by peace-lovers provide examples. Thus much work must be done to coordinate, standardise, modify and adapt the entire range of methods to the requirements of class struggle and to develop a common anti-monopoly strategy.

(2) The development of a common strategy for the 'labour side' of the intrasocietal correlation meets profound difficulties. The diverse and somewhat scattered methods of *economic* struggle, which, in some instances, are combined with political demonstrations must be changed and welded into a single coordinated *political* struggle.

Marxist-Leninist writers often exemplify such an organisational and strategic unity of different classes and strata of society, as well as political movements, by the so-called 'popular front' — for instance, those in France and Spain before the Second World War.

Modified methods

In our times both of the protagonists use modified methods and forms of class struggle. The methods by which the ruling social groups in the developed industrial countries act to preserve and strengthen the governing socio-economic and political systems naturally change as the societies evolve. The ruling élites explain their policy in general statements about the national interests; they regard the preservation of the system as the basic national purpose. In Marxist-Leninist theory, these methods are considered to be class struggle methods used by the governing élites in pursuit of their interests. Any concession made by the rulers — for instance, an increase in the democratic rights of the population — is interpreted as being exacted by the ever more powerful working-class side of the intrasocietal correlation of forces. The influence of the socialist world system on internal developments in non-socialist countries is also strongly emphasised.

The new methods of the 'rulers' are said to consist of the following:
(1) A gradually increasing cooperation between monopolies and the state which leads to a fusion of these two instruments of the financial and industrial oligarchy into a new form of capitalist rule: that of state-monopoly capitalism. 'The monopolies use the state primarily for their enrichment. The state places advantageous orders with them and reduces their taxes... The state subsidises industrial enterprises or branches of industry which have become unprofitable for private capital or which need large capital investments (e.g., railways and coal mines), and exploits them in the interests of the monopolies.[44] The state increases its control of the basic areas of the national economy —

finance, heavy industry and natural resources — not only to increase profits but also to regulate the economy in order to rectify the anarchy of production and to improve the planning of production and distribution, to avert economic crises and mass unemployment and arrest the growing impoverishment of a part of the population.

(2) Utilisation by the ruling class of some of the extra profits to increase salaries and improve the living conditions of the population.

(3) A concession by the ruling class of a gradual increase in formal democratic rights.

These measures accompanied by intensified indoctrination are intended to eliminate the premises for revolutionary outbursts.

The proletariat and its allies should not reject such reforms merely because their original purpose is to preserve and strengthen the capitalist system, say the Marxist-Leninists. They should attempt to use the reforms against the rulers and exploit the concessions made by the monopolist bourgeoisie to develop the class struggle. For instance, the nationalisation of some kinds of natural resources or industries may be used to help the majority of the population to gain more influence over the private sector, and over economic planning and to propose alternative plans;[45] they can also use their participation in the local and central organs of administration to increase their influence on foreign policy and other matters.

One of the new methods consists in exploiting the internal split in the bourgeois class, — parts of which have interests conflicting with those of the monopolies — and in making an alliance with it concerning individual questions. The anti-capitalist front thus becomes an anti-monopoly front.

In general, however, the proletariat must take into account that the intrasocietal correlation of forces has become complex, that there are no conditions for an immediate socialist revolution, and that it is necessary to work out strategic and tactical methods for the *transitory periods* of a revolutionary transformation of society. '...the majority of the working people of developed capitalist countries aim at principal democratisation of the social and political system, but they are not yet ready for the struggle for consistent socialist goals'.[46]

Because of all the above-mentioned difficulties, the concepts of strategy and tactics of revolutionary struggle in our times, and the basic strategic and tactical principles for it are repeatedly defined and redefined in the programmatic documents of Communist parties and their international meetings.[47]

Fluid structure of the correlation in developing countries

Difficulties of a sociopolitical assessment

Most of the developing (i.e., post-colonial) countries have undergone revolutionary changes of a national and social character. They have acquired political independence and destroyed many of the feudal and colonial socio-economic relationships. However, in several instances, neither the revolutionary transformations nor the society which has emerged from them have had a clear-cut class character. Democratic revolutions there (which in Soviet writings are called bourgeois-democratic) have been intermixed with 'socialist transformations', and both have been carried out against the background of liberation from colonial rule, which has also been viewed as a kind of revolutionary change.

Several of these societies were not, before the revolutions, 'classical' societies consisting of two basic antagonistic classes; in other words, they did not fit the classical Marxist-Leninist typology of socio-economic formations. In particular, they were not capitalist societies in the traditional sense: they had neither a strong industrial bourgeoisie nor a mature working class. On the contrary, the so-called intermediate social strata — the commercial bourgeoisie, officials and intelligentsia — were playing an increasing role in economic and political affairs. In many countries the peasantry still played a significant role in the economy. These premises have continued to influence social development in the post-revolutionary period: neither the bourgeoisie nor the working class have suddenly become clearly defined social organisms with definite and conscious class interests and strong leaderships. The revolutions did not immediately change this amorphous structure. There began a slow and gradual process of reshaping the social structure and crystallising the principal social forces (cf. Chapter 4).

The emergence of a number of new states in the years of the rapid growth of the national liberation movements was presented as the great triumph of Marxist-Leninist theory, which had predicted such a development, and of those socialist states which had politically supported the movements and hoped to gain new allies in the global struggle against imperialism. In the initial studies, the general assessment of the character and role of the new states was positive. However, as more and more new countries in the Third World have moved closer to the Western camp, the assessments have become more cautious. At the same time, attempts have been made to explain this unexpected development in terms of Marxist-Leninist theory.

The new countries definitely did not fit the classical Marxist-Leninist typology of the five historical socio-economic formations, since Soviet writers were loath to call them capitalist, yet could not include them as a whole in the socialist category. Several writers refused to view them as a construction of a transitory type, since such a formation had no place in Marxist-Leninist theory. Nor could they be regarded on the whole as a group of countries following the path from capitalism to socialism. Their current domestic and international policies zigzagged in an erratic manner. They wandered between groups which supported either the Western or the Western bloc or even the group of completely neutral countries. They underwent sudden domestic transformations with changes in the governing élite and in the direction of socio-economic development.

The variety of regimes and the levels of socio-economic development and of the changes in them impelled Soviet writers to present many kinds of classifications. Some of them were based on the state of the economy, others on the traditional sociopolitical scheme which included the two basic categories of the capitalist and socialist systems. The problem of the global assessment of the developing countries was solved in various ways in these classifications: some writers called them 'mixed countries' or 'transitional countries', the latter term being used to imply that sooner or later a transition to socialism would take place.

Heterogeneity of the protagonists

In the developing countries both sides of the correlation of class forces are extremely diversified, since the socio-economic structures vary from those with survivals of feudal and caste relations (in Asia and North Africa) and tribal structures (in Africa south of the Sahara) to relatively developed capitalist relations (in Latin America). In the Marxist-Leninist terminology the political superstructures in these societies range from feudal-theocratic regimes, through reactionary military dictatorships to multi-party, relatively democratic systems, and finally, to revolutionary states.

The peculiar feature of the 'labour part' of the social equation in developing countries, say the Marxist-Leninist writers, is that wage workers constitute, on the average, only 30 per cent of the population (60 per cent in Latin America, 30 per cent in Asia, and less than 20 per cent in Africa). Moreover, this is a heterogeneous class, consisting of three different elements: (1) the industrial proletariat, (2) office workers, officials and allied groups and (3) plantation workers, day labourers and others. In some countries, the modern proletariat is some-what less numerous than the office workers, officials and similar 'status groups' in trade and the services and much less numerous than the agricultural workers employed on capitalist and semi-capitalist planta-tions and farms. Farm hands and day labourers in the Third World constitute about 45 per cent of all wage earners.[47] There are substantial differences in the objective status of the three groups of wage-earners (for instance, most of the officials enjoy various socio-economic and political privileges) and consequently their class consciousness has been largely corrupted by the ruling élite.

Two factors operate on behalf of the growing community of interests — and thus the cooperation — among various groups of wage-earners.[48] First, there is the inflation and the relative over-population, which adversely affects all wage-earners. Second, there is an accelerated process of 'proletarianisation' of various groups in the population and therefore the overall number of working-class people has increased in the last 15—20 years by 70—100 per cent. This development also has disadvantages, the Soviet writers say, since there has occurred a temporary decline in the relative size of the *regular core* of the industrial proletariat with its high class consciousness, which is the motive force in the revolutionary struggle. There are also other disadvantages, such as the concentration of hundreds of thousands of workers in large enterprises that usually are situated in capitals, ports and a few big cities which restricts the working-class movement to a relatively small territory and holds back the development of a broad alignment of the workers with the rural areas and small towns.

The social heterogeneity of the 'labour part' of the correlation of forces also means their ideological heterogeneity. The privileges of a part of the office worker group, the dual status of most agricultural workers, who are simultaneously wage-earners and small proprietors (or aiming to become small proprietors), the varying situations of the industrial workers themselves, some of whom, the top layer of skilled workers, defect from the mass of proletarians — all these circumstances make it extremely difficult to unite them in a single 'force'.

The background of temporary alliances of the proletariat with the middle sections of the population, and particularly with the peasants and the petty bourgeoisie, which have varied in different countries and different periods, make an assessment of the intrasocietal correlation of forces at a given moment or in a given period even more complex and thus also render difficult the choice of methods in the political struggle.

Possible paths to socialism

This conclusion is said to be justified by the prospects of developments in the countries of the Third World. Since most of these countries have been in a state of social and economic backwardness — which in Marxist-Leninist theory would place them in a pre-capitalist or early-capitalist stage of development — three possibilities for their inevitable development towards socialism may be foreseen:

(1)   The traditional development through the capitalist socio-economic and political systems as a necessary intermediate stage on the way to socialism;

(2)   A quite unorthodox — non-capitalist — path of development leading directly towards socialism; with this, the capitalist stage could be by-passed;

(3)   Another unorthodox path, leading the countries in question through a non-capitalist *intermediate* stage. In this stage, for instance, all banking, transport and other key industries would be nationalised, as also all foreign monopolies and foreign trade. Radical land reforms would eliminate all feudal or semi-feudal institutions and privileges. State economic planning would be introduced and economic policy would favour the productive forces in the country.

(A mixture of these two unorthodox approaches is also conceivable, according to the Marxists. This would correspond to the current state of development in some countries of the Third World. In these, either 'state capitalism' or elements of 'national socialism' is developing. However, the final direction is not firmly established there.)

It is hardly possible therefore, to make generalisations about the *structure* of the correlation of the intrasocietal forces in the developing countries and the *methods* to be used in the class struggle there. Only the main *tendencies* can be noted, such as the gradual numerical, organisational and ideological growth of the labour side of the social equation. However, the specific correlation of the intrasocietal forces in each country or in particular groups of countries must be separately analysed.

Some historical experiences

Marxist-Leninist scholars study the history of the working movement to discover principles of strategy for use in the process of extending and strengthening the 'labour side' of the correlation of intrasocietal forces and also to exploit the possibilities which an advantageous correlation provides in times of acute crisis pregnant with revolution.

Three kinds of revolution have been a frequent topic of analysis: the first is exemplified by the Paris Commune; the second, called bourgeois-democratic revolution, is exemplified by the revolts of 1905 and February 1917, in Russia; and the third by the revolution of October 1917 in Russia. The class struggles in the periods between the two world wars, after the Second World War and at the present time, have also provided a topic.

The following points about the Paris Commune are said to be of great interest:[49]

(1)   It was the first workers' revolution in which the proletariat con-

stituted the main motive force; therefore it succeeded, although only for a short time;

(2) A positive result of that revolution was to give the petty bourgeoisie — for instance, shopkeepers and small entrepreneurs, officials, the intelligentsia and craftsmen — a place in the government; this was the first attempt to build an alliance of the proletariat with other strata;

(3) The middle sections of society took an ambiguous attitude towards the revolution; they played an intermediate role: some of them followed the upper bourgeoisie, while others sided with the proletariat. But even the position taken by the latter elements was equivocal and vacillating and as the armed struggle increased in intensity they began to drop away;

(4) The main cause of the defeat was that the proletariat was not adequately prepared for revolution, it was not sufficiently organised and ideologically ripe. There was no workers' party and the influence of petty-bourgeois ideology — for instance, of Proudhon's ideas about class cooperation and of Blanqui's conspiratorial tactic — was great;

(5) The economic conditions negatively affected the material basis of the revolution: the revolutionary forces possessed no advanced means of production.

However, the overall conclusion is that the alliance between the politically conscious and well organised working class and the intermediate strata — the peasantry, small urban proprietors, craftsmen and working intelligentsia (including officials) — is always a condition for the success of a proletarian revolution.

The revolt of 1905 demonstrated the need to prepare for revolution and once more confirmed the importance of having allies:

(1) The proletariat had a revolutionary party and was ideologically better prepared than in any previous revolutionary actions; yet the ideological and organisational preparations were not sufficient;

(2) In particular, the efforts to unite workers, peasants and soldiers into a single revolutionary movement were not altogether successful. Many peasants lacked an understanding of the aims and strategy of the revolution and this affected the behaviour of the army, which consisted mainly of peasants. The army on the whole remained on the side of tsarism.

(3) The last-mentioned factor represented an important addition to the theory of revolution-making: at the time of the revolution *at least a part of the armed forces must be won over to the workers' cause* and be on the revolutionary side of the class struggle. This condition was partly fulfilled in the following revolution — the bourgeois-democratic revolution of February 1917 in Russia — in which the united workers and soldiers were able to establish a single revolutionary organisation, the Soviets of Workers' and Soldiers' Deputies and consequently overthrow

the tsarist regime. However, the state power passed at first to the bourgeoisie, since the proletariat and the peasantry were not sufficiently organised and conscious of their class aims and failed to cooperate. On the other side, the enemy — the tsarism and the upper bourgeoisie — were still strong enough to crush the organisations of the working class.

In the view of the Marxist-Leninists all these experiences were used in the *October Revolution.* The following may be regarded as the most important:
(1) The Bolshevik Party succeeded in convincing the overwhelming majority of the working people, including some of the peasantry, that revolution was the only way to escape war and oppression;
(2) The Party correctly judged which social forces the working class could mobilise against tsarism and capitalism. It succeeded in isolating the petty bourgeois parties from the working masses, in depriving them of all influence on the course of events and in making compromises with those forces which joined the revolution;
(3) The Party's great victory lay in spreading the revolution to the army and navy; the defeats in the world war, which were presented by the Party as being caused by the criminal and anti-national behaviour of the government and the military leaders, largely contributed to the armed forces' support for the revolution; the efforts for peace were welcomed by the broadest strata of the nation;
(4) The party forecasted and announced several basic social and political reforms which gained much support for the revolutionary rulers in the critical first period after the victory. The most valuable reforms were those in aid of the peasants, who were the allies of the proletariat.

Criticism of the intrasocietal balance-of-power theories

The Marxist-Leninist concept of intrasocietal forces is inseparably connected with the theory of society divided into antagonistic classes and developing through class struggle. All other theories are said to view society as an aggregate of groups which may have conflicts of interests, however these conflicts are not rooted in the class-division but in other differences — for instance, in different kinds of production with which the groups in question are associated. In many theories the existence of differences or inequalities in social status is assumed but either their origin is not analysed, or it is said to result from genuine inequality of individuals. Various theories of the 'stratification' of society either into a plenty of strata or into large groups but connected with 'status', 'power', and similar criteria help to obscure the picture of society.[50] The interaction of the components of society, which are mostly called social groups, produces a kind of *balance of power*, according to these non-Marxist theories; it helps to create stability in society, in spite of social conflicts.[51] No correlation of *opposing* forces is here involved, nor does the balance of power determine the forms and methods of social struggle and its outcome.

The ideas of the socio-economic balance between social groups are said to be complemented by theories of 'pluralistic democracy', which advocate the division of political power between various groups and their organisations. 'Pluralism' denies that class struggle is the driving force of historical development and replaces it by harmonious coexistence and regulated cooperation between social groups or strata with different, and even conflicting, interests. The formal manifestations of political pluralism are free elections and the existence of several political parties, some of which are in opposition to the government. This theory is said to include the assumption that the state apparatus is a non-class body which mediates between various social groups and tries to maintain a balance between them.[52]

The criticism of the theories of the intrasocietal balance-of-power theories, including the concepts of 'political pluralism', may be summarised in the following points:

(1) There can be no balance of power in non-socialist societies. In developed capitalist countries, theories of this kind disguise the absolute power of the monopolies.

(2) In most developed capitalist countries the struggle of two or more political parties does not mean a struggle of antagonistic social forces with conflicting interests. The successive transition of government power from one party to another does not mean a change in the social position of the classes. Such changes do not affect the power of the monopolies. The so-called free elections divert the attention of the exploited masses from the struggle for their basic interests.

(3) The state apparatus is a class apparatus. Two recent developments are (a) the extension of the functions of the state (for instance, its greatly increased intervention in financial and economic affairs) and (b) the increasing ties between the state and the monopolies, which increase and strengthen the role of the state as the instrument of the élite of capitalist class.

(4) The state is an instrument of the status quo. Its activities all aim at stabilising and strengthening the existing socio-economic system.

(5) A functional division between the state apparatus and non-governmental bourgeois or pro-bourgeois organisations, which is one of the postulates of the theory of political pluralism, does not weaken the power of the monopolies. It renders such power more flexible and effective.

All these criticisms reveal the basic contrast between the philosophy underlying the concept of the correlation of intrasocietal forces as acting on behalf of the revolutionary transformation of society and the theories which, in the Marxist-Leninist view, underlie various concepts of the intrasocietal balance of power and purport to justify the preservation of the capitalist system and to promote such a policy.

Conclusions

The analysis of experiences and of the current significance of the correlation of intrasocietal forces results, in the view of Marxist-Leninist writers, in the following general conclusions:

(1) The role of a social group in the correlation of intrasocietal forces depends on the following factors:

its objective economic and associated social interests;

awareness of these interests;

cognition of the possibilities of realising them — i.e., of the conditions of social struggle (for instance, the assessment of adversaries, allies, their relative strengths) and the foreseen development of events; choice of an appropriate strategy and tactics of struggle as regards strategy, there is a need to establish a hierarchy of interests, and a sequence of their realisation.

In short, the role of a social group depends on both the objective conditions and subjective factors such as cognition and awareness of the group's interests and the specific situation, and the choice of appropriate action.

(2) Both sides of the equation of sociopolitical forces — i.e., of the correlation of intrasocietal forces — have their constant components and both possess temporary allies in particular periods and/or in particular issues. A potential ally can be made a real ally only if one has an appropriate strategy to link him to one's own cause. The worsening economic and/or social situation of the 'middle strata' or the oppressed nationalities is not a sufficient motivation to bring them into the anti-imperialist camp. The dual nature of the 'middle strata' make them susceptible to conservative propaganda (which can, for instance, demagogically exploit the failures of liberal-bourgeois or even monopoly élites) and cause them to side with the proletariat only in times of acute crisis. Even then, only some of them can be attracted. Peace movements may support the anti-monopoly camp in questions of arms control or the reduction of nuclear armaments, while acting against it on the issue of radical social reforms and generally they may not be inclined to undertake any organisational cooperation with the Communist parties.

(3) The complex determination of the position of particular social groups in the social struggle has brought about some change in the simplistic scheme of class relations in the so-called capitalist society

presented by orthodox Marxism. Instead of the correlation of two antagonistic classes, which relegates all others to the status of secondary forces, Marxist-Leninist writers now present a more general framework for the social struggle, an alignment of social forces, which — although it has two poles and tends towards polarisation — consists of many components. Even the basic antagonistic classes are undergoing a process of stratification, which necessitates ideological and organisational measures for their consolidation. The capitalist state, for instance, is becoming a body whose mission is to provide a compromise between the conflicting interests of the various factions of the proprietary class, to brake and absorb the contradictions, to coordinate the political activities of the factions and to develop an 'aggregate' domestic and foreign policy.[53] Thus the polarisation into two opposing camps has begun to be treated as a *tendency* rather than an established configuration.

(4) It seems that the concept of the correlation of intrasocietal forces may help to explain why, in a certain country at a certain historical moment, conditions develop which favour a socialist revolution and why they are exploited (or not) by revolutionary forces. The scheme implied in the works of Marxist classics, which concerned a simultaneous revolution in several of the most developed capitalist countries, was not realised. Thus other explanations were sought for the October Revolution and the subsequent socialist revolutions. However, the orthodox thesis was preserved, according to which a socialist revolution ripens when the relations of production become a brake on the forces of production and when, therefore, social development requires a change in the relations of production and in the superstructure. Since imperialism is such an outmoded system, hindering the growth of the forces of production, it is said, a revolution is inevitable and imminent.

However, contrary to this proposition, no revolutions have occurred in the developed countries and none seems imminent there. To explain why a revolution broke out in Russia, a moderately developed country, the law of the necessary correspondence of the relations of production to the forces of production was insufficient. Another law was invoked by way of explanation: the above-mentioned law of the uneven development of capitalism. This has not only an internal but also an international aspect; both will be discussed in Chapter 6, but here one effect of the law should be mentioned. The uneven development of capitalism and the sharpened competition between particular imperialist countries makes impossible a simultaneous revolution in all the developed countries, which are on different levels of development. On the other hand, it makes possible an attack against a capitalist regime in one of the weaker countries, under favourable circumstances, when some direct causes of a revolution are present — for instance an economic crisis or a defeat in war accompanied by economic destruction, such as occurred in Russia in 1917. These objective conditions ought, however, to be exploited: they ought to interact with the *subjective* premises of revolution. When the ruling class loses control of the economic and political situation, the oppressed masses ought to exploit their advantage.

(5) Two basic lacunae in the contemporary Marxist-Leninist analysis of the correlation of intrasocietal forces may be noted. One is the above-mentioned exclusion of socialist society from the analysis since, in the Marxist-Leninist view, this is free from the basic division of society into two antagonistic parts. The other is the lack of an analysis of the intrasocietal correlation in society which is in a transitory inter-formational phase of development *(perekhodnaya mezhformatsionnaya stadiya).* [54] Such a society possesses features of two formations: both the preceding (i.e., lower) formation and the subsequent (i.e., higher) formation which will replace it. We may distinguish here three kinds of intrasocietal correlation of forces: that within the remnants of the old formation, that within the emerging new formation and that between the antagonistic social forces of both of them. Since the struggle is carried on simultaneously on all fronts, the interaction of the three correlations is very complex indeed.

(6) Finally, as we have seen, and as we shall see in the analysis of the correlation of international forces, the interaction between the intra-societal and the international correlations has been conceptualised only in very general terms and no statements about the respective regularities have been made.

Notes

1. Engels' functional definition of the state is well known: 'an organization of the possessing class for the protection of it against the non-possessing class' ('The origin of Family, Private Property and State', in Marx, Engels, *Selected Works,* I, II. Moscow, p. 291). 'As the Marxist-Leninist science indisputably proved, the dictatorship of the economically governing class is the essence of each state; it (the class — JL) uses political power for the protection of the existing economic system and for the suppression of resistance shown by class antagonists'(*Istoricheskii materializm i sotsialnaya filosofiya sovremennoi burzhuazii,* 1960, p. 378).

2. *Bolshaya Sovetskaya Entsiklopediya,* 2nd ed., vol. 33. It is a type of relations between classes and peoples with respect to the state authority. This aspect of relations is the most fundamental; it expresses the basic interests of these classes (A. Vishnyakov, 'Politika KPSS:nekotorye teoreticheskie voprosy', *Kommunist,*

     1973:10, p. 52).
3   Janos Kadar, in *S.M.R.*, 1981, p. 49.
4   Shakhnazarov, 1984, p. 55.
5   *Leninism and the World Revolutionary Working-Class Movement*, 1976, p. 500.
6   *The Theory and Practice of Proletarian Internationalism*, 1976, pp. 30—2.
7   Shakhnazarov, 1984, p. 102.
8   *Leninism and the World Revolutionary Working-Class Movement*. Shakhnazarov, *The Destiny of the World. The Socialist Shape of Things to Come*, Progress Publishers, Moscow 1979; *Fundamentals of Political Science*. Textbook for primary political education, Progress Publishers, Moscow 1979 (2nd printing); L. Moskvin, *The Working Class and Its Allies*, Progress Publishers, Moscow 1980; *Sovremennyi kapitalizm i rabochii klass: kritika antimarksistskikh kontseptsii*, Politizdat, Moscow 1976; A.N. Melnikov, *Sovremennaya klassovaya struktura SShA*, Izd. 'Mysl', Moscow 1974; *The Working Class of Capitalist Countries and the Scientific-Technical Revolution*, Peace and Socialism Publishing, Prague 1969; *Mezhdunarodnoe rabochee dvizhenie*, V.V. Zagladin, A.A. Kutsenkov, eds, Politizdat, Moscow 1976; Zarodov, 1983, Ch. III; Shakhanazorov, 1984, pp. 55; V. Krasin, 1985.
9   Bunkina, 1970, p. 11 ff.
10 Cf. Ch. II.3.C and III.I.D. in this study.
11 Frederick Engels, 'From Paris to Berne' in Karl Marx, Frederick Engels, *Collected Works*, Moscow, Vol. 7, pp. 519—20.
12 V.I. Lenin, *Polnoe Sobranie Sochinenii*, Moscow, vol. 27, p. 103. Cf. Seleznev, 1982, p. 62.
13 Seleznev, 1982, p. 61.
14 Ibid., pp. 62—5.
15 K. Ostrovityanov, 'Tvorcheskaya moshch' Leninskoi mysli i kapitalizm nashikh let', *Kommunist*, 1981:7, p. 86. Cf. Seleznev, 1982, pp. 58 ff.
16 Shakhnazarov, 1979, pp. 257—9.
17 Melnikov, 1974, pp. 257—9.
18 Seleznev, 1982, p. 61.
19 Zarodov, 1983, Ch. III.
20 'Class Alliances and Political Blocs', *W.M.R.*, 1980:10, p. 68.
21 Seleznev, 1982, p. 5. Cf. Krasin, 1985, Essay Five: 'Class and Political Alliances'.
22 Cf. Isaac Mintz, 'Revolution and the Intelligentsia', *W.M.R.*, 1981:12, Cf. Krasin, ibid.
23 'Class Alliances and Political Blocs', 1980; Exekias Papaioannou, 'Concerning International and National "Supra-Class" Alliances', *W.M.R.*, 1981:8.

24 Papaioannou, 1981, p. 8.
25 Wimmer, 1979, p. 44.
26 Ibid., p. 49.
27 *Fundamentals of Political Science*, 1979, p. 55; Krasin, 1985, pp. 89—93.
28 Moskvin, 1980, pp. 11—12. For a detailed analysis, see Nadel, 1982. He writes: 'The middle strata of bourgeois society include one intermediary social class (petty bourgeoisie) and a number of social groups: persons of liberal professions, semi-proletarians, who are simultaneously hired workers and owners of small enterprises, and hired workers who do not own means of production but differ in some respects from the working class; this basically concerns the representatives of intelligentsia' (p. 88).
29 *Zapadnaya Evropa v sovremennom mire*, vol. I, Moscow 1979, p. 274.
30 'Class Alliances and Political Blocs', *W.M.R.*, 1980, p. 75. V.I. Lenin, *Dela*, vol.. 39, p. 453. Lenin also pointed out another set of three classes under capitalism: the bourgeoisie, the petty bourgeoisie and the proletariat ('Can the Bolsheviks Retain State Power?', *Collected Works*, vol. 26, p. 96).
31 'The Middle. Strata: Whom Are They With?', *W.M.R.*, 1982:12. Krasin sees a division of the urban middle strata into new and traditional ones: the petty traders, shopkeepers, owners of small enterprises, artisans belong to the latter, various layers of intelligentsia, workers by brain in industry and state administration and those employed in the sphere of services to the latter. (1985, p. 91).
32 Nadel, 1982, pp. 429—38.
33 'Class Alliances and Political Blocs', 1980, p. 67.
34 *Protsess ...*, 1981, p. 90.
35 Seleznev, 1982, p. 55.
36 Mintz (note 21), 1981, p. 14.
37 *Collective Works*, vol. 2, p. 335.
38 Wimmer, 1979, p. 46.
39 Moskvin, 1974, Chs. VI—VIII; Shakhnazarov, 1979, Ch.IV (especially p. 259).
40 *Leninism and the World Revolutionary Working-Class Movement*, 1976, p. 395.
41 Golub, 1979, p. 24 (Fr. Engels quoted from *Selected Military Works*, Russian translation, p. 643).
42 Ibid., Ch. Three: 3 and 6—9.
43 Cf J. Lider, *Military Force*, 1981, Ch. 4.
44 *Fundamentals of Political Science*, 1979, p. 419; *Mirovoi revolutsionnyi protsess i sovremennost'*, 1980, p. 393.

45 Bunkina, 1970, 'Conclusions'.
46 *Mirovoi revolutsionnyi protsess i sovremennost*, 1980, p. 393. Cf. Ch. Seven; 3. 'Metodologicheskie, teoreticheskie i sotsialno-istoricheskie osnovy sovremennoi strategii i taktiki kompartii' and 4. 'Novye istoricheskie usloviya i problemy strategii revolyutsionnogo rabochego dvizheniya. Internatsionalnaya stategiya kommunisticheskogo dvizheniya'.
47 Ibid., esp. pp. 392–3, 395–6.
48 *Leninism and the World Revolutionary Working-Class Movement*, 1976, Ch. V, 'The Working Class of the Developing Countries'.
49 Moskvin, 1974, Ch. I. 2.
50 Cf. Ch. II. Cf. Galkin, 1982, Nadel, 1984.
51 Löwe, 1973, pp. 48–52.
52 Kuz'min, 1983, p. 11. Cf. Krasin, 1985, pp. 42–6. He also criticises the 'pluralistic model' of building socialism.
53 *Protsess ...*, 1981, p. 89.
54 Seleznev, 1982, pp. 8 ff.

PART III
CORRELATION OF WORLD FORCES

5 Correlation of international forces: general assumptions

Agenda

Three assumptions seem to underlie the Marxist-Leninist concept of the correlation of international forces:

(1) International relations form an extension of the domestic political struggle for class and national interests; there is a close interrelation between the domestic and external policies of any class.

(2) The correlations of intrasocietal and international forces produce a mutual impact.

(3) The interaction of the domestic and internationalist role of the working class occupies a special place in both kinds of correlation.

The concept of the correlation of international forces has recently attracted increasing attention and it seems to have acquired the status of a category. Thus, for instance, in 1975 and 1977 the East German political monthly *Deutsche Aussenpolitik* published two studies on this correlation, defining it as a 'category of class struggle which covers both the relation of the natures of the two opposing forces and that of their material, politico-moral and military potentialities'.[1] The correlation of international forces is said to exceed by far the area of interstate relations: it constitutes the *entire* relation of the forces of the two antagonistic systems — that is, of two different socio-economic formations.

To take another example, in a collective study published by the Soviet Academy of Science, the correlation of class forces and class policies — i.e., the correlation between the international bourgeoisie and the international working class — is considered to constitute the highest level of international political relations. Moreover, as a very broad and complex concept expressing a basic relationship which greatly influences the course of all international and domestic events, it should be considered a category:

> 'The determining Marxist-Leninist category, which permeates the analysis of all three levels of international political relations, and consequently the analysis of the process of forming and implementing the foreign policy of capitalist states, is the correlation of the two forces of the two socio-economic systems. This correlation cannot be reduced to a comparison of the parameters of military power, for instance as basic as nuclear-missile power with regard to its impact on contemporary international relations. It is a broad and complex class sociopolitical category. It should be viewed as a correlation of the class, social, economic, political, ideological, military, ethical and other forces in the two socio-economic systems of our times.'[2]

In the analysis of the correlation, constantly new aspects of it and factors affecting it are discussed, such as the roles of ideology, policy and strategy.

Categories and kinds of relation of international forces

Categories

Two basic categories of the relation of international forces may be conceived of in the Marxist-Leninist social philosophy:
(1) The relation of forces (balance of power) in an international system consisting of homogeneous states.
(2) The relation of forces in an international system consisting of states with different socio-economic systems representing two successive socio-economic formations; these constitute two sub-systems.

In the second case, three types of relation of international forces coexist. One of these encompasses the international system as a whole and is the relation of forces between states representing the two formations (or the two antagonistic systems). The other two lie within the sub-systems; these two, in our epoch, constitute the relation of forces among the capitalist states and the intrasocialist relation.

To distinguish in this study between the traditional relation of forces of a few capitalist powers and the contemporary relation of forces of the two antagonistic systems, the former is usually called the 'relation of forces' or 'balance of power', while that between the systems is called the 'correlation of world forces' (see Chapter 6). The notion of the 'relation of international forces' will be used as a *general* concept covering all kinds of alignment of forces in the international sphere.

Kinds of relation of international forces

On the contemporary scene, the following kinds of relation of forces in the international sphere are conceivable:
(1) the correlation between world-wide antagonistic camps (including most of the developed countries); a variant of this would confine the correlation to the two superpowers which represent the main power in the two camps;
(2) the relations of power between groups of states in particular regions (regional relations of forces) and sub-regions;
(3) the relations of power between individual states, especially in two variants: within a coalition (alliance) of states or outside it;
(4) the relations of power between protagonists other than states.

While attention is focused mainly on the correlation of forces between the joint power of the two antagonistic systems, the comparison of the power of individual states and the relation of forces between groups of states in particular regions and sub-regions are also considered.[3] The former may influence, for instance, the relations within the opposing camps and thereby their composition and, in the final account, their joint or composite strength. It also affects the relations between individual states belonging to the opposing systems, the chief of these being the power-relation between the superpowers. The relation of forces between the states of the Third World which, in the Soviet view, took the socialist path to development and the states associated with the capitalist world is also examined.[4]

The set of the kinds of international relations and of the respective relations of international forces has been further elaborated as a *hierarchical system*. It includes global relations (and the global correlation of forces), regional, sub-regional, inter-group and bilateral interstate relations (and the respective relations of forces).

In the sphere of *global international relations* various alignments of forces between five states or groups of states are said to play important roles: those between the United States, the Soviet Union, China, Japan and the states of Western Europe. These five components form various structures which profoundly affect international relations as a whole: (1) the bipartite structure consisting of the United States and the Soviet Union; (2) tripartite structures of the United States — Soviet Union — China and the US — Japan — Western Europe; (3) the structure including all five components; and (4) a six-party structure in which the five power centres are supplemented by the developing nations.[5]

However, it is said that for a long time to come, the basic correlation of economic, political and military forces — namely, the relations between the two opposing socio-economic and political systems and their alliances, NATO and WTO — will have the most influence on international relations at global level. This correlation is multi-dimensional and it affects all levels of international relations and all regions, but the essence of it is the correlation of the forces of the states belonging to the two opposing alliances. This bipolar structure will not be transformed into any multi-polar structure; it will exist simultaneously and parallel to multi-polar structures and will greatly affect them and interact with them.

A section of this study deals with a Marxist-Leninist criticism of non-Marxist theories which view the world as a multi-polar system of 'centres of power'. The existence of several such centres has recently been admitted by Soviet politicians and analysts, but it is maintained that they do not form the *basic* structure of international relations.

It is accepted that international relations, viewed as a 'system, structure and process', combine bipolarity with multi-polarity and that the conflict between the two antagonistic blocs, though basic for the system as a whole, is not the only one, since there is also the conflict between 'imperialism' and the developing countries; moreover, the traditional conflict among various imperialist states and power centres still continues. This does not constitute, however, the *basic* conflict of our times.

As regards the *regions and sub-regions,* these are said to be political rather than geographical concepts of which the boundaries may vary according to the complex of political problems which are the subject of conflict. A political region has common political problems; however, these may change. The same geographical regions may appear in different contexts depending on the political problems concerned. Sub-regions have the same characteristics; however, they cannot easily be separated from the regions. In spite of the political characteristics ascribed to them, regions and sub-regions are referred to in Soviet writings by their geographical names — for instance, the regions of the Near East, the Middle East and the Far East, the Mediterranean, Central America, South Africa and South-East Asia, and the sub-regions of the Eastern Mediterranean, the Persian Gulf, the Indian Peninsula, Southern Europe and Scandinavia.

The concept of the 'group level' of international relations and the respective correlations of forces may become relevant on the occasion of various problems in various regions. Benelux, ASEAN or OPEC are examples of such formal or informal groups of states: relations in NATO or the European Economic Community or between them are also mentioned.

Finally, there exist bilateral relations, which constitute the lowest level of international relations and, at the same time, the basic substance of the international structure. Here again, the relations of the superpowers which, directly or indirectly, affect all levels of international relations, are the principal ones.

Nature of the correlation

The correlation of international forces at any level is regarded as an *objective category*. It reflects objectively existing conditions in the international sphere and objective historical tendencies. However, the development of the correlation of forces is not spontaneous and automatic, but depends largely on the politics — i.e., actions — of states. These may, for instance, accelerate the growth of some components of the forces in order to compensate for an inferiority in others.[6] The correlation has an objective value, although it is differently perceived and assessed by particular protagonists, and even by particular sections of the governing classes or other groups in capitalist countries.

The correlation of international forces has a *multi-level structure* which includes all the basic components of state power. Non-Marxist concepts are criticised, which either reduce the correlation to military factors or assume a loose multitude of components and the intangible character of some of them, and propose vague and ambiguous components and parameters for inclusion in the measurement of the correlation. The latter comprise 'the geopolitical situation', 'the economic potential', 'the spiritual health of the nation', 'territorial and ecological resources', 'the quality of the country's leadership', 'techno-scientific potential', 'military power' and so on. In these concepts, the components and parameters are simply enumerated and no hierarchy is given.[7] The Marxist-Leninist concept, on the other hand, consists in clearly defining all the basic potentials and presenting the sociopolitical and the structural-functional characteristics of the protagonists as the basis of the forces being compared.

The correlation of international forces is a *dynamic category*. It continuously changes, but not always rectilinearly, smoothly and at the same rate. The principal changes which characterise the beginning of a new period are leap-like. Parallel to the general tendency which represents the historical development of society, partial and temporary tendencies may also be noted which are mutually contradictory and sometimes also in conflict with the general tendency. The development of the relation of forces on the global scale may also proceed unevenly on some of the lower levels.[8] These general characteristics will be discussed in more detail below, with regard to the Marxist-Leninist concept of the correlation of world forces.

Impact

The differences between the initially mentioned categories of the correlation of international forces cause the different impacts of these correlations on world developments.

The impact of the relation of forces (balance of power) in a non-socialist formation, being in accordance with the character of the formation, favours developments that are typical of it, such as the struggle for spheres of influence and profits. Thus a change in the balance of power between the great imperialist powers leads to wars concerning a redivision of the spheres of influence; such wars produce a further change in the balance of power which, after some time, leads to new crises and new wars. Stability and the balance of power are relative and they are possible only in some periods; moreover, they are also 'regulated' by wars.

Changes in the relation of international forces and wars connected with these changes, do not under these conditions alter the structure of international relations or the intrasocietal correlation of forces or the aims underlying the international rivalries and struggles.

The basic changes in the relation of international forces connected with the emergence of a socialist state (and then of a whole socialist system) changed the international system itself: it began to consist of states belonging to two different socio-economic formations. The balance of power among a few of the most developed imperialist countries as the determining feature of the international system was replaced by the correlation of forces between two opposing systems. A new kind of confrontation was said to arise, which was concerned not with spheres of influence but with the future of mankind. All further changes, such as the collapse of the colonialist system or the restructuring of international relations were connected with changes in the correlation of world forces. These changes did not necessitate wars and did not bring about new wars. On the contrary, they reduced the likelihood that the imperialists might unleash wars.

The very nature of the impact of the correlation of international forces underwent a change: the changes in the correlation brought changes in the conditions under which the laws of the international class struggle operate: the strategic positions of the opposing camps, their potentialities and the forms and methods characterising their confrontation. For instance, the confrontation between capitalism and socialism, which is called in Marxist-Leninist theory a law of our times, more often takes the form of ideological struggle and domestic revolutions than of interstate wars.[9]

Correlation of intrasocietal and international forces: mutual impact

International relations as an extension of domestic political struggle

In Marxist-Leninist theory and policy, political struggle in the domestic sphere is projected into the international relations. Generally, the struggle of the two antagonistic classes on the domestic front reflects and effects the international struggle of the 'world bourgeoisie' and the 'world proletariat' (or 'world working class'). The foreign policy of states is fundamentally affected by the domestic alignment of class forces and the actual state of the class struggle.

The first and principal novelty of our times is the emergence of a new component of the 'world working class' in the form of socialist states which, like the bourgeoisie, use their state apparatus as a basic instrument in the international class struggle.

Second, the working class and its allies in the capitalist countries have appeared on the international arena as new and independent protagonists. They enter the field of international relations not only through the relations of states but also parallel to them and independently of them. Their impact is exerted through the common actions of workers in different countries, the international activities of Communist parties and trade unions and also indirectly through the common actions of the intelligentsia of various countries which partly belongs to the working class and which often acts in support of the international working class.[10]

Therefore, in the Marxist-Leninist view, the basic correlation of political forces in the contemporary international system may be interpreted as not only and not mainly that of individual states or coalitions of states but 'first and foremost as the correlation of contemporary class forces — namely, the international working class and the bourgeoisie, the forces of socialism and capitalism'.[11] This kind of international relations directly affects the character of international politics regarded as primarily the arena of the struggling class which have shaped the international system. The alteration in the balance of power between socialism and capitalism is mainly a change in the relationship of class forces.[12]

It seems, however, that, as implied in the writings of some Soviet analysts, the impact of the international working class on the course of world events has been weakened by its extreme differentiation.

The world proletariat consists of two main contingents: the free working class of the socialist countries and the proletariat of the non-socialist states which is fighting for its emancipation... The working class of the non-socialist world is heterogeneous. It includes the proletariat of the industrially developed capitalist states, which has been tempered in class battles, and the budding working class of the countries fighting to consolidate their national independence. Naturally, they operate in different conditions and employ different forms and methods of struggle.[13]

However, the negative effects of this differentiation are toned down by Marxist-Leninist writers.

Mutual impact of the two kinds of correlation

Since, in practice, states and coalitions of states are the protagonists whose activities are primarily taken into account in the Marxist-Leninist (and particularly the Soviet) analyses of international relations, the above-mentioned propositions about the class content of the international rivalry seem to concern the *essence* of international relations, as Marxism-Leninism sees them, while the correlation of state powers may be interpreted as the basic *form* in which the essence manifests itself.

This brings us to the second way in which the domestic correlation of forces is projected into the international arena: through the foreign activities of states. The close interrelation between the domestic and foreign policies of a class-state is one of the basic premises in discussions concerning the connection between the correlations of intrasocietal and international forces. Domestic interests are regarded as primary: to the governing class, the pursuit of external interests is subordinate to and/or complementary to domestic aims and policies. Although the defence of sovereignty — which is usually officially presented as the basic aim of foreign policy — is said to be in the interests of the entire nation, it is at the same time, and perhaps primarily, motivated by the desire of the ruling class to defend their rule in their own independent state; thus it connects both the domestic and the external interests of the governing class. In the pursuit of other interests — economic and strategic assets and ideological influence — the primacy of the interests of the ruling élite comes clearly to the fore.

Having secured an advantageous correlation of intrasocietal forces, the ruling class in many cases makes an alliance with states of the same social character for the pursuit of common international interests. Thereby it contributes, or attempts to contribute, to the creation, or strengthening or maintenance of a favourable correlation of forces in the world and/or in a particular region. Such a correlation may provide conditions for taking action or counter-action in the domestic affairs of individual countries where the class struggle takes an acute form. Any change in the intrasocietal correlation of forces — the most radical

130

being a revolutionary change in the entirety of the socio-economic and political system — affects the correlation of international forces and, vice versa, any modification of the correlation on the world scale may decisively affect the course of international developments in a country which is undergoing a crisis.

Differences

The differences in the character of the two kinds of correlation — the intrasocietal and the international — are also a subject of analysis. A basic difference is that in the relationships between the basis and superstructure. The international system has no socio-economic basis that is common to all nations, nor any superstructure similar to that in domestic society. While the socio-economic relations between the classes in society directly reflect productive relations, and this in turn affects the superstructure, the relations between states and even international classes, social organisations and movements, can be seen as deriving from the relations of production in a very indirect way.

'International relations are *secondary* and *tertiary phenomena*, which, in general, are *derived and transmitted* — i.e., non-primary — conditions of production.'[14] These words of Marx concerned international relations merely as regards their connection with economic production but taken out of context they were used by some Soviet writers in a general way to describe international relations as a special and independent sphere of social relations which cannot be explained in terms of the basis-superstructure relationship. This situation makes the analysis of the class contradictions on the international arena and of the forces which represent them even more complex and difficult than the analysis of these features in the domestic setting. The economic basis is said to affect only 'in principle' critical international events such as crises and wars.

Domestic goals and proletarian internationalism

To Marxist-Leninist politicians and theoreticians, the conceptual problem of the interaction between the correlation of intrasocietal forces and that of international forces was connected with the practical problem of the interaction between the proletariat's pursuit of domestic and of international goals. This issue may be presented as a set of questions: How can the aim of bringing about a domestic revolution be combined with the aims of the international revolutionary movement? How can the defence of other national interests — of which the proletariat is said to be the only true defender — be combined with the international duties of the proletariat? Should one of these missions be subordinated to the other?

Proletarian internationalism

All these questions are answered in terms of proletarian internationalism which is said organically to combine the domestic and international missions of the proletariat. Class internationalism means the mutual solidarity and mutual assistance evidenced by the national groups in an international class in both their domestic struggle and their international activities. Internationalism is an ideology and policy, the respective attitudes and social feelings of the class in question which extend beyond the framework of domestic class boundaries.[15] True internationalism presumes both a community of all basic interests and the independence and equality of the national detachments of a 'world class'.

These two features are present only with regard to the working class. The bourgeoisie of various countries has some common but at the same time also many contradictory interests springing from their rivalry and their tendency to extract maximum profit from other countries. Therefore 'the bourgeoisie as a class is inherently nationalist. It is unable to base its relations on equality and cooperation between national groups'.[16]

Contrary to this, as Marxists assert, 'Proletarian internationalism is mutual solidarity and assistance, comradely cooperation which presumes the independence and equality of the individual parties and non-interference in each other's internal affairs'.[17]

To some Marxist writers the preference shown by the bourgeoisie for its domestic class interests means that this cannot be regarded as an international class. Only the proletariat has organised the relations between its various national groups in a way which enables it to act as a world class.[18] However, in spite of being nationalistic and egoistic and unable to pursue a true internationalist policy in crucial world questions, the bourgeoisie attempts in its actions to maintain a solid front against the world working class.

In the Marxist-Leninist view, proletarian internationalism nowadays takes *four basic forms*. As Andrei Gromyko says, the ideas of proletarian internationalism have been first realised in Soviet society, where the inter-nations and inter-nationalities relations have been freed from class and national antagonisms.

Second, he considers that proletarian internationalism has achieved its higher form in relations between the socialist states: it has become 'socialist internationalism',[19] which means cooperation and unity of action among all the socialist states in both the domestic and the international spheres.

Third, proletarian internationalism means the solidarity of the socialist states and the workers in capitalist countries in their struggle for a socialist revolution. And, finally, it means the solidarity of the socialist states with the struggle of the peoples of colonies and dependent countries for their social and national liberation.[20]

The last two forms of proletarian internationalism assume an extended form in the solidarity of all the *anti-imperialist* forces in their struggle for democracy, socialism and peace.

However, this does not mean that the former needs to be replaced by the latter. It is just proletarian internationalism which makes the struggle of broader popular masses realistic: it provides the struggle with an orientation, consistency and material power in the form of the socialist states.[21]

National and international interests

The proletariat's internationalist class character involves unity and interdependence in its pursuit of domestic and internationalist interests, say the Marxists. Thus Janos Kadar says that, 'In our opinion, the idea of proletarian internationalism harmoniously combines national and international interests, because the achievements of the individual parties strengthen our movement and the strengthening of the international Communist movement helps the individual parties.'[22] (Since the domestic class interests of the proletariat include national interests and since domestic society is often called in political and sociological literature national society or 'nation', the Marxists often refer to domestic interests as 'national interests'.)

The relationship of the national and international reflects the interaction of two objective processes: (1) the growth of the significance of national inputs to social progress and national specifics of class struggle: and (2) the growing internationalisation of all fields of social life and the growing role of the international factor in the resolution of the revolutionary tasks in individual countries.

This interaction can take various shapes in various periods and various countries. However, in spite of the differences, no revolutionary action can be successful in a purely national framework, isolated from the action of the international revolutionary forces. The forms of the interaction of the national and the international can be various, but the necessity for it has repeatedly been confirmed.[23]

Although international interests coincide with the domestic interests of the revolutionary movement and the policies of the various proletarian national detachments, and their parties should organically combine them, this is not necessarily true of all the short-term interests. It may happen that short-term domestic interests conflict with the long-term international ones.

One should distinguish here between the policies pursued by the working class in socialist and non-socialist countries. The lack of coincidence between some domestic and internationalist interests may concern only the non-socialist countries. To them internationalist interests may not coincide (indeed, they may not always even be compatible) with all the domestic interests of the working class, but only with its fundamental substantial and long-term interests. To socialist nations, domestic and internationalist interests are identical. Correctly understood, the interests of each socialist nation fully coincide with internationalist interests.

There are two corollaries of this relationship between the domestic and internationalist interests of the working class. The first is the relationship between the *general* regularities of the revolutionary movement, of revolution and of the build-up of socialism and their *national* features. The second is the relationship between the Communist parties' pursuit, on the one hand, of the domestic goals and, on the other, of international revolutionary goals. Both matters reflect the Marxist-Leninist assertion that the relationship between the domestic and the internationalist aspects is not an abstraction of merely academic interest: the answers to the main questions concerning the revolutionary movement depend on a correct understanding of this. These matters therefore merit attention.

Socialist revolution: general regularities and specific national features

Can we detect any general regularities in the revolutionary movement and particularly in the socialist revolution and the build-up of socialism? And, if the answer is in the affirmative, do these regularities exist under any national conditions? Some Marxist-Leninist writers answer the first question in the negative. Since every revolution, they say, has unique national features and exhibits so many specific features it seems impossible to establish general laws concerning revolutionary processes and the development of socialist societies. Each crucial step towards socialism cuts across what were up till then considered to be general uniformities.[24]

The prevailing and officially established view, however, is that there do exist objective laws of revolutionary movement, socialist revolution and socialist construction. From this follows the need to work out policies for their realisation in particular national conditions — that is, to adapt the general experiences, conclusions and guidelines to specific domestic conditions. At the international conference on theoretical matters, entitled 'The Dialectics of the National and International in the Working Class Movement', held in Hungary in May 1981, many delegates considered that the inevitably specific features of every revolution and the unique features of the socialist build-up in individual countries could not be an argument for denying the general uniformities that objectively govern these processes.

The dialectical link between the objective laws of social development and the concrete forms in which they are manifested, it was said, make equally intolerable both the voluntary neglect of international universal experience and the dogmatic adoption of it as a ready-made solution for all cases. And, as one writer put it, every socialist revolution and every socialist society reveals the common substance of all socialist revolutions and socialist societies and the general uniformities inherent in this type of social revolution and social system.[25] Indeed, these are merely general directives. The question of *how* to adapt them to the conditions of individual countries has been left to the Communist parties there.

Which experiences of the revolutionary movement in various countries can be regarded as universal and can be applied by each national detachment of the working class?[26]

First, there is the very necessity to wage a revolution, without which no basic change in the social, political and economic position of the working masses is possible. Any social-democratic, reformistic and evolutionary theories should be rejected.

Second, the revolution must consist of the establishment of working people's power followed by the transfer of property by basic means of production to society as a whole.

Third, the revolution can be performed either by armed violence or by peaceful means. Several revolutions were accomplished in the latter way, owing to a complex of favourable circumstances: the victory of the Soviet Union over the fascist powers, the existence of a powerful socialist state close to the countries where the revolutions took place, and the intensification of the general crisis of capitalism.

Fourth, the revolution must be directed by a revolutionary party; the unity of the ranks of the working class greatly contributes to the success.

Fifth, the revolutionary government must immediately begin the process of accomplishing socialist transformations or direct preparations for such transformations: nationalisation of several industries, introduction of elements of planning, organisation of control over remaining capitalist firms, accomplishment of several reforms such as the reform of the courts, taxation policy, election law, and so on.

Sixth, special attention should be paid to economic planning, with the aim of satisfying the growing material and spiritual requirements of the people, and laying the material foundation for socialist principles in all areas of society.

Finally, the common experience of all revolutions is the necessity for gradual implanting the socialist consciousness, combatting all varieties of racist, fascist, chauvinist and other inhuman ideologies.

National and international revolutionary goals

Some researchers have questioned whether the relationship between domestic and internationalist goals and policies may be reduced to a simple subordination of the former to the latter.

Four positions may here be discerned. The prevailing and officially adopted position, the orthodox one, was expressed by Konstantin Zarodov, then Chief Editor of the *World Marxist Review,* who criticised the attempts to reduce the multi-faceted dynamics of the changes in the correlation of the national and international to the statement that, whereas the elements of international class organisation once used to prevail in the revolutionary movement, a concern for the national interests and rights of the peoples and the independence of the Communist parties was now coming uppermost. Zarodov asserted that the Communist parties always connected the national interests of their peoples with the international interests of their class and he concluded: 'It is far more important to understand how this independence (of Communist parties-JL) can help to achieve the common internationalist aims of the revolutionary forces.'[27] Zarodov also stated that, without the support of the internationalists, 'the peoples of the socialist community countries would face more difficulties in their struggle and work, while the working class of the industrialised capitalist countries and the peoples of the erstwhile colonies and semi-colonies would be unable successfully to build on the gains secured in fierce battles'. Indeed, he concluded, they might even lose those gains.[28]

Another scholar states that internationalism plays the key role in the Party's life and activity.[29] In yet another wording, the class approach is to regard the international as the key, the primary element in the correlation of the domestic and international. The national (i.e. domestic) element relates to the international as a part to the whole, as the particular to the general.[30] If short-term interests of the domestic struggle conflict with long-term international ones, priority must be given to the latter. 'Marxism-Leninism teaches the necessity of subordinating the national interest to the common interest.'[31]

The second approach, which is the opposite of the previous one, emphasises the exceptional significance of developing the national-patriotic component of the ideological and political struggles of the Communist parties in combatting bourgeois anti-Communist propaganda: the latter seeks to present the Communists as an anti-national force, bending their people's interests to some alien external will.[32]

Other Marxists consider that one should not insist on ranking one of these approaches above the other, nor try to find out which of the two sides of the dialectical unity of the domestic (national) and international should be regarded as primary and which as subordinate and secondary. They are *inseparable and equally important.* One must recognise the equal significance of the two truths: that the revolutionary movement can develop only on national soil, and that it cannot develop successfully otherwise than in a close international interaction with similar or kindred movements in other countries.[33]

Finally, the most pragmatic view seems to be that the question of the priority of one or the other element in relations between the domestic (national) and the international should be decided in accordance with the concrete historical situation.[34]

The various positions seem to have one assumption in common. This means that *nationalism* which is as a rule called 'bourgeois nationalism' and which is regarded as a set of ideas quite different from patriotism — the latter being interpreted as the pursuit of real national interests accompanied by patriotic feelings — is incompatible with internationalism. Nationalism is said to be a hindrance both to domestic socialist development and the common international revolutionary struggle. It is considered insufficient to assert this incompatibility in programmes or studies: nationalism must be fiercely *combatted.* A consistent struggle against nationalism is the main characteristic of an international approach to interstate relations in the socialist camp and in international relations in general.[35]

The above-mentioned considerations may seem abstract but they are not. They reflect a dilemma which several Communist parties are facing. In recent decades the problem of the role of national interests of the whole society in the entire spectrum of the class revolutionary interests of the proletariat has come to the fore in various countries. To gain allies and to strengthen the anti-monopoly side of the correlation of intrasocietal forces the working class must take into account the national feelings of the population and their perception of national interests which in most countries do *not* coincide with revolutionary feelings and perceptions. Thus, with regard to 'national' goals and priorities, the Communist parties, it has been maintained, should not only use this term in the sense of 'domestic revolutionary', but should also include in it the national-patriotic perceptions of the majority of the population.

Notes

1   Martin, 1975, 1977.
2   *Protsess* ..., 1981, p. 56. 'The main watershed in present-day international relations continues to run along the class front. Whatever the changes in the policy of various imperialist powers, this line ultimately provides the only true key to the nature of international relations at the present stage. The balance of forces between the two systems, which has changed on a global scale, is directly expressed in the sphere of international politics. *It has become a material factor of immense weight, the solid foundation which has attached global importance to the socialist countries' foreign policy not only from the standpoint of the example it sets, but also in terms of the depth and scope of its influence on the whole present-day system of international relations. There is now a real possibility not only for putting on the agenda the crucial international problems of our day, the problem of war and peace above all, but also for mapping out practical measures for their solution.'* (Kapchenko, 1984, pp. 104—5).
3   *Mezhdunarodnye konflikty sovremennosti*, 1983, Ch. II.5.
4   Ibid., p. 145.
5   Ibid., pp. 146—7.
6   Ibid., p. 151.
7   Ibid., pp. 152—3.
8   Ibid., pp. 150—1.
9   Martin, 1977, p. 25.
10 V.S. Semenov, 'Sotsialnye klassy i mezhdunarodnye otnosheniya', in *Sotsiologicheskie problemy mezhdunarodnykh otnoshenii*, 1970, pp. 69—71.
11 Cf. Shakhnazarov, 1980.
12 '... the formation of world order is a process which develops as a result of the changing correlation of forces between the main factors participating in the international arena'. These factors are: states and their alliances, large-scale international movements (communist, national-, liberation, social-democratic, non-aligned, etc.), international organizations, the mass media, or, to be more exact, the public opinion which is formed by the media. 'In the final analysis, social class and group interests, under the guise of national or even international interests, are the basis of this correlation of forces (i.e., in the world — JL). Thus an analysis of the present and forecasting the future world order must certainly include an assessment of the correlation of class forces in the world' (Shakhnazarov, 1984, p. 8). He also asserted: '... it is not the interaction of states which lies at the basis of the changing correlation of forces, but the struggle between the two social

systems. This is not limited to the interstate level but involves the most varied social and political forces, penetrates borders and intersects social strata' (ibid., p. 54).

13   *Fundamentals of Political Science,* 1979, p. 419.
14   Karl Marx, *A Contribution to the Critique of Political Economy,* Progress Publishers, Moscow 1977, p. 215.
15   *The Theory and Practice of Proletarian Internationalism,* 1976, p. 67.
16   Ibid., p. 14.
17   Janos Kadar, addressing the Berlin Conference of European Communist and Workers' Parties 1976, quoted in 'The International and National in the Working Class Movement', *W.M.R.,* 1981:8, p.49.
18   *The Theory and Practice of Proletarian Internationalism,* 1976, p. 15. Cf. Krasin, 1985, Essay Nine: 'The International and the National in the Revolutionary Process'.
19   A. Gromyko, 'V.I. Lenin i vneshnyaya politika Sovetskogo Gosudarstva', 1983, pp. 15 ff.
20   Socialist internationalism is the lawful level of development of the international solidarity of working class in the historical conditions under which it has become the ruling class, and its Marxist-Leninist parties have become the ruling parties (Gromyko, ibid., p. 16).
21   Gromyko exemplifies this form of internationalism by the agreements on friendship and cooperation between the Soviet Union and India, Syria, Angola, Ethiopia, Mozambique, Afghanistan (sic!) and other countries (ibid., p. 24).
22   Zarodov, *Leninism and Today's Problems of the Transition to Socialism,* 1983, pp. 96–7.
23   Kadar, ibid. (Note 17).
24   Cf. *W.M.R.,* 1981:10, p. 68.
25   Zarodov, in *W.M.R.,* 1981:10, p. 71.
26   One of the main themes in Zarodov, 1983.
27   Cf. Zarodov, 1983, Ch. IV.4: 'Features of the Revolution'; Shakhnazarov, 1982, Ch. 7: 'Unity or Diversity?'
28   Ibid., p. 80.
29   Janos Wat, in *W.M.R.,* 1981:10, p. 64.
30   Hans J. Kleven, in *W.M.R.,* 1981:10, p. 67.
31   *The Theory and Practice of Proletarian Internationalism,* 1976, p. 70.
32   This view was expressed by many speakers at the above-mentioned international theoretical conference on the dialectics of the national and international in the working-class movement (*W.M.R.,* 1981:10, p. 64).
33   Khristo Maleyev, ibid., p. 65.

34 K. Kipkovics, ibid., p. 65. 'In each concrete instance', writes Shakhnazarov, 'the correct correlation must be found between the different manifestations (national and international — JL) of one and the same class interest. Of course, at times there is a certain objective conflict between present and future interests and this makes for a difficult choice.' There is no general formula, he continues, which would allow such problems to be resolved (1984, p. 102).

35 *Razryadka mezhdunarodnoi napryazhennosti i ideologicheskaya bor'ba*, 1981, pp. 32—3.

6 Correlation of world forces

Development of the concept

Classical concept

In classical Marxism, two basic forces in the world — the international proletariat and the international bourgeoisie — were in conflict concerning the future of mankind. The simultaneous revolution in all countries — or at least in all the developed countries — was expected to entail the disappearance of nation-states as separate political units. The victorious proletariat was assigned the mission of doing away with national boundaries.[1] With this aim, the proletariat of all countries which had a common foe would fight that foe as a united international force.

This scenario represented an embryo of the idea of the two mutually hostile camps on the world scene. It differs from the current concept of the rivalry of two antagonistic political camps, the core of which constitutes national or multi-national states. Nevertheless, the idea of the world proletariat and the world bourgeoisie as two basic adversaries has not disappeared; it is included in the modern concept either as an underlying idea or as a variant of the juxtaposition of the two camps, or even as a broader concept in which the rivalry of the two camps represents only one front of the world-wide struggle of the two international classes.

Lenin and Stalin: states as protagonists in the international revolutionary struggle

Although Lenin did not abandon the idea of the final disappearance of nation-states, after the victorious October Revolution he posited that, for the defence of the power that had been seized and for the development of socialism and ultimately of communism, the establishment of a strong state was indispensable. He therefore introduced the concept of the state of proletarian dictatorship of which the primary function would be to crush the resistance of the overthrown classes and to defend the gains of the revolution against enemies within and outside the state. Lenin assumed that the revolution would not triumph simultaneously in all countries, and not even in all of the developed countries. Its first victory would snap the weakest link in the 'imperialist chain'. The revolutionary state would have to defend itself against more powerful states. Lenin also considered the possibility of the emergence of a very different type of state from another front of the anti-imperialist struggle — i.e., from a victorious national-liberation movement.

Lenin's concept implied the division of the world after the victory of the revolution into countries belonging to two different systems. This would be an asymmetric structure, since a single proletarian dictatorship would be set against all other states. He regarded this condition as transitory, however, expecting the revolution to spread, sooner or later, throughout the world.

Since the colonies, as the economic hinterland of the industrial nations, also formed part of the capitalist system, the national liberation struggle of the colonial and dependent peoples against international imperialism was part of the world-wide anti-capitalist struggle. The ideas about the two antagonistic systems and about the national liberation forces as allies of socialism and part of the anti-imperialist forces were included in the contemporary Soviet paradigm of the world system and in the concept of the correlation of international forces.

Two new and unique paradigms were emerging: (1) the composition of the world and the identification of its basic component parts and their relationships on the basis of individual states and groups of states belonging to different socio-economic formations — i.e., the capitalist and the socialist *systems (blocs) of states*: and (2) the composition of the world on the basis of world-wide *sociopolitical camps:* these might include states, peoples which had not yet gained formal independence, classes within states and international movements.

Stalin developed the idea of building socialism first in one particular state and he placed in the focus of all his arguments the contradictions between the Soviet Union and capitalist states. He developed — and, indeed changed — the concept of the state as the main component of a superstructure built on a socio-economic foundation, and reflecting it, into the concept of the state as an active force which was assigned the mission of gradually transforming the basis.

In the international perspective, certain elements in Stalin's approach paved the way for the modern concept of the two world-wide rival camps and the correlation of world forces as the motor of international development. To Stalin, the world had definitely split into two camps — the imperialist camp and the socialist camp, the latter being headed by, and indeed embodied in — the Soviet Union. He regarded the contradiction between the Soviet Union and the capitalist countries (which before the Second World War were called 'the capitalist encirclement') as the basic contradiction of the epoch. He maintained that the strengthening of the Soviet Union was the *precondition* of the future triumph of socialism throughout the world. He viewed internal contradications in the capitalist countries as the main asset operating in favour of the Soviet Union. Proletarian internationalism became centred on the Soviet Union: internationalism was interpreted as the support offered to the Soviet Union by the Communist parties throughout the world and vice versa. Stalin made a threefold division of the countries of the world into the exploiting countries, the exploited countries and the Soviet Union. In his view, some members of the first two groups could be treated as allies of the Soviet Union. However, although he included both the struggle of the working class in the developed countries and the national liberation struggle of the peoples of the colonies and dependent countries in the set of the internal contradictions of the capitalist camp operating in favour of the Soviet Union, he played down their role in the calculus of the forces of capitalism arrayed against socialism.

Despite some differences, the modern concept of the correlation of world forces contains important elements of Stalin's concept of the world — principally his division of the international system into two opposing camps. Indeed, in his last years Stalin sketched the main features of the modern concept. He also contributed to the idea that this correlation is the main driving force in world developments and that in the everyday rivalry of the two camps, it determines the substance of the domestic and foreign policies of the countries in both camps.

When Stalin advanced the initial ideas of the concept the Soviet Union was still the only representative of the socialist part of the world. After the Second World War, the concept of two opposing camps became the basic premise of Soviet foreign policy.

Krushchev modified this concept:

(1)   He saw the world as being divided into three groups of states: the developed capitalist, the underdeveloped and the socialist states. In another perspective he also made a division of the world into two zones: the zone of peace and the zone of war. By including the under-developed countries in the zone of peace Khrushchev was trying conceptually to separate these countries from the developed capitalist ones.

(2)   Peaceful forms of the rivalry between the two opposing world camps were presented as the basic ones; the theory of the inevitability of war was revised in several essential respects.

(3)   All countries were included in the set of active protagonists in the field of international relations.

Modern concept

Basic assumptions

In the 1970s and 1980s the concept of the correlation of world forces took its final form. One set of assumptions concerns the altered shape of the contemporary international system, the other the basic forces and basic fronts of the world-wide struggle.

The changes in the shape of the international system may be summarised as follows:[2]

(1)   The world has become *heterogeneous*: it consists of states having different socio-economic systems.

(2)   Instead of the group of homogeneous *Great Powers* which exerted the decisive impact on the course of most world events, partly through the mechanism of a balance of power, there are now two *systems* opposed to each other in their socio-economic and political domestic structures, doctrines and policies. The relations between the two systems constitute a quite new type of interstate relations. Not only the main events in the international system but the whole course of its development is now affected by the interaction of the two opposing camps.

(3)   The relations within the socialist system of states represent a revolutionary new type of friendly relations, a mode for the future world system.

(4)   The *number of states* which influence the course of world events has grown enormously.

(5)   The *means* of influencing the course of international affairs have become more *diversified.* Instead of being complementary to military force they often operate as independent factors (for instance, economic

weapons, ideological instruments and so on).

(6)   In consequence, new *groups* of states have begun to operate as collective protagonists: the OPEC countries, the Islamic countries, the non-aligned countries, etc.

(7)   The permanent politico-military *alliances* are also a new feature of international relations.

(8)   Apart from the multitude of new states, *other new protagonists* have entered the political scene — for instance, certain great international movements (see below).

(9)   Public opinion concerning certain issues (e.g., Vietnam and Chile) is becoming the *world opinion* which plays in these issues a significant and unprecedented role.

(10) The *global character of several problems* currently awaiting solution (peace, the protection of the environment) requires global solutions.

New characteristics

In the Marxist-Leninist view, the correlation of international forces in our times is said to differ from the balance of power in the so-called period of the domination of imperialism with regard to the following features.[3] :

(1)   The balance of power reflecting a *rivalry* between *several* great imperialist powers has been replaced by the *bipolar* correlation of forces expressing the *antagonism* of two international class forces: those of world socialism and imperialism.

(2)   The objective of a re-division of spheres of exploitation has been replaced by the struggle for the 'to be or not to be' of capitalism.

(3)   The domination of imperialism has been replaced by the growing impact of socialism on the basic development tendencies in the system.

(4)   The qualitative indices of the correlation of international forces have acquired a dominating position in relation to quantitative indices. While previously the more or less measurable power of a state determined its ability to impose its will on other states and its place in the world hierarchy, and thereby determined the relative strengths of the opposing forces, the situation has now radically changed:

> The impact will be determined much more by the class character of the mutually opposing forces and thereby by the character of the problems which the confrontation concerns.[4]

(5)   The relative impact of particular components of the relation of international forces has changed: the impact of the military component has diminished, while the importance of the economic, sociopolitical

and moral-ideological components has increased.[5]

(6) The protagonists have changed. Instead of states with their statically-interpreted military power, the sides in the correlation now include states, groups of states, international movements, classes, popular masses and parties. Their strengths should be understood as real forces which can actually be used as well as their developmental tendencies.[6]

All these differences will be discussed below in connection with the concept of the correlation of world forces.

The new shape of the international system gives rise to several analytical and empirical questions. Four of these, connected with the Soviet concept of the correlation of world forces, will be discussed: the protagonists in the correlation, their forces, the dynamics of the correlation and its role in world developments.

Two main adversaries

The correlation of the two main opposing sociopolitical forces in the contemporary world has been described by individual Marxist-Leninist, basically Soviet, writers in four alternative (but, in a sense, complementary and hierarchically combined) forms[7]:

(1) As the correlation between the two antagonistic systems: capitalist (or 'imperialist') and socialist. The socialist system is described as follows: The socialist countries have the same type of economic basis: social ownership of the means of production; the same type of political system: the rule of the people who are headed by the working class; a common ideology — Marxism-Leninism; common interests in the defence of their revolutionary gains and national independence from encroachments by the imperialist camp; and a great common goal — Communism.[8]

(2) In an even broader interpretation, as the correlation between 'the forces of peace' and 'the forces of war' (in a variant, between the forces of 'socialism and peace' and the forces of 'imperialism and war').[9]

(3) As the correlation of forces between the two superpowers (mostly in military analyses).

(4) In the principal region of confrontation — i.e., Europe — as the correlation between the Warsaw Treaty Organisation and the NATO states.

(Occasionally, instead of a two-party correlation, the 'alignment' or 'deployment' of world forces was presented as a constellation of groups of states — for instance, including the imperialist powers, the smaller capitalist developed countries, the developing countries of the Third World and the socialist countries. This kind of relations characterises the *configuration* of the actors in the international scene and their forces rather than the *comparison* of their strengths.)

The emphasis on the above-mentioned alternatives in the presentation of the correlation of world forces has been changing. In the descriptions and analyses dating from the 1940s and 1950s, the two antagonistic systems were usually the counterparts of the correlation, but since military power was all the time in focus the comparison was, in fact, reduced to the correlation of power of the two leading states — i.e., the superpowers, which possessed the crucial military instruments, strategic nuclear weapons. In the 1960s, as the number and influence of the newly independent countries increased, the two camps were still considered to represent the opposite sides of the correlation (although the countries of the Third World were regarded as potential allies of the socialist camp).

In the 1970s, the concept of the bipolar structure was *a casu ad casum* complemented by comments about new centres of power in the capitalist world. The correlation of world forces was often presented under a new name: as that between the forces of peace and of war.[10] The socialist and the imperialist countries were the respective centres of these forces. Most of the non-aligned countries, the progressive international political movements (the working class movement, the national liberation movement and the peace movement) were regarded as the natural allies of the socialist camp. The other side of the equation included political and non-political institutions and movements of a reactionary character: churches, the 'fascist international', the 'revisionist international', and so on.[11]

(The Marxist-Leninist evaluation of the Social-Democratic movement was changing and it varied in relation to the different international issues and conflicts. In general, however, it was negative:[12] The Social-Democratic ideology is essentially designed to adapt the working-class movement to the interests of the bourgeois system, states a textbook on politics; although in their programmes the Social-Democratic parties claim to be working to overthrow capitalism, their leaders are generally opposed to any revolutionary transformation of society. They maintain that capitalism can be either 'improved' or 'corrected' by the introduction of partial changes or reforms which intially do not affect its substance.[13]

Marxist-Leninists also believe that if, on some issues, the Social-Democratic movement may be regarded as an ally, this is due to the fact that it includes proletarians who by no means wish to perpetuate the capitalist order but are fighting for the rights of the working class.)

In another approach, the correlation to be assessed is said to be that of two 'world-wide classes': the world working class and the world bourgeoisie. The national groups of these international classes are component parts of the global forces. International political movements are here included in the world classes; for instance, the international

Communist movement is a part of the world working class.[14]

In one version of this approach, the world working class is said to consist of (1) socialist states, (2) the working class in capitalist countries, (3) the working masses in the Third World countries.[15] In yet another version, the working class in the non-socialist countries is divided into that in the advanced industrial countries of North America, Western Europe, Japan and Australia, and in other countries which are economically underdeveloped and struggling to consolidate their national independence.

Some writers use the terms 'world socialism' and 'world capitalism'. The following forces are included in the concept of 'world socialism': (a) the socialist countries, (b) the socialist-oriented countries, (c) the Communist movement, (d) all revolutionary forces which are united and interact with other social groups and political movements of an anti-imperialist character.

The concept of 'world capitalism' includes: (a) the group of developed capitalist (also called imperialist) states, (b) countries with poorly developed economies which may be regarded as capitalist-oriented, (c) various interacting conservative and reactionary political movements.

In a narrower sense, the term 'socialist world system' means the group of 15 socialist states, and 'capitalist world system' means the aggregate of states in which capitalism is the reigning system.[16]

In general, the different pairs of adversaries in the different kinds of the correlation of international forces discussed reflect different fronts and levels of the international struggle, or a combination of them; thus one can analyse the correlation of the two opposite social systems, the correlation between imperialism on the one side, and the international working movement and the national liberation movement on the other, or between the forces of war and peace.[17]

The classification of international forces may also be based directly on the Marxist-Leninist view of the contemporary epoch as a transitory one which includes three kinds of states: the two coexisting rival camps representing different socio-economic formations and the countries of the Third World which are in a state of constant flux and are undergoing a transition towards either capitalism or socialism. These countries do not represent a third camp or a new centre of power but oscillate between the two camps.

Hierarchy instead of alternatives

The various types of correlation, which result from an analysis of it from a number of angles, can be summarised in a set with a decreasing scope:[18] (1) the correlation between the opponents of war and those forces who favour a military way of resolving international contradictions; (2) the correlation between all the anti-imperialist forces and imperialism; (3) that between world socialism and world capitalism (or the world working class and the world bourgeoisie); (4) that between the two systems: the forces of the socialist community and the major imperialist states (or between the two alliances); and finally (5) between the two superpowers (the latter term not used by Soviet writers). Not all who fight against war take an anti-imperialist stand; there are realistically-minded imperialist circles also. Likewise not all who struggle against imperialism are adherents of socialism. For instance, in the Soviet view, the Social-Democratic movement has in the main taken a positive stand in the matter of international *détente* and many of its prominent leaders backed the transition from the Cold War to peaceful coexistence; however, the movement as a whole is against communism and calls for an unclear 'third way' — an alternative to both capitalism and socialism — which in practice means the defence of capitalism.[19]

The different kinds of correlations of world forces may be seen as the *sui generis* hierarchy. Within the correlation of the forces of war and peace, the correlation of world capitalism and world socialism plays the main role; within the latter relation the correlation between the two systems is the determining;[20] and the correlation of the forces of the superpowers is the core of the intersystemic correlation.[21]

In Soviet publications concerning the correlation of international forces three assumptions have been reflected — namely, those about (1) the global role of the Soviet Union as a superpower, (2) the Soviet role in Europe as the most potent in this region and (3) its dominance in the socialist camp.

One uniquely important power-relation has, in recent decades, received much attention: that between the Soviet Union and socialist China. This has not been conceptualised, since the 'case' of China is presented as 'non-typical'. China under its present leadership is neither a socialist nor a capitalist state. It is therefore outside both the normal dichotomy of 'socialism-capitalism' and the relationship within the socialist camp. However, this new kind (or rather, instance) of relation of power now plays a significant role in any world equation of military power and, naturally, also in current Soviet doctrine and policy. It ceased to be merely an atypical case in the intra-socialist alignment of power and gradually developed into a component of the alignment of forces on the world scale: in Soviet statements and analyses China is nowadays presented as an informal ally of the 'imperialist camp'.

Although the correlation of world forces is basically a concept in international relations (and according to Marxist-Leninist theory precisely *because* of this) it combines international political characteristics with social-class features:

(1)   The correlation is that between two opposite systems in the *class* respect:

(2)   It includes and is affected by domestic class forces — namely, the correlation of intrasocietal forces in the particular countries. For instance, the class struggle in developing countries, depending on its outcome, affects positively or negatively the anti-imperialist side of the world equation;

(3)   The correlation is affected by the international class movements acting directly as classes — for instance, the international cooperation of Communist parties and conservative parties and the actions of trade unions and international monopolies (or associations of monopolies);[22]

(4)   The classes also act through the state apparatus in the member states of the two opposing coalitions.

The interpretation of the bipolar structure of the world as being based on class distinctions and therefore also ideological distinctions possesses, in the view of the Soviet Union, the following important political and propagandist advantages:

(1)   The socialist side of the correlation of world forces, although it includes socialist states as coherent entities, may also be presented as 'cutting across' the capitalist world, in the sense that anti-capitalist forces are at work *within* the bourgeois states. Moreover, the capitalist powers are also engaged in internecine conflicts. Therefore the power of the bourgeois side of the world equation of forces cannot be regarded as the cumulative power of all its components.

Although the countries of the Third World constitute a complicating factor, since they 'wander' between the two camps, and their inclusion in one or the other camp depends on the concrete domestic and international situations, the Soviet policy-makers are inclined to regard almost the entire Third World as an ally of socialism (see the next section).

(2)   While the content of the correlation of forces in individual countries is determined by the characteristics of the governing socio-economic and political system and the stage of society's development and level of production, the content of the correlation of international forces may be presented as primarily determined by the character of the epoch. The main contradiction of the epoch involves the struggle of the main antagonistic classes of the given socio-economic formation (structure), and consequently it determines the identity of the main

antagonistic forces of the international system. One of these is the principal defender of the status quo, the other the principal carrier and champion of social progress.[23]

(3) The presentation of the correlation of world forces as that between social forces rather than states makes it easier to justify the Soviet programme of peaceful coexistence of states, which is said to be based on the equality of the two greatest powers and the sovereignty of all states. The Soviet Union's struggle to make further political and strategic gains, even by more or less directly intervening in the internal affairs of other states, has been presented as a manifestation not of the superpowers' rivalry but of the international class struggle and the support given to the class forces of progress.

(4) The 'bipolar' concept has also the advantage, in the Soviet view, that the political and philosophical propositions connected with it reinforce each other. All the propositions of philosophical materialism and the laws of dialectics and historical materialism are said to apply fully in this concept and to provide guidelines for interpreting the impact of the correlation of world forces on international development. Thereby they confirm the value of Marxism-Leninism as the *true* philosophy of society.

(4.1) The bipolar world structure based on a class criterion is a *unity of objective and subjective values.* The military and the politico-moral potential, the level of the economic and political developments and the shares of the industrial and agricultural production on both sides in world production (both in absolute figures and rates of growth) may be regarded as objective values. National liberation movements, the international workers' and Communist movements as well as reactionary international organisations, with their impact on world processes, are also objective items in the correlation. The competing ideologies and the political strategies and actions may be considered the subjective components.[24]

(4.2) The rivalry of the two systems (and in a sense also their cooperation) is said to be subject to the operation of the *law of the unity and the struggle of opposites.* Gradual quantitative changes in the correlation to the advantage of world socialism lead to radical qualitative changes and to the superiority of socialism in certain important respects which, in turn, leads to the restructuring of international relations. For instance, the domination of the great Western powers has finally disappeared. The constant shrinking of the capitalist system leading to its complete disappearance means the 'negation' of capitalism by socialism. Such a mechanism of development manifests the operation of the laws of *the transition of quantitative changes into qualitative ones* and of *the negation of negation.*

(4.3) The use of the concept of the correlation of world forces as a sociological (or sociopolitical) category (or at least a basic concept in international relations) which expresses the operation of objective laws also aims at presenting the development of the international balance of power as being dictated by these laws. Since these operate with the force of necessity, the constant change of the balance in favour of socialism is stated to be inevitable and irreversible. At the same time the category-status of the concept of the correlation of forces — i.e., as a *basic feature* or the contemporary international system and of non-socialist society — makes it easier to justify the expansionist policy of socialist states and the allegations of class struggle in the capitalist countries. In other words, Marxist-Leninist theory maintains that the correlation of forces between the bourgeoisie and the working class in particular countries will continue to develop in a law-like manner (i.e., according to objective laws of class struggle) to the advantage of the workers until it results in a social revolution. The latter will mean the victory of the 'new' over the 'old' and a reversal of the previous domination of the bourgeoisie. The same reasoning may be applied to international relations. Thus the final switchover to the advantage of socialism is seen as inevitable and irreversible in each country and in the international system as a whole.

(4.4)   Moreover, by presenting the correlation of forces as a sociological (or sociopolitical) category, the claim of the Soviet Union to lead the socialist camp and the entire world camp of revolutionary forces is also becoming law-like. The centrifugal tendencies in the socialist camp can be condemned as weakening the anti-imperialist side of the world equation of forces. Since the correlation of forces between the United States and the Soviet Union is extended from that between two states into that between two historical forces and historical tendencies, and since it is presented as the main manifestation of the class struggle, which follows the laws of history, the Soviet Union has the duty to fight for equality with, and then superiority over, the United States, the latter being the leading force in the declining system.[25] This confirms the superpower status of the Soviet Union.

(4.5)   In the framework of the international class struggle, which is governed by sociological laws, the correlation of world forces determines in a law-like manner *two* important developments: one of these is the advance of *socialism* and of the process which accompanies it — the liberation of peoples from colonial oppression; the other is the promotion of *peaceful* interstate relations. These two processes are said to be closely interrelated. The correlation of forces, which is becoming increasingly advantageous to socialism makes possible peaceful coexistence, which, in turn, facilitates the further advance of socialism.

Here, as in other fields of human activity, the expression 'determines' should not be taken as automatically prejudging the course of events. In Marxist-Leninist theory the historical processes and missions dictated by the laws of dialectical materialism can be accomplished only through human action — in this case, through a conscious struggle of peoples in conjunction with the active policy of the Soviet Union and its allies.[26]

The latter must aim at achieving further changes in the correlation of world forces and at peaceful coexistence. These two basic missions and policies necessitate two basic kinds of action differently related to armed violence. The advance of socialism requires the active support of the socialist states — principally of the Soviet Union — and of all movements towards socialism *in the individual countries* even if they lead to armed violence. The support may take political, ideological, economical and, if necessary, military forms. Thus the strengthening of peace means the development of peaceful relations solely *between states.*

(4.6)   Finally, according to Marxist-Leninist analysts, the correlation of forces has also acquired an ethical value: its development in favour of socialism is *just* since it accords with the laws of social development and progress. As a corollary, the attempts ascribed to the United States to regain a military and overall superiority in conflict with the operation of historical societal laws are considered by Soviet politicians and writers to be reactionary and unjust.

'Internal' balance of forces

On each side of the intersystemic equation there is also an 'internal' balance (alignment) of forces. Soviet analysts deal basically with that in the 'imperialist camp'. The changing balance of forces between the United States and its West European allies (the 'transatlantic balance') is said to develop in a way which is unfavourable to the United States and which negatively affects cohesion within the Western Alliance.[27] After the total American supremacy in the economic and military fields in the post-war decade, Western Europe grew stronger and achieved economic independence and it now remains dependent only on the American nuclear guarantee. Economic differences have come to the fore, weakening the cohesion of the Alliance. The military requirements of the two pillars of the Alliance are likewise no longer identical.

The political assessments and policies also have been following gradually diverging paths. The Europeans plan to continue and even strengthen the *détente* with the socialist states, which they feel gives them a kind of immediate security and certain advantages in pursuing their economic and all other everyday interests. Unlike the Americans, they play down the dangers of the developments in the Third World, and they have begun to doubt that military power, such as that of the USA, greatly affects the outcome of all conflicts in the world. These and other differences in interests, assessments and policies are said to be weakening the Western side of the world equation.

Soviet writers tone down tendencies in the socialist camp which in fact somewhat resemble those said to be typical of the West and which arise partly from the great discrepancy in military and economic power between the Soviet Union and its allies: (1) the tendency of the USSR's allies to reduce their dependence on the dominating ally; (2) their assessment of the dangers from the West which is much less dramatic than that made by the leaders of the Soviet Union.

Contrary to the description of the decreasing cohesion in the 'imperialist bloc', the socialist bloc is said to be increasingly cohesive. Since it is based on close political, economic, techno-scientific and military cooperation, its combined power far exceeds the sum of the component state powers. While the combined efforts of the imperialist bloc is limited to certain fields of foreign and military policies and the production of war material — and in other areas such efforts may even be weakened by sharp competition — the socialist bloc combines all aspects of national powers.

Developing countries: 'world socialism' replaces the national working class

In the bipolar scheme which underlies the entire Marxist-Leninist philosophy of development within the national society and the contemporary theory of international relations, developing countries (or the 'underdeveloped countries' or 'countries with underdeveloped economies', as they are also called by some Soviet writers,)[28] constitute a different and separate analytical problem, as also a different practical problem for the policy-makers.

To preserve the thesis that, despite its heterogeneity, the Third World as a whole may be seen as associated with the socialist camp, this association is occasionally called 'anti-imperialist forces' or 'forces of peace'; or it is said to include all forces which constitute the 'resources of socialism'. In Shakhnazarov's above-mentioned scheme, as we have seen, 'world socialism' includes, *inter alia*, 'socialist-oriented countries'[29] and 'other political forces working for the establishment of the socialist system'. In other studies the expression 'countries following the non-capitalist path of development' has been used.[30] Apart from the states with markedly rightist or dictatorial governments, all developing countries may be included under such a broad and ambiguous heading.

Another terminological measure is to write about the 'forces of social renovation'. These include two kinds of movements: the Communist movement, which Marxism-Leninism presents as the most influential political force of our time with the mission of carrying out a socialist revolution in developed capitalist countries, and the national liberation movement, which has the task of promoting national democratic revolutions in underdeveloped countries.[31] 'The forces of social renovation' are regarded as belonging to the anti-imperialist side of the correlation of world forces.

The most difficult theoretical problem concerns the thesis that even the capitalist-oriented developing countries constitute 'resources of world socialism', since sooner or later they will undergo socialist transformations. These countries form a heterogeneous group. Some of them lack an all-embracing and fully developed social system of any specific type; the variety of modes of production characterised by historically different coexisting forms of ownership and social production entails the coexistence of different classes and social groups. After the national liberation, the political superstructure may include the feudal and capitalist elements on one side and the revolutionary-democratic and socialist elements on the other.

Here, however, two groups of countries may be distinguished. One of them includes economically relatively developed countries with a relatively numerous working class. They are mainly in Latin America. These countries will sooner or later undergo a socialist revolution according to the traditional model of social progress, say the Soviet writers. The other group includes countries characterised by economic backwardness, nationalism and the influence of religion — attributes which raise serious obstacles in the way of a socialist revolution. Moreover, they have no substantial working class which could lead the movement towards socialist transformations.

However, in this situation Soviet writers produce another theoretical solution: 'In agrarian countries the role of the proletarian vanguard of the liberation movement can be played by the socialist world system'.[32] Thanks to the existence of *'world socialism'* and the advantage which they derive from the *new world balance of power,* the developing countries will acquire material and political support which will replace the proletarian leadership on the spot and prepare the way for non-capitalist development.

In spite of terminological refinements and theoretical modifications, the thesis that the Third World countries as a whole are an ally of the socialist camp and an item on the anti-imperialist side of the world equation of forces can hardly be regarded as a scientific generalisation.

In the first decade of the wave of anti-colonial revolutions, the very fact that these were directed against the Western powers, and that the Soviet Union had no colonial past in the strict sense appeared to make all newly independent countries potential or actual allies of the socialist camp. The Soviet leaders (first Khrushchev and then Brezhnev) thought it wise to give some assistance and support to any Third World country almost regardless of its domestic policies, alignment of intrasocietal forces, and structural development tendencies. The generally anti-imperailist foreign policy of nearly all these countries was a sufficient reason for considering them to be pro-socialist. Even those countries which rejected the Soviet model of modernisation and socialist development — if they concurrently rejected the Western-capitalist way and chose their own way (which was sometimes called national-socialism) — were thought to be participating in the anti-imperialist struggle. If the communist movement in a country was attacked but the state was externally anti-imperialist, the latter still was judged according to its relations with 'imperialism' — that is with the world class struggle.

In the 1970s the Soviet Union, while continuing to support each anti-imperialist manifestation in the Third World countries, concentrated on supporting their struggle against 'Western exploitation' and tried to step up its economic cooperation with them — independently of their domestic structure and policies. One of the aims was to satisfy the Soviet Union's own economic requirements.

With all the modifications in the factual policies pursued *vis-à-vis* the various Third World countries, some general attitudes have outlasted all the setbacks and unexpected developments. These are deeply rooted in the main principles of Marxist-Leninist theory and are not lightly to be dismissed. They are: (1) the policy of treating the Third World as an ally of the socialist camp; (2) the belief that the Third World is moving towards socialism.

To sum up, the path of the developing countries towards socialism is seen as a gradual process in which one country after another will be detached from the group of capitalist Third World countries. Admittedly, reversals are regarded as possible, since, as Soviet writers assess, parliamentary democracy is always pregnant with sudden 'rightist' changes and since the imperialists may undertake or inspire a counter-revolutionary action by means of economic pressure, political blackmail or outright aggression. However, the main trend is irreversible: the advantages of socialism in the correlation of world forces will create an economic, political and psychological climate in which the need for fundamental reconstruction becomes self-evident. Therefore, the final conclusion is that the course of the revolutionary process depends largely on the relation of world forces.[33]

Two arguments for this thesis were added as regards the group of the developing countries. First, the economic developments so far have shown that the capitalist countries cannot help them to make any substantial economic and cultural progress. Second, the growing number of the countries in which the governments declare socialist aims testifies to its rightness. Recent history 'makes it plain that the movement from capitalism to socialism is spreading across the world. This has now become so obvious that it can be accepted as an axiom.'[34]

Forces

The second great analytical issue in the concept of the correlation of
world forces concerns the *forces* which constitute the global power of
the rival camps and form the basic object of the comparison.

No single kind of power

According to Marxist-Leninist theory, these forces cannot be limited
to the armed forces (or military power) nor to any other *single* kind of
power or relationship, whether economic, political or ideological. They
represent the complex of all the material and non-material forces in
societies.[35]

First, since the individual countries and the camps in their entirety
have begun to embody not only national but also social qualities, which
differ in the different systems, the assessment of these systemic differences should be included in the global assessment.

Second, the impact of economic factors (including the techno-
scientific potentialities) on the global state power in both peace and
wartime has greatly increased. *Inter alia*, this is one of the preconditions of the successful prevention of war, and of surviving any war
that may occur.

The content of the economic power to be compared is variously
described by different scholars. Shakhnazarov enumerates the following
components: the gross per capita product, the productivity of labour,
the growth rate, the level of industrial production (particularly in
metallurgy, power generation, engineering, chemical industry, radio
electronics and other leading branches of industry), the level of technology, labour resources and the skill of the work force, the number of
specialists and the success of theoretical and applied science.[36]

Third, the impact of ideology and of the political awareness of the
masses on global state power is growing (see below).

In the Soviet view, the increasing role of the non-military components of the correlation of world forces also reflects the fact that in the
international system a constant struggle between the basic socio-
economic antagonists is proceeding on numerous fronts: economic,
political, ideological and others.[37] This struggle varies continuously
in intensity, with different forms of it coming to the fore, and the non-
military components of the world correlation exercising their various
kinds of influence.

The great variety of the component equations in the correlation of
world forces involves a great disparity of the methods applied in world-
wide competition, in both struggle and cooperation, and their very
different impacts. The increase in material power does not always make

the protagonist capable of a more active policy. The immense growth of military power on both sides of the world equation, for instance, has a paralysing effect and prevents any major action. (This is, naturally, beneficial for mankind.) In contrast, political and ideological activities and penetrations may gradually undermine the adversary's assets, both domestic and international, his political influences and strategic positions.

Determining character of the system

All the above-mentioned components of the global power of a state or a camp depend on the way in which they are created and mobilised and this is said to be determined, in the final analysis, by the character of the socio-economic and political system. The following factors are to be taken into account: the level of economic development and the solidity of the economic structure, the scope of cooperation between the different social classes and strata, the amount of support given by the population to the government, the political and ideological unity and strength of society and the efficiency of state power.[38] With regard to the whole alliance, the character of the system determines whether the combined power is greater or smaller than the simple sum of the component state powers, whether it is weakened by the internal contradictions or whether it contributes certain new values connected with the cooperation and mutual support given by the member states.

For instance, the internal contradictions *between the imperialist powers,* emerging not only from the direct competition between them but also from the different strategies adopted in relation to the socialist countries, are said to diminish the resultant power of the imperialist system as a whole.[39] Contradictions also exist *in the particular capitalist countries* which diminish the global power of that camp. Apart from the class contradictions, which always weaken the power of any capitalist state, the following contradictions and conflicts have been pointed out in Soviet writings[40]: the conflict between the fear of nuclear war among peoples and their fight for peace, on the one hand, and the arms race engaged in by the Western governments on the other; the conflict between the opposition of the popular masses to armed interventions and the adventurist policy of some Western governments; conflicts of interests between that section of the ruling class which seeks broader economic contacts with the socialist countries and the military-industrial complex which opposes *détente;* finally the rivalry between the particular services in the armed forces.

Does the traditional emphasis on military force remain?

All the new ideas mean that the traditional Marxist-Leninist approach, in which military power was the basic object of analysis in the comparison of the power of states, is now regarded as obsolete.[41] However, the new position is reflected in conceptual discussions rather than in descriptions of concrete developments. The traditional emphasis on military power continues to characterise the more authoritative political utterances and scientific writings concerning the current situation and the politico-military developments in the world. One typical statement reads:

> The establishment of the dynamic balance of strategic forces between the USSR and the USA substantially limits the military activities of imperialism in the international arena and compels it to take into account the peaceful policies of the socialist community of states... Thus military power remains one of the principal instruments of government foreign policy; its role and effectiveness, together with other means, depend on the specific international political situation and the specific balance of forces developing in the world, or in particular regions.[42]

The level of the strategic forces and the economic and technoscientific potentials (which make it possible to maintain and develop these forces) are regarded as the most important items in the 'military opposition' of the two rival systems in the world. The traditional approach is still valid in politico-military analyses and planning.

Role of ideology

Among the intangible values contributing to the global value of the correlation of world forces, ideology is considered to play an essential role.

The Marxist-Leninists consider that international relations include ideological relations — the ideological cooperation of states having the same class ideology and the ideological conflicts between states of different types.[43] The struggle between capitalism and socialism is said to be waged in three interconnected spheres: the economic, the political and the ideological one. Thus both the ideological cooperation within the two camps and the clash of two basically conflicting ideologies — the socialist and the so-called bourgeois — constitute an important item in the correlation of world forces.

When the Marxist-Leninist politicians and scholars present the concept of peaceful coexistence, as a rule they stress that while wars are to be avoided, peaceful coexistence is accompanied by economic competition and ideological struggle.[44] Indeed, in several statements ideological struggle under the conditions of peaceful coexistence has been proclaimed the basic form of intersystemic competition.

The Western and particular American authors have always been criticised for asserting that ideological struggle makes peaceful coexistence fragile if not impossible and that *détente* must include weakening or even ending of ideological struggle. In their view, if ideological struggle continues, and even intensifies, it means that the struggle between the two antagonistic systems is only 'redistributed' from one sector to another one; the relaxation of tensions in one sector leads automatically to more intense tension in the other one.[45]

In the early 1980s, in all the Soviet political and military studies, the Americans began to be accused of focusing on ideological struggle.[46] However, the anti-Communist propaganda of the West, takes the distorted form of ideological struggle — the so-called 'psychological warfare'. It includes justification of the foreign and military policy of the United States and its allies by the necessity for defence against Soviet military buildup.

(Actually, in Western political science, the ideological differences between the two camps have also begun to play a significant role in explaining their rivalry but 'power considerations' still occupy the main place and many researchers try to reduce the aggregate of the contradictions between states with different domestic systems to those connected with the pursuit of power and power position to the detriment of the ideological considerations.[47])

Soviet scholars admit that 'it is extremely difficult to construct an exact, subtle distinction between Cold War, "psychological warfare" and ideological struggle'.[48] Arbatov calls psychological warfare a peculiar form of ideological struggle.[49] However, in innumerable books, studies and articles they make such a distinction, attributing ideological struggle to the socialist countries only and 'psychological warfare' to the 'imperialist' ones.[50] The latter are said to wage 'ideological sabotage',[51] to resort to 'inadmissible methods of propaganda aggression'.[52] to propagate 'militarism, violence, racism, aggression or any form of national exclusiveness',[53] to substitute 'war ideology'[54] and 'militant anticommunism'[55] for a genuine struggle between two world outlooks.

The substitution of the various forms of psychological warfare for genuine struggle of ideas has been repeatedly condemned.[56]

Ideological struggle is defined as a struggle of ideas and ideologies in general, and of foreign policy ideologies in particular.[57] Marxist-Leninist theory, however, does not go beyond general formulae about the struggle of ideas or views of the world situation as the essence of the ideological confrontation of the two world systems and does not

160

explain the differences between ideological struggle, on the one hand, and ideological diversion and psychological warfare on the other. Generally, it is stated that the question of war or peace is now the basic object of the ideological struggle.[58] This struggle is carried on by all peace-loving forces against imperialism, militarism and the arms race which, as the Soviet critics maintain, has recently been stepped up by the imperialist camp.[59]

It may be suggested that in practice ideological struggle against the 'imperialist' ideology is reduced to a polemical campaign against America's foreign and military policies and its domestic system. Moreover, in their criticism of Western policy, Soviet politicians and scholars reduce one by one the possible forms which ideological struggle could take.

(1) Thus it is stated that 'the Soviet Union has always maintained that the ideological struggle should not be introduced into interstate relations or used as a brake in tackling acute international problems'.[60] 'Our country is against ideological differences being transplanted into the area of international relations', Andrei Gromyko has noted; such a policy leads to dangerous confrontation.[61] Remarks by the American President and his closest advisers attributing to the Soviet Union the urge to achieve world domination or accusing it of accelerating the arms race, are described as direct 'psychological warfare' against the USSR which violates the norms of international law and the corresponding articles of bilateral agreements and understandings.

(2) Further, it is said that the United States and other imperialist powers endeavour to bolster their foreign policy by propagandist methods and that such 'public diplomacy' designed to win the sympathy of the broad sections of the public for the policy of the imperialist powers is an instrument of psychological warfare, rather than of ideological struggle.

(3) An important feature of the ideological struggle today is the effort by strategists of psychological warfare in the West to shift the ideological struggle to the territory of socialist countries.

In order to erode socialism from within and break the unity of the socialist states, they use all means of overt subversions, even the most unscrupulous ones.[62]

They use ideological discussion 'as a pretext and cover for outright subversive activity: sending agents who distribute leaflets calling for the overthrow of the existing government, financing anti-government activity, trying to make the population hostile to its government, etc'.[63]

(4) Within the capitalist countries, the unbridled ideological campaigns of bellicose anti-Communism and anti-Sovietism, are designed to create hostility towards socialist countries, towards peace and international cooperation.[64]

161

(5)   The criticisms of the Soviet Union in Western publications are also condemned. These are described as 'highly malicious remarks by professional Sovietologists and liars about the Soviet Union and the socialist system'.[65]

The aim of this literature is to present the Western countries, and in particular the United States, as bulwarks of peace and democracy and their system as a humane one and, at the same time, to discredit the socialist countries and their home and foreign policies in the eyes of the public. The Soviet writers bring these themes of Western propaganda under the general heading of 'anti-communism'.

As regards the methods used in 'psychological warfare', three kinds of propaganda are enumerated, called 'white', 'black' and 'grey'. The first of these is 'official propaganda spread by the official mass media', the other two consist of all kinds of false information about the adversary.[66] Again, the aims and the methods — and especially the 'white propaganda' — hardly differ from those in the 'anti-imperialist' propaganda of the socialist countries, which is presented as a means of ideological struggle.

Thus both official statements and the writings of Sovietologists which are said to serve the anti-Communist and anti-Soviet ideological campaign in the United States and other Western countries, as well as both the ideological struggle in the international arena and antisocialist propaganda disseminated in socialist countries are condemned as *not* belonging to the sphere of ideological struggle. What else remains? It seems that, in the Soviet view the only proper means of ideological struggle are those used by Soviet politicians and writers in official statements, books and articles to accuse the United States of everything evil, the anti-imperialist propaganda disseminated in capitalist countries, and so on.

Likewise, it *is* ideological struggle when socialist countries are concerned to extend the influence of Marxist-Leninist ideology to the working masses of other countries. They defend its purity, they unmask bourgeois ideology and demonstrate its scientific hollowness and reactionary nature.[67]

Arbatov writes that 'ideologies constantly clash both on the global scale and in many individual countries', and that 'ideology and propaganda may also be used as instruments of a certain policy, particularly a policy of subverting and destabilising other societies, which means psychological warfare'.[68] However, there is no difference in the contents of these two activities: spreading anti-capitalist (or 'anti-imperialist') propaganda in capitalist societies, which is fully approved by the theorists of peaceful coexistence, has just the same aims that Arbatov ascribes to psychological warfare. The spreading of anti-capitalist propaganda in capitalist countries is called ideological struggle, while the spreading of corresponding propaganda in socialist coun-

162

tries is called psychological warfare. *Quod licet Iovi, non licet bovi* (Seneca)

In the framework of Marxist-Leninist theory this opposite assessment of ostensibly similar policies is fully explicable, however. *All* ideological campaigns and actions undertaken by the Western powers are unjust and constitute a distorted form of ideological competition, i.e., psychological warfare, since they aim to defend imperialism, they are against progress, against the laws of history, against the main direction of social development. And *all* respective policies of the socialist countries, which are the carriers of progress, are just and justified.

Summing up, although the scientific interest in the issue of ideological struggle as an important front of intersystemic competition and a significant item in the correlation world forces is beyond doubt, the Marxist-Leninist analysis of the very *concept* of this struggle seems to be a weak point in the *theory* of the correlation. In Soviet policy, however, it certainly is a strong point.

Internal mechanism in 'world socialism'

Although an anti-communist ideology underlies all the activities of the imperialist camp, only a temporary convergence of interests in that camp can be achieved, according to Marxist-Leninist analysis.

It is weakened by constant interstate struggles for divergent economic, political and strategic interests: struggles between the great powers and between the United States and its allies, as well as by attempts to form regional groups in Western Europe and to create new centres of power, such as Japan.

The socialist side of the world equation, on the other hand, although it consists of three parts, is not similarly torn or weakened by internal separatistic tendencies. On the contrary, it is said, the different contributions by the various participants enrich the common power and the common policy.

Centripetal tendencies

Three ideas underlie the centripetal tendencies in the socialist camp. In the first place, strong centripetal incentives in the system of socialist countries arise from the needs of the members of the system and from the requirements of the system itself. The socialist countries started from widely differing initial positions, as regards both their external environment and the level of their internal development — primarily the economic but also the sociopolitical level. All of them, in varying degrees, needed economic support and cooperation with other members

163

of the system. This coincided with the development requirements of the system as a whole. Difficulties in the economic development and in achieving a correspondence between the socio-economic basis and the superstructure, as well as between the various elements in the basis, made the need for cooperation more urgent:

> At every stage in the building up of socialism and communism, the socialist countries try to solve the complicated problems of correspondence between the basis and the superstructure, between politics and economic, ideology and material living conditions, centralism and democracy, personal and social interests, but primarily the degree of correspondence between the forces of production and the relations of production. Each country attains such a degree of correspondence chiefly through its own efforts and resources. However, the vast scale and complexity of the tasks of socialist and communist construction, on the one hand, and the possibilities of socialism as a system, on the other, demand ever closer cooperation and cohesion among the socialist countries.[69]

Second, the basic interests of all three component detachments of 'world socialism' have become binding interests: they require the close association and cooperation of all the nations belonging to this camp.[70] These interests include[71] the strengthening of socialism on a world scale, the banning of wars, the protection of the environment, the prevention of dangerous and widespread diseases, the exploration of space and the oceans and seas, control of the earth's climate and the transformation of the vast deserts and swamps into flourishing regions.

Third, although the breadth of the international communities and international movements differs and changes with time, as also does the content of their interests, there exists at every stage of social development one *main* interest that is common to all of them. In the interwar period this was the defence and strengthening of the first socialist country. Now it is the defence of the system of socialist states and the furthering of its expansion, as well as a new aim common to all countries: the defence of peace in the world.

Principles of proletarian internationalism

The interaction of all the components of 'world socialism' for the realisation of the above-mentioned aims is based on a system of principles that constitutes the so-called *proletarian internationalism*.[72] The revolutionary solidarity of the proletariat, the unity of the workers of the entire world and the subordination of national interests to the international interests of the revolutionary movement are the three basic principles. A corollary to the last of these is that the struggle for national sovereignty and equality among nations is subordinated to the international proletarian struggle. It is pointed out that sovereignty should be evaluated in terms of the class interests of the proletariat and the extent to which it is of use in accomplishing the common revolutionary tasks of the international working class.[73] If the acquisition of sovereignty by a given population would serve the interests of the proletariat, it should then be striven for.

Marxist-Leninist analysts hold that an independent solution of questions affecting a nation's domestic affairs, its socio-economic, political and cultural matters and its relations with other peoples must not be achieved at the cost of the world proletariat and the international communist movement. If any danger of this arises — such as happened in Czechoslovakia in 1968 — the socialist countries have a moral responsibility to the world proletariat and the international communist movement to remove it. This also applies to *each* Communist party — which is responsible to all sections of the modern world revolutionary movement. The same may be said concerning the principle of equality. This cannot be transformed into an abstract and absolute idea: nations are equal when they act in a spirit of solidarity as parts of a single revolutionary army. The principle of equality serves to unite the revolutionary forces in nations, which represent their interests in the best way.

Other principles include:

(1) the principle of the equality and sovereignty of all the nations that are allied for the common defence of socialist gains;

(2) the self-determination and voluntary union of the peoples of these countries;

(3) the fraternal cooperation of the peoples in the task of socialist construction;

(4) the strengthening of the unity and solidarity of the world socialist system;

(5) the unity of will and action among the communist and workers' parties;

(6) the close unity of the forces of socialism and of the working-class and national liberation movement in the struggle for peace, national independence and social progress;

(7) the struggle against bourgeois nationalism and chauvinism.

Underlying philosophy

Three ideas of sociological methodology are said to underlie the mechanism of the interaction of the components of world socialism. In the first place, the basic value of all these principles consists in their *serving the class interests* of the proletariat.

165

Second, *they are not voluntary* scientific or political constructions: they reflect the objective relationships of class struggle on the world scale.

Third, it is an *internationalist duty* of all members of the revolutionary community to observe these principles. This duty is defined as the totality of obligations of the national contingents of the working class, the communist and workers' parties and the socialist fatherlands to the world's revolutionary forces. The obligations are based on the above-listed principles of proletarian internationalism.

Soviet writers admit that the functioning of all the above-mentioned principles encounters many obstacles. These arise, they say, from the ideological bourgeois offensive which spreads nationalism and the resiliency of nationalistic views and feelings — remnants of the formerly prevailing bourgeois ideology. The struggle to overcome nationalistic prejudices is regarded as a complex and lengthy one; however, its outcome is certain, since it reflects laws and inevitabilities of the objective social development.[74]

Difficulties

Soviet politicians and researchers admit that the development of the socialist communtiy of nations is encountering many difficulties, some of which are inherent in the process of building such a community, while others are caused by the impact of the world capitalist system.

The then Vice-Premier and Minister of Foreign Affairs, Andrei Gromyko, wrote in 1983: 'The countries of the socialist community, in the course of their development, are encountering some serious difficulties. This development proceeds through untrodden paths, through the struggle of the new with the old, through the resolution of internal contradictions and through the elimination of illusions and mistakes.'[75]

One of the external causes of these difficulties is the international situation, which hinders the development of the socialist community. The socialist countries are acting in the conditions of an intense class struggle between two systems and are subject to brutal pressures exerted by the imperialists. Soviet political and military analysts assert that in the 1980s the United States has intensified its 'indirect strategy' which aims to disrupt the socialist camp by means of ideological and economic pressures.

The external pressure and the internal processes connected with the scientific-technological revolution have resulted in increased economic difficulties. 'In the present conditions', writes Menshikov, 'considerable difficulties are engendered by the worsening international situation, the need for large defence outlays, and the imperialist circles' attempts to follow a policy of sanctions with respect to the socialist countries.

Other problems are connected with the new stage of the scientific and technical revolution, the development of new industries and introduction of new technologies'.[76] The internal difficulties are of qualitative rather than quantitive character. Faced by the socialist countries they include a depletion of extensive sources of growth, demographic processes which tend to reduce the influx of manpower into economy, the growing cost of the extraction and transportation of mineral raw materials and energy, and the need for balanced efforts to boost efficiency, intensify the economy, and accelerate scientific and technical progress.[77]

However, these difficulties can be jointly tackled by the socialist countries. With their *increasing integration,* it is said, they can overcome the most complicated obstacles to economic development and achieve the optimal utilisation of all resources. It is pointed out that the common efforts hitherto made and the aid given by the Soviet Union 'which has an enormous scientific and technological capability' have led to the elimination of 'backwardness' in particular socialist countries which was inherited from the capitalist system of production and that the gap between the individual European countries of the CMEA has narrowed considerably. One of the next aims will be to speed up the development of Vietnam, Cuba and Mongolia, through a socialist industrialisation programme, which will be supported by the socialist community as a whole.[78]

The struggle against the above-mentioned difficulties requires a common strategy. The economic 'summit' of the CMEA countries in Moscow in 1984 adopted a single strategy and elaborated long-term guidelines for interaction and the development of socialist integration. The resources of the community will be concentrated and the efforts coordinated in the crucial fields of technological development: electronics, manufacture of automation facilities, robots and flexible automated systems, nuclear power engineering, development of new materials and technologies, and biotechnology. The main link in this strategy is the creation and application of a fundamentally new technology.

This will involve strengthening cooperation in the creation of new industries which determine long-term technological progress and also result in long-term cooperation in agriculture and consumer goods production. It was decided to prepare a 15-20 year Comprehensive Programme of Scientific and Technological Progress aimed at speedily introducing scientific and technological advances through joint efforts.[79]

Contradictions or distinctions?

Soviet politicians and writers also admit that there are contradictions between the component parts of 'world socialism' and even between the socialist states. However, these are presented as *non-antagonistic contradictions* which are not rooted in the struggle between antagonistic classes and the struggle between states representing such classes. In most analyses of international relations, only the possibility of the emergence of some 'differences' (*raskhozhdeniya*)[80] between the socialist states has been noted, but in individual studies addressed to a narrower circle of social and political scientists, the existence of contradictions and conflicts between socialist states has been admitted.[81] Such contradictions are said to have two kinds of causes: objective and subjective. The objective contradictions arise from differences in levels of economic development, in social structure (where there are different levels of sociopolitical development) or in the international position (where, for instance, there are differences between the global interests of the Soviet Union and the regional or local interests of its allies).[82] However, these are not viewed as contradictions: the differences of interests can and must be settled 'on the basis of proletarian internationalism, through comradely discussion and voluntary fraternal cooperation'. Although 'there have been cases in which internationalism took a back seat in relations between socialist countries'[83] the difficulties were overcome. In this context China is said to be an exception.

It is said to be the deliberate policy of the Communist parties to prevent the contradictions from reaching the 'open' stage of conflicts. As socialist states come closer to one another, and the system as a whole becomes increasingly united, contradictions will disappear. A few of them may persist or re-emerge, since each development must result in certain contradictions.

Latent conflicts become open ones only with the operation of subjective factors, such as the violation of the principles of socialist development and of cooperation between socialist states. The former arises from ignorance or neglect of the laws of economic and social development (cf. Chapter 2); for the latter kind of violation nationalism is mainly responsible. All of these represent non-antagonistic contradictions which can be resolved before they reach the stage of open conflicts. China provides the only example of a different development quoted: the economic backwardness of the country is the objective factor, the anti-socialist policy of the present Chinese leaders is the subjective factor and the main cause of the development of contradictions and of latent conflicts into open ones. With this exception, the increasing cohesion of the socialist camp is always held to be the basic 'law' or 'regularity' (*zakonomernost'*) of inter-socialist state relations.[84]

Since, in this view, the above-mentioned contradictions do not generate a struggle but rather stimulate comradely discussion and cooperation, one may doubt that they really are contradictions, Soviet scholars say. They are more like differences arising from the specific interests of states.

The assessment made by Marxist-Leninist analysts seems to be questionable, however, since several conflicts in the socialist camp *did* occur, which could but reflect certain interstate *contradictions*. The negation of their existence and thus the absence of any proposals for the solution of them makes such a solution even more difficult.

In polemics against Western accusations that the Soviet Union maintains unequal relations in the socialist camp, Soviet writers:

(1)   quote Marxist-Leninist theories and official statements concerning the equal rights of all members of the socialist coalition,

(2)   state that equality means equality of political rights and the observation of sovereignty, rather than 'physical equality' which is impossible to achieve and which anyway would lead to the attribution of varying degrees of importance and different roles to the members of the alliance.

The world socialist system, the socialist community, in which all the member states are equal in terms of their international legal status, does include distinctions as to the size of their respective territories and population, the availability of their natural resources, their economic scientific and technological potential, defence capability, culture and so on.[85] At the same time Soviet writers condemn the 'anti-communist assertion' that there exists a political inequality in the socialist system.[86]

In general it may be said that the ideas concerning the internal mechanism of the development of 'world socialism' seem to constitute the most orthodox part of the theory of the correlation of social forces. In spite of the growing awareness among the Communist parties of significance of the national factor in the relationship between the national and international interests, feelings, processes and fronts of struggle, the international factor continues to be presented as taking precedence over the national one. The orthodox formulae about the priority of the socialist revolution over national developments and consequently about the priority of revolutionary interests and aims over national ones are often repeated.

Internal mechanism in 'world capitalism'

Agenda

World capitalism, like world socialism, is said to be highly dynamic and changing in some basic ways; these affect the internal configuration on that side of the world equation of forces and its aggregate power.

Four processes analysed by Marxist-Leninist writers in various publications and on various levels of generalisation will be discussed here:[87]

(1)   The 'leaps' in the economic and political developments in particular capitalist countries, according to 'law of the uneven development of capitalism' stated by the Marxist-Leninists;
(2)   The processes connected with victories and defeats in war;
(3)   The effects of social revolutions and the loss of colonies;
(4)   The influence of the socialist world system and the changing correlation of world forces.

'Uneven development' of capitalism

The operation of the above-mentioned law of the uneven development of capitalism (Chapter 4) means that the power position of different states in the international system varies in an irregular way. The changes usually begin in the economic field; because of the uneven development, some capitalist powers advance beyond others in a leap-like way. The law began to operate with an increased and qualitatively new force in the phase of imperialism, when capitalism spread over almost the entire world and became an international system in the strict sense of the word, with a world market, a world division of labour and a domination of financial capital.

The world, even then, was not a uniform world, however. At least six different areas could be distinguished with regard to the development of the economic and political systems: three highly developed areas: central Europe, the United Kingdom and the United States; two less developed areas: Russia and East Asia; and colonies in which capitalism was developing rather slowly.

The uneven development generated rivalries between the imperialist powers for markets and spheres of capital investments, which occasionally led to wars for a redivision of the world of colonies and dependent countries. In this connection Soviet writers discuss some new phenomena reflecting the new situation after the Second World War.

The uneven economic development of the capitalist countries may be illustrated by comparing the growth of industrial production in the United States with that in the countries of Western Europe. In the decades before the First World War (1870-1913) American production grew twice as fast as that in the countries of Western Europe (about 4.3 per cent per year as against 2 per cent). The relation became even more advantageous to the United States in the period 1913-37, and during and after the Second World War (1937-48), when America's production increased by about 79 per cent while that of the Western Europe fell by 7.5 per cent. One result of this was that, although in the mid-nineteenth century Western Europe accounted for 75 per cent of industrial production in the world, and the United States for only 20 per cent, the respective indexes were 50 per cent versus 35 per cent in the years before the First World War and, after the Second World War, America could boast of more than half of the industrial production of the entire capitalist world. However, in the two decades from 1948 to 1967 the relative growth of production in Western Europe was 5.9 per cent per year, while that of the United States was only 4.7 per cent. Another example of uneven development was the rapid growth of the West German and Japanese economies after the Second World War.

In recent decades the various effects of the techno-scientific revolution and the different degrees and forms of state-monopolist intervention in the economic process have been partly responsible for the uneven development.

Political developments

However, the changes in the political power position of individual capitalist states in the international sphere do not always reflect changes in their economic development.

According to Soviet writers this situation may be explained as follows.

(1) Political changes do not keep pace with the economic developments. Agreements and regulations which corresponded to the previous alignment of forces cannot immediately be changed.

(2) There can be political reasons for which the states cannot or will not take political advantage of their increased economic power (West Germany is the example of the first case, Japan of the second).

(3) The development of other components of state power, such as military technology, affects also the political power position. America's political influence is greatly enhanced by its near-monopoly in the field of nuclear missiles.

(4) Various international and domestic developments of a non-economic kind greatly affect the alignment of political power of capitalist states.

Wars, revolutions, loss of colonies

The uneven pattern of development in the capitalist countries led to *wars* which aimed at a redivision of the spheres of influence. These wars resulted mainly in a weakening of the imperialist world *as a whole*, say Soviet analysts: on the other hand, however, they brought about a relative correspondence between the power of the state and its international position — i.e., a temporary balance of power. Since this type of war is no longer waged, both these effects have, in recent decades, disappeared.

The collapse of the *colonialist system* has also produced various effects. It has resulted in the shrinking of the imperialist section of the world and the weakening of the economic position of former colonial powers. It also led to the weakening of their military and strategic positions — for instance, the loss of bases — in the Third World. This development brought about changes in the correlation of intrasocietal forces in the former metropolitan countries, such as a loss of power for those strata of the bourgeoisie who profited mainly and most directly from the colonies and the growth of class consciousness among the working masses. It also stimulated interstate and international contradictions.

On the other hand, the loss of the colonies stimulated the restructuring of the domestic economy and the search for new paths to economic development — for instance, in the United Kingdom and France. It also led the imperialist countries to combine their forces and efforts in the search for new forms of collective 'neocolonialism'. However, it may be said in general that the interstate contradictions continued to grow — both those arising from the rivalry of particular imperialist powers for a division and redivision of the new influences in the Third World and those between former colonies and combined forces of imperialism.

Finally, national and social *revolutions* are a potential threat to the contemporary alignment of forces in the imperialist countries of the world, since the progress of each new state along the path to socialism weakens imperialism as a whole and its positions in particular regions.

Influence of the socialist system

The influence of the socialist system on changes in the alignment of power in the capitalist system and on its power as a whole is said to be constantly growing. This does not directly affect the laws, regularities and processes in the economic development of the non-socialist world, however. It acts *indirectly* in the political sphere: internationally, by cooperating with a part of the imperialist camp and by disrupting its unity, and internally by stimulating the political awareness and strengthening the role of the working masses.

Centrifugal and centripetal tendencies

All the above-mentioned factors and particularly the laws of capitalist development, the changing international situation, including the changing correlation of world forces, the impact of the socialist system and the initial phase of the restructuring of international relations, as well as the policy of the principal imperialist powers, have decisively affected both the centrifugal and the centripetal tendencies in the capitalist world. As usual, Soviet writers discussed two areas in this world: (1) its imperialist core, consisting of the United States, Western Europe and Japan and (2) the developing world.

To take the second part first, Soviet analysts say that in the post-war period the ties between the developing world and the imperialist centre have been loosening. The beginning of the anti-colonial struggle with its clearly anti-imperialist content separated the former colonial world from the imperialist powers politically and, to a great extent, also militarily. The efforts to create a network of politico-military alliances and bases which would cover the whole capitalist world petered out; only NATO survived. In the developing world, some countries chose the socialist way of development; others, because of interstate conflicts and wars, never came to constitute a cohesive part of the capitalist world. When the developing countries took a common position in political and economic questions of global importance it was often an anti-imperialist policy.

In an attempt to enhance the cohesion of the imperialist side of the world equation of forces main efforts were made for strengthening American-West European cooperation in NATO. The outcome of these efforts has been discussed in innumerable publications, but we can only summarise here some of the basic points.

(1)   Two developments altered the balance of power in NATO and consequently in the 'imperialist world'. The first was connected with the changed correlation of world forces: America lost its invulnerability to nuclear attacks and its nuclear guarantee to NATO began to be questioned. The second development was 'internal' — namely, the rapid economic recovery in Western Europe.

(2)   Both these developments gave the European members more influence in the Alliance, and particularly in establishing its force posture.

(3)   Both developments also provided grounds for resisting the American attempts to extend NATO's obligations to extra-European territories and to make this organisation an instrument not only of regional but also of global American policy.

(4)   In France, a change in the internal alignment of forces generated separatist tendencies and weakened its links with the Alliance.

(5)   The European members of NATO began to pursue more independent foreign policies, especially in their contacts with the Soviet Union and its allies; they increased their economic contacts with the Eastern bloc.

(6)   Internal developments, and particularly the growth of the anti-nuclear movement, limited the freedom of manoeuvre of the West European governments in the military activities of the Alliance.

(7)   The centrifugal tendencies came to a climax in the period of maximum détente, in the mid 1970s. Subsequently, the United States and

the conservative forces in Western Europe increased their efforts to achieve greater cohesion in the Alliance and to step up its military efforts. Moreover, during the last two decades the tendency towards the consolidation of the Western countries has been apparent in the increasing internationalisation of economic relations, the development of interstate enterprises, increased economic integration and the international division of labour.

To sum up, two tendencies have characterised developments in the Western bloc. One is the trend towards consolidation; the other is an intensification of various centrifugal processes and actions, of rivalries and of contradictions. The extension of American business activities into West European countries promoted both of these tendencies.

Summary and two general conclusions

Changes in the correlation of world forces and an awareness of the disastrous consequences of inter-imperialist wars greatly diminished the probability of the outbreak of such wars. Instead, the inter-imperialist struggle has taken new forms — for instance, of economic competition — and is carried on between (1) imperialist powers which compete for economic influence in the post-colonial world; (2) the same protagonists which compete for economic influence in the developed countries; (3) monopolies which are supported by state apparatuses; (4) integrated groups of capitalist countries (EEC, EFTA) and individual powers, such as the United States and Japan. A common phenomenon is the combination of the power of suprastate monopolies with the power of states.

Two general conclusions concerning the analysis of the internal mechanism of the alignment of forces within the imperialist camp are usually drawn by Marxist-Leninist writers. First, they consider that the contradictions between imperialism and socialism constitute the basic contradiction of the contemporary epoch, but this does not eliminate the *internal conflicts in imperialism,* of which the principal one is interstate rivalry. Second, this rivalry does not eliminate the possibility of an armed conflict *between these systems.*

Dynamics of the correlation

Dynamic character of the correlation

As we have seen, the correlation of world forces is extremely dynamic and the constant changes in it arise from many sources and elements. There are changes in the power of both of the protagonists under

174

comparison — that of superpowers and of their alliances — as well as of the structure of the alliances, and even the membership of particular states. The importance of the particular components of power varies (cf. the increase in the role of the techno-scientific component in our time); and the global framework in which the correlation is assessed — the politico-military world structure and situation — also develops.

The global framework exercises the determining influence on the dynamic of the correlation. In the Soviet view, the world develops towards socialism, and the global correlation of forces is constantly changing in favour of the socialist system. These are interrelated processes: the increasing strength of the socialist alliance, the growing importance of the anti-imperialist policy of the post-colonial countries and the growing contradictions in the imperialist camp *contribute* to the general trend towards socialism.

There are temporary recessions, admit Soviet scholars.[88] In the early post-war period the reactionary forces in Western Europe had certain successes: the events in Yugoslavia and afterwards in other socialist countries weakened the cohesion of the socialist camp and brought about a kind of relative balance of strength between the two systems. Later the anti-Soviet shift in Chinese policy meant a serious obstacle to the growth of the common socialist strength and reactionary changes in some countries of the Third World weakened the national liberation movement as a whole and its progressive role in the world alignment of forces.

There are also shifts in *regional* relations of forces, resulting from changes in the position and actions of particular states, as well as changes in the policy of political or other groups and movements; these forces may be regarded as unstable allies of the anti-imperialist camp which have not taken a definite position.[89]

Both the dynamic character of the correlation of world forces and the shifts in regional correlation contribute to the fact that the outcome of *individual* political events cannot be predetermined and predicted. It is said to depend on the actual 'parallelogram of forces' resulting from the interaction (or rather intersection) of three policies *and* the military power backing them: (a) of the antagonistic systems; (b) of particular states engaged in the conflict;[90] and (c) of revolutionary and counter-revolutionary movements, local and global, which influence the course of regional events.[91]

On the other hand, the outcome of individual conflicts cannot decisively affect the dynamics of the correlation of world forces. A single defeat of revolutionary forces does not testify to the weakness of the world progressive forces, nor does a victory won by them mean their final triumph, or even the early prospect of it.[92]

The same may be said concerning the general trend in the correlation of economic forces, which is to the advantage of socialism but is subject to temporary recessions. A certain acceleration in the rates of economic development of the imperialist countries in particular periods may to some extent defer the date of the achievement of the economic superiority by socialism; it corrects the Marxist-Leninist forecasts of the economic competition between the two systems. The imperialists may also exploit disagreements in the socialist camp, individual mistakes and failures on the part of the revolutionary forces.[93]

The main trend is presented as clearly oriented and inevitable: since the creation of the first socialist state the correlation of world forces has periodically undergone major shifts in favour of socialism. The dynamic character of the correlation of forces and its clear orientation allows us to assess various policies, Soviet scholars point out. Any policy which tries to preserve the existing correlation is reactionary, since it contradicts the laws of social development.[94]

Three dynamic components

The socialist states, the international workers' movement and the national liberation movement have been mentioned as three component parts of the socialist ('progressive' or 'peace-loving' or 'anti-imperialist') side of the world equation of forces. Thus together with the comparison between socialist and capitalist states, the second correlation included was that between the international workers movement and the international cooperation of monopolies, capitalist states and bourgeois parties and the third correlation was that between the national liberation movement and states emerging from it, and the colonialist or neo-colonialist powers.

These three components of the world correlation of forces may be considered both separately and jointly. The rivalry between the socialist and the capitalist states, the combats waged by the international working movement and the national liberation struggle constitute more or less independent fronts of combat, with victories and defeats, and the importance of these in the overall anti-imperialist struggle may vary in different periods. Yet they all at the same time participate in a common struggle and are components of the same side of the world equation. All of them contribute to the general movement of mankind towards the final transformation into communism.

According to the Marxist-Leninists the correlation of world forces which creates favourable conditions for this general tendency, accords with and expresses the laws of social development.

Four shifts in the correlation of world forces

(1) *The embryonic phase*   The correlation of social forces as a category was implied in the mechanism of the theory of class struggle. To Marxist-Leninists, each social struggle, domestic or international, operates with this category.

Initially, however, the term 'correlation of forces' was used only occasionally and in a general way. A careful calculation of forces was made by the leaders of the revolutionary movement in the everyday struggle and before any major action, but without any theoretical generalisations. The same may be said about the comparison of forces in the international arena. Although the so-called international working class was set against the international bourgeoisie in various theoretical and propagandist contexts, the concept of the relation of international forces was not discussed in much detail.

(2) *First shift and the emergence of 'capitalist encirclement'*   The October Revolution in 1917 caused the *first great shift* in the relation of international forces, according to the Marxist-Leninists. For the first time in history the correlation of social forces acquired an *interstate* (and in Marxist-Leninist theory, an international) dimension. Lenin wrote in 1921: 'In the economic and military respects we are materially immeasurably weak but morally — with regard to the real relation of forces of all classes in all states rather than to abstract ethics — we are stronger than all the others'.[95] However, the term 'capitalist encirclement' began to be used in political analyses and especially, in propaganda rather than 'relation of forces'. The latter term was introduced in judging the domestic development in particular capitalist countries.

(3) *Two camps have emerged*   The *second great shift* took place after the Second World War. It was connected with the defeat of three major capitalist powers and the weakening of others, and with the emergence of a whole group (called a system) of socialist states.[96] This became a political camp under the absolute domination of the USSR. At the same time the rise of the United States to the status of a capitalist superpower which was beginning to play the chief role in the non-socialist world contributed to the polarisation of the international system into two camps. Two groups of states, including almost all the developed industrial countries, with their markedly different socio-economic systems and antagonistic policies, and led by two super-powers, created a new structure in the international system. The correlation of forces as a sociological (or sociopolitical) category had acquired two coexisting and interconnected aspects: the *domestic* and the *international*.

(4) *Collapse of colonial system*   The emergence of a large group of independent states in the 1950s and 1960s, which resulted from the 'explosion' of the anti-colonial (or, in Marxist-Leninist language, the 'national liberation') movement, was viewed as the *third basic shift* in the relation of international forces. This also marked the beginning of the third period in the so-called structural crisis of the world capitalist system. The new states were regarded as the 'natural allies' of the socialist camp in its so-called anti-imperialist struggle. The correlation of social forces had acquired an additional, 'national liberation' dimension. More and more frequently it was called 'the correlation of world forces'.

(5) *Strategy parity*   In the early 1970s, Soviet and other Marxist-Leninist politicians and writers began to point out a *fourth basic shift* in the correlation of world forces: the attainment by the Soviet Union (and consequently by the entire socialist camp) of military-strategic parity with the Western camp.[97] This was said to be occurring at the end of the sixties and in the early seventies. It was the first time in history that a *military* development rather than a great sociopolitical change in the world structure was specified as constituting a basic shift in the correlation of world forces.

(6) *Differences between the shifts*   These circumstances direct our attention to some general differences between the four shifts in the correlation that have been mentioned. The first three shifts were said to be connected with, and correspond to, the *three succeeding stages in the structural crisis of the world capitalist system*. The fourth shift caused simply by the *military build-up* of the Soviet Union. At the same time, the first three changes were said to be connected with the *internal* weaknesses of capitalism: the October Revolution and the emergence of the group of socialist states after the Second World War were caused by the domestic class contradictions and by the contradictions among capitalist states, while the collapse of the colonial system — by the contradictions between the colonialists and the oppressed peoples. Thus the three shifts in the correlation of world forces were caused by the internal weakening of one side and the strengthening of the other one. The fourth shift was said to result from the absolute growth in the power of the socialist camp, which was greater and more rapid than the concurrent absolute growth in power of the capitalist world. The zero-sum game has been replaced by a more complicated model.

Thus it appears that there are two kinds of changes in the correlation of world forces: (1) either one side is getting stronger at the cost of the other or (2) the strength of both is increasing, but unevenly, and thus the *relative* strength of one of them is increasing.

It seems that in the 1980s two changes in the exposition of the 'shifts' and of their final outcome can be discovered. The first is that the importance of the third 'shift', i.e., of the emergence of the newly independent post-colonial countries has been somewhat toned down. Some writers did not include it in the set of decisive events which were tantamount to the beginning of a new phase in the world correlation of world forces and in the transition of the world towards socialism. Zarodov, for instance, characterises the third period not by the collapse of the colonial system and the emergence of the camp of post-colonial countries but as one of consolidation of the positions of socialism which had spread to new countries.

Zagladin simply omits the third 'shift' and the third 'period' and links the three stages in the balance of world forces with the October Revolution, the emergence of the socialist system and the achievement of military-strategic parity between socialism and imperialism.[98]

This change in emphasis may perhaps be explained by two motives. One is the opposition to the Chinese emphasis on the national liberation movement as allegedly the main revolutionary force of our time, equally or even more important than the communist movement. The other is the conclusion that the developing countries, in spite of their anti-imperialist biases, will not automatically ally with the socialist camp. In the 1980s the role of these countries as a natural political ally of the socialist camp has been somewhat toned down.

Shakhnazarov writes that imperialism still controls many of these countries[99] and Zagladin recalls that most developing countries are now part of the world system of capitalism. The character of their future social development is not predetermined and it will 'affect the overall balance of forces *in one way or another*'[100] (italics added).

Influence on world affairs

The following influences of the correlation of world forces are pointed out by the Marxist-Leninist analysts:
(1)   Prevention of wars, especially intersystemic wars;
(2)   Social and national revolutions;
(3)   Restructuring of international relations;
(4)   Arms control.
(5)   Peaceful coexistence.

Influence on international conflicts

Marxist-Leninist analysts believe that the correlation of world forces which is advantageous to 'world socialism' has a positive impact on international conflicts.[101] In general, this correlation has limited the conflicts, and particularly those between the two antagonistic camps. It has lowered the level, the intensity and the scale of the use of military means in the conflicts which took an armed form. In many cases, such as the Israeli/Arab war of 1973, it has led to a localisation and de-escalation; in others it has influenced a transition from military operations to negotiations as in the Greece/Turkey conflict over Cyprus; it has led to a large decrease in the likelihood of conflicts in Europe, and in some cases to the liquidation of conflicts (for instance, with regard to Berlin).

However, the correlation of world forces is only one of the factors that affect the outbreak of international conflicts and it cannot eliminate them as a social phenomenon. Other and more important objective factors preclude the elimination of conflicts. First, these are the objective contradictions in the capitalist societies and between them, as well as those between the two antagonistic systems. These will always generate conflicts, and the correlation of world forces can only diminish the probability of their outbreak in the form of open hostilities and effect their de-escalation, if they break out. Second, there are subjective factors motivating the outbreak of open international conflicts, such as the foreign policy of the imperialist states and various domestic motives and pressures such as the demands of the military-industrial complex. The impact of the pro-socialist correlation of forces may cut both ways: it may reduce the motivation and the readiness to unleash open conflicts but it may also generate attempts by the imperialist states to reverse by force the general trend of development.

Third, the mutual restraint on the use of military force on the global level[102] and by the most powerful countries against one another, may generate regional and local armed clashes aiming to resolve various conflicts that are rooted in the long colonial period; the great powers may aggravate such conflicts by competing for political, strategic and economic positions and by supporting their formal and informal allies — i.e., waging wars 'by proxy'.

Finally, the traditional roots of conflicts within the group of imperialist powers have remained. While the Cold War increased the solidarity of these powers in the face of a 'common threat', the inter-imperialist differences of interest became more conflict-generating under the conditions of *détente*,[103] and in the 1980s they have further increased because of the intensified economic competition. The Federal Republic of Germany, France, and Japan have been gaining economic strength and this growth has been attended by attempts to increase political influence and to create a corresponding military potential. Some Soviet scholars posit that the centrifugal tendencies in the imperialist world as a whole — like those in NATO — are unlikely to lead to armed conflicts in a foreseeable future,[104] others, however, are not so certain.

180

'Knowing the bellicose nature of German and Japanese imperialism', writes Shakhnazarov, 'there can be no doubt that this will be followed by the demand for a redistribution of spheres of influence', and therefore: 'Conflict, including military, is possible and inevitable if the present tendency towards a redistribution of power continues in the imperialist camp.'[105]

Prevention of wars

All the sources of wars have subsisted according to the Marxist-Leninists, since capitalism in its imperialist stage has survived in large areas of the world. Yet no major war — and, in particular, no war between the antagonist systems — has broken out. The reason for this is said to be the increasingly pro-socialist correlation of forces in the world. The Marxist-Leninists believe that it would be sheer suicide for the imperialist camp to start a nuclear missile war against the socialist camp. It is not only that a comparison of purely military forces promises no imperialist victory in such a war. They consider that in the capitalist countries political control over the general course of war and especially over military operations would be extremely difficult to achieve; the coordination of political, economic and military efforts would be much more difficult than in socialist countries; finally, the resistance among the masses of the population in the capitalist countries would make it impossible for their governments to keep control of them, not only for the maintenance of the armed forces but also for the maintenance of any sociopolitical rule at all.[106]

However, though the socialist camp could use such a war to achieve the ultimate victory over imperialism, the costs and losses would be enormous and therefore peaceful coexistence would be a better way to bring about the final triumph of socialism throughout the world. The contemporary correlation of world forces, including the strategic nuclear parity between the superpowers, effectively prevents an intersystemic war.[107]

A corollary issue is the prevention of wars between particular states belonging to the opposing systems. Such a war would cause the immediate outbreak of an intersystemic war; thus the contemporary correlation of world forces effectively prevents this also.

Local wars raise a different problem. Soviet writers describe three kinds of local wars which differ in the sociopolitical sense. One kind consists of interstate local wars in the Third World which break out for various national and social reasons, but are rooted in the period of colonial domination. The correlation of world forces cannot eliminate the danger of such wars completely; in some cases they break out because of the regional alignment of forces, but in most cases because of the complex local political-military situation.

The second kind includes wars that are waged for national liberation; these sometimes turn into internal wars with foreign intervention or, at least, active military support given either by progressive forces to the insurgents or by imperialist powers to the former colonial power or a regime which is closely connected with it. It is because of the pro-socialist correlation of world forces that, in constantly recurring instances, the oppressed peoples of the colonies have achieved independence without open armed intervention by the colonialist powers.

The newly independent countries are facing the enormous task of economic development under conditions of backwardness and lack of economic support from outside. They also face the danger of imperialist military intervention or indirect support of reactionary forces in their territories. However, to Soviet writers it is clear that with the present correlation of world class forces, the liberated countries are able to resist imperialist dictation and achieve just — that is, equal — economic relations. It is also clear that their already substantial contribution to the common struggle for peace and the security of the peoples is likely to grow.[108]

The third kind of local war is an internal revolution of either national or social or mixed character, in which the danger of intervention by the great powers is also considerable. The general view of Soviet theorists is that the correlation of world forces cannot prevent the outbreak of such internal — or mixed internal/international — wars, it may only affect the likelihood of an armed intervention in them, prevent an escalation and contribute to the termination of them. For instance, the Iranian revolution was carried out under a favourable domestic and regional correlation of forces, and the pro-socialist correlation of world forces made it impossible for the United States to intervene militarily. This situation greatly influenced the victory of the revolutionary forces. On the other hand, it prevented the escalation of a local armed conflict into a major war, which might have spread to the entire Persian Gulf area and even developed into a world war.

This assertion is connected with the assessment of the character of military interventions — either just or unjust — and with the likelihood of their occurrence. The Soviet complex of ideas concerning the impact of the correlation of world forces implies that socialist states have the right to support any national or socialist campaign of liberation; such was the view taken of Cuba's support of the embattled government of Angola and the USSR's support of Ethiopia in its war against Somalia. However, similar support given by the United States to the counter-revolutionary forces in various Latin American countries was condemned as highly unjust. The Soviet writers state that in all cases where the correlation of world forces permits, interventions of the latter kind will be combatted or prevented.

182

Correlation of world forces and revolutions

The increasingly pro-socialist correlation of world forces does not hinder the outbreak of revolutions. On the contrary, in the Marxist-Leninist view, these will positively influence the development of the international system. The further changes in it will result not from interstate wars but from revolutions, which will extend the frontiers of the socialist system throughout the world.

In the classical political and military literature revolution was viewed as a by-product of certain destructive wars. The fathers of Marxism, who were against wars because they caused suffering among the workers and great cultural damage, nevertheless accepted that some wars may ultimately have had positive consequences in the social sense — i.e., revolutions — or at least have created very favourable conditions for revolutions. Moreover, the revolutions could not have occurred without some kind of armed violence, and the armed uprising usually was followed by a civil war.

However, with the contemporary correlation of world forces, interstate wars — and particularly those between the coalitions of developed countries — may cause unprecedented destruction and endanger all the hitherto achieved gains of socialism. They could eventually destroy socialism and reverse the process of human development. From now on socialism must try to advance along the path of *internal* developments, not only through new forms of armed struggle in the domestic sphere but also through new forms of non-violent political struggle.

Restructuring of international relations

The process of restructuring international relations from the balance of power of a few great capitalist states and their dominance to the formal equality of more than 150 equal states and world system based on two antagonistic camps, with the socialist camp constantly gaining in strength and influence on world affairs, is regarded by Marxists as a 'law-like' process that impels the world towards socialism.

In the Marxist-Leninist view, this process is leading the world away from international relations based on 'positions of strength' and the dictates of great powers and towards relations in which the sovereignty of each state is respected and its interests taken into account. It is also leading away from confrontation to actual peaceful coexistence and cooperation.[109]

This is a relatively long *process,* however, the Soviet authors say. Some consider that it includes the entire period of the coexistence between states with different socio-economic systems. The emergence of the Soviet Union marked the beginning of the process, and the transformation of socialism into a system of states, which has radically changed the correlation of world forces, greatly hastened it.[110] Some premises of the restructuring have already been fulfilled: the impact of imperialism on the course of world affairs has declined and the great capitalist powers can no longer unleash a world war; a large section of the world is already enjoying a new kind of international relations.[111] Others say that the restructuring began in the early 1970s with *détente*, the strengthening of European security and the improvement of American-Soviet relations.[112] All the Soviet writers consider that the processes connected with the restructuring of international relations have affected internal developments in the 'imperialist camp' — *inter alia*, they have sharpened all the inter-imperialist contradictions.

Arms control and the correlation of world forces

The arms control negotiations, particularly SALT, have seemed to be fully compatible with Marxist-Leninist ideas about the correlation of world forces and with its corollary, the theory of peaceful coexistence. Soviet writers have stated that the SALT negotiations should aim to:
(1)   reduce the strategic arsenals and the resources devoted to nuclear armament;
(2)   strengthen the parity in the offensive strategic nuclear capabilities of the two main adversaries, thereby enhance the strategic stability;
(3)   help to prevent a thermonuclear war;
(4)   help to control crisis situations;
(5)   facilitate further arms control negotiations concerning all other kinds of weapons.
    Western politicians and writers think, however, that to Soviet leaders the SALT negotiations were to serve the same aims as those served by the advantageous correlation of world forces. In this context, the purposes of participation in these negotiations would be the following:
(1)   To favour the Soviet political and military strategies by improving their capacitites to fulfil their aims. In particular, the SALT negotiations were to improve the survival outlook for the Soviet control apparatus — i.e., the government, party and military leaderships;
(2)   Gradually to improve the global correlation of strategic nuclear forces to the advantage of the Soviet Union and thereby improve the situation for the covert or open use of conventional forces and non-military means of pressure;[113]
(3)   Thereby to open the way to new political and psychological gains;
(4)   To use in furtherance of these aims not only the *results* of the SALT negotiations but also *the fact of participation in such negotiations.* These would constitute a smoke-screen for a rapid Soviet military

build-up;

(5) To use the negotiations as propaganda for the peaceful policy of the Soviet Union and a condemnation of the 'aggressive policy' of the United States and NATO.

These were considered to be the real aims of Soviet diplomacy in the arms control negotiations and they were sharply criticised by many Western politicians and writers and used as a weapon against those at home who wished to curb the arms race. The common theme was that the United States should try to correct the negative global military balance by building up certain important weapons-systems, and that the SALT negotiations were only tipping the balance more against the West. Much of the argument was devoted to a group of problems concerning the USSR's acquisition of a 'thermonuclear war-winning capability'. The critics maintained that, in future, the Soviet bloc might use their new superiority in important fields of strategic nuclear weaponry in one or another military scenario. History showed, they said, that when a country achieved military superiority it was always tempted to exploit this, even when such superiority formed no part of its political grand design.

(Such arguments seem to this author to be unjustified, since no superiority in any component of nuclear strategic capabilities can be a sufficient incentive for any country to take the risk — amounting to a certainty — of being destroyed. In this respect, the present correlation of military forces may be regarded as representing, regardless of any possible changes, a factual stable balance of terror.)

The parity between the two superpowers was said to have rendered obsolete the entire strategy of NATO, since the US nuclear umbrella had disappeared. The strategic balance between the superpowers had led to a strategic imbalance in Europe, which might be the principal theatre of war.[114]

On the whole, therefore, the SALT negotiations were considered by some Western writers to be counter-productive, and to contribute to the maintenance of Soviet superiority instead of leading to parity. They would accelerate the arms race instead of slowing it down and they would only heighten the tension.

In contrast to these pessimistic and critical comments, Marxist-Leninist writers said that the pro-socialist correlation of world forces — especially its military component — and the successful deterrence of the West from military enterprises, were factors impelling the United States to engage seriously in arms control negotiations. At the same time that state of the correlation in which the side aiming at peaceful coexistence was equal, if not superior, to the 'world forces of war', favoured the attainment of positive results.

All the above-mentioned influences of the correlation of world forces culminate in its impact on the 'law-like' process which develops in the realm of international relations and which is, in the Soviet view, peaceful coexistence. Soviet writers occasionally state that peaceful coexistence is not a particular political programme but rather a *law* in our times, according to which there is no alternative to peace among the nations of the world. War has become too dangerous and is counterproductive for all the participants.

The 'law of peaceful coexistence' favours socialism, since in a peaceful world — and thanks to the favourable correlation of world forces — socialism can constantly achieve new victories in its economic, ideological and political struggle against capitalism. However, this means that the struggle will continue. The theory of the inevitability of war has now been replaced by the assumption of the inevitability of the ideological struggle between states with different social systems under conditions of peaceful coexistence.[115]

Peaceful coexistence constitutes a set of ideas about the aims of a policy of peace and about how it can be achieved, and at the same time it means the policy itself. The cornerstone of this theoretical and practical construction is the assumption that the socialist camp has grown strong enough to overcome imperialism and the forces working for an imperialist peace or an imperialist war.

Never before have the fate of millions of people, the direction and results of the class struggle inside particular countries so greatly depended on the alignment and correlation of world forces, on the state of international relations, and on the way major international issues are settled. This, say the Marxist-Leninists, is because the course internal processes take in individual countries and the very existence of these countries largely depend on whether a new world war with the use of nuclear missiles can be averted.[116]

However, the Marxist-Leninists accept that the advantageous correlation of world forces is only one of two complex and interconnected groups of factors which have much to do with the prevention of interstate wars.[117] The other group concerns processes in the productive forces: the ongoing scientific and technical revolution and its technomilitary consequences.

The development of the productive forces has also meant the development of military technology and this has made war an extremely dangerous adventure. The growing importance of the international division of labour, the development of foreign trade and of international economic contacts and the increase in the independence of the economies of the various countries also favours the cause of peace.

The shifts in American policy, the ups and downs in cooperation between the NATO states, the unexpected developments in several countries of the Third World, and other events have apparently modified the Soviet thesis of the direct and unequivocal impact of the correlation of world forces. Without changing the basic proposition about the decisive impact of this correlation in the *long run* on the *general* course of events, and on the principal issue of the prevention of an all-out war, they have begun to point out some limitations on the impact.

In the first place, the correlation of world forces is not the only factor that affects the strategy of the imperialist powers. Various international and domestic factors of an economic, social, ideological and moral-political nature also produce their effects. The international division of labour, international trade and relations with developing countries are among the main external factors. Second, the subjective factor — the policy of governments — also plays an important role. The impact of the correlation of forces on such strategy is affected by (a) the perception of national interests; (b) class interests and aims among the governing élites and different perceptions of the possibilities of realising them; and (c) the requirements of domestic policy.

Third, the subjective assessment of the correlation of world forces, combined with the perception of domestic and international class interests, may push policy into quite different political channels. In the view of Soviet authors, for instance, the pro-socialist correlation of world forces in the early 1970s, combined with the Soviet insistence on *détente,* moved Presidents Nixon and Ford *towards* accepting such a policy; this contributed to the partial successes of the *détente* era. Afterwards, however, under the conditions of the same correlation, and in spite of it, the militaristic clique in the United States, fearing a further deterioration of the correlation, turned the policies of Carter and Reagan *against détente.*[118] In the former case, the ruling élite decided to accept the fact of the changed correlation and to adapt itself to this state of affairs; in the latter case they decided to try to reverse the trend. Thus the class character of imperialist policy may produce different variants of the political line.

Finally, in spite of the steady change in the correlation of world forces to the advantage of socialism, imperialism is still strong. Thus the global assessment of the outcome of the hitherto acquired advantages has been toned down. While previously world socialism was said already to gain advantage over world capitalism, now it has been stated that 'there is today, for the first time in history a rough balance between imperialism and its opponents. That means that the world has reached a kind of watershed in its transition from capitalism to socialism.'[119]

The change in the correlation of forces in the favour of socialism

187

'does not necessarily have to be continuous', writes Shakhnazarov. 'In today's complex and varied world longer or shorter delays are possible in this historical process, or even temporary setbacks. The rate of change can be uneven and deviations from the general line indicated by the objective laws of history cannot be excluded. Finally, only primitive determinists would exclude the possibility of phenomena which could cut short the progress (the simplest example of such a phenomenon is a world nuclear war)'.[120]

Therefore, although the correlation of world forces is steadily changing in favour of socialism, there are still no grounds for claiming a decisive advantage over imperialism.[121] It continues to dominate in a large group of developed capitalist countries and by several neo-colonial methods it exploits the riches of the countries of the Third World and directly or indirectly controls the policy of a number of them. All class forces which are hostile to social transformations are on the side of imperialism, and there are also forces which oscillate between the imperialist and socialist world-wide camps.

Therefore, although the main direction of development is predetermined, and although under the existing correlation of world forces the possibilities of imperialism to act in an arbitrary way have been sharply reduced, the danger of various types of war breaking out has remained.[122] In particular, local aggressive wars initiated or instigated by imperialist powers cannot yet be excluded. Moreover, Soviet scholars began to warn against a simplified way of assessing the correlation of world forces and against the view that constantly new victories of socialism are predetermined.

The assessment of the correlation of world forces is incomparably more complicated than that of the correlation in a particular area and at a particular time. It is difficult to take into account the great number of factors which contribute to forming this correlation, some of which have a variable magnitude and are capable of behaving in unforeseen ways. The path of development of the historical process, with sudden turns which defy the imagination, is hardly to be calculated and predicted. It is only a retrospective analysis of the international relations and of the *direction of social development* which allows to assess the correlation of world forces and the chances of the class forces which oppose one another in the world area.

This statement by G. Shakhnazarov,[123] one of the leading theorists of the concept of the correlation of world forces, contrasts sharply with his own numerous analyses of the state of this correlation, its component parts, their expected development and their concrete impact on world affairs.

However, he still asserts that just with this approach there can be no doubt that the correlation of world forces in the world is steadily changing (although at different rates and not without the occurrence of the reverse phenomena at different times) in favour of socialism.

Notes

1 'Only the proletarians can destroy nationality' ('Das Fest der Nationen in London' in Karl Marx and Friedrich Engels, *Historisch-Kritische Gesamtausgabe,* Frankfurt-Berlin, Marx-Engels Verlag, 1927—1932, vol. 4, p. 460). To be sure, Marx and Engels often mentioned that even after a world revolution certain inequalities in the conditions of life (for instance, springing from the differences in the geographical conditions) between particular countries, provinces or other kinds of political units would remain, but they would not be political. Horizontal diversity would not lead to a horizontal division into separate administrative units, i.e. quasi-states. Cf. Kubalkova, Cruickshank, 1980, pp. 49 ff.

2 Some examples from an extensive bibliography: Bunkina, 1970; Shakhnazarov, 1978; Inozemtsev, 1978; *Protsess formirovaniya i osushchestvleniya vneshnei politiki kapitalisticheskikh gosudarstv,* 1981; *Mezhdunarodnye konflikty sovremennosti,* 1983.

3 Cf. Martin, 1975, 1977; Bunkina, 1970; Shakhnazarov, 1974, 1977, 1979, 1982, 1984; Tyushkevich, 1974; Zhurkin, 1974; Kortunov, 1977, 1978; Tomashevskii, 1971, Ch. 3; Arbatov, 1973, 1983; *Problemy voennoi razryadki,* 1981; *Mezhdunarodnye konflikty sovremennosti,* 1983.

4 Martin, 1977, p. 28.

5 Martin, 1975, pp. 1960—3. The main theme in Sheidina, 1984.

6 The Russian term is *sootneshenie sil v mire;* concerning an equilibrium of power, the term *ravnovesie sil* is used.

7 Cf. Note 3.

8 *The Road to Communism,* Foreign Languages Publishing House, Moscow 1961, p. 465; *The Fundamentals of Marxist-Leninist Philosophy,* 1982; *The Basics of Marxist-Leninist Theory,* 1982, Ch. XX.

9 *Voennaya strategiya,* 1st ed., 1962, p. 3; 2nd ed., 1963, p. 3; 3rd ed., 1968, pp. 7—8.

10 Shakhnazarov, 1974, 1977; Tyushkevich, 1974.

11 Shakhnazarov writes that the particular international events are determined by the interaction of three policies: those of the antagonistic systems, of particular states and of international movements (1977).

12 Cf. Ch. II.4. C and D. in this study.

13 *Fundamentals of Political Science,* 1979, pp. 434—5.

14 *The Theory and Practice of Proletarian Internationalism*, 1980, p. 12.
15 Sergiyev, 1975.
16 Shakhnazarov, 1979, pp. 45—6.
17 Ibid., p. 46.
18 Cf. Zagladin, 1985, p. 70.
19 Shakhnazarov, 1982, pp. 70, 80 a.o.
20 Zagladin sees it as the decisive factor in the struggle for peace (1985, p. 70).
21 For instance, Tomashevskii, 1971. Martin writes: 'In the framework of the general international correlation of forces the relation between the USSR and USA has a special importance, USSR exerts the decisive impact on the international correlation of forces' (1975, p. 1963).
22 Shakhnazarov, 1974, 1977. In the latter study he also includes the public opinion which in particular cases can significantly influence the course of events (e.g., as it did in the Vietnamese war, he says).
23 *Sovremennaya epokha i mirovoi revolutsionnyi protsess*, 1970; *Fundamentals of Political Science*, 1979; *Mezhdunarodnye konflikty sovremennosti*, 1983.
24 Lebedev, 1980, p. 104.
25 Aspaturian is apparently wrong when he writes that according to the Soviet view the correlation of world forces is determined by social and historical processes in which the policy of states is only a component and that it can be affected *only marginally* by state policy; that it derives from many variables which operate independently of state policies. The opposite is true: a conscious policy on the part of states — for instance, both the United States and the Soviet Union — is regarded as the *key* factor affecting the correlation of world forces. Aspaturian contradicts himself when he writes that Soviet leaders know that 'the most direct and quickest way to affect the correlation of forces is to increase one's military might' (1980, pp. 10.11).
26 Thus the assertion by Bialer that in the Soviet view the advance of the cause and the increase of the forces of socialism represents a historical process and that peaceful coexistence represents a political strategy of the Soviet Union seems unnecessarily to stress the distinction between a 'process' and an 'active policy'; here the 'process' is also a result of an active policy (1980, p. 243).
27 One of the main themes in Bunkina, 1970. Cf. a detailed analysis of the centrifugal and centripetal tendencies in NATO and their impact on the doctrine and policy of the alliance in Khalosha, 1982. Cf. *USA, Westeuropa, Japan-imperialistische Zentren der*

Rivalität, IPW-Forschungschefte, 1/1976, Staatsverlag der DDR, Berlin.

28   Shakhnazarov, 1979, p. 40.

29   *Afrika: strany sotsialisticheskoi orientatsii*, Izd. 'Nauka', Moscow 1976.

30   *Razvivayushchiesya strany: zakonomernosti, tendentsii, perspektivy*, Moscow 1974.

31   Shakhnazarov, 1979, Ch. IV.

32   Ibid., p. 321.

33   Ibid., p. 326.

34   Ibid., p. 325.

35   A. Filuyov, 'In the labyrinth of numbers', *International Affairs*, 1974:7; he reviews the study of Bruce M. Russett, (ed.), *Peace, War, and Numbers*, Sage, London 1972. 'According to the Soviet concept, the correlation of forces between the two systems is a correlation of their *class* forces and not of their military strength .... The correlation of class forces includes such elements as: the economic potential and the solidity of the economic structure of society; the extent of cooperation between its different classes and strata; the population's support for the government; the impact and efficiency of state power; the political and ideological unity and strength of society; the amount of cooperation and cohesion of the states and the political forces in the system as a whole' (Voslensky, 1975, p. 2). '... bourgeois political thinkers, as a rule, ignore the class essence and content of international relations and the class character of a state's foreign policy. They take great pains to conceal the fact that the foreign policy of a state expresses the interests of the ruling class. That is why most bourgeois specialists in international affairs reduce the correlation of forces in the world to mere estimates and comparisons of the states' economic and military potentials' (Sergiyev, 1975, p. 100). And further: 'Contrary to the concepts of bourgeois politologists, Marxist-Leninist theory proceeds from the fact that the category of correlation of forces in the world cannot and should not be reduced to the correlation of the military potentials of states, and that in the final analysis this is no more than the correlation of class forces in the world-wide system of international relations' (p. 100). Lenin is quoted concerning the necessity of analysing and taking into account the correlation of power between the world's two basic forces: the world working-class and the world bourgeoisie (p. 100).

36   Shakhnazarov, 1984, p. 53. Cf. the components of the technical potential described by Sheidina, 1984, p. 36.

37   One of the main themes in Sheidina, 1984.

38   'In politics', writes Shakhnazarov, 'attention is paid to the broad-

ness of the social base of the state power, the way in which it is organised, the constitutional regulation of relations between government and legislative bodies, the ability to take efficient decisions, the extent to which the population supports the domestic and foreign policy, the presence or absence of opposition' (1984, p. 59).

39 Tomashevskii, 1971. He terms it 'indirect sources' of military power. The military strength of each capitalist country is potentially directed against socialism and social progress, and in this sense it is a component element in the total military power of imperialism. But at the same time the military power of individual countries conflicts politically, to a certain degree, with the military power of imperialism as a whole and seriously inhibits the political use of this power against the international socialist system and other forms of social progress *(Voennaya sila i mezhdunarodnye otnosheniya*, 1972, p. 219).

40 Tomashevskii, 1971; Arbatov, 1973.

41 Sergiyev, 1975:5, p. 102.

42 *Voennaya sila i mezhdunarodnye otnosheniya*, 1972, pp. 222—3.

43 Kosolapov, 1983, Ch. I.1: 'Ob'ekt issledovaniya. Dialektika ob'ektivnogo i sub'ektivnogo v mezhdunarodnykh othosheniyakh i vo' vneshnepoliticheskom protsesse gosudarstva'. Cf. Shakhnazarov, 1984.

44 Shakhnazarov, 1984, p. 79.

45 Ibid., pp. 70—1.

46 Shakhnazarov, 1984; Kapchenko, 1985; Sheidina, 1984, Ch. Four.

47 Theorists of balance of power emphasise that in a system based on it 'military power considerations outweigh ideological considerations' (Padeldorf, et al., 1976, p. 311). 'Balance of power politics reject ideological prejudices and commitments because they introduce rigidities and distracting elements into the balancing of power. States must be ready to re-examine their own interests and shift alliances based closely upon the calculation of power in the service of national interests' (ibid. pp.312—13). In the balance of terror period (1948-mid 1960s) and the emergent tight bipolarity 'the ideas concerning the priority of ideological considerations' are negated (p. 312). Such ideas are rooted in the treatment of 'ideology' and 'ideological differences' quite differently from the Marxist-Leninist theory. In the above-mentioned comments ideology simply means a kind of *national political doctrine* which is different from the Marxist-Leninist concept of *class ideology.* The latter sees in the world two contrary ideologies, the bourgeois and the proletarian one, capitalistic and socialistic, while in Padeldorf's approach ideological

differences mean differences in national interests, and any shift in alliance rooted in conflicts of national interests can be named change in ideology. Cf. Shakhnazarov, 1984, Part II, Ch. 3.

48 Shakhnazarov, 1984, p. 81.
49 Arbatov, 1983, p. 143.
50 Kirshin, 1982; Kapchenko, 1983; Kortunov, 1983; Tolkunov, 1984; Ziborov, 1984; Shakhnazarov, 1984.
51 Ziborov, 1984.
52 Tolkunov, 1984, p. 45.
53 Shakhnazarov, 1984, p. 80.
54 Kortunov, 1983.
55 Vidyasova, 1984; Puchkovsky, 1983.
56 *Razryadka mezhdunarodnoi napryazhennosti i ideologicheskaya bor'ba*, Akademiya Nauk SSSR, Izd. 'Nauka', Moscow 1981, p. 33.
57 Ibid., p. 32. 'The process of the struggle of ideas is objective and it cannot be eliminated' (p. 34).
58 N. Kapchenko, 'The Problem of Preserving Peace and the Ideological Struggle', *International Affairs*, 1983:7, the main theme.
59 The Soviet policy of *détente* set against the US policy of preparations for war is the main theme in *Razryadka mezhdunarodnoi napryazhenhosti i ideologicheskaya bor'ba*, 1981.
60 Kapchenko, 1983, p. 9.
61 Gromyko, 1984, p. 568.
62 Kapchenko, 1985, p. 47.
63 Shakhnazarov, 1984, p. 80.
64 Kapchenko, 1985, p. 47.
65 Ibid., p. 11.
66 Y. Kashlev, Y. Kolosov, 'Psychological Warfare — A Weapon of Reaction', *International Affairs*, 1983:10+.
67 Kirshin, 1982.
68 Arbatov, 1983, pp. 142—3.
69 V. Kulish, 'Socialist International Relations: Substance and Development Trends', *International Affairs*, 1983:7, p. 87. Cf. Ryzhkov, 1984; Rybakov, Shiryayev, 1984.
70 *The Theory and Practice of Proletarian Internationalism*, 1976, Ch. 2; Kulish, 1983, p. 87.
71 Cf. *The Theory and Practice of Proletarian Internationalism*, 1976, pp. 80—1.
72 Ibid., Ch. 2.
73 Ibid., p. 57.
74 Ibid:
75 1983, p. 18.
76 Menshikov, 1984, p. 99.
77 Rybakov, Shiryayev, 1984, p. 22.

78 Rybakov, Shiryayev, 1984, p. 21; Ryzhkov, 1984, p. 8.
79 Ryzhkov, 1984; Menshikov, 1984; Rybakov, Shiryayev, 1984.
80 Cf. Inozemtsev, 1978, p. 40.
81 *Razryadka mezhdunarodnoi napryazhennosti i ideologicheskaya bor'ba* V, 1981, Ch. VIII. 4, pp. 318—25.
82 *The Document of the 1969 International Meeting of Communist and Workers' Parties*, in Shakhnazarov, 1979, p. 175.
83 Shakhnazarov, 1979, p. 176.
84 Inozemtsev, 1978, p. 40.
85 Y. Novopashin, 'Socialist International Relations and Anti-communism', *International Affairs*, 1983:10, p. 62.
86 Ibid., pp. 60—2. Novopashin accuses V. Kubalkova and A.A. Cruickshank (1981) for advocating the view that states have been born even more unequal than individuals; he takes, however, this sentence out of context.
87 One of the main themes in Bunkina, 1970. Cf. *Mezhdunarodnye konflikty sovremennosti,* 1983.
88 Tomashevskii, 1971: 'Problema sootnosheniya sil v mirovoi politike', pp. 61—101.
89 'Therefore, when calculating the correlation of forces, it must be taken into consideration that the international arena has its own type of "wandering" values, which in each concrete case can significantly influence the outcome of events' (Shakhnazarov, 1974, p. 87).
90 Tomashevskii, 1971, pp. 230—1.
91 'In each concrete case and at each given moment the intersection of the course followed by the social systems, the policies pursued by countries, and the line of action of revolutionary, counter-revolutionary and intermediate movements forms an intricate pattern of forces predetermining the outcome of current international events' (Shakhnazarov, 1974).
92 Therefore 'it would be highly imprudent to draw general conclusions on the basis of individual facts. For example, the victory of the Cuban revolution in 1959 cannot be regarded as a sign that socialism had achieved an absolute preponderance of strength over imperialism, just as the fascist military coup in Chile in 1973 cannot be regarded as evidence of the reverse. It is only the totality of events considered from the standpoint of their dynamics that can give ground for a correct judgment of the balance of strength in the world and, most important, of how that balance is changing' (Shakhnazarov, 1974, p. 51; Cf. 1977, p. 92).
93 Bunkina, 1970, p. 120.
94 'The Soviet concept of the correlation of forces contains only one — but certainly very important — predetermined point: the

final victory of socialism on a world scale. The consequences of this is the following approach to the correlation-of-forces problem: since the laws of history prescribe a constant shift of the correlation of forces in favour of the socialist system, only such a development of the correlation of forces is legitimate; to attempt a social and political change in the opposite direction, or even to preserve the existing status quo in the correlation of forces, is a "modern version of the imperialist policy of exporting counter-revolution" ' (Shakhnazarov, 1974, p. 44). The preservation of the balance of power in the world today is, from this point of view, precisely the same as the previous "liberation" and "roll back" doctrines (ibid.). While the bourgeois politologists contend that 'any state seeks by its foreign policy to "stabilize" the system of international relations — i.e., to retain this system in its initial state', Soviet scholars see in it an outcome of diverse policies, which result in a momentary balance at the moment within a general trend towards development, this development being of 'natural character' (Sergiyev, 1975).

95 W.I. Lenin, *Werke*, Bd. 33, Berlin 1971, p. 133.
96 A West German writer asserts that the second shift in the correlation of international forces took place on the eve of the Second World War, when the Soviet Union, which just achieved internal stability, became an important participant in the conduct of world politics (Walter Schilling, 'Die sowjetische Einschätzung der internationalen Machtverteilung', *Europäische Wehrkunde*, 1970:9, p. 426).
97 Martin writes that the achievement by the Soviet Union of superiority in several fields of military technology was in the early 1970s of great importance for the shift in the correlation of international forces (1975, p. 1707).
98 Zagladin, 1985, p. 73. Cf. Zarodov, 1981, Chapter II.
99 Shakhnazarov, 1984, p. 61.
100 Zagladin, 1985, p. 70.
101 *Mezhdunarodnye konflikty sovremennosti*, 1983, Ch. II.5, especially pp. 153—70.
102 The main theme in Sheidina, 1984, is that the United States have been compelled to shift the emphasis from the use of military to non-military means in foreign policy.
103 Ibid., pp. 160—1.
104 Sheidina, 1984, pp. 45 ff.
105 Shakhnazarov, 1984, p. 93.
106 For the impact of domestic factors on the process of formulating and accomplishing foreign policy of capitalist states see *Protsess formirovaniya i osushchestvleniya vneshnei politiki kapitalisticheskikh gosudarstv*, 1981, Chs. II and IV.

107 '... it is not the absolute strength of imperialism that is shrinking but its relative strength as compared with socialism. Imperialism as a system has constituted, and still constitutes, a threat to peace and social progress and any underestimation of it may prove fatal' (Sanakoyev, Kapchenko, 1976, p. 144).

108 Kortunov, 1977; Bykov, Razmerov, Tomashevskii, 1981, Ch. III. 'For Peaceful Coexistence and Cooperation'. 'The class character of contemporary international relations also determines the substance of *détente*. As a direct outcome of the continuing change in the balance of power in favour of socialism, it is a consequence of a world social progress, while it simultaneously promotes the development of that progress' (Kortunov, 1977, p. 105) 'The change in the balance of power has become the foundation for peaceful coexistence. The adaptation of this principle by capitalist states constitutes their reaction to the new world situation' (Sanakoyev, Kapchenko, 1976, pp. 84—5).

109 *Mezhdunarodnye konflikty sovremennosti*, 1983.

110 Cf. Bykov, Razmerov, Tomashevskii, 1981, pp. 34 ff.

111 One of the main themes of Kortunov, 1977. The bourgeois politology writes much about the crisis of international relations, but it is only the crisis of imperialist foreign policy; this necessitates the restructuring of international relations (p. 105). One of the main effects of the shift in the correlation of forces in favour of socialism is that it has created conditions for a fundamental restructuring of international relations. The power of the socialist communtiy is said to be the cause of such restructuring and the motivating force behind further changes in that direction (N.I. Lebedev, *A New Stage in International Relations*, Pergamon Press, Oxford 1978. Translated from Russian, 1976, the main theme of Ch. 2: 'Fundamental Changes in the World Balance of Power Affecting the Present Reshaping of International Relations'). Cf. L.I. Brezhnev, *Leninskim kursom*, Rechi i stat'i, Politizdat, Moscow 1978, vol. 6, pp. 115.

112 *Problemy voennoi razryadki*, 1981, pp. 11—13.

113 E.g. 'The Politburo utilizes arms talks ... as part of its grand design to further alter the correlation of forces in its favour' (Frank R. Barnett, 'Preface' to Paul H. Nitze, James E. Dougherty, Francis X. Kane, *The Fateful Ends and Shades of SALT. Past... Present... And Yet to Come*, Crane, Russak, New York 1979).

114 Raymond Aron, 1980.

115 Khalosha, 1982, p. 6.

116 *Fundamentals of Political Science*, 1979; Shakhnazarov, 1979, 1981.

117 Tomashevskii, 1971, Ch. 5. Cf. 3D in this chapter.

118 *Mezhdunarodnye konflikty sovremennosti,* 1983, pp. 156—8. Cf. *Problemy voennoi razryadki,* 1981, pp. 12—16.

119 Zagladin, 1985, p. 74.

120 Shakhnazarov, 1984, p. 18.

121 Ibid., pp. 61—2.

122 Ibid.

123 Shakhnazarov, 1984, p. 60. He also writes that the correlation of forces in the world cannot be measured and assessed accurately by means of merely a comparison of the resources of the protagonists, i.e., statically. Their measurement and assessment requires seeing it in a broad historical framework, and including in the assessment the expected change according to the content of the epoch. Our epoch, which is the epoch of the revolutionary transformation of capitalist society into communist, presupposes a change in the correlation of forces to the detriment of capitalism and in favour of socialism. This has been the constant feature of all world politics since October 1917 (1984, p. 18). Sanakoyev writes that in assessing the alignment of class and political forces in the world arena 'one should take into account not only economic and military factors but also the prospect for the social and political development of mankind as a whole' (1983, p. 19). Moreover, again Shakhnazarov, in a world which changes rapidly under the influence of both social and techno-scientific revolutions the real weight of the opposing forces cannot be measured in their static form, without account being taken of their potentials. Relying on the indices of development (tempo, rhythm), probable changes in resources by a particular date may be predicted. This facilitates the calculation of the correlation of forces in a particular area and at a particular time. It also facilitates the prediction of the course of events in concrete situations and at given moments. These depend on the intersection of the course of social systems, the policy of states, and the line of action of revolutionary, counterrevolutionary and intermediate movements (ibid., pp. 59—60).

124 Ibid., p. 61.

7 Correlation of world forces and other paradigmatic concepts

Criticism of balance-of-power concepts

Traditional criticisms

In Marxist-Leninist writings the concept of the correlation of world forces is set against the Western theories of the 'global balance of power'.[1]

This contrast may be compared with that between the concept of the correlation of intrasocietal forces and the non-Marxist theories of the intrasocietal balance of power (cf. Chapter 4).

The validity of the basic assumption underlying the so-called philosophy of power (or of political realism) was often questioned; the principle of this philosophy was that the drive for power as the motivating force of international relations must lead to the establishment of a balance of power which stabilised the world situation (cf. Chapter 2.)

Several objections to these and other — actual and alleged — positions have been raised, namely:

(1)   Balance-of-power theories over-emphasise military power as the determinant of the total power of states and groups of states. They disregard such factors of power as the socio-economic and political system and the policy pursued by the particular state, or states;[2] they also ignore moral-political potentialities. They disregard the laws of social development, which are a potent objective determinant of international relations.

(2)   Balance-of-power theories are based on a false — or at least an outmoded — view of the international system. They emerged at a time when the world of great powers consisted of homogeneous states and they ignore the view of the contemporary world as an arena for the struggle of two main historical social antagonists — states with different socio-economic and political systems, which are striving for the leading role in the world community. They also disregard the influence of dozens of smaller states on the course of events and the influence of international sociopolitical movements.

(3)   Instead, the balance of power theories propose various artificial models based on the concept of the interplay of a number of great powers which establish a kind of power balance as the main framework and structure of the international system. One suggested model is the 'triangle', consisting of the United States, the Soviet Union and China. Another is the 'Pentagon', the same three powers plus Western Europe and Japan. There is also a model which is a combination of two triangles, that of rivalry (the United States, the Soviet Union and China) and that of cooperation (the United States, Western Europe and Japan). There is a combination of a 'Western' triangle (the United States, Western Europe and the Soviet Union) with an 'Eastern' quadrangle (the United States, the Soviet Union, China and Japan).[3]

All such models are regarded by the Marxist-Leninist writers as distortions of the real picture and the real correlation of forces between the rivals.[4] They ignore the class differences between the main protagonists in the world struggle, and consequently they ignore the class nature of international relations. These relations, however, provide the medium for an internationalised class struggle in which the rivalry of the two antagonistic systems is the principal motive force. In other words, models based on a *fragmentation* of power divert attention from the basic division of power between the two camps, which represents the main contradiction of our epoch — from the dynamics of the basic relation of forces and from the main trend in the world's development. The replacement of the real picture of the world by the power concept permits a camouflage of the class content of imperialist foreign policies;[5] it also aims to take the ideology out of international relations.[6]

Moreover, the criteria by which the 'powers' are defined are highly dubious. If military power is a criterion, then Japan falls out of the model. If political and economic power and the capability for waging a common, consistent and strong policy are the basis, Western Europe which is internally discordant and whose members wage policy following their own interests and often compete in the economic field, cannot be included.

(Besides, if groups of countries formed on a political, geographic, economic or other basis can be regarded as centres of power, then one has to recognise the same quality in Latin America, the Arab oil-producing states, and other groups.)

These inconsistencies may be explained by the diversification of power which now consists of many components or takes many forms; this results in 'asymmetries' in power when a country may be economically very strong while militarily weak (e.g. Japan), or vice versa: economically weak but in some military respects strong (e.g. China and India which possess nuclear weapons).[7]

The theory of two blocs, which is a variant of balance-of-power theories, does not satisfy the Soviet critics either.[8] This theory asserts that East and West form two opposing centres of power which together determine the resolution of the most important conflicts. It disregards the social nature of the opposing camps and the fundamental difference in their aims and the role of the world, reduces them to traditional interstate alliances and attributes to them similar power-politics. The historical competition of the forces of progress and the forces of reaction is here replaced by a geopolitical opposition of two groups of states which wage a 'normal' power game.

(4) Such an approach also diverts attention from the real causes of conflicts and wars, which reside in the character and policy of the imperialist states. It replaces the effective efforts for the prevention of war by the illusory idea of the balance of power.[9] In the traditional version, war was regarded as a necessary means of regulating international conflicts and — paradoxically enough — as one of the means of preserving the balance of power and thereby maintaining a relative stability in international relations. This idea is said still to lie heavy on the contemporary versions of the balance-of-power theories. It helps to perpetuate war as a phenomenon inherent in social life.[10]

(5) Balance-of-power theories ignore the impact of several powerful factors other than states. They cannot explain the emergence and impact of the new factors affecting international relations such as the international communist movement, national liberation movement, non-aligned movement, peace movement, political movements associated with various religions (primarily Christian and Islamic), and others.

Nor can they explain the dual role played by the social-democratic movement with its dual class nature and internal struggle between the right and left wings. There is no place in these theories for such factors as the world public opinion and mass media, with their both structural and functional character, which have acquired an autonomous influence on the international climate and the resolution of particular issues.[11]

(6) Balance-of-power theories have always been used by the great capitalist powers to justify their policy of domination.[12] While claiming to play the role of 'balancers' — states that ensure equilibrium — the great powers in fact aimed at controlling world policy. They interfered in relations between other countries in order to make significant political and economic gains for themselves. The United Kingdom

played such a role in the nineteenth century, and the United States has attempted to do likewise in our times.[13] This policy was supported by traditional geopolitical ideas which interpreted and justified the foreign policy of the great powers in terms of their geographical location.[14]

Accordingly, the balance-of-power theories in the past neither prevented wars aiming at *conquest* and the transformation of a system (or rather a region, such as Europe) into an *empire,* nor protected the *independence* of states. On the contrary, they contributed to the dependence of weak states on the powers which were members of the balance-of-power system. Nor did they provide conditions for establishing and maintaining the international institutions on which an international order might be based; one recalls the impotence of the League of Nations.

(7) Balance-of-power theories have acquired a particularly reactionary character in the present situation, and for two main reasons. First, they have been used to justify the build-up of a network of anti-socialist blocs and bases and to make preparations for war against the socialist countries. The United States pursued this policy also with another aim: to increase its political and military influence on its allies.[15] Second, these theories have been used to justify the suppression of movements that strive for national liberation or social revolution on the grounds that changes in the internal structure of states — and consequently in their posture in international affairs — may change the world balance of power in favour of socialism.[16]

In sum, these are theories pursuing the preservation of the political and socio-economic status quo, which means the 'containment' of socialism.[17]

(8) The balance-of-power concept presupposes a free play of forces — a game, in which each participant aims at increasing its power by making alliances. Every state plays at its own risk and takes into account basically its own rules. The wars to which such balance-of-power games lead — and which are one of the methods in the game — have not changed much in the international situation in the nineteenth century, but in our times they may lead to the destruction of civilisation. The stake would be not less or more power but the survival of the human race. Stability can be achieved only by a concerted action undertaken by all states and aiming at the elimination of all interstate wars.[18]

(9) In view of the actual state of the correlation of world forces, balance-of-power theories and the respective models have no chance of being realised. There is no equal distribution of power between a number of states; no state has the strategic advantage of being a 'central balancing mechanism'; and, since war is too dangerous, no constant 'adjustment' of the balance of power by means of war is possible.[19] On the contrary, the rivalry of the imperialist powers makes it almost impossible to achieve a stable agreement concerning a division of the

spheres of political, economic and military influence, even within the capitalist part of the world.

(10) Finally, it has been said, all balance-of-power theories regard power separately from the aims to which it may be used and their relation to the direction of world development. Power of any social or political force, which acts on behalf of social progress, i.e., the revolutionary transition of society and of the international system from capitalism to socialism acquires an *additional strength,* indeed it is becoming invincible, since it acts in accordance with the operation of inexorable objective laws of history. This force takes sides with the future against the past, with the new against the old, with the progressive against the reactionary. In the long run, the *direction* of the action i.e., of the application of power, determines its outcome. This is particularly important in our transitional and revolutionary epoch.[20]

Modification of Soviet position

The gradual development of the theory of international relations by Marxist-Leninist — and particularly Soviet — writers, even if it has not softened the criticism of the traditional and contemporary Western balance-of-power theories, has led the Marxist-Leninists to accept certain systemic features of international relations system linked to balance-of-power ideas, although in their writings such theories have acquired a quite different interpretation (see Chapter 2).[21]

The point of departure of the modified Marxist-Leninist approach is the acceptance of the fact that there exist certain regularities characteristic of the mechanism of the functioning of the international system which are inherent in its very structure. The principal 'law' is that concerning the maintenance of a dynamic balance. The existence of a politico-military balance between states is the basis of the normal functioning of the entire interstate system. It serves the maintenance of the system as a whole, the preservation of its principal features and characteristics in the process of its functioning and development. It is based on the interaction and balance of two contradictory elements: the changeability of particular elements (or states) and the relative stability of the ties between them (i.e., of the structure of the entire system).

Since there is no supervisory and controlling authority, the international system belongs to the class of systems which are governed by a spontaneous self-regulating mechanism. The balance results from the interaction of a multitude of conflicting interests, aims and actions of states and coalitions of states. There is never an absolute balance, but only a *tendency* to establish such a balance which proceeds through an unlimited chain of non-balanced conditions.

The forms of the operation of the 'law' of maintenance of the balance are different in different epochs. The concept of a bipolar dynamic balance in our epoch may be accepted by Marxism-Leninism, but only on condition that it be regarded as merely a transitory structural-functional aspect of the system. By this the Soviet writers seem to mean that the opposite *social* characteristics of the two main forces of the contemporary world which involves a continuous change of the system towards socialism must be emphasised as the other — and perhaps the most important — characteristics of the international system.

It should also be noted that Soviet writers see *three* meanings in the term 'balance of power'. One is the relation of forces in the international system as a certain *objective condition,* and the manifestation of the above-mentioned objective law. The second is the *politics of the balance of power* engaged in by particular bourgeois states. Such politics usually aim at changing the balance in favour of particular states.[22] The third meaning is the reflection of the objective law in theoretical and political *thinking* which takes the form of various political and theoretical conceptions and — if officially adopted — of state *doctrines.* In the Soviet view, the doctrines of 'containment', of 'roll back', of 'massive retaliation' and the like, which were said to aim at preserving the balance of power, in fact were used to justify a determined policy pursued by the imperialist states, which endangered the balance of power.

The other theoretical 'concession' to the theory of the balance of power is the acceptance by Soviet writers of the *bipolarity* of power as characteristic of the contemporary form of the international system. However, they point out that power cannot be reduced to military power and, besides, that this bipolarity is very vulnerable to a policy of destabilisation, should one of the two pillars aim at superiority; any gain by one side would mean the defeat of the other side. In practice, it is the imperialistic 'pillar' which is said to be trying to introduce a permanent imbalance into international relations.

Basic differences remain

However, the differences between the concepts of the balance of power, some versions of which may be tolerated in Marxist-Leninist writings, and the dominating concept of the correlation of world forces, remain. To all the above-mentioned distinctions which are rooted in the different philosophies of international relations, and in the first line to the social heterogeneity of the opposing world forces (the balance-of-power theory traditionally dealt with homogeneous states), a further distinction should be added. This points to the different views of the very nature of balance of power. While balance of power in the form now accepted by the Soviets means, first, a transitory balance, and, second, some rough equality of power — although dynamic and attained through the interaction of many imbalances — the correlation of world forces does not. It means an inherent qualitative *superiority* of one force — the socialist one — and at the very least a clear *tendency* of this side to grow ever stronger. This is said to reflect the objective development of the international system, in spite of all the transitory balances in particular periods. With this basic difference, both concepts coexist in contemporary Soviet theory.

Criticism of the Chinese paradigm

The Marxist-Leninist concept of the correlation of world forces is also set against the Chinese one, which has developed from Marxist views but is said to be degenerating into a kind of anti-Marxist version of balance of power theory.[23] This concept differs from the Marxist-Leninist views in its assessment of the main contradictions of our epoch, of the world structure, the characteristics of the basic social forces, the direction of world development and the role of armed violence in this.

Early versions

Although in the period immediately following the successful Chinese revolution the picture of the world struggle between socialism and imperialism in the political literature of China showed the former as being headed by the international working class and in this resembled the Soviet model, another concept very soon came to the fore. According to this, the struggle for national liberation, rather than the policy of the socialist states and the working-class revolutionary movement, constituted the main front of war against imperialism. The successful outcome of this struggle would represent the first stage of the world revolution, the second being a social revolution in the developed countries.

In the earlier version of this concept, which was presented in the late 1950s and 1960s, the world balance of power was viewed primarily as that between the 'world villages' (the underdeveloped countries of Asia, Africa and Latin America) and the 'world cities' (the capitalist countries of North America and Western Europe). In a later version two changes were introduced. First, the Soviet Union was presented as an imperialist state, which had ceased to function as a socialist state and had begun to compete with the United States for world domination. Second, the lesser capitalist countries were presented as a separate group. Both the 'world villages' and the lesser capitalist countries were described as being the objects of rivalry between the two superpowers.

In this framework — parallel to the main struggle of national liberation against imperialism, and as a part of the world struggle for revolution — a fight was going on between the superpowers to acquire spheres of influence. Thus at least three kinds of balance of power should be taken into account: (1) as regards the struggle for world revolution, the relation between the forces of national and social revolution and those of counter-revolution; (2) as regards the struggle of both the 'villages' and the lesser capitalist countries against the hegemonist policy of both superpowers, the balance of power between these two groups, and (3) the balance between the superpowers themselves.

'Three worlds' theory

In the 1970s, these ideas developed and resulted in a picture of the world as consisting of *three* camps called 'worlds'.[24] Mao Tse-tung wrote:

> In my view, the United States and the Soviet Union constitute the first world. Japan, Europe and Canada, the middle section, belong to the second world. We are the third world. The third world has a huge population. With the exception of Japan, Asia belongs to the third world. The whole of Africa belongs to the third world, and Latin America too.[25]

Mao was said to have presented here a new classification of world political forces and one which he regarded as necessary for the establishment of a new global strategy for conduct of revolutionary struggle.

The three main protagonists of the contemporary world, to which any concept of an alignment of world forces must relate, are described as follows.

The two 'imperialist superpowers', which constitute the *First World*, 'have become the biggest international exploiters, oppressors and aggressors and the common enemies of the peoples of the world'. Of these two, the Soviet Union is presented as 'the most dangerous source of world war'. This is because the Soviet Union is following on the heels of the United States and aims to re-divide the world by taking from the United States areas under the latter's control. The United States, which wants to protect its interests in the world, has gone over to the defensive in its overall strategy. The Soviet Union, which wants to expand, has decided to attack. Since the Soviet Union is inferior to the United States in economic strength, it must rely chiefly on its military power in order to expand. Because of the unprecedented centra-

206

lisation of the economy in the Soviet Union and the creation of a state-monopoly capitalist economy and a fascist dictatorship regime it is easier for this state than for the United States to put the entire economy on a military footing and militarise the whole apparatus of the state. Both of the superpowers are said to be competing to subjugate the Third World.[26]

The socialist countries and the oppressed nations of the *Third World* are the main force combatting imperialism and hegemonism. The workers' movement in the countries of the First and Second Worlds and the anti-imperialist fighters in the Third World support one another. It should be noted, however, that, in this concept, the workers' revolutionary movement in the developed capitalist countries must for the present remain at the stage of regrouping and gathering strength, since there is yet no revolutionary situation for an immediate take-over of state power.

In the Chinese view the Third World plays a leading role in the fight against imperialism, in spite of the differences in the social and political systems and in the level of economic development of the countries of that 'world', and in spite of the disputes and the armed conflicts that have occurred between them. China belongs to the Third World because it is both a socialist and a relatively poor but developing country.

The developed countries situated between the two 'worlds' described above constitute the *Second World*. They oppress and exploit the developing nations but are at the same time controlled and bullied by the superpowers. They have a dual character and represent an opposition to both of the either worlds. The socialist countries of Eastern Europe are included in this group: they are not regarded as socialist but are called 'East European countries'.

Topicality of the theory

Mao's death and the great changes subsequently made in the fields of economics and administration have not changed the basic tenets of the theory underlying the Chinese world policy, say the Marxist-Leninists. The rapprochement with the United States has confirmed and reinforced the political implications of this. Concluding an analysis of Chinese foreign and domestic policy, two Soviet researchers write: 'Everything seems to indicate that Maoism as the sum of ideological goals and practical actions will be shaping the main guidelines of Peking's political course for a long time to come and that no new crisis phenomena in Chinese politics will bring a rapid and fundamental change in the country's foreign or domestic policies'.[27]

In another collective work it is stated that the theory of the 'three worlds' has become 'the very core *(serdtsevina)* of the present foreign-policy-doctrine of the Maoists'. This theory constitutes a natural phase of the transition of the Maoist leadership to a counter-revolutionary policy.[28]

It is said that the developing militarisation of China and the continuing indoctrination of the people with the ideas of social-chauvinism and nationalism seem to fit the theoretical bases of political and military doctrine.

Criticisms of the Chinese views

The various criticisms of the Chinese concept of the world structure and world balance of power may be considered under three headings (1) the theoretical and ideological differences between this concept and that of the correlation of world forces; (2) the motives underlying the Chinese concept; (3) the political implications of this concept.

The first criticism concerns *the shift from the socialist focus* in the revolutionary struggle *to the national focus*. The Chinese consider that the national liberation struggle is replacing the revolutionary struggle headed by the working class and that the former 'socialist camp' has ceased to exist. 'In their view, the historical conditions do not require that it should be reestablished.' Not only the Soviet Union but the East European countries as well have ceased to be socialist. Class struggles in particular countries are said to have no impact on the global class struggle, which is dominated by the struggle for national liberation in various areas. A corollary is that the Third World has become the principal power that is capable of transforming the world. Second, the Chinese see no basic differences between the international *bourgeoisie* and the *working class* in general, and between their policies in particular; neither of them is regarded as monolithic; they are split and include both 'progressive forces' and diehards.

Moreover, in the Chinese concept class criteria have been abandoned in the assessment of the character of particular states. States have ceased to be either capitalist or socialist: now they are described as large or small, rich or poor, developed or underdeveloped, but without any sociopolitical characteristics.[29] The disregard of the domestic system and policy as the criterion of the classification of states and the denial of the dependence of foreign policy on the domestic structure lead to a grouping of states that is not based on their class character. They are not seen as belonging to socio-economic blocs consisting of states with a similar class structure. They are seen as 'worlds' — amorphous groups of states without any socio-economic common denominator. States having widely differing class characteristics are therefore classified together — for instance, the United States and the Soviet Union (in the 'First World'); United Kingdom and Czechoslovakia (in the 'Second World'); or China and Kenya (in the 'Third World').

A theory akin to this, which is a variant of the traditional 'power theories', asserts that the basic balance of power in the world is that between the rich countries of the North and the poor countries of the South. The confrontation of power of these two camps must lead to a physical clash, and superiority of power will determine the outcome. Soviet scholars condemn this Chinese theory (they call it a theory of 'petty-bourgeois leftist revolutionaries')[30] as substituting a contradiction that is sharp and important *per se* but derivative and secondary for the main contradiction of the epoch, that between capitalism and socialism. It attempts to divide the two greatest and allied revolutionary forces of our times — the international working-class movement and the national liberation movement — into national compartments and to make them opponents. Moreover, any action according to this theory would be suicidal to the 'South' which would be inevitably crushed by the powerful 'North'. All this is pure phantasy, however, since both 'camps' are abstract concepts, which would never take material shapes.

It is no wonder that in the Chinese paradigm the concept of the class division of the world and the *class struggle* for the future of mankind has *disappeared.* The world balance of power, which was formerly seen even by the Chinese as being based on a relation between the forces of the two antagonistic blocs of socialism and capitalism (or imperialism) no longer exists. Not only have the protagonists and the fronts of combat radically changed but the boundaries between them have become fluid. No hard and fast formulae can be laid down for distinguishing between the political forces in the world.

The concept of the correlation of world forces has been replaced by the concept of the struggle between the two imperialist powers for spheres of influence and the subjugation of peoples rather than for or against the sociopolitical reconstruction of the world on the basis of socialism.

Three political ideas and *three motivations* underlie this concept, it is held. The first is its sharp *anti-Sovietism,* which is crowned by the assertion that the Soviet Union has become a fascist state and the main instigator of wars in the world.

Therefore, say Soviet politicians and writers, 'the main thesis of the concept of "three worlds" is an appeal to all states to create a "united front" against the Soviet Union. This should include the United States'. The Maoists aspire to the ideological and leadership roles in the anti-socialist coalition.[31] The second motivation is the Chinese *drive towards world hegemony.* In China both the foreign policy and the domestic policy of indoctrination of the population convey a sense of the special role of the Chinese nation which was once on 'the summit of world civilisation' and of superiority to other nations. China prefers to observe the struggle of the two systems 'from the outside'. It may side with one of them or with one of the superpowers, according to circumstances; and finally it will emerge as the all-powerful state which can decide in the great questions affecting mankind. The third underlying idea of the Chinese paradigm is the *omnipotence of armed violence* as the ultimate means usable in all political conflicts in the domestic and international spheres — and the tendency to use this means.[32]

The basics of the Soviet criticism is that in the Chinese approach violence means armed violence, and revolution means armed revolution.[33] 'Maoism would like to push the variety of forms of the class battles of the proletariat and bourgeoisie and of socialism to the Procrustean Bed of armed force.'[34] Mao's statements that 'guns breed power' and that 'the world can be remodelled only with the gun' — which, according to the critics, underlie the Chinese ideology and policy — can only mean a glorification of armed violence.[35]

Finally, with regard to the *political implications* of the theory of the 'three worlds', the following criticisms have been made:

(1) The concept excludes the socialist world from any independent role in the international arena; the socialist countries are lumped together with the capitalist ones.

(2) The concept aims at splitting the socialist camp and undermining the unity of action of the anti-imperialist forces as a whole.[36]

(3) It sees China as cooperating with reactionary right-wing nationalistic states in the Third World.

(4) It sees China as an ally of the imperialist bloc in fight against socialism.[37]

(5) The concept of the 'three worlds' accepts the inevitability of a world war and directly supports the forces moving towards war. China confirms the implications of the theory of 'three worlds' in practice by openly preparing for a third world war.[38]

Assessment of the 'dependency' paradigms

Unlike their opposition to the balance-of-power concepts and the Chinese 'three-worlds theory', the Marxist-Leninist writers do not directly set the concept of the two world camps against the so-called 'theories of dependency'.

The ideas that are common to the many variants of the latter kind of theories may be presented in simplified form as follows:

(1) The world is divided not on the basis of geography, states, systems of government and so on, but according to the dichotomy of Centre and Periphery. The industrially developed nations constitute the Centre, the underdeveloped countries the Periphery. The Periphery has its corrupt indigenous élite, a bourgeois or semi-bourgeois stratum, which is connected and cooperates with the Centre. The Centre must be treated as a whole, since the whole Centre participates in the exploiting

relationship. (Only a few theorists see a duality also in the Centre — i.e., its division into centre and periphery.)

(2) The relationship between the Centre and the Periphery is characterised by the dominance of the former, the unequal distribution of wealth in its favour and its exploitation of the periphery.

(3) The relationship is therefore an asymmetric one, which allows the Centre to grow at the expense of the Periphery.

(4) The Periphery can change its dependent relationship, according to one group of theorists, by its own efforts, without changing the entire world system of interdependence between nations. A possibly larger group of theorists, however, consider that the entire world system must be changed 'at one go'.

The Marxist-Leninist — mainly Soviet — criticism of this view of the world structure is implied rather than openly expressed. Admittedly, Marxism-Leninism has some ideas in common with the 'dependency' theories, namely:

(1) The bipolar division of the world into 'exploiters' and 'exploited' which resembles the Marxist-Leninist assumption about the two 'world classes';

(2) The basic role of the uneven economic development of states and nations;

(3) The condemnation of the Periphery's élites as profiting, together with the Centre, from exploitation;

(4) The partial coincidence of the anti-Centre essence of the 'dependency' theories with the anti-imperialist essence of the Marxist-Leninist paradigm.

However, both the criteria of the division and the resulting world structure and the membership in the component parts of it, are questioned. The 'dependency theories' are criticised for the following deficiencies:

(1) They ignore the domestic socio-economic system and domestic social structure as the criterion of the world-wide division. They ignore capitalism and socialism as the basic antagonists and states with different domestic systems as the basic components of the opposing camps;

(2) They ignore the stratification and the internal struggle in the developed countries. The 'Centre' should be replaced by 'imperialism', i.e. by the governing economic-financial-military-political élites of a few leading imperialist powers;

(3) They disregard the heterogeneity of the Third World and the existence of rich countries there;

(4) They replace class criteria by the poor-rich (or underdeveloped-developed) dichotomy which leads to placing the Soviet Union and other developed socialist countries in the exploiting Centre;

(5) As a result of all these errors, the 'dependency theories' cannot propose a suitable way to end the exploitation and the underdevelop-

ment of the majority of countries in the Third World.[39]

As a corollary, it is said, too little attention is paid to the fact that the underdeveloped countries will have to get out of their 'underdog position' by their *own efforts* and by carrying out *social changes* (or even revolutions) at home.

Soviet writers also attack the critics of the 'dependency theories' who dismiss the argument that underdeveloped countries are poor because they are dependent. Likewise they disagree with the thesis that the exploitation of underdeveloped countries could and should be removed by increasing and enchancing relations of interdependence and by a large-scale interpenetration of the developed and underdeveloped sections of the world. Paradigms based on such interaction are said not to reflect the reality of our times, which means the rivalry between the antagonistic systems and the capitalist states; inequality of states; the lack of success in the attempts of a takeover of the functions of states by international and transnational organisations, and so on.

In their general assessment of the 'dependency theories', Soviet scholars see the entire relationship between the underdeveloped and the developed countries as a secondary rather than a primary front of world relations (the primary being the socialism-capitalism relationship), and therefore the 'dependency' paradigm must be wrong.

Western criticism of Soviet concepts

The Western criticism of the Soviet concept of the correlation of world forces[40] is in many respects 'symmetrical' to the Soviet criticism of Western theories of the global balance of power: the accusations are often similar.

Several Western criticisms concern the unscientific, and even misleading character of the concept of correlation of world forces.

(1) The concept of the correlation of world forces is based on a falsified picture of the international system as being allegedly governed by 'historical laws' that prejudge its development towards socialism.

(2) The Soviet concept is said to over-emphasise military power as the core of the total power ('forces') and to disregard the other components, particularly the economic potential.

At the same time, an apparently contrary criticism is expressed: that the Soviet leadership emphasises the combination of all means of state power. Previously, when the Soviet Union was inferior to the other states in the global relationship, the *strategy* of using a combination of means had to compensate for this. Now, because of the enormous increase in Soviet military power, the combination may serve as a powerful adjunct to *other* means of policy. The Soviet Union can achieve many of its political aims without resort to armed violence.[41]

This criticism seems to be only allegedly opposed to the initially mentioned, since here also military power plays the central role: without the threat of its use the use of the non-military means would be ineffective.

(3) The correlation is not measurable. There is a deliberate deception in the talk about a certain *assessment* of the correlation of forces when only a few components — the strategic-military and, in some respects, the economic component — are relatively measurable. It is even more deceptive to speak of a pro-Soviet global correlation, when only in one component — the strategic-military one — can there be anything like a global parity, or even a superiority in certain aspects, and when the latter must be viewed in conjunction with economic and other deficiencies.

(4) It is also a deception to speak about the irreversible character of the correlation, while it could be changed — even in the military component — in the reverse direction, if only the United States were to make an appropriate effort.

(5) While exaggerating the differences of interests in the Western alliance, the Soviet concept fails to mention the contradictions and disagreements in the socialist camp, or it reduces them to 'differences in national specifics' or in 'the levels of economic development'.

(6) The unscientific character of the concept is shown by the fact that the Soviet Union presents it in different forms to different audiences: to its supporters it says that the correlation of world forces is very advantageous, to the West that the East neither has achieved nor strives for superiority.

Another group of critical comments concerns the usefulness (or 'instrumentality') of the concept of the correlation of world forces as a direct means of policy.

(1) The concept in question is used by the Soviet leadership to justify both current and long-range policies of aggression. Several accusations are made under this heading.

  (a) The Soviet Union uses the concept of the correlation of world forces as a means of maintaining its domination in the socialist camp;

  (b) It uses the concept to justify the arms race and the accelerated build-up of its military power;

  (c) It justifies each act of aggression by 'historical laws' which oblige the Soviet Union to extend the sphere of socialism.

(2) The concept provides a convenient framework for making political and military demands. The allegedly advantageous global correlation of world forces is used as a pretext for demanding a global role for the Soviet Union — i.e., the right to co-decide on all problems and conflicts in the world. Assuming the position of strategic 'parity', the Soviet Union have also made several military demands in the course of SALT

negotiations. The Soviet Union is also trying — not without success — to achieve a military superiority in Europe, explaining this by its need to maintain *global* equality with the United States.

(3) The concept is used as a propagandistic means for separating Western Europe from the United States.

(4) The concept is a politico-propagandist means for winning over and influencing the countries of the Third World.

It helped the USSR in the 1960s and 1970s to undertake several steps to increase its activities, first economic and then military, in the Third World.

The final judgement is that the concept of the correlation of world forces (1) justifies aggression, (2) favours wars by explaining their outbreak as governed by 'laws of history' and (3) encourages the arms race.

To explain this Soviet emphasis on the correlation of world forces, Western researchers suggest that since the Soviets feel that they are *weaker* than the West in *global* terms, they use the concept to stimulate and justify their own efforts in all fields of state activity which relate to the military build-up and to slow down the Western military effort.

It should be noted, however, that, as it was mentioned above, the Western assessment of the Soviet approach to the concept of the correlation of world forces is not consistent. For instance, in one criticism, the Soviets, fearing that in purely military terms they might be surpassed by the West — especially if the United States were to place more emphasis on a military build-up and if the individual Western military potentials were united — include several non-military factors in the concept of the correlation: the economic, the ideological, the unity in the Soviet bloc as compared with the disunity in the West, the strength of the international working movement, the anti-imperialist forces in the Third World, and so on.

In another criticism, the Soviets' approach is contrary to that described above: they consider that they can achieve parity, or even a global superiority, only in military power,[37] and thus they make a maximum effort to catch up with the West and surpass it in this respect. This provides a rationale for their build-up in the military field, which is their greatest achievement.

It is odd that both assertions *a casu ad casum* are made in the same studies.[43]

Correlation of world forces versus global balance of power: differences in concepts

Agenda

The differences between the Soviet and the Western approaches concern, apparently, the following aspects:
(1) The protagonists: the socio-economic systems and international movements in the Soviet approach versus the blocs, superpowers and other great powers in the Western interpretations; a bipolar structure versus a multipolar one;
(2) The character of the correlation: the emphasis in the concept on the intangible class characteristics versus the emphasis on measurable parameters of power;
(3) The view of the international system: cooperation and rivalry between the antagonistic systems versus an anarchical behaviour of states; the emphasis on the domestic roots of international behaviour versus the basic impact of the international features of systems;
(4) The underlying philosophy of international development: the dynamic character of the correlation and of a world that is moving towards socialism versus the view that events are happening in a relatively stable world that is influenced by the stabilising functions of the balance of power and the growing economic and cultural interdependence of nations.

The differences in terminology may seem to be formal; they are also diminishing in number since in recent Soviet studies, particularly those published in English, the term 'balance of power' has been used *a casu ad casum* and, on the other hand, in several Western studies we note the term 'correlation of forces'. Concepts, however, must be viewed in conjunction with the political philosophy which underlies them and with the different meanings attached to the formally similar key terms in the formulae which are set against one another.

Protagonists

As regards the protagonists — the opposing sides in the correlation — the traditional concept of the balance of power as being confined to Europe was replaced in Western political philosophy in the years immediately following the Second World War by the relation of forces of the two opposing camps — first, those concentrated on the European continent and, second, the rival forces throughout the world. A new but apparently secondary component of the world configuration is the amorphous group of less developed countries that includes the non-aligned nations of Africa, Asia and Latin America. The political and economic heterogeneity of these countries and the weakness of most of them diminish their power of action as a kind of 'third force'.

This concept had been complemented by a gradually emerging and developing picture of the world as a system of 'centres of power'. Apart from the two superpowers, Western Europe, Japan and China have been described as the new centres. These ideas were reflected in the models of a multi-polar world discussed earlier in this study.

On the other hand, in spite of the sharp criticism of any ideas of multipolarity of power in the Soviet writings, the Soviet politicians and scholars could not deny the growth of new power-centres in the world, the fact of the significant development of the economic and political strength of Western Europe and Japan, for instance, and in some respects, also of China. They have not denied — they often even stress it — that Western Europe is becoming more independent of the United States, and is moving away from some American policies. They also have accepted that Japan, with the rapid growth in its economic strength, assumes a larger and more independent role in the international system.

Differences exist, however, regarding the *meaning* of the emergence of the new centres of power. In Western literature, there is an inclination to build 'models' of a multi-polar world. The Soviet authors admit that there is a process of redistribution of global economic and political power but first, this does not renounce, they say, the *basic* opposition between world socialism and world capitalism, and, second, they also place an insistent emphasis on the continuing *military bipolarity*. They obviously expect that the Soviet Union and the United States will remain infinitely in a class by themselves. Although Soviet diplomacy can only benefit from the declining position of the United States in the non-Communist world (which, of course, is approvingly described and evaluated in Soviet writings), it is not interested in the creation of a self-sufficient European military community possessing its own strategic-nuclear arsenal, nor in the conversion of Japan into a military power possessing independent nuclear weapons. It prefers a world in which there are two camps and two powers in control of them to a world with several centres of power, some of which would be equal, or nearly equal, to the Soviet Union.

The Soviet opposition to the emergence of new centres of power is specially concerned with China. While constantly pointing to the growth of China's military force as a danger to world peace, the Soviet politicians and theorists refuse to regard China as a great power, and to recognise its status as one of the powers which determine the world's development.

The Soviet view of the Third World countries, discussed above, ascribes to it a rather passive and derivative role, basically as a potential ally of the anti-imperialist camp. It is stressed, however, that in political and economic questions this group generally takes an anti-imperialist line. Yet it cannot be viewed as the third socio-economic system, since these countries are in transition to one of the two world-wide antagonistic systems, either capitalist or socialist. As a whole, they may be regarded as a component of the anti-imperialist front.

Forces

The concept of the correlation of world forces by definition includes the entire range of forces at the disposal of the two antagonistic systems; for instance, on the 'anti-imperialist' side of the world equation they include all the forces which can be used by socialist states, by the so-called exploited masses in the non-socialist countries, by national liberation movement, and so on. They apparently, at least in theory, far exceed armed forces of groups of states. Likewise, in theory, the Western proponents of the concept of the world or global balance of power stress the importance of both military power and the economic and other non-military potentials.

But turning from general concepts to the actual assessment, we see another picture. In both approaches the *superpowers* and their *military power* continue to be the main protagonists and the main items in the correlation. Each side describes how its strategic nuclear forces neutralise the other, how its diversified conventional forces can act and counteract in various regions and how its naval forces oppose those of the other side on the seas and oceans. These are also the main items taken into consideration in the SALT and other negotiations on strategic nuclear weapons, where other components of the world balance of power — i.e., other states and non-military values — are regarded as secondary.

> The possession of a strong strategic superiority has always been one of the chief prerequisites for the pursuit of an active foreign policy, since the very recognition of this superiority by other states often forced them to agree to certain (and at times considerable) concessions, or to submit to the demands of their more powerful rivals.[44]

This statement in an authoritative study on the role of military power in international relations (although with the implication that it only concerns the Western position) may well characterise the Soviet approach, and it is an answer to the question of what forces are considered to constitute the essence of the world correlation. In both approaches, despite the acceptance of the importance of the economic potential, of the ideological instrument and of the cultural values, military force is still regarded as the determining factor in the balance, at least with regard to the main contemporary problem – the prevention of a world war, or 'victory', if it breaks out. Both approaches seem to assume that while we are witnessing the emergence of a political multi-polarity, a bipolar relationship in the military field still remains the basic one and should be regarded as the main item in the correlation of world forces.

Soviet scholars occasionally advance ideas closely related to those of the balance-of-power theory. They state, for instance, that 'irresponsible' bellicose actions by any state will be countered by other states if they see the danger of a disturbance in the balance of power and a threat to their interests; this is considered an argument against the 'subjectivist' and 'voluntarist' concept of international relations, but it unintentionally reveals the Soviet view of the relatively balanced distribution of power in the international system, and of the 'balancing mechanism', which consists of actions undertaken by the most powerful states in order to thwart any attempt to disturb the balance.[45]

Views of the international system

Balance of power theories originated in a world of homogeneous states, which had similar socio-economic and political systems. Modified in our times and to an increasing extent related to the two antagonistic camps, they stress the 'antagonism' in a quite different way from that of Marxist-Leninism. They set 'democratic' states against 'dictatorships' rather than capitalist societies against socialist ones, asserting that the basic feature of the states in the Soviet camp is not the socio-economic socialistic system (which, in their view, is far even from socialist theories) but an authoritarian system characterised by the absolute rule of a new élite. To the Soviet theory and politicians this is not only a falsification of reality but also a false methodological approach to the systemic differences between the two opposing camps. The alleged and formal characteristics of the political authorities are substituted for the basic socio-economic differences between the domestic systems of states. This is said to be a modification of the traditional approach which sees in all states essentially homogeneous entities, differing only in their forms of political rule. Such an approach may also be regarded as a modification of the interwar approach when (even in the view of some Western analysts of the balance of power theories[46]) the differences between the 'ideologies' of 'democratic' states and the 'authoritarian' ones (Germany, in the first place) were considered to represent the dividing line between the states which took sides in the contemporary balance of power.[47] A related difference seems to be that, while in the Western concepts states are in actual fact treated as homogeneous *entities*, in the Marxist-Leninist theory the non-socialist states represent antagonistic societies, internally divided, and their power depends on the alignment of domestic forces. Though the impact of domestic struggle on foreign policy has been in the two recent decades pointed out and analysed by Western scholars, its impact on the world balance of power has been more or less omitted in analyses of the latter subject.

Apart from their different view of the nature of states, the two concepts take a different approach to the essense of the two camps. Marxism-Leninism views the camps as the expression of the domination of two definite socio-economic systems in two parts of the world. The common actions of the member-states of the systems are necessarily rooted in their common domestic system and ideology, since the foreign policy of each state is determined by its domestic structure. The correlation of world forces is that between socio-economic systems, not states. The West views the opposite camps as groups of states whose similar socio-economic policies are composed in different ways: the Eastern bloc is united forcibly by the Soviet Union and constitutes a group of satellites under the Soviet dictatorship. The Western camp and its core — NATO — is said to be a freely united group of democratic states. The balance of power is that between these differently composed groups of states and not between socio-economic systems.

And certainly a real difference in the compared concepts is that while the concepts of the world balance of power are limited to inter-state or inter-coalitions relations, the correlation of world forces is said also to include a multitude of protagonists other than states, the international revolutionary movement with its national contingents and the national liberation movement with its state and non-state components. This emphasis reflects at the same time the emphasis on the class characteristics of the two opposing camps.

Philosophies and perspectives

The basic and underlying difference between these concepts, as among all other general political ideas in the two opposing camps, is that between the radically different social and political philosophies. The prevailing Western approach to the problems of the balance of power is based on the assumption that the drive for power motivates both domestic developments and the international behaviour of states. The global balance-of-power theories assume that the peculiarities of the international system greatly affect the behaviour of states: because of the anarchy of the system, which may be viewed as a kind of jungle, each country is doomed to self-sufficiency and self-reliance in the pursuit of its interests. For this purpose all states must strive for power; the drive for power leads to interstate conflicts, including wars. Thus the rivalry of the superpowers is seen as a manifestation of the normal dynamics of polarised great-power rivalry in which the Soviet Union, as a revisionist power,[48] challenges the United States for primacy, while the latter tries to preserve its global spheres of influence on the basis of its politico-military superiority in important respects as well as economic influence.

In the balance-of-power theories all changes in the global balance of power are interpreted in those terms — for instance, the gradual change in the bipolar military balance in favour of the Soviet Union or the continuing extension of the power rivalry into the Third World.[49] Even internal changes in the Soviet Union are explained in terms of the struggle for power: the fall of Khrushchev is presented as the transition from a personal dictatorship to a more pluralistic and consensual leadership under Brezhnev. The explanation of Soviet behaviour as being nationalistically motivated also contrasts with the Marxist-Leninist explanation of the behaviour of states in terms of class interests.

Marxism-Leninism assumes that the behaviour of states is primary determined by their internal structure. The structure and features of the international system are a product of the domestic socio-economic systems and therefore are greatly affected by the struggle between countries with different systems.

As regards further perspectives, in the prevailing Western literature, the balance of power — whether between a number of great powers, or the two superpowers, or the two antagonistic camps — is regarded as a condition of preserving the status quo (if not for ever, at least for a considerable period). This can be set against the Soviet concept of the dynamic correlation of forces, which not only assumes a constant change in favour of the socialist system, but also regards that change as a factor which promotes the ultimate victory of socialism.

This distinction is also rooted in the different social and political philosophies, and reflected in the respective political doctrines. Marxism-Leninism, and its main proponent, the Soviet Union, views the world as moving towards a classless society, and that view is considered a law of history. The correlation of forces between those aiming at such a revolutionary transformation of the world, and those who oppose it, *must be dynamic;* it changes with the accumulation of victories of the socialist forces.[50]

In the opposite philosophy and doctrine, political ends are not so structurally concrete and so future-oriented. The social development towards greater freedom, equality and justice, is an unending process of doing whatever is possible and taking one step at a time; it is an evolutionary process. The sociopolitical equilibrium in particular states, and the political balance in the world based primarily on the balance of state powers with military power as their most important component may be constantly strengthened and improved, and there is no need to change all of it by revolutionary means. The existing states, with their internal structure, and the international system, are the 'givens' which have to be preserved.

Since the structure of this system has changed, first from multi-polar to bipolar, and then to a combination of a politically multi-polar and militarily bipolar alignment of forces, the aim of policy is *to establish the form of power balance best suited to our time.*

Thus, while Marxism-Leninism sees in this process *a permanent contest* between two world-wide forces and two antagonistic social systems, and in these terms assesses the role of the correlation of world forces and the significance of any change in it, Western scholars and politicians speculate on the *evolutionary nature* and constantly new distribution of power.

In the Marxist-Leninist view, the continued emergence of new fronts of competition and, on the other hand, of new areas of cooperation, is of essential importance. However, they state, these emerging phenomena, which make the world more interdependent, do not change the basic direction of its development through the competition of the two systems.

In other words, while the Soviets view international relations as a *process,* as developing and acquiring a completely new structure, which must be protected and fostered by the progressive forces, the political realist philosophy regards them as a relatively stable *system* which preserves its basic shape and can only gradually be corrected and adjusted to the changing conditions.

It should be noted, however, that the actual differences between the two approaches are sometimes obscured in Soviet criticism by its focus on the alleged ones. A good deal of the criticism has been levelled against ideas which, even in the West, are regarded as obsolete, such as (a) the negation of the great ideological and systemic difference which divides the world, (b) the use of war as a balancing mechanism and (c) the overestimation of the role of military force. There are many more formal similarities between the Marxist-Leninist concepts of the correlation of social forces and the balance-of-power theories than Soviet researchers admit; the actual differences must be sought primarily in the basic differences of interests and ideologies.

In sum, however, in spite of some similar views of the global balance of power or the correlation of world forces these two concepts are expressed by antagonistic camps and ideologies. They cannot have much in common given the deep gulf in the respective world outlooks and the political philosophies and doctrines which reflect differences in basic long-range interests.

Notes

1 Shakhnazarov, 1974, 1977; Karenin, 1971; A. Topornin, 'The Balance of Power Doctrine and Washington', *SShA: Ekonomika, Politika, Ideologya,* 1970:11. *Protsess formirovaniya i osushchestvleniya vneshnei politiki kapitalisticheskikh gosudarstv,* 1981, Ch. III.3. 'Funktionirovanie sistemy mezhdunarodnykh otnoshenii'; Cf. J. Lider, *On the Nature of War,* 1977, 1979, Ch. XIV.
1977, 1979, Ch. XIV.

2 The treatment of states in 'balance of power' theories as homogeneous unities is regarded as one of basic characteristics of them predetermining their non-scientific character. All states are placed on equal footing like abstract mathematical values and the class differences in their socio-economic systems — and consequently in their policies — are not taken into account (Cf. Sanakoyev, Kapchenko, 1976, pp. 145—7).

3 V. Kortunov, 'Razryadka napryazhennosti i retsidivy "kholodnoi voiny" ' *Krasnaya Zvezda,* 14 January 1976. Filuyov, 1982, sharply criticises Western contentions that the possibility of war decreases when a bipolar balance of power replaces the multi-polar one, as well as that it increases with such a change. Another theory holds that in our century the possibility of war decreases as some states increase their superiority in power to others; and this promotes stability in international relations. This is the main idea in 'Capability, Distribution, Uncertainty and Major Wars', by J.D. Singer, S. Bremer, and Y. Stuckey, in Russett, Bruce M., ed., *War, Peace and Numbers,* Sage, London 1972. Kortunov, 1977, after mentioning 'geometrical allegories' and commenting that they have either a military-political, an economic, or a regional basis, wholly depending on the author's subjective views, asserts: 'Most Western politicians incline to a model of the world in which the pattern of forces will be determined by a contest between several conflicting power centres: the United States, the Soviet Union, China, Western Europe and Japan' (p. 107). Apart from these traditional 'power centres', many new ones have been proposed, including India, Brazil, Iran and Saudi Arabia (p. 108).

4 The criteria of the 'centres of power' are very various: the possession of nuclear weapons, or a large economic potential, or large population, or great natural resources, etc. (Kortunov, 1978, p. 315).

5 Two errors are here mentioned. Either the competition of the two systems is reduced to an apolitical conflict of the two greatest powers for world hegemony (the bipolar structure), or the emerging structure of international relations is presented as an apolitical competition of many countries and coalitions, independent

of their sociopolitical systems (the multi-polar structure) (Kortunov, 1978, pp. 311–12). Apparently, the term 'apolitical' is here used to mean a disregard of the differences in the socio-political systems.

6　Kortunov, 1977, p. 108.

7　Sheidina, 1984, p. 54. The emergence of new centres of power may increase the threat of war, since they may aim at the redivision of the spheres of influence. In the Third World, new groupings of states increase the danger of war by their announced policy of combatting 'subversive activities' (Serebryannikov, 1982, p.10). New totalitarian regimes affect negatively the arms control negotiations (Burlatskii, 1982, p. 64).

8　Shakhnazarov, 1984.

9　Sheidina, 1984.

10　The bellicose character of such concepts is said to consist in their view of the world as the arena of an antagonistic struggle between 'centres of power' which must lead to wars. The authors of such ideas expect a war between China and the Soviet Union (Kortunov, 1978, pp. 312–15).

11　Shakhnazarov, 1984, pp. 23–32.

12　The classical example of an alleged positive impact of the balance of power on the preservation of peace – i.e., the peace in Europe after the Congress in Vienna in the nineteenth century – was characterised by (1) its reactionary character (as expressed in the struggle against the revolutionary forces in Europe), and (2) its instrumentality to the domination of the great powers. Besides, even the period in question was not free of wars, e.g., the Crimean War 1853–1856 and the French-German War of 1870–1871 and it led to the First World War (Kortunov, 1978, pp. 317–18).

13　'What we call the imperialist policy of the "balance of power" is something different – namely, the perfidious foreign policy of a state which aims at setting other countries against one another thereby securing for itself the profitable position of arbiter ... the state that controls the balance holds the key position in the balance-of-power system, for on this position depends the outcome of the struggle for power. For this reason the state is called "the arbiter" of the entire system, which decides who is to win and who is to be defeated' (Topornin, 1970, p. 2). 'The "balance-of-power" policy has always pursued the aim of creating the best opportunities for implementing this or that state's hegemonistic plans, and in effect it amounts to no more than a veiled desire for world domination. This has been most frequently expressed in attempts (of the most powerful state – JL) to act as an arbiter between two powers, thereby securing preponderant positions with the minimum expenditure of effort and resources'

(Kortunov, 1977, p. 109).

14 Karenin, 1971; Topornin, 1970, pp. 3 ff.
15 Karenin, 1971, analysed the balance of power policy of the United States from the end of the nineteenth century, and concluded '... the politics of the "balance of power", as before, has an anti-Soviet and anti-communist character and, in the final analysis, it aims at the seizure of world power by the American imperialists' (p. 169).
16 In particular, Soviet scholars criticise all concepts of local and limited wars as serving to justify the preservation of the balance of world forces (e.g., S. Krasilnikov, Introduction to the Russian edition of H. Kissinger's *Nuclear Weapons and Foreign Policy/ Yadernoe oruzhie i vneshnyaya politika/*, Izd. Inostrannoi Literaty, Moscow, 1959, p. 5—32).
17 'The doctrine of the balance of power in the framework of either a "bipolar" or a "multipolar" world . . . aims at the preservation of the international, and consequently also of the sociopolitical, status quo. It counts on the continuance of the traditional expansionist policy of the capitalist states and of the unjust and undemocratic system of international relations' (Kortunov, 1978, p. 321).
18 Filuyov, 1972, Conclusions.
19 Kortunov, 1977, p. 109. The alliance of China with imperialism and the preparation for a new world war are the most frequent accusations. 'China is now the only country in the world whose leaders openly and even demonstratively call for the unleashing of a new world war' (Kortunov, 1978, p. 309). Both the theory of the 'three worlds' and the concept of the two 'superpowers' aim at presenting the Soviet Union as the main danger to world peace, and they suggest that a new world war is inevitable (Apalin, 1976; Apalin, Mityayev, 1980). Cf. Zamkovoi, Filatov, 1981, pp. 282—4.
20 Shakhnazarov, 1984, pp. 46—8.
21 *Protsess formirovaniya i osushchestvleniya vneshnei politiki kapatalisticheskikh gosudarstv*, 1981, Ch. III.3: 'Funktsionirovanie sistemy mezhdunarodnykh otnoshenii'.
22 'Actions of a bourgeois state in its foreign policy as a rule aim at creating a certain advantageous correlation of forces, even if this does not correspond to the regularities of the system (ibid., p. 283).
23 The literature of the subject is too voluminous to be listed here. For some items, see bibliography. Some Chinese publications discussed and criticised are the following: 'Soviet Social-Imperialism — Most Dangerous Source of World War', *Peking Review*, 15 July, 1977:29; 'Chairman Mao's Theory of the Differentiation

of the Three Worlds is a Major Contribution to Marxism-Leninism', *Peking Review*, 4 November, 1977:45; Huang Hua, 'The International Situation and China's Foreign Policy', *Peking Review*, 6 October, 1978:40. To exemplify the criticism, as summarised by I. Alexeyev, and G. Apalin: China's theory of 'three worlds' is a variant of the concept of a multi-polar world structure. China's foreign and military policy is characterised by: (1) a pathological anti-Sovietism, a total ideological and political confrontation with the Soviet Union and the socialist community, and subversive activity against them; (2) the search for a mutual understanding with reactionary, right-nationalistic regimes in Asia, Africa and Latin America; (3) the increasingly unprincipled formation of a bloc with any reactionary force of imperialism on a common platform of struggle against the policy of *détente;* (4) the stepping-up of the attempts, together with the opponents of *détente* in the imperialist camp, to intensify world contradictions and to create and use situations of conflict for aggravating tensions ('A Soviet Assessment of China', *Co-existence*, vol. 15, pp. 46—54); cf. *Maoizm—ideinyi i politicheskii protivnik marksizma-leninizma*, Moscow 1974; Apalin, Mityayev, 1980.

24 Cf. *Razryadka mezhdunarodnoi napryazhennosti i ideologicheskaya bor'ba*, 1981, Ch. VIII.3. 'Teoriya "trekh mirov" kak ideologicheskoe obosnovanie vneshnei politiki maoistov'; Bykov, Razmerov, Tomashevskii, 1981, Ch. VI: 'Against Peking's Hegemonistic Policy Course', Apalin, Mityayev, 1980, the main theme.

25 'Chairman Mao's Theory ...' (Note 23).

26 Ibid.

27 Apalin, Mityayev, 1980, p. 230.

28 *Razryadka mezhdunarodnoi napryazhennosti i ideologicheskaya bor'ba*, 1981, p. 308.

29 Apalin, Mityayev, 1980, p. 111.

30 Shakhnazarov, 1984, pp. 42—4.

31 *Razryadka mezhdunarodnoi bezopasnosti i ideologicheskaya bor'ba*, p. 309.

32 Kapitsa, 1969; *Kritika teoreticheskikh kontseptsii Mao Tsze-duna*, 1970; Yepishev, 1974; *Filosofskoe nasledie V.I. Lenina i problemy sovremennoi voiny*, 1972, Ch. 3.3; Apalin, Mityayev, 1980.

33 Maoism is said to reduce the entire class struggle to armed violence: 'According to Maoists, class struggle is violence, violence and violence' (Yepishev, 1974, p. 85). The apologia for violence justifies the policy of internal and external militarism which is followed by the contemporary Chinese leaders (p. 86). This approach leads to the theory of inevitability of a new world war which has become the basic principle of the Chinese foreign policy

(Zamkovoi, Filatov, 1981, p. 310). Cf. Apalin, Mityayev, 1981, Ch. One. 3: 'The Absolutisation of Force'.

34 Apalin, Mityayev, 1981, p. 28.

35 Cf. J. Lider, *Military Force*, 1981, 'Criticism of the Chinese views' in Ch. 10.

36 Bykov, Razmerov, Tomashevskii, 1981, p. 56.

37 *Razryadka mezhdunarodnoi napryazhennosti i ideologicheskaya bor'ba*, 1981, p. 57.

38 Apalin, Mityayev,. 1981, Chapter Three.

39 Cf. *The Soviet Union and the Developing Countries*, R.E. Kanev, (ed.), John Hopkins University Press. Baltimore, London 1974, Cf. Kubalkova, Cruickshank, 1981, Chs. 3 and 4.

40 Some items of the abundant bibliography: Michael J. Deane, 'The Soviet Assessment of the "Correlation of World Forces": Implications for American Foreign Policy, *Orbis*, Fall 1976, (vol. 20 nr.3), pp. 625—36; Id. 'Soviet Perceptions of the Military Factor in the "Correlation of World Forces" ', in *International Perceptions of the Superpowers Military Balance*, Donald C. Donald, (ed.), 1978; Vernon V. Aspaturian, 'Soviet Global Power and the Correlation of Forces', *Problems of Communism*, May-June 1980, pp. 1—28; Bialer, 1980, 'The Arms Race and the Correlation of Forces', pp. 241—53.

41 Robert L. Pfaltzgraff, Jr., 'Soviet Military Strategy and Force Levels, in *The Soviet Union in World Politics*, Kurt London, (ed.), Westview Press, Croom Helm, Boulder (Colorado), London 1980, p. 294.

42 'The Soviets ... do not see this parity as being assured once and for all ...'. 'With regard to the general relation of forces they still consider themselves to be weaker than the West, still feel strongly the need for a maximum effort to catch up with the West. This, as a matter of fact, provides one rationale for their purely military build-up effort, an area where they can show the greatest successes, and which in their perception at least partly counterweighs their strongly perceived economic and technological inferiority *vis-à-vis* the West' (Bialer, 1980, p. 245).

43 Cf. Bialer, 1980, p. 145.

44 *Voennaya Sila i Mezhdunarodnye Otnosheniya*, 1972, p. 38.

45 Tyushkevich, 1975, p. 116.

46 Cf. William J. Newman, *The Balance of Power in the Interwar Years 1919—1939*, Random House, New York 1968; Geoffrey Barraclough, *An Introduction to Contemporary History*, Penguin Books, Baltimore, Maryland, 1968, Ch. IV: 'From the European Balance of Power to the Age of World Politics'.

47 Ibid.

48 Osgood writes: 'For historic, ideological, and internal political

reasons, the Soviet Union seeks to "fill every nook and cranny in the world basin of power" (in Kennan's words)' (1981, p. 5).

49 Osgood, 1981, pp. 2 ff.

50 Soviet authors note that while, during the domination of capitalism in the world, international conflicts were emerging and were resolved mainly in accordance with the correlation of forces between the national groups of bourgeoisie, and were confined to the framework of inter-imperialist contradictions, now they have assumed a definite class character and have become a part of the competition between the world forces of progress and reaction. In turn, the outcome of the particular conflicts affects the correlation of world forces (Kortunov, 1978, p. 272). Cf. *Mezhdunarodnye konflikty sovremennosti*, 1983, Ch. IV: 'Sistema vzaimodeistvii mezhdunarodnykh konfliktov sovremennosti'.

PART IV
MILITARY DIMENSION

8 Correlation of military forces: introductory remarks

Concept

Correlation in war and peace

In the military perspective, the correlation of forces is a fundamental concept. Warfare means a clash of physical forces and its immediate purpose is to destroy a part or the whole of the enemy forces in order to achieve such an advantageous correlation of forces as makes it possible to achieve the goal: that is the enforcement of political demands on the enemy. At each level — whether strategic, operational or tactical — the aim of each protagonist in a war is to achieve favourable correlation of forces at the beginning of combat and to change it even more to his advantage by military actions. The lower the level of action, the greater is the relative importance of the purely military correlation of forces (which means, roughly, the comparison of the quantity and quality of the armed forces engaged), and the smaller is the relative role of the political, economic and other factors affecting the course of the operation. An exception is the moral-psychological factor which at all levels forms an integral part of the combat quality of units.

The war perspective has, therefore, been the traditional one in analyses of military force and the correlation of military forces. Although the peaceful uses of the military instrument are as old as armed conflicts, they have generally been ignored by military theoreticians. The correlation of military forces has always been a factor behind political strategies and activities, and diplomatic intercourse, but the impact of this factor was rarely a topic of military discussion.

As the role of deterrence and other uses of military force in peacetime gained in importance, it was more openly recognised that both the real and the perceived correlation of military forces profoundly affected the shape and effectiveness of policy. It was asserted, however, that the assessment of the correlation and its influence in peacetime was connected with the effectiveness of a potential, direct and open use of military force in war, as perceived by the adversaries. For instance, the comparison of the preparedness and capabilities of both parties for fighting a general nuclear war may influence the management of global crises or arms control negotiations. A perceived correlation of forces that would be advantageous to one side in wars short of total, plays an even greater role in the management of crises which may engender such wars. This is a telling argument in crisis negotiations.

Narrow and broad interpretations

The correlation of military forces may be conceived of in a *narrower* sense as the relation of the armed forces possessed, together naturally with their arms and equipment.[1] However, in the perception of military force by political and military leaders a *broader* concept seems to dominate. In this, the forces under comparison include at least five components:
(1) The armed forces available;
(2) The military-economic, military-scientific and military-technological potentialities;
(3) Mobilisation potentialities;
(4) The doctrinal strategy of using the armed forces available;
(5) Civil defence.

All these components contributing to the global value of the military instrument have a complex structure and are closely interrelated. Thus, for instance, the assessment of the armed forces available includes: (1) the quantity and quality of the strategic nuclear forces; (2) those of nuclear forces below the strategic level (e.g., theatre nuclear forces); (3) those of conventional forces; (4) those of reserves; (5) the organisational structure (composition) of the armed forces; (6) the doctrinal linkage between all these elements, and particularly between the nuclear and the conventional forces; (7) the vulnerability of nuclear forces — and particularly strategic ones — which is one of their basic characteristics.

The mobilisation potentialities include not only the possibilities of a rapid reinforcement of the forces in being at the start of the hostilities or crisis, and of a continuous reinforcement of them and replacement of the units during the hostilities, but also, more generally, the capacity to mobilise economic resources. This must not be limited to a quick conversion at the time of an acute crisis and imminent war but must seek to ensure the organised conduct of war by making the economy as nearly invulnerable as possible to attack. The doctrinal strategy goes far beyond the strategy for the initial period of war to foresee several alternatives in further stages and to prepare for these.

The principal link between the components of the forces under comparison seems to be the interdependence between the armed forces and their doctrinal strategy, On the one hand, the strategies of the adversaries, and their interaction, greatly affect the military posture of both of them and the correlation of forces. On the other hand, doctrinal strategy is much influenced by the correlation of armed forces, actual and perceived. The latter influences the politico-strategic planning and plans for economic and techno-scientific development in relation to military needs.

Particular components of the correlation of military forces play different roles in preventing or waging different types of war, and in managing different crisis situation. The strategic nuclear forces which determine the assessment of the correlation in all discussions concerning an all-out war have relatively little influence on the ideas concerning limited local wars. On the other hand, civil defence — which up to now may have seemed unimportant for preventing an all-out nuclear war, and for waging it — becomes more important in comparisons of the forces in wars short of total which have been prevented or fought, or which may be fought.

In the broader concept of the correlation of military forces, both the material basis of using military forces and the will to use them are relevant. 'Forces' mean here both what a given protagonist possesses and what he is prepared to do in the non-material sense; the latter includes the *will* to act, the *organisational abilities* and, as mentioned above, the *strategy* prepared.

Component (partial) military correlations

For strategic planning in general and military operations in particular regions and at particular levels, as well as for preparing adequate force postures for these uses, it may be well to distinguish between the correlation of armed forces and means at the strategic level, the operational level and the tactical level. Further, the correlation may be assessed in each category of armed forces: the strategic nuclear forces, the theatre nuclear forces and the conventional forces. Finally, the correlation of military forces may be assessed in relation to particular geographical regions and possible theatres of military operations.

The overall or global correlation of military forces may be considered to consist of the capabilities on all these levels of military art or in all categories of armed forces, or in all the possible areas of conflict. The partial assessments do not obscure the global one; on the contrary, they may indicate and clarify the critical items in the global comparison. For instance, in the 1970s and 1980s, changes in the correlation of military forces between NATO and the Warsaw Treaty Organization, in conjunction with the changes affecting the correlation of forces of the superpowers in the Middle East, the Carribean area and the Far East, greatly affected the global correlation of forces between West and East and created a new East-West strategic configuration.

An additional viewpoint concerning the global correlation of military forces may be found in Marxist-Leninist publications. The basic component of this correlation — namely, between the military forces of the members of the two opposing blocs — may be complemented by other correlations, which also affect the 'correlation of military forces between socialism and imperialism'. These are the military forces of the following states:[2]

(1) The other formal and informal allies of the superpowers. In this respect, the developments in Vietnam, Cambodia and Laos in the 1970s not only changed the regional alignment of forces in Asia, but were also advantageous to socialism throughout the world. On the other hand, the actions of Israel against the Arab states and of South Africa against Angola as well as the growth of Japan's military power, were said to be advantageous to 'imperialism'.

(2) The newly independent countries of the Third World. The growth of the military forces of the 'socialist-oriented' countries is naturally to the advantage of world socialism; the contrary effect is produced by the military build-up in the capitalist countries of the Third World, which are inclined to cooperate with the Western powers.

(3) China is a special case; its military strength is said to be nowadays on the side of the anti-socialist world forces.

Correlation of military forces versus correlation of world forces: independent, subordinate or pars pro toto

The military correlation may be viewed as either a value in itself which can be analysed separately or as only a part of the correlation of global powers — political, economic, ideological, techno-scientific and so on — of the adversaries.[3] Also conceivable is a variant in which the correlation of military forces is the principal component of the overall correlation which determines the global assessment. On occasion, it is used *pars pro toto* to mean the global correlation.

The importance of the correlation of military forces as the *principal* component in the correlation of world forces is always maintained when Soviet politicians, military leaders and writers describe the rapid change in the correlation of forces in favour of socialism. This, they say, has greatly reduced the danger of an all-out world war and may even eliminate it in the end. The Soviet Union is said to have rapidly built up a military machine which has neutralised that of the potential imperialist aggressors. Although in the post-war period pro-socialist changes occurred in *all* areas — socio-economic, political, techno-scientific, ideological and military — it was the radical change in the correlation of military forces that determined the development of the new strategic situation in the world and the attainment of the most important goal of international relations: the prevention of an all-out world war.[4]

The assessment of the way in which the correlation of military forces relates to the fulfilment of political aims by military means is of extreme importance. Therefore the political intentions must be included in the assessment of the real value of military forces and of their correlation. Certainly, one may dismiss such a view of political intentions by saying that these can change — they may depend on the specific crisis situation — and, besides, they may be misunderstood. However, a neglect of the *specific* aims must lead to a consideration of *all* the theoretically conceivable missions of military force and to an attempt to build up a military force to fit all circumstances. The super-powers must, in such a case, include in their war preparations 'the worst case', i.e., an all-out war which begins with a surprise attack and a multitude of variants of major and minor wars in all conceivable theatres of military operations. In reality, however, foreign and military policies must reduce this all-comprehensive scope by taking into account the following factors: the *real* political *intentions* of possible adversaries, the *choices* available to them and the probable course of action, the probable *aims* of war if it breaks out, and the probable *strategy* of the protagonist *vis-à-vis* his adversary in pursing the aims of war.

However, certain stable characteristics of the long-range policy should be taken into account. One such characteristic is the basic aim of the United States to preserve the international status quo, *vis-à-vis* the basic aim of the Soviet Union, deriving from Marxist-Leninist ideo-logy, which is to hasten the perhaps distant, but inevitable, transforma-tion of the international system. These doctrinal aims involve long-range missions of the forces under comparison which are relevant to the assessment of their effectiveness and to the comparison of their strength.

All the concepts mentioned above refer to the correlation of forces in the international arena. The problem of the correlation of military forces in intrasocietal conflicts — and particularly in revolutions and civil wars — has not received attention in the Marxist-Leninist literature. Therefore it has not been discussed in this study. It may be suggested that since the intrasocietal policy of classes, strata and their alliances is regarded as an extremely important kind of policy, and since intrasocietal conflicts and wars are classes in the respective categories of conflicts and wars, the general ideas about the correlation of military forces based on international conflicts and wars should also apply to intrasocietal developments, with the necessary modifications which each such application requires. This seems to be an item on the agenda of analyses.

Correlation of military forces, parity and stability

Parity and stability

The concept of the correlation of military forces in peacetime is closely linked to two other concepts which play a large role in military research: those of military parity and of military stability. Military parity is one of the possible values of the correlation of military forces.[5] It may be a component or an aspect of the global parity in power of two states or coalitions of states — that is, of the equal aggregates of their military, economic, political, techno-scientific and other potentials or forces (the latter meaning mobilised potentials or potentials in action). The term 'equal' here means 'roughly equal' or 'approximately equal', since the individual components are hardly measurable and there is always an assymmetry in some of them with regard to the two states (coalitions) under comparison. Since a parity of two antagonists means the absence of expectations of political gains from an open armed clash between them — and therefore only a small probability of war — *stability* is regarded as almost inevitably resulting from parity. This term has been in vogue in Western analyses, and it is occasionally used in Soviet writings. The parity of the superpowers or of the opposite blocs in a particular region may mean that neither of them can openly use military force without encountering an effective resistance by the other side.[6]

In this reasoning the concept of military superiority, which is full of intangible values, would mean an obvious capability to carry out successful military actions or to threaten such actions. It may therefore be used to attain political goals without a resort to open war. For instance, it may be held that after the Second World War, and up to the end of the 1950s, the United States had a military superiority in nuclear strategic weapons, and up to the mid 1960s also in conventional weapons in the extra-European territories, since it could move conventional forces to the places of conflicts much faster and in greater quantities than could the Soviet Union. Many commentators on America's foreign and military policy say that it was unwise not to take advantage of such superiority. Some writers consider that in factual military actions superiority, at least in some levels and regions, can more easily be tested and proved than parity; therefore parity may be called 'the absence of superiority'.

Particular aspects of parity and stability

To underline (1) the difficulties of *measuring* the correlation of military forces, (2) the dynamic character of the particular components of this and (3) the difficulties in speaking about stability as an absolute and permanent condition, terms concerning only particular aspects of parity and stability — or particular 'parities' or 'stabilities' — have also been used.

Apart from global military parity (which is followed by global military stability) the terms used include:
(1) strategic parity (and stability), (2) deterrent parity (stability), (3) arms race parity (stability) and (4) crisis stability.

Among these terms, strategic parity and (global) military parity are those most often used (sometimes interchangeably) in Soviet writings. The concept of 'stability' is also sometimes used. However, another concept is preferred: that of 'parity in security' or 'equal security'. 'Security' seems to be preferred in Soviet writings not only because it sounds defensive but also because it does not conflict with the assumption about the inevitable *change* in the international system in favour of socialism in the long run, which is connected with the tendency of the global correlation of forces to change in favour of socialism. As distinct from this meaning 'stability' may be associated with the preservation of the international status quo.

Deterrent parity (stability) has usually meant that the main adversaries have had an equal power to deter each other from a major war, or at least from a surprise attack that would initiate such a war. In practice, this term has been linked to strategic parity. An arms race parity (stability) means that no achievement in the arms race can lead to the attainment of a superiority which would make it possible to launch a war without a great risk of a total destruction.[7] Crisis stability means that, because of military or strategic or deterrent parity, it would be extremely risky, even in periods of acute crisis, to resort to an open use of military force which might escalate to a major war.

Multi-compartmental military balance

One conclusion to be drawn from these preliminary definitions is that a military balance should be a multi-compartmental and multi-level one. The comparison of the military forces of the countries which possess an entire range of armaments and forces, goes beyond strategic nuclear forces or global conventional forces to include theatre nuclear forces in various regions, theatre conventional forces, general purpose forces stationed at home, strategic defence forces and other components. Paradoxically, strategic parity may even contribute to a kind of instability on other levels, since it may permit the exploitation of a superiority in other components — for instance, in conventional forces — for the attainment of particular political or politico-military aims. The same may result from the possession of a military advantage in a certain region. While a strategic parity constrains each superpower from directly confronting the other, it allows one of them to exploit a regionally or locally advantageous situation for a military action — as in the Soviet occupation of Afghanistan or in several actions by Soviet allies (interventions by proxy) in Africa. Thus no parity in a single component — not even the principal one, strategic parity — can be substituted for global equality in order to ensure global stability.

Relative value of the correlation

Varying effects on different conflicts and wars

The third conceptual issue is the effect of the correlation of military forces on different states of international relations. The correlation of the same value may produce different effects in different kinds of conflicts.

Distinctions should be made between (1) the correlation of military forces of the potential adversaries in a time of peaceful and relatively smooth rivalry and cooperation; (2) the correlation in a time of crisis, in which several 'correlation indicators' acquire a special importance (for instance, the availability of appropriate forces at the right time in the crisis area); and (3) the correlation of military forces in wartime. A further distinction should be made between different types of crises and different types of war. For instance, we know little about the effect of an overall rough equality of forces on the outcome of crisis management by the sides in the correlation, nor about the opportunities available to the sides in the different variants of the opening stage of hostilities in a general nuclear war, or a specific conventional war. Obviously, all these effects depend on the value of the component correlations or aspects of the global correlation as related to specific conflicts and areas.

As regards the course of military operations, the effects of the correlation of military forces analysed are generally divided into those in the particular phases of war, with the focus on the initial period. In a general nuclear war, the correlation of military forces *after* the first nuclear exchange receives particular attention.

Different values in different missions

Summing up, we may say that the value of the correlation of military forces can be assessed in relation to three main functions in international relations: to back negotiations, to deter a protagonist from an open armed conflict, or to win a war. The possibility of exerting an influence on domestic conflicts by the threat of intervention or by fulfilling such a threat, may be regarded either as an aspect of these functions or as a separate function.

In the Western theory and practice it has become common to distinguish between the forces which serve deterrence from war and those which may be used to fight a war. Western critics of American military policy have said that since the forces assigned for deterrence were not identical with those assigned for war — which was in their view the basic error of American military policy — the focus, in practice, was on the former. Therefore deterrence could not be effective, since forces which were not prepared to fight could not deter either.

More generally, it may be said that the value of military force — in its entirety and in each of its components — and in relation to the adversary's military force — is assessable only together with the missions assigned to it and with the strategy for their fulfilment, in the broader framework of the politico-military intentions and policies.

Applying this proposition, for instance, to a strictly military mission in a given expected theatre of military operations, we may say that the superiority of NATO in tactical nuclear weapons — before the Soviet Union annulled it — was advantageous to the strategy of massive retaliation. These weapons represented an additional means of deterrence against war by ensuring that the response would be a nuclear one and that an escalation to a general nuclear war attack would follow. However, in the strategy of flexible response even a quantitative superiority in tactical nuclear weapons would mean no substantial advantage to the strategy of deterrence and to combat.

The final problem in this is the dependence of the actual value of the correlation of military forces — i.e. of the influence it can exert — on the perception of it by both sides in the correlation.

Perception depends on several factors.

(1)   The data available and the choice of the data which are regarded as valid. Military forces, and the correlation of these, produce both physical and psychological effects. In war the psychological effects are the result of the physical ones. In peacetime the psychological effects result from the expected physical ones.

(2)   The interpretation of the term 'hardware'. The perception refers not only to the amount of the hardware but also to the interpretation of information about it. The interpretation is a complex problem, depending on the choice of the indicators, the number of them and the order in which they rank. The ideological position of the researcher greatly affects the analysis, assessment and perception: what he wishes to see and to emphasise.

(3)   Changes in the correlation of military forces which have much more influence on perception than does the existing state of affairs, even if the latter already includes great discrepancies. After some time, however, when the changed components have become a constant part of the new correlation, they cease to attract special attention. Perceptions, one may say, have a long life.

(4)   The choice of the supposed effects of using armed forces in war which are to be emphasised; these may vary. Values of the particular weapons and forces are measured in relation to those effects which are regarded as the most important ones. However, various researchers differ as to which effects are the principal ones, besides they have various points of reference, scales of values and so on.

(5)   This very incomplete set of factors affecting the perception of the value of military force also includes the understanding of the adversary's way of thinking, his policy, intentions and so on. This affects the protagonists' perceptions of each other's military power and its adequacy with regard to the aims pursued.

Notes

1   Lukava, 1984; cf. 'Sootnoshenie sil i sredstv' in *Voennyi Entsiklopedicheskii Slovar'*, 1983, p. 691.
2   Geiling, 1982, pp. 9—10.
3   Cf. J. Lider, *Military Force*, 1981, Ch. 10; Bykov, Razmerov,

Tomashevskii, 1981, Ch. I.2; 'Nuclear arms and delivery vehicles are becoming an ever more important component of the correlation of world forces, which is the objective basis for the development of international relations' (ibid., p. 18). Moreover, the authors state that strategic parity (or, in a broader sense, global military parity) between socialism and imperialism is an *effect* of changes in the correlation of world forces.

4 Bykov, Razmerov, Tomashevskii, 1981, Ch. II.2, especially pp. 50–1; cf. *Mirovoi revolutsionnyi protsess i sovremennost'*, 1980, p. 106. This is also the main proposition in Geiling, 1982.

5 Lukava, 1984, p. 20; 'Nuclear parity means the maintenance of rough equality of the adversaries in nuclear potentials, forces and weapon systems' ('Yadernyi paritet' in *Voennyi Entsiklopedischeskii Slovar'*, 1983, p. 843).

6 Bykov, Razmerov, Tomashevskii, 1981, p. 52. 'The current world strategic balance is clearly not to the liking of the most aggressive groups in the imperialist camp. Their military doctrines have always been geared to the most diverse use of force — from the threat of force to overt military intervention. The new situation has drastically reduced the sphere of such actions' (ibid.).

7 Thus: 'Whatever the difference in the structure of the opposing strategic forces, they were dynamically balanced, which meant that neither side can attain decisive superiority' (ibid., p. 51).

9 Soviet approach

Concept

Definition and interpretation

Soviet military thought departs from the assumption that the correlation of military forces is a highly important analytical concept, which even constitutes a category in itself. This concept is also regarded as an aspect of a category of a higher order — namely, the correlation of intrasocietal and international political forces, since any military action is a form of social action undertaken for political purposes.

The correlation of military forces and means is defined as a comparison of the combat power of the adversaries, which makes it possible to determine the degree in which one side is superior to the other.[1] The correlation should be assessed by comparing the qualitative and quantitative characteristics of the opposing forces. This entails an interpretation of *combat power* as the basis of comparison. Combat power is regarded as the principal component of all military power in the broad sense; it determines the course and outcome of particular military operations and even of the war as a whole;[2] this, of course is also of extreme importance for the evaluation of military power in peacetime.

Political criteria of comparison

In the discussion concerning the identity of the protagonists in the correlation of world forces (Chapter 6) it was pointed out that in this concept the main adversary or adversaries of the Soviet Union or of the socialist camp is the United States, or NATO, or all the potential enemies covered by the terms 'imperialism' and 'forces of imperialism and war'.

According to Soviet theory and policy, the basic reason for trying to achieve an 'adequate' correlation of military forces is to ensure what is called 'security' and, to achieve this, the military forces of the Eastern bloc must be at least equal to those of *all* its potential adversaries. Thus the comparison of the forces of the superpowers which is usually made in Western analyses, is very inadequate in the Soviet view. Soviet political and military leaders, and of course also the military analysts, make three kinds of comparison concerning: (1) the military forces of the superpowers; (2) the forces of the two alliances; (3) the forces of the Soviet Union and China. It would be the task of the socialist forces, especially those of the Soviet Union, to ensure security in three kinds of war — namely, (1) in a highly improbable but still conceivable general war involving the Soviet Union and the United States; (2) in a war in Europe; and (3) in a war in the Far East. Moreover, there are missions to be accomplished by the Soviet military forces which are not declared but factual — for instance, to maintain the Soviet domination in Eastern Europe, which requires an additional military deployment. Forces must be assigned for the defence of the territories in the rear and lines of communication to the first line of defence. Forces are also necessary for neutralising any disloyal acts committed by distrusted allies. Finally, the global aspirations of the Soviet Union, which came to the fore in the 1970s and 1980s, require adequate forces to meet challenges arising from limited and local conflicts throughout the world; this mission also has not been 'officially' stated.

These very varied missions make the measurement of the correlation of military forces a very complex task: an advantageous correlation must include adequate forces for the missions *in their entirety*. We shall discuss this matter in Chapter 12.

Political aims of comparison

Soviet writers often point out that the basic aim of the comparison of military forces is political and not scientific, practical and not theoretical. Among the problems which are discussed by the Marxist-Leninist teaching on war and army the preservation of the military strategic equilibrium between the Soviet Union and the United States, and between the two respective alliances, has gained special significance, they say. This is because the rough equilibrium of combat potentialities of the two alliances — their strategic nuclear forces, medium range nuclear forces and conventional forces — makes possible the prevention of nuclear war.

Military strategic parity also makes it possible to *reduce* the military potential of both sides and to establish the parity on lower levels, provided that such reduction be based on the principle of equal security for them.[3] However, say the Soviets, the United States aims at achieving military superiority and several decisions in the early 1980s have testified to this policy (cf. Chapter 9). Thus instead of concentrating the scientific and political efforts on the achievement of agreements on arms reduction, the socialist states must make continuous efforts to match the constantly new American challenges.[4]

Forces and means compared

Concepts

The interpretation of the nature of the forces and means under comparison is closely connected with the Marxist-Leninist theory of military power in the broader framework of state policy, and with that of combat power as related to war. The content of these concepts, as analysed by this author in a separate study[5] may be summarised in the following points.

Among many definitions of military power, the most official one, which is given in the Soviet military encyclopaedia, states that military power is 'the aggregate of all the material and spiritual forces of a state (or coalition of states) and the ability of the state(s) to mobilize these forces for the purpose of attaining war aims; it is the expression of the military, economic, techno-scientific and politico-moral potentials'. Military power is directly embodied in the armed forces.[6]

In this and other definitions, three problems which are crucial to the concept of military power are not resolved: (1) its status as a correlative value or an absolute magnitude or both; (2) its potential capacity in a future war as compared to its current real value; and (3) its scope — i.e., its relation to the total power of the state, whether it is equated with the latter or constitutes only the strictly military part of it, or something in between. However, independently of the answer, all of these aspects of military power may be used in the comparison of forces. It may be suggested that the lack of unambiguity facilitates the flexible use of various interpretations according to the needs of the specific comparison or of political propaganda.

As for the structure of military power, this has been in a state of continuous reconceptualisation. At first the components of military power were equated with the five permanently operating factors in Stalin's famous formula (1942): stability of the rear, the morale of the army, the number and quality of divisions, the armament of the army and the organisational ability of the army commanders. Subsequently, the factors were often reformulated and restructured into three: economic, political and military. In some studies, the military power of the state is said to consist of two basic potentials: the material and the spiritual.[7]

Finally, however, the set which is most commonly used nowadays consists of four potentials that are said to represent the main fields of social activity: economic, techno-scientific, moral-political and military.[8]

It seems that, in more recent times, the relative nature and the dynamism of military power have been emphasised. The use of it is said to depend on the specific international situation, on the alignment of forces in the world and in society, and on the doctrine and policy of states. In various phases of the preparations for war, and during war the component potentials can be transformed into actual power in various degrees; some components may to some extent be replaced by others. The other unsettled point is the *hierarchy* of the components. The economic potential is often viewed as the basis of all military power; the politico-moral potential is said to permeate all elements of military power and determine the degree to which they are realised; the military potential directly expresses the ability of the country to wage war. The techno-scientific potential is said to be realised through all the other potentials. The expressions 'the basis', 'permeates all elements', 'determines', or 'directly expresses' are far from constituting criteria for a definite hierarchy.

In many studies the military potential occupies the first place. This may be partly because the importance of the *available* military means of waging war or supporting policy causes the writers to emphasise the existing forces; besides, in war the military instrument naturally plays the main role, since it is the principal means of destroying, partly or entirely, the military potential of the enemy.

It seems that the lack of clarity partly reflects the difficulty of assessing the *value* of military power. The global amount of military power can hardly be assessed in absolute terms, since it consists of many very differently evaluated elements, including intangible values.

Moreover, it may be suggested that while, in the past, the *utility* of military power could be conceived of as *proportional* to the absolute *magnitude* of armed forces, nowadays *the direct proportionality has disappeared.* To put it very roughly, the utility depends on the correspondence between the means and the ends (or tasks), and thus not nearly so much on its total amount as on the *versatility* of armed forces and the ability to use them *flexibly* and immediately at the time and place of a conflict. The possibility of the use of military power in the framework of the relation of two *coalitionary* military powers and their world competition certainly does not make the assessment easier.

To overcome the difficulties connected with the concept of military power as either a correlative value or an absolute magnitude, or both, the Soviet writers have simplified their analyses of the particular *components* of military power by focusing on their absolute values.

Armed forces

As regards the core of military power — i.e., the armed forces — the basic characteristics of their value was divided in Stalin's formula (cf. p. 246) into three 'permanently-operating factors': the quantity and quality of the division, their armament and the organisational abilities of their commanders. In the years of the great doctrinal debate, 1953—5, and afterwards, a new combined notion was gradually conceptualised; the three 'factors' were united, the interpretation of them was changed and new components were added. The quantity and quality of divisions was replaced by the quantitative and qualitative characteristics of the armed forces, with an explanation that the divisions symbolised the armed forces in their entirety; similarly, the organisational abilities were said to symbolise the commanders' abilities as a whole, and even more: to represent the preparedness for war manifested by the total agglomeration of armed forces. While the notion of armament — naturally — was not changed, nuclear weapons became the measure of its magnitude. 'Stable' new components were added: space, geography, time, reserves of manpower and weapons, and the like, as well as some transitory factors connected with a concrete instance of war: a favourable strategic position, or a preparation in advance for initiating war (for instance, as correct deployment of the armed forces).

Descriptions of the particular components also contained new interpretations and elements; for instance, the quantity (size) of armed forces was described as consisting of (a) the global size of armed forces available at the beginning of the hostilities in the main direction; (b) the global size of armed forces available during the whole war; and (c) the number of trained combat reserves. The level of military art was included in the quality of armed forces, later also the correspondence of the organisation of armed forces to the needs of a modern war, and, likewise, the politico-moral consciousness of the troops. The 'organisational abilities' were said not only to encompass the ability of the commanders to train troops, organise the combat, organise and train the reserves and organise all kinds of supplies, but also to represent the ability of the political leadership to organise preparations for war on the basis of a knowledge of military science.

The above-mentioned changes expressed not only the reaction against the thesis concerning the five permanently acting factors which — in the face of the German offensive — had pointed out the main concern of the Soviet leadership about strengthening the rear, increasing the number of troops, providing sufficient armaments and radically improving the management of the armed forces, but which afterwards turned into expressions of a rigid dogmatic theory. The changes were connected with the realities of the nuclear age and its approaching missile period — a fact which explained, for instance, the inclusion of the 'transitory components' connected with the possibility of a surprise nuclear attack, and such stable factors as territory (space and geography), which also might play a large role in defence against nuclear strikes.

Military potential

In the following years, these changes led to a definite and increasing emphasis on 'forces in being' — i.e., on the actual armed forces which the state possessed before the war or, in another variant, on their combat power; while, in some individual definitions, the notion of 'potential' was still maintained and military potential was defined as the maximum possibility of a state to mobilise armed forces wholly equipped and prepared for a modern war, in others a conceptually opposite view was expressed. This meant that the actual armed forces which the state had at its disposal at the beginning of a war were considered to represent its real ability to conduct military operations and its combat power and were therefore presented as the main component of its military potential. In this case, the potential was, in fact, replaced by the actual power.

The main tendency, however, was to combine both of these approaches. The military potential was, as a rule, presented as including all possible components: the actual forces with their combat power, the possibility of rapid mobilisation of new forces to complement the existing ones, and also the possibility of supplementing them during the war; the supply of the proper quantity and quality of armaments and equipment to the armed forces was implied in such definitions and descriptions.

For instance, in several authoritative publications the military potential was defined as that which expresses the maximum ability of the state (or coalition) to maintain and improve its armed forces, to increase their combat power, to supply them with trained manpower and modern military equipment and all sorts of materials, especially in wartime; this was complemented by the statement that the military potential was embodied directly in the armed forces, in their combat power. The basic definition was that 'the military potential includes the combat power of the existing armed forces and also the military-mobilisational possibilities of the state (coalition)'. Recently, it has often been stated that the military potential is the *leading* component of the military power of a socialist state (or, in the Soviet terminology, of its defensive capacities), although the traditional assumption that it derives from the economic conditions and from the scientific technical potentialities has also been repeated.

The leading position assigned to the military potential is sometimes reflected in the leading place assigned to it in the list of potentials which make the military power, and even the global state power, or by the special statement that the outcome of war depends primarily on the correlation of the strictly military forces. In some publications all the other potentials are said to affect the course of war *through* the military potential.

Combat power

Of the two component parts in the definition of the military potential, combat power is in the focus of the analysis, while the military-mobilisational possibilities are considered to be the factor that conditions the maintenance and increase of combat power.[9]

Combat power is defined as the aggregate of the material and politico-moral combat factors which determine the condition of the armed forces and their ability to perform their both offensive and defensive tasks. These factors are: the number and quality of the troops; their politico-moral condition and training; the quantity and quality of their military equipment and weapons; the fire power and mobility of troops; the numbers of the commanding cadres and their abilities; and, finally, the level of military science.[10]

In modern war, the core of the ability to conduct successful combat is the ability to survive. 'This is the ability of the forces to overcome the effects of the enemy's means of destruction, to maintain their combat capability at the needed level and, in the event that it is lowered, to restore it.'[11]

It is pointed out that there are no adequate criteria by which the combat power of the armed forces of states or coalitions of states can be compared and assessed in relation to one another, even if the assessment is confined to quantitative indices and values. The lack of criteria makes the assessment even more difficult if some qualitative values are included. The main difficulty lies in the asymmetry between the structure of similar units and the need to compare apparently similar but, in fact, dissimilar units. The comparison of armaments raises further difficulties. It is also hard to compare imponderables like the quality of leadership, the organisation and training of forces and the state of morale. With regard to conventional forces, there are always uncertainties in estimating the readiness of the conventional strength which will be available at a time of international crisis and impending armed conflict. The dependence of the actual combat power on factors such as time, space, location and climate also varies in different armies, and this makes comparison even more difficult. In short, the availability of combat forces and the influence of geography must be carefully qualified with regard to questions of where, when, and for how long.

The significance of the availability of forces ready for immediate combat has resulted in the use of another concept, namely *combat readiness.* This is defined as such a state of the armed forces which ensures that, at any moment and in any situation, they will be able immediately to begin combat actions and successfully carry out the assigned tasks of rebuffing and decisively crushing the aggressor's forces'.[12] Combat readiness is said to be the link between the potential military power (might) and the real one.

Combat power and combat readiness depend on the level of military theory.[13] This forecasts the strategic shape and content of the possible war, the trends in the development of armaments and ways of waging combat actions, the impact of rapid techno-scientific progress on the organisation and structure of the armed forces and their military art. Military theorists study the conduct of wars, including local wars, which occur in our times, and partly on the basis of their military exercises, they assess the changes taking place in the organisation, structure and military art of the 'imperialist' armies. They develop the theory of training and instructing the military personnel whose knowledge, skill and high spiritual qualities determine, in the final account, the value of combat power and combat readiness.

In the Soviet assessment, the impact of factors external to armed forces on their combat power is extremely significant. These are the quality of the state leadership, the morale of the population and the abilities of the economic system to meet the requirements for costly and sophisticated weapons.

Analysis

Correlation in peace and war

Traditionally the analysis of the balance of military forces has focused on war. The growing significance of the relation of international forces — and, in its final version, the correlation of world forces — required an analysis of the military component of the latter kind of correlation,

250

which related basically to peacetime.

However, the focus on war remained in the war-oriented definitions of military power mentioned above, especially when the correlation of military forces was discussed as a separate topic. This was perhaps partly explained by the difficulty of measuring military power in peacetime. It is action — the use of military force in open hostilities — which is regarded as most clearly demonstrating its actual value.

As regards both peacetime and wartime conditions, Soviet writers and politicians have developed two lines of discussion: one of these was conceptual while the other concerned the actual state of the military correlation. The conceptual discussion differed in the two fields concerned. With regard to war, the inquiry was extended to include the impact of the military correlation on the course and outcome of war, which might be expressed in the form of propositions having the status of law. In relation to peace, the discussions focused on the meanings of parity and superiority, and their impact on international military stability. They also concerned the prospects of deterrence against various types of war and of arms control and disarmament.

In both areas, the usual subject of analysis was the correlation of military forces between the two superpowers, and often, parallel to this, between the NATO and the WTO forces. As regards peacetime, in practice the emphasis has been on the correlation of strategic nuclear forces, with the addition of the theatre nuclear forces when the problems of the so-called strategic parity or strategic balance were discussed. A special topic of analysis in the early 1980s was the correlation of the intermediate-range nuclear forces. Discussions on the correlation of conventional forces have been usually viewed as a component of the above-mentioned global comparison, but in the negotiations about the reduction of forces in Central Europe they were kept separate.

As regards war, the analysis is most often divided among the three levels of the so-called laws of the correlation of forces concerning: (1) war as a whole; (2) warfare; and (3) particular levels of warfare, categories of operations, character of warfare and participating forces, environments, and so on.

Features of analysis

The Soviet inquiry into the concept of the correlation of military forces — at times called, as traditionally, military balance — seems to reveal the following features:
(1) In the actual analyses, the comparison is usually confined to military force in the strict sense of the word; other items are dealt with in the form of general statements about the impact of political, economic or systemic factors.

(2)   Accordingly, although the correlation of military forces is said to be a part of the overall correlation, which is closely connected with other components, the course of the military analyses is reversed: they discuss the impact of military force on the course of political events, and mainly on political strategy.

(3)   The analysis of the impact of the correlation of military forces on the course of war is confined, as a rule, to the military aspects. The lower the level of military action, the greater the significance ascribed to the purely military indicators of the correlation.

(4)   Some Soviet writers attempt to include the concept of the correlation of military forces in more general and more theoretical discussions on the nature of war and warfare. They are trying to discover recurring patterns and dependences in armed struggle, which may be expressed as laws of war and warfare and then translated into principles of successful action. The correlation of military forces — which is one of the key concepts in the military studies — should also be analysed in this perspective.

One of the first effects is that the impact of the correlation of military forces has been included as a key factor in the contents of the principal so-called laws of war and warfare. In this perspective, the main ideas concerning the correlation of military force will be recapitulated below (a more detailed analysis is given in a separate study by this author).[14]

(5)   Like their Western counterparts, Soviet researchers, military men and politicians are concerned with the problem of measuring the correlation of military forces. Their main preoccupation is to measure the strategic nuclear forces, although it seems that they give more attention than the Western side to other components of military force.

(6)   Finally, it should be noted that all the Soviet analyses of the correlation in question are highly political. The dominating proposition in Soviet writings is that in all main components of 'forces' (which are the key values in the comparison) the Soviet state and the Soviet armed forces are superior to the probable adversary. The correlation of military forces, which is increasingly advantageous to the Soviet Union, is regarded as greatly affecting Western military doctrines and, more generally, obliging the Western policy chiefs to make retreats and revisions. Some Western analysts regard the underlying attitude here as evidencing a desire to achieve a war-winning capability. Whether this is true or not, it shows the attention which military policy-makers are paying to all the components of the military power of the Soviet state. Consequently, they emphasise the need to seek a comprehensive concept of the correlation of military forces which omits none of its important components.

Notes

1 'Sootnoshenie sil i sredstv', in *Sovetskaya Voennaya Entsiklopediya'*, vol. VII, p. 445; 'Correlation of forces and means is an objective indicator of combat power of the belligerent sides, which permits an evaluation of the degree of superiority of one of them over the other one. The correct calculus of the correlation of forces and means contributes to taking well-founded decisions, to creating in time and to maintaining the necessary superiority over the enemy in chosen directions. It is determined by the comparison of the qualitative and quantitative characteristics of small units, units, formations, and weapons of one's own forces and those of the enemy. It is calculated on strategic, operational and tactical scales in the entire battle zone (region), in the main and secondary directions' ('Sootnoshenie sil i sredstv', *Voennyi Entsiklopedicheskii Slovar'*, 1983, p. 691). 'Correlation of forces and means: the aggregate of indices permitting evaluation of the relative strength of the friendly and hostile troops by comparative analysis of the quantitative and qualitative characteristics of troops organization, performance data, armament and combat material, as well as other indices that determine the combat readiness and combat capability of the troops' *(Slovar' osnovnykh voennykh terminov,* Voenizdat, Moscow 1965, p. 210). Cf. Lukava, 1984, p. 20.

2 'Boevaya moshch' in *Sovetskaya Voennaya Entsiklopediya*, vol. 2, p. 513. 'The combat power of the armed forces together with the mobilisatory potentialities of a country, constitutes its proper military potential. This potential, in a condensed form, expresses all the material and spiritual potentialities of the country' (Bondarenko, 1976, p. 197). Cf. *Kurs marksistsko — leninskoi filosofii,* E.A. Khomenko, M.I. Yasyukov, eds, Voenizdat, Moscow 1974 (2nd ed.), p. 487.

3 The main theme in Lukava, 1984, especially p. 23.

4 Lukava, 1984, Cf. S. Borisov, 'Belyi dom pod znakom militarizatsii i shovinizma', *Kommunist Vooruzhennykh Sil,* 1981:3, pp. 81—5.

5 J. Lider, *Military Force,* 1981.

6 *Slovar' osnovnykh voennykh terminov,* 1965, p. 42.

7 Tabunov, 1982, p. 20. He enumerates four basic spheres of social life: economic, social, political and spiritual (p. 21).

8 Cf. J. Lider, *Military Force,* 1981, Chs. 7 and 8.

9 Ibid., pp. 172—3.

10 Cf. Savkin, 1972, p. 111; *Marksizm-Leninizm on War and Army,* 1972, p. 250; *Kurs marksistsko leninskoi filosofii* (Note 2), p. 487.

11   Lukava, 1984:2.
12   Cf. Lukava, 1984:2.
13   Ibid, the main theme. Cf. 'K novym rubezham boegotovnosti', *K.V.S.*, 1984:23.
14   Cf. J. Lider, *On the Political and Military Laws of War*, 1979.

10 Impact in war

Agenda

The physical clash of forces constitutes the basic front of war; thus the correlation of military forces in armed struggle (warfare) plays the most direct and decisive role. This was the reason for the thorough Soviet inquiry into the impact of the correlation of forces on the course and outcome of war as a whole and specifically on armed struggle and its particular aspects. The analysis resulted in the establishment of three sets of propositions concerning this impact in a 'codified' form, which were presented as *laws.*[1]

A collective work on the Marxist-Leninist philosophy and methodology of military theory and practice states: 'In the final account, the correlation of material and spiritual forces of the combating sides conditions the course and outcome of war. This general, indeed universal, law operates through a system of laws of war and armed struggle'.[2] It is then explained that these laws express the essential dependences between, on the one hand, the course and the outcome of war and, on the other, the military power of states, which expresses the sum of their potentialities. Let us examine the manner in which the Marxist-Leninists approach the formulation of these laws.

Concerning the way in which the causes, course and outcome of war depend on the correlation of forces, they consider three groups of laws:[3]

(1) *General laws of war* which relate to war as a whole and as a socio-political phenomenon occurring in all epochs. These express the essen-

tial, internal, necessary and repetitive relations of war to the basic areas of social life — economic, political, ideological and others — as well as the internal relations between the structural components of war. They operate differently with regard to states having different social systems.

(2) *General laws of warfare (armed struggle)*, which are also called *specific laws of war*. These express the way armed struggle depends on the political content of war, on the development of the economy and of military technology, of human resources and other factors.

(3) Individual (particular, specific) *laws of warfare* related to particular levels of armed struggle (combats, army and front operations), the categories of armed struggle (offensive and defensive operations), the character of armed struggle and forces (regular or irregular forces and operations, civil defence), the environments in which warfare is carried on (air warfare, land warfare, sea warfare) and so on.

Some writers call the aggregate of these three groups 'laws of war', others call the particular groups 'laws of war', 'laws of warfare' and 'laws of the effectiveness of armed struggle'. The first group of laws is analysed in the Marxist-Leninist teaching on war and army, the second in the general theory of military science, and the third is the subject of the particular fields of military art.

Laws of the dependence on the correlation of forces constitute a significant part of each of these groups of laws (see below).

General laws of war related to the correlation of forces

Laws of the dependence of the course and outcome of war on the correlation of forces

The codification of the dependence of the course and outcome of war as a whole on the correlation of the aggregate of social factors — political, economic, ideological, moral-psychological, techno-scientific and military — is the result of a lengthy conceptual development, through many discussions and changes. This began with the analysis of the factors which determine war and the principal front of war — armed struggle. The scientific and practical interest in such an analysis was, from the early stages of the development of Soviet military thought, dictated by political and ideological necessities: those of describing and emphasising such determinants of the fate of war as the Soviet state and its army, in an early stage of their development, could rely on. It reflected the economic reality (not promising at that time) and the very limited possibilities of providing the armed forces with armament and equipment.

Thus, in the first post-revolutionary years, when the technology and armament basis were poor, theory stressed the importance of the political and moral factors, which were presented as determining the course and outcome of war; scholars and politicians also emphasised the value of the new revolutionary quality of the armed forces. As industry began to expand, the role of the economy and of the strength of the rear in the description of the 'factors of victory' also grew. Through the whole interwar period the superiority of the Soviet state and socialist system in the *aggregate* of factors determining the course and outcome of war as a whole was emphasised.

In 1942 Stalin formulated the thesis on the five permanently-acting factors determining the course and outcome of war. The thesis was closely connected with the concrete contemporary political, military and economic tasks of the country and its army: it pointed out the direction of main efforts, and also aimed at raising the spirit of the people and army in a very dangerous situation. It was in fact a set of political and economic *postulates and directives,* called 'factors'.

However, it was at the same time considered, and afterwards in fact became a basic theoretical proposition delimiting the scope and defining the main ideas of all military research and military theory. It was called a 'thesis', 'proposition' and the like, but was treated as a law, and the main one, since it pointed out the main dependence in war, the set of factors regarded as determining its course and outcome.[4]

After Stalin's death both the validity of the 'permanent-factors-thesis' and its law-like status as determining the scope of military theory, were questioned and many changes were gradually introduced. The term 'thesis' was replaced by 'formula' , the expression 'permanently acting' was abandoned, 'determining' was replaced by 'influencing' and the five factors were soon reformulated and restructured into three: economic, political, and military (called factors, potentials, possibilities, and the like). Another change was the admission of the role of so-called transitory factors. (cf. Chapter 9.)

At the end of the 1950s and during the 1960s and 1970s, the following tendencies in the development of the theory can be identified:

(1) The replacement of the five 'permanent' factors, which were very different as regards their scope, structure, and force of influence, by the potentials representing the main fields of social activity — the economic, techno-scientific, moral-political (sometimes called ideological) and military.

In some studies the politico-moral potential was replaced by three other potentials: the social, the political and the spiritual.[5] The social potential was defined as expressing the social — primarily class — structure of society and consequently the degree of cohesiveness in the relations between classes and nationalities, as well as between society as a whole and social collectives and individuals. The political potential expresses the potentialities for waging war arising from the political system; and the spiritual potential expresses the potentialities rooted in the spiritual life of society, and primarily in the moral and political awareness of the classes.

This change is of special importance with regard to the correlation of military forces, and even to the correlation of world forces, since it emphasises the importance of the socio-economic and political systems as the *basis* of the entire power, military and global, of a state or a coalition.[6]

(2) Changes in the content and structure of the potentials according to the conditions and requirements of the nuclear missile age — for instance, the emphasis on the techno-scientific potential, on the possibilities of automating a good deal of human activity, the dominance of the nuclear missile armament in the military factor, etc.

(3) The increasing role of military potential proper, with emphasis on the nuclear missile 'forces in being'.

(4) Rejection of automatism in the interpretation of the thesis: potentials do not *ensure* victory in an automatic way, they must be transformed into real factors, actual forces superior to those at the disposal of the enemy.[7]

(5) The replacement of the absolute size of potentials (factors, etc.) by the *correlation of forces.*

(6) Finally, application of a 'more objective approach: laws and dependences have begun to be presented as acting on both sides.

As the number of publications devoted to the problem increased, new proposals were put forward concerning the formulation of a single *unified law* which would express all the given dependences as a whole.

In the 1960s, the old formula on the five permanent factors, after several modifications, was transformed into a formal law. The factors were described as dynamic and changing, depending on the degree to which the corresponding potentials were exploited; in other words, factors were presented as potentials transformed into real forces.

The law was phrased in three alternative ways:

(1) In the most general form, as the law of the dependence of the course and outcome of war on its *material and spiritual* basis, or on the *correlation of military power* regarded as representing the *whole power of the state in war:* 'The dependence of the course and outcome of war on the correlation of military forces of warring sides, regarded dynamically, and taking into consideration the political aims of the parties, is the general law of war.'[8] In another wording, this was called the law of the determining role of the correlation of the material and spiritual forces of the warring sides.[9] .

It was pointed out, however, that the ethical or spiritual superiority over the enemy can manifest itself and affect the course and outcome of combats or operations only *through* the material force of the weapons applied. Thus the moral superiority was to be *transformed* into a material superiority which would lead directly to victory. This was called 'the dialectics of the moral and material forces in armed struggle'.[10]

(2)   In a more detailed form, war was said to be dependent on the *correlation of the entirety* of the economic, scientific, politico-moral and military forces proper, and on the ability of a protagonist to *change* this correlation in his own favour.[11]

(3)   Finally, the new law was presented as a *set* of partial laws, which express the dependence of the course and outcome of war on the correlation of the economic potentials of warring sides, their techno-scientific potentials, their socio-political systems, their politico-moral potentials and their military potentials.[12]

In the military encyclopaedia,[13] and other authoritative works[14] four laws of this kind are formulated:

(1)   The dependence of the course and outcome of war on the correlation of the *economic forces* (potentials) of the warring sides (coalitions). The economic conditions which, in the final account, determine the level of development of the military science and military power of the belligerents, were said to be in all epochs the decisive factor; in our times, the outcome of war depends more than ever on the development of the material production.

(2)   The dependence of the course and outcome of war on the correlation of the *scientific (or techno-scientific) potentials* of the belligerents. This law also now operates more effectively than ever, since science has become a direct productive force. Technology is here regarded as a component part of science.

(3)   The dependence of the course and outcome of war on the correlation of the *politico-moral (or moral) forces and potentials* of the warring states (coalitions). Nowadays, when the warring sides possess the means of mass destruction and (can use) mass armies, this law operates with special force.

In a more general form this law has been expressed as the law of the dependence of the course and outcome of war on the correlation of the social and politico-moral forces and potentials of the warring states (coalitions). The addition of the term 'social' is here of special importance: the law is said to express the impact of the *social and political systems* of the warring sides, of the *social structure* of the state, of the *correlation of class forces* and of the institutions in the *superstructure.*[15]

Here we find a direct connection between the military dimension of the correlation of forces and its sociological dimension, which was mentioned in Chapter 1.

The conclusion drawn from the above is that the essential processes of war are determined by the political aims and by the correlation of the economic, scientific, social, politico-moral and strictly military forces.[16]

(4)   Last but not least, the dependence of the course and outcome of war on the correlation of the military forces (potentials) of the warring sides. Here military force is conditioned by the economic, social, politico-moral, scientific, technical and strictly military potentials.

Those writers who distinguish between six factors, or components of military power, accordingly formulate six laws of the dependence of the course and outcome of war: on the correlation of economic forces of the belligerent states (coalitions); on the social system, social structure and social forces of the states (coalitions); on the political systems of the states (coalitions); on their spiritual forces; on the correlation of the techno-scientific factors among the belligerent parties; and on the correlation of military factors.[17] The difference between this set and all others also consists in emphasising the dependence on factors rather than on potentials (factors being defined here as 'realised potentials').

No final set of laws has been agreed on and, in particular, no choice has been made between a single law stating the dependence of war on the correlation of all forces (potentials), considered as the entire state power, and a set of laws stating a set of dependences of war on the correlation of particular forces (potentials).[18]

A compromise has been proposed in a textbook for officers (in 'Officer's Library'). At first, four laws have been presented stating the dependence of war on the following correlations: (1) that of economic forces; (2) that of scientific potentials; (3) that of social and moral political forces; and (4) that of military forces. These laws have been said to be aspects of a more general law: the law of the decisive role in war of the correlation of the material and spiritual forces of the belligerents.[19]

As we see, the terminology has not been finally established. The shift in emphasis from factors to potentials in the late 1950s was followed by concentration on 'forces in being'. This was quite natural under the conditions of the nuclear missile age, but finally no clear priority was established. Up to now the terms 'factors', 'potentials', and 'forces' have often been used interchangeably. The authors of the *Marksistsko-leninskaya filosofiya i metodologicheskie problemy voennoi teorii i praktiki* consider that potentials, or components of military power, represent only possibilities which should be realised. This is not always accomplished, however. They propose the term 'military readiness of the country' and 'combat readiness of armed forces' to describe the capability of a state instantly to enter a war.

They also use the term 'factor' to mean potentialities set in motion which become motive forces of warfare. Factors are these parts of potentials which a protagonist has succeeded in transforming into active forces. The capability of a state to make such a transformation depends on both objective potentialities and subjective forces: the organisation of the leadership and management, the politico-moral

260

condition of the society and armed forces and the degree of realism in the military-political doctrine.[20]

It is interesting to observe that Soviet theory stresses the interdependence of these laws and of more general propositions about the correlation of world forces. This is done in two perspectives. First, it is stated that the change in the correlation of world forces in favour of socialism affects changes in the laws of war, and in particular in the laws of correlation of forces, since the influence of the international ties of the warring sides on the course and outcome of war must be included in the set of the above mentioned factors affecting the final fate of war.[21]

Further, it is considered that an *active policy* may profoundly affect the correlation of forces during a war. The outcome of war depends not only on the correlation of the military might of the countries or coalitions of countries, but also on a protagonist's ability to change the international situation to his own advantage and to create a military superiority at a given place and take advantage of it. Here the political strategy is closely linked to the military one.[22]

Basic law of war

As the research into all of the above-mentioned laws developed, proposals were made concerning the formulation of a single unified law which would express the sum of the dependences of war on the correlation of forces *combined* with the dependence of war on policy, which is the basic content of another group of general laws of war. One such proposal concerning the dependence of war as a whole on the material and spiritual (or non-material) basis of war or on the correlation of military powers has been mentioned earlier.

Two other proposals were also put forward. One of them described the determining influence of the *political content* or war on its character, course and outcome as the basic law or war, i.e., it did not include the dependence on the correlation of forces.[23] This was perhaps a modification of a much earlier formulation proposed by Popov in his treatise on the laws of war,[24] in which he stated that the determining influence of *politics* on armed violence was the basic law of war.

The second proposal *combined* the law of the determining influence on war of the *correlation of forces* with the law of the determining influence of the *political content* of war. In a collective study, the basic law of war was described as: 'The law of the determining influence of the political content of war and correlation of forces of the mutually opposing sides on the character, course and outcome of war'.[25] This formula and similar ones[26] tell us more than a simple sum of the two component laws since they assert the interaction and interdependence

261

of both the political goals of war and the correlation of forces (which are primarily military ones). Goals, to be realistic, must depend on the appropriate correlation of military forces, and both the goals and the correlation change in the same direction and affect war in the same direction, since both depend on the character of the sociopolitical system.

Finally, in a compromise proposal, a textbook for officers posits that *two laws* — that on the determining role of the political aims of war and that on the decisive impact of the correlation of the material and spiritual forces of the belligerents — decide of the sociopolitical character of war and its dynamics (i.e., its course and outcome). This assertion is supplemented by two propositions. First, the course and outcome of war are said to be determined by the *whole system of laws*, not only by the most general ones. Second, an additional important law is formulated: historically wins the belligerent who represents the new and more progressive social and economic system and effectively exploits the potentialities inherent in it.[27] The authors of *Marxistsko-lenininskaya filosofiya i metodologicheskie problemy voennoi teorii i praktiki* propose a similar pair of laws.[28]

To sum up, it seems that the basic law of war has not yet been finally established and the search for it continues. Whatever the outcome, the correlation of forces will play a decisive role in its formulation.

Part of a broader system

The laws of the correlation of forces, together with other laws of war and armed struggle, are part of a broader system of laws which operate in war. These are philosophical laws (such as the law of the unity and struggle of opposites), sociological laws (such as the laws of class struggle or of the dependence of victory in just wars on the unity and cohesion of world revolutionary forces)[29] and strictly military laws. The interconnection of these laws links even closer the correlation of military forces with the correlation of intrasocietal and international forces in the framework of the correlation of world forces.

Why do the formulae differ?

Differences in the formulation of the laws are explained by Soviet researchers as follows.

The objective laws of war and warfare are independent of the will and consciousness of men as regards their content and form. When cognised by men, they are formulated as scientific laws; since they reflect objective laws, they are objective as regards their content, but since they are analysed by different researchers, holding possibly divergent views concerning the hierarchy of issues and the importance of particular aspects, the analysis results in various formulae.[30] Apart from this explanation, the reason why there exist various formulations of laws which obviously differ not only with regard to their form but also in their *content* (which includes, for instance, in the laws of the correlation of forces *various factors* affecting war and warfare), seems to be that the theory of the correlation of forces is in a state of constant flux and — as a theory — perhaps only *in statu nascendi.*

Lacunae

The Marxist-Leninist theory of the laws concerning the impact of the correlation of forces on war has significant lacunae. Both the global correlation of forces (the 'world' one) and its military component have extended their impact on war beyond the course and outcome of hostilities to cover *the outbreak of war* as well as its *prevention.* Soviet political and politico-military literature devotes primary attention just to the impact of the correlation of world forces including its crucial military component on the prevention of war and emphasises the restraining influence of the present state of the correlation. (Cf. Chapters 6 and 7.) Soviet military theory, however, which declares its interest in the laws of the genesis of war, has not dealt with the impact of the correlation of forces on the outbreak of various types of war. It seems like a paradox that the impact of the correlation of forces on the course and outcome of wars which are becoming unlikely is analysed, defined and redefined and has acquired the status of law, while the impact of the correlation of forces on the genesis and also the prevention of war has no place in the analysis and in the respective group of the laws of war.

General laws of warfare (armed struggle) related to the correlation of forces

Law of the dependence of the effectiveness of armed struggle on the correlation of forces

To turn to the impact of the correlation of forces directly participating in a military operation, battle or combat on the course of fighting, this has been formulated as the law of the dependence of the *effectiveness of armed struggle* (or, in another wording, on the course and outcome of armed struggle) on the correlation of forces. It was presented in two variants. According to the narrower concept the course and outcome of armed struggle (operation, battle or combat) depends on the correlation of the *combat power* of the troops directly participating in it:[31] at any given moment in the development of any operation, battle or combat, the shape it takes will favour the side whose forces have a greater combat power than the enemy's.[32] The correlation of forces on a particular sector of the front at a certain time may differ from the global correlation of the armed forces which are fighting against each other.

In a much broader interpretation, rather concerning large actions, the winning side in a military operation will be that which is superior in means and forces — i.e., in the complex of all the political, economic and strictly military factors.[33] (Here there is no clear difference between a general law of war which operates with all sociopolitical, economic and strictly military forces which constitute the military power of a state and a law of armed struggle which concerns only the factors which affect combat power.) Some proponents of the latter law consider it to be *the basic law of armed struggle,* since only a superiority in combat power enables the forces to assert their own appropriate methods of combat, to exploit fully the terrain and the time factor, to seize the initiative and to achieve further changes in a correlation of power that is to their own advantage.

Other laws of armed struggle

The correlation of forces is presented not only as determining the whole course of development taken by the operation, battle or combat but also as affecting conditions for the action of other laws of armed struggle.[34] These serve the attainment of a favourable correlation of forces. One such law holds that in any military action the troops which *forestall* the enemy in deploying forces into combat and operational formations and outpace him at the beginning of the action will gain a considerable advantage.[35] Another law asserts the essential dependence of the course and outcome of each military action on the concentration of the main efforts of the participating forces *on the decisive axis.* Yet another law asserts the necessity to *unevenly* deploy the means and forces along the front line.[36]

The above-mentioned statements about the determining influence of the correlation of forces and other interconnected laws of armed struggle provide a representative example of the way in which the common experience of combat is raised to the status of a law.

'Forces' mean combat power in action

As we have seen, in most descriptions based on the narrower concept of the law of the effectiveness of armed struggle the term 'forces' means the combat power of the troops directly engaged in the given action,[37] and therefore includes all the quantitative and qualitative characteristics of means and forces, together with the level of military art at their command.[38] However, some writers recall that in the final account the amount of combat power depends on the country's economic and psychological potentialities and on the political content of the war.[39]

In some writings particular features of the correlation of forces as a relationship in armed struggle are described:

(1) Although the correlation of forces on a tactical scale is part of an analogous balance on an operational scale, the latter being, in turn, a part of the global strategic balance of military powers, such a relationship is valid only 'in principle'. The correlation of forces on any lower level, and especially on the tactical one, is relatively independent of the more general balance, and a situation may arise when a favourable tactical correlation of forces is created in spite of an unfavourable global balance.

(2) Since armed forces consist of various components and various combinations of them, different components play the decisive role in different situations. Numerical superiority is frequently the determining factor, but in many situation other components — e.g., combat morale — may prevail.

(3) The correlation of forces is extremely dynamic: it changes as conditions change, for instance as a result of successful — or unsuccessful — combat operations. The higher the level of fighting, the greater the influence of social, economic, scientific and other conditions, and on the strategic level — of the international politico-military situation. The size and rates of the change also depend on the form of combat and the weapons used. The correlation of forces changes more quickly and dynamically in air and tank battles, and it may change extremely rapidly and radically in any combat involving nuclear missile weapons. These enable the troops to alter the correlation of forces suddenly from an unfavourable to a favourable one, but also simultaneously on the operational and strategic scale, and not only on the tactical one.

The most interesting fact about the interpretation of the concept of the correlation of forces — i.e., combat power — as a law-like factor determining the course and outcome of each military action is that it includes the ability of the commander to *create* and to *use* the favourable correlation — i.e., create the conditions for victory.[39] Thus also at this level of the use of military force the concept of the correlation of forces includes *action* as an integral component.

Nuclear conditions

The mechanism of the operation of the law of the effectiveness of armed struggle has profoundly changed under the conditions of the nuclear age. Nowadays it is not the initial correlation of combat forces which determines, or at least greatly influences, the final outcome of a military action but the ability quickly to change it in one's favour through fighting. This is now considered possible and necessary because of the availability of nuclear weapons and the high degree of mobility of the troops; the former can destroy the combat power of the enemy, the latter makes it possible quickly to take advantage of the results of nuclear strikes. Changes in the correlation of forces can now be achieved in minutes, and even seconds.[40]

Such changes in the mechanism of this law may affect its objective content. If this mechanism could previously be expressed by the formula: correlation affects the outcome of fighting, it should now, perhaps, be replaced by a more complex formula — namely, initial fighting, partly depending on the initial correlation, affects the resultant correlation, which in turn determines the outcome of the fighting as a whole.

Pitfalls of the analysis

The laws of the correlation of forces that relate to warfare engender an analytical (and thus also an empirical) danger. In the assessment of the impact of the comparison of forces, there is a tendency to overestimate and thus over-emphasise the quantitative comparison of the military forces and to regard fire-power as its main criterion, to the detriment of not only such intangible values as the abilities of the commanders and the moral condition of the military personnel, but also all the components of military art. However, a situation is conceivable in which it is the *strategy* of using the available military force (and also lower levels of military art) that determines the outcome of armed combat. This may happen particularly in a war involving the use of nuclear weapons when both sides possess great (or even an over-kill) capacity, and therefore have an approximately equal destructive power. Even if one side is initially slightly superior in destructive power, the other may win because it has a better strategy, operational art or even tactics. In both cases the 'correlation of forces' either ceases to be the determining factor or it remains such a factor only in combination with strategy and military art as a whole.

Admittedly, military art, and particularly strategy may be implicitly *included* in the concept of the correlation of military forces as an intangible value, and it seems that it is so included by some Soviet writers.

However, they might more appropriately state it explicitly in presenting the concept, and perhaps also include strategy or military art as a whole in the texts of the laws of the correlation of forces.

Correlation of forces and military art

Mutual impact

It is not only that military art greatly affects the actual value of the correlation of military forces: the impact is mutual, since a favourable correlation of forces widens the possibilities of military art and makes it possible to select the most expedient variants of the operations — for instance, in a nuclear war the best variant of a nuclear strike;[42] to create conditions for a variety of combat actions; to manifest flexibility in the creation of the combat formation and operational organisation of the armed forces; to enlarge the possibilities of combining fire and manoeuvre; to make a better use of space, time and the other factors which influence military operations.

Moreover, a favourable correlation of forces *on one level* enlarges the possibilities of military art *on other levels.* Here also essential changes in the interpretation of this proposition may be observed. Consider the traditional formula: 'A superiority in the relationship of forces on the higher level creates favourable conditions for successful military actions on lower levels, and the possibility of establishing a superiority of forces in military actions on a lower level contributes to the change in the relationship of forces on the higher level.'[43]

In this context the development of nuclear weapons introduces a significant change. In all forms of military actions in the past and in the conventional wars of the present the relationship of forces has been changing fairly smoothly from the tactical level through the operational level to the strategic level, but now it is becoming possible by means of nuclear strikes to change the relationship of forces simultaneously on the strategic and operational-tactical levels.[44] As we have mentioned, an advantageous correlation of military forces widens the possibilities of military art, but it is also necessary that military operations be conducted in a *special manner:* a protagonist must try radically to change the correlation in his own favour. It is necessary to take measures which can change the correlation *at the very beginning* of an action, for instance by a pre-emptive attack — a surprise attack which will make impossible for the enemy to use all his forces. The most expedient action, of course, would be to destroy some of them before they dispatched to the scene of combat. Another conceivable action would be to destroy, or at least damage, the enemy's command, control and communication systems.

In other words, a type of military art should be accepted and practised which from the very beginning of a war and during it *constantly aims at improving the correlation of forces.*

Principles of military art based on the correlation of forces

The final subject under this heading is the impact of the correlation of forces on the principles of military art. In Soviet theory these principles are defined as basic ideas concerning the successful conduct of armed struggle and the basic recommendations for organising this.[45] They are connected with the correlation of military force in a double way.

First, the *plan* of any military operation or combat is established on the basis of the knowledge of laws of war and principles of military art. The principles are reflected in manuals, regulations and instructions. In the prevailing Soviet view, the principles of military art are considered to be a direct reflection of the laws of armed struggle. They are said to derive from the laws and to correspond to them exactly.[46]

For instance, the law which holds that the course and outcome of armed struggle depend on the correlation of forces of the belligerents, and the corollary statement that victory will go to the side which succeeds in concentrating superior forces and means at the decisive place at the decisive moment, involve the corresponding principle of the concentration of forces and means superior to those of the enemy at key sectors and at appropriate times.

Other principles of military art should also facilitate to create, in the final account, a favourable correlation of forces in the beginning of an operation (combat) and, moreover, to change it further in his favour in the course of the action and as the result of this.

Second, while the laws of war and the principles of military art form the theoretical basis of the plan of an operation (combat), its *direct* basis consists of the concept of the action ordered by a higher chain of command and adapted by the commander. The order and its adaptation are based on the assessment of the actual correlation of forces. This is here included both in the theory — which is distilled from experience and the conclusions drawn from the development of military technology and military art — and in the recognition of the actual situation, on which the plan of the concrete action is based.

Notes

1 Cf. J. Lider, *The Political and Military Laws of War,* 1979;
Serebryannikov, 1982, Ch. IV.

2 *Marksistsko-leninskaya filosofiya i metodologicheskie problemy
voennoi teorii i praktiki,* 1982, p. 284.

3 Serebryannikov, 1982, pp. 155—7.

4 *O sovetskoi voennoi nauke,* 1964, p. 292. Cf. Popov, 1964, pp. 34
ff. for the criticism of this proposition.

5 This is 'the established view' according to the authors of
*Marksistsko-leninskaya filosofiya i metodologicheskie problemy
voennoi teorii i praktiki,* 1982, p.285.

6 Ibid., pp. 286—7.

7 'Potential means the true possibilities of a country (coalition)
which can be exploited for the conduct of war. War constitutes a
very complex set of phenomena and processes, and the possibilities may be transformed into reality, or may not ... The notion
of the "factor" is very broad, it means the role of each material
and spiritual element of the objective world in war phenomena and
processes'. Thus each effort or condition which in some way
affects the course and outcome of war can be regarded as a 'factor'
(Prokop'ev, 1965, pp. 212—13); 'Potentials and their elements, set
in motion when aggression by an opponent is possible, or in the
course of war, become factors — i.e., driving forces, and conditions
of victory or defeat'(*Marksizm-leninizm o voine i armii,* 1957,
p. 246); 'The moral factor ... is the moral potential in action'
(Il'in, 1969, p. 8; in the same words: Tabunov, 1980, p. 30).

   Serebryannikov writes that military power depends on the
ability to mobilise the potentials — all the material and spiritual
potentialities of a country — which in turn depends on the character of the sociopolitical system (1982, pp. 146—7).

8 For instance, 'The dependence of the course and outcome of war
on the correlation of military force of warring sides, regarded
dynamically, and taking into consideration the political aims of
the parties, is the general law of war' (*Marksizm-leninizm o voine
i armii,* 1957, p. 245). Lenin presented the law of the dependence
of the course and outcome of war on the correlation of the
material, moral-political and military potentials (N. Azovtsev,
'V.I. Lenin — osnovopolozhnik sovetskoi voennoi nauki', *K.V.S.,*
1968:8; c.f. Azovtsev, 1971).

9 *Voina i Armiya,* 1977, p. 154. 'The war experience in different
historical epochs demonstrates that the relation of the material
and moral forces of the warring armed forces always constitutes
the deep basis of the course of combat and its final outcome'
(*Metodologicheskie problemy voennoi teorii i praktiki,*

1969, p. 321).

10 *Metodologicheskie problemy voennoi teorii i praktiki*, 1969, p. 322.

11 Ibid., Chapter XIII entitled 'Dialektika sootnosheniya sil v vooruzhennoi bor'be', pp. 297—318. Lenin pointed out that all components of the correlation of forces, all material and spiritual forces of both fighting parties, had to be taken into account (S. Ivanov, 'V.I. Lenin i sovetskaya voennaya strategiya', *K.V.S.*, 1970:8).

The law is also described as the dependence of victory and defeat on the correlation of *military power* of the warring sides. Its discovery has been attributed to Lenin (*Filosofskoe nasledie V.I. Lenina i problemy sovremennoi voiny*, 1972, p. 138). Here military power is seemingly considered the entire state power engaged in war.

12 'Voina' in *Sovetskaya Istoricheskaya Entsiklopediya*, Izd, Sovetskaya Entsiklopediya, vol. 3, Moscow 1963, p. 622.

13 'Zakony i obychai voiny', *Sovetskaya Voennaya Entsiklopediya*, Vol. 3, pp. 375—7; Cf. 'Zakony voiny', *Voennyi Entsiklopedicheski Slovar'*, p. 262.

14 *Voina i Armiya*, 1977, pp. 154—8.

15 Ibidem., p. 156.

16 Ibid., p. 157.

17 *Marksistko-leninskaya filosofiya i metodologicheskie problemy voennoi teorii i praktiki*, 1982, pp. 302—4.

18 Note that other dependences have also been formulated as laws — for instance, the dependence of the course and outcome of war on the correlation of the 'condition of the rear' in the warring countries (Skirdo, 1970, p. 97).

19 *Marksistsko-leninskoe uchenie o voine i armii*, 1984, pp. 73—6.

20 Ibid., pp. 290—1, p. 294.

21 'Zakony i obychai voiny', loc. cit., p. 378.

22 Cf. Morozov, Tyushkevich, 1967.

23 Serebryannikov, 1982, p. 156.

24 Popov, 1964.

25 *Voina i Armiya*, 1977, p. 154.

26 'The political content of war and the correlation of forces decisively influence the origin of war, its character, its course and outcome' (Morozov, Tyushkevich, 1967). Tyushkevich writes: 'The law of the unity of the determining influence of the political goals and the correlation of forces of warring sides can be regarded as the basic law of war, expressing its nature. It stresses the fact that war is waged by opposing sides for opposing goals, but these goals are founded on a certain correlation of forces as on their objective basis ...' (1975, p. 231). Cf. *Filosofskoe nasledie V.I.*

Lenina i problemy sovremennoi voiny, 1972, pp. 137—9:
The two above mentioned laws are presented as general and universal by Skirdo, 1970, pp. 97—9.

27 *Marksistsko-leninskoe uchenie o voine i armii*, 1984, p. 76.
28 *Marksistsko-leninskoya filosofiya i metodologicheskie problemy voennoi teorii i praktiki*, 1982, pp. 304—6.
29 *Marksistsko-leninskaya filosofiya i metodologicheskie problemy voennoi teorii i praktiki*, 1982, pp. 301—2.
30 *Marksistko-leninskoe uchenie o voine i armii*, 1984, p. 77.
31 Popov, 1964, p. 77. He also presented a complementary law which related victory to the concentration of the main efforts on the decisive axis (p. 81). In a later study, both laws received a modified wording: 'The course of a battle, engagement, or operation depends on the relationship of the material and morale of the belligerents; this, too, is a basic law of armed struggle', and 'The course and outcome of a battle, engagement, or operation depends on achieving superiority over the enemy in the decisive sector at a decisive moment; this, too, is a law of armed struggle' ('The Principles of Military Art and the Laws of Armed Struggle', *Soviet Military Review*, 1966:3, p. 3).
32 *Metodologicheskie problemy voennoi teorii i praktiki*, 1969, p. 323; Savkin, p. 110.
33 S.N. Kozlov et al., *O sovetskoi voennoi nauke*, Voenizdat, Moscow 1964, (2nd ed.), p. 316.
34 *Metodologicheskie problemy voennoi teorii i praktiki*. 1969, p. 323; Savkin, pp. 110—11.
35 Popov, 1964, p. 97. Zakharov, 1967, pp. 48—9, contends that this law, which he regards as one of the basic laws of armed struggle, underlies the principle of surprise.
36 *Metodologicheskie problemy voennoi teorii i praktiki*, p. 335; '... the effectiveness of the actions of troops depends on the nature, strength and direction of strikes delivered by them' may serve as an example (*Marxism-Leninism on War and Army*, 1972, p. 318). Cf. Tuyshkevich, 1968, pp. 13—14.

   Popov, who also presents this law is, however, inconsistent since he later contends that the law of the dependence of the course and outcome of each military action on the concentration of the main efforts on the axis of the main strike is universal in the sense that it is exploited by the commanders not only when the correlation of forces is unfavourable or when the forces are equal, but also when one of them has a clear superiority over the enemy on the whole front (1964, p. 84). Thus the character of this law as a corollary to the law of the correlation of forces is here negated.
37 Tyushkevich uses the expression 'balance of military power' (1968), Savkin terms it 'correlation of combat might', or 'combat

power' (p. 111), Zagladin 'balance of military power' (1985).

38 Tyushkevich, 1968, pp. 13—14.
39 Tyushkevich contends that the correlation of forces (balance of military power) is determined, in the final analysis, by economic conditions and circumstances; therefore it is a reflection of the law of the determining influence of the correlation of forces of warring sides on the course and outcome of war (ibid., p. 74). Engels is quoted as stating that victory or defeat depends on the size and quality of population and on the equipment available (*Marxism-Leninism on War and Army*, 1972, pp. 317—18).
40 Morozov, Tyushkevich, 1967.
41 One of the main themes in *Voennaya strategiya*, 1962, 1963, 1968; *Nauchno-tekhnicheskii progress i revolutsiya v voennom dele*, 1973, and others.
42 I. Anureyev, 'Determining the "Correlation of Forces" in Terms of Nuclear Weapons', *Voennaya Mysl*, 1967:6, after *Foreign Press Digest* (Nr. 0112/68, 11 July 1968, pp. 35—45).
43 *Metodologicheskie problemy voennoi teorii i praktiki*, 1969, pp. 304—5.
44 Ibid.
45 Popov, 1964, p. 122; *O sovetskoi voennoi nauke*, 1964, p. 324; *Marxism-Leninism on War and Army*, 1972, p. 321. '... the principles of military art are to be understood as the basic ideas and most important recommendations for the organisation and conduct of battles, operations, and war as a whole, suitable for practical use in all basic forms of troop combat activity. It is accepted that the basic principles of military art include those which are valid for all three of its parts — tactics, operational art, and strategy' (Savkin, 1972, p. 1). 'The basic initial propositions of military art are expressed in its principles, which are common for military operations on the strategic, operational and tactical scale, since they express the practical ways of the application of the objective laws of war' ('Voennoe iskusstvo' in *Voennyi Entsiklopedicheskii Slovar'*, 1983, p. 140).
46 Savkin, 1972, p. 52; *Marxism-Leninism on War and Army*, 1972, pp. 321—2. 'Laws of military science answer the question, what are the conditions and ways, the forces and means of conducting armed struggle. Principles answer the question of what to do and how to do it, in order to exploit the laws of armed struggle. Therefore, principles are recommendations, directives for action... and are formulated on the basis of the cognised laws of armed struggle' (Azovtsev, 1970, p. 30).

11 Impact in peacetime

Significance of the global correlation of military forces

Agenda

The primacy of the socio-economic and political factors and transformations in the development of domestic and world affairs is the message of Marxist-Leninist theory. However, the extreme importance of the military component of the correlation of forces has always been emphasised. Since the October Revolution it has played an essential role in all the basic stages of the revolutionary movement. Lenin is quoted as saying that revolutionary forces must be able by their military organisation and preparation not only to seize power by military means but also to be able to defend it. This was initially related to the defence of the October Revolution against the internal and external enemies of the first socialist state. The military inferiority of that defence was the primary concern of all its leaders and ideologists; the first result was that the Soviets had to accept the Treaty of Brest-Litovsk under which the young revolutionary state made great territorial concessions in order to survive.

In the following period, the main political aim of Stalin was to preserve the state with its still inferior military power, *vis-à-vis* the 'capitalist encirclement'. In the initial period of the German-Soviet war the Soviet military inferiority to the German invaders resulted in heavy defeats; great efforts were then made to change the correlation of military forces and the gradual successes in this undertaking conditioned

273

the gradual changes in the fates of war. After the war, the inferiority in nuclear weapons, and in the 1950s in the means of delivery, were the main Soviet concerns. The achievement in the early 1970s of the so-called strategic parity was therefore described as one of the basic shifts in the correlation of world forces — which was an extraordinary theoretical and ideological proposition, taking into account the above-mentioned basic assumption of Marxist-Leninism about the primacy of socio-economic and political factors as determining the course of domestic and world affairs. This may perhaps be explained by the fact that the establishment of strategic parity was regarded by Soviet politicians and scholars as a determining change in the correlation of world forces which permitted the initiation of a new and much more active and assertive policy on a global scale. This marked the very beginning of Soviet *global policy.*

In the current international relations, the global correlation of military forces is regarded as the principal instrument for implementing the programme of 'peaceful coexistence'; the general impact of the correlation of world forces was discussed in Chapter 6. The correlation of military forces is regarded by the Soviet establishment both as continuing to change in favour of the socialist camp and as decisively promoting all the basic aims of peaceful coexistence. The following advantages are mentioned in Soviet political and military literature:

(1) The global correlation of military forces prevents interstate wars between the states belonging to the two opposing camps;

(2) It affects the global military strategy concepts of the United States and NATO and limits their possibilities.

(3) It cannot prevent wars in the Third World, but it prevents military interventions by imperialist powers which might involve an escalation to an intersystemic conflict.

(4) On the other side, a correlation that is advantageous to the USSR enables that state to give full support to national liberation movements and to states that are friendly to the socialist camp.

(5) It creates a framework favouring ideological rivalry.

(6) It creates, in Europe, favourable conditions for the development of economic cooperation with the Western countries.

Concept of strategic parity

In Soviet publications concerning the correlation of forces, particularly the military ones, the concept of military parity occupies a prominent place. Since military forces are hardly measurable and, indeed, hardly comparable (see Chapter 12), the interpretation of the concept of military parity is crucial. Parity, in the Soviet view, seems to have two meanings.

In the broader concept, it means the rough overall military equality of the two superpowers, with or without the forces of their allies, but rather including the latter. The narrower concept called 'strategic parity' means the rough equality in strategic nuclear forces of the two superpowers. Recently this has been complemented by various concepts of a nuclear balance in the so-called European theatre of possible military operations — which is also called the Eurostrategic Nuclear Balance or the balance of TNF.

The characteristic features of the Soviet interpretation of the concept of strategic parity are as follows:

(1)   Strategic parity does not mean a complete symmetry — i.e., parity in all the basic components of strategic nuclear forces.

(2)   It does not preclude a disparity in conventional forces.

(3)   It does not involve — indeed, does not even imply — a parity in the global correlation of forces (correlation of world forces), with all its intangible — structural, ideological and other — values.

(4)   Strategic parity does not mean military parity in all the particular regions. It is possible to create a regional or a local superiority and utilise this to achieve a political and military *fait accompli.*

(5)   Strategic parity is largely a qualitative concept and it is not easily amenable to measurement (Chapter 12).

(6)   One may speak indirectly of strategic parity, if the strategic power of the adversaries is sufficient for them to destroy each other.[1]

Strategic parity is not military parity

The comparison of the military forces of the countries which possess an entire range of armaments and forces exceeds strategic nuclear forces to include theatre nuclear forces in various regions, theatre conventional forces, general purpose forces deployed at home, strategic defence forces and other components. Parity in one component of course does not mean equality in the entirety of military forces. Paradoxically, strategic parity — i.e., parity in strategic nuclear forces — may even contribute to the exploitation of a superiority in other components — for instance in conventional forces — for the attainment of particular political or politico-military aims. The same may result from a military advantage in a certain region. While the existence of a strategic parity restrains the superpowers from directly confronting each other, one of them may exploit a regionally or locally advantageous situation for a military action — as the USSR did when occupying Afghanistan and as Soviet allies did when carrying out actions (interventions by proxy) in Africa.

Soviet politicians and analysts have also begun to speak and write about 'military equivalence' or the parity of military potentials, using these terms interchangeably with 'strategic parity'.[2]

The broader concept of 'military parity' or 'military-strategic balance' (*militärstrategische Gleichgewicht*) is used to mean parity in three respects: (1) a dynamic parity of nuclear strategic forces between the superpowers; (2) a rough parity in medium-range nuclear weapons in Europe; (3) a rough parity in the NATO and Warsaw treaty conventional forces (including, apparently, battlefield nuclear weapons).[3]

Soviet politicians and writers use interchangeably both of the terms 'military parity' and 'strategic parity' mainly when considering the relations between the two superpowers and, more recently, between NATO and WTO.

In the first years after the Second World War it was emphasised that in modern times a war cannot be won with a single kind of weapon and this implied the need to develop comprehensive military force; that was the time of the American monopoly and growing superiority in nuclear weapons. Subsequently, however, and in contradiction to their previous arguments, the Soviet leadership began to use their achievements in the field of nuclear weapons as the main line in their propaganda about the correlation of military forces said to be constantly changing to their advantage. The Soviet conventional build-up was always toned down, and seemingly for different reasons in different periods. In the first post-war decades, the great Soviet superiority in the number of conventional forces in Europe was played down, since it was the main Western argument for a comprehensive expansion of both the nuclear and conventional forces. For quite different reasons no Soviet comparison of the conventional forces in the extra-European territories was made: the Soviet Union was inferior there in its capability of projecting conventional forces over great distances. In the following decades, the conventional superiority in Europe continued to be played down — *inter alia*, because of the negotiations for the mutual reduction of armaments and forces there. The rapid build-up of the Soviet capability of projecting conventional forces to the Third World was not emphasised either, to avoid 'helping' the Western politicians and military leaders with their warnings of the growing Soviet menace there.

Thus, although the all-embracing scope of the correlation of military forces and consequently of the multi-dimensional character of military parity/superiority was always accepted and sometimes mentioned, in practice the discussion of the issue was reduced to the strategic nuclear forces. The arms race in this field seemed to need much less justification than in other fields. The real and alleged achievements with regard to strategic nuclear parity were considered to support foreign policy (which was beginning to take a global form) and to strengthen the Soviet position in the negotiations for arms control and disarmament.

The Soviet leaders considered their achievement of *strategic parity* as being tantamount to the achievement of an *overall military superiority* which in turn was regarded as essential to the establishment of an advantageous global correlation of forces. It is not by chance that from the beginning of the 1970s the term 'correlation of world forces', in the sense of being advantageous to the socialist camp, has become the most frequently used concept in Soviet writings on international and military affairs.

Two groups of advantages have been attributed by Soviet politicians and analysts to the position of strategic parity: one of them is said to be enjoyed by all parties in the world-wide rivalry, the other favours the socialist camp.

Among the first group of advantages, strategic parity:
(a)   makes it possible to avoid a nuclear war ;
(b)   makes military interventions by the two great powers dangerous and thus prevents them; it renders highly improbable the escalation of a local war to an all-out conflict;
(c)   makes it possible to slow down — and eventually to stop — the arms race;
(d)   opens the way for a gradual arms reduction — provided that the balance of power can be preserved;
(e)   clears the air for political *détente* and an increase in the economic and cultural cooperation between states belonging to the opposing camps.

Soviet politicians and writers considered that the *USSR* derived two basic advantages from strategic parity: it provided security against the worst kind of war conceivable; and it deterred the Americans from 'blackmailing' by means of military pressure and similar forms of compulsion. Other advantages, which have been implied in Soviet publications and apparently also demonstrated in practice, may be described as follows.
(1)   A strategic parity which deters both of the great powers from risking a direct military confrontation allows for a broad spectrum of indirect and covert uses of military power. These may range from supporting revolutionary, leftist or simply pro-Soviet forces in Third World countries that are troubled by domestic disorders or external pressures (which in Soviet literature is called 'countering imperialist aggression' or 'increasing Soviet prestige and influence'), through helping them to establish a revolutionary regime (by proxy — for instance, using Cuban troops) and finally to establishing a definitely client regime (as in South Yemen). The latter may provide a permanent strategic infrastructure to strengthen Soviet influence and to support possible military operations in the future.

In short, a parity in strategic nuclear weapons allows the Soviet Union to exploit its superiority in conventional weapons and regional favourable circumstances in order to undertake military and para-military actions in vast areas of the Third World.

(2) A strategic parity is of advantage in carrying out a policy of incrementalism — i.e., of exploring and exploiting opportunities as they occur (or are created), and profiting from the lack of a reaction from the Western nations, because of their fear of a direct confrontation. Although the Soviet Union may also face such a risk, its ability (together with its allies) to act rapidly and react flexibly is much greater than that of the United States, because in socialist countries there is no need to take account of domestic public opinion.

(3) The USSR has also used strategic parity to gain a strong position in Europe: to strengthen its dominance in Eastern Europe, its influence on the course of Western European affairs, its position in negotiations on economic and political issues, and in negotiations concerning arms control. The need to preserve military equilibrium in Europe is used as a formal pretext for the military build-up.

(4) In general, a strategic parity can be used to paralyse enemy actions by the Soviet threat. In the 1970s it was partly responsible for the American inaction in Angola, Ethiopia and other African trouble spots.

(5) Finally, by virtue of its factual and asserted values, strategic parity supports Soviet global policy and its propaganda about the superiority of the socialist system.

Parity, stability, security

Strategic parity serves to preserve temporarily the political status quo between the main adversaries and, more generally, it is a factor *stabilising* their relations. However, this means different things to the different adversaries. To the Soviet Union the achievement of strategic parity has meant an increase in its global security, particularly in Europe. This was accompanied by the confirmation of Soviet domination in the Eastern part of the Continent, particularly in the Helsinki Agreement. On the other hand, it seems that the strengthening of the status quo in Europe has brought no radical change in Soviet global policy either in Europe or in the developing world: the Soviet Union continues to be devoted to the mission of changing the world status quo. Moreover, military parity, while it creates stability globally and in certain regions, may be treated by the Soviet leadership as a basis for future political offensives, since it may enable further changes to be made in favour of socialism without the open use of interstate armed violence, and in some instances without domestic armed revolutions. Soviet satisfaction with the confirmation of the status quo in Europe was connected with the shift of emphasis to the political offensive in the Third World. However, it may be asked whether, even in Europe, the USSR's policy of gradually strengthening its influence on, and positions in, the Western area has really been abandoned.

Significance of strategy

In the Western view, Soviet long-range policy exploits the strategic-nuclear parity. While Western writers doubt that there exists a Soviet 'grand design' for such a purpose, they assert that the Soviet Union possesses an operational strategy which allows for the maximisation of the available capabilities and the exploitation of opportunities as they occur. The Soviet leadership continues to regard military force as a means of peacetime policy.

However, Western researchers encounter here several questions, which up to now have not been answered. Since the West also considers military force to be a backdrop for policy, it is worth asking why the Soviet Union in so many cases is capable of more effective action: this must have certain structural and conceptual causes. Has the Soviet Union more effective strategic concepts? Can it plan better? Does the Soviet Union use means of politico-military strategy which are not available to the West? (as Soviet theorists assert). These and other questions may be placed on the agenda of research.

A comment may be made here. It seems that the view of some Western researchers that the Soviet Union treats strategic or military parity as a compensation for its inferiority in *all* other components of state power is too simplistic. These writers fail to see the achievements of the Soviet Union in various social — economic, cultural and educational — areas; they fail to take account of the power of the ideological and political propaganda which may become a very effective instrument of foreign policy, particularly in the Third World. The developing countries are seeking ways of quick development not only in economic and cultural but in all social respects, and the influence of Soviet achievements cannot be neglected.

Impact on the prevention of wars

Correlation of military forces and peaceful coexistence

The impact of the correlation of military forces on the prevention of wars is felt in the framework of the influence of the correlation of intrasocietal and international forces; this matter was discussed, in general, in Chapter 6. Since military force plays a particularly significant role in the accomplishment of the military aspects of peaceful coexistence, we may examine some related issues.

Restraints on particular types of war

(1)   As regards the prospects of the outbreak of domestic armed revolutions, when the progressive classes consider that the correlation of intrasocietal forces — particularly the military ones — is in their favour, they may decide on a political offensive or even a military attack in order to seize government power. The rulers may answer with measures that result in a civil war or they may decide not to resist, if they see no prospect of winning it. The same may be said, in the Marxist-Leninist view, of the national liberation struggle. It may happen that when the colonialist forces are inadequate — i.e., when the correlation of military forces is highly disadvantageous to them — they may feel obliged to a retreat without a war.

Both Soviet reasonings must be complemented in our times by the inclusion of the correlation of world forces — particularly their political and military components — and the correlation of regional military forces. The *complex* of the correlations of intrasocietal, regional and world forces determines the forms which the domestic struggle for social and/or national liberation may take.

The first Communist revolutions (e.g., the October Revolution) encountered fierce resistance from the rulers, who found allies in other capitalist countries. The international correlation of forces was seen as being highly advantageous to capitalism, and several governments decided to support the anti-revolutionary forces in Russia. This led to a long and bloody civil war.

In our times, *both sides* in an intrasocietal or/and anticolonial struggle may acquire such support. However, in favourable circumstances (an internal military stalemate and a mutual political and/or military neutralisation of the potential interventionist powers) revolutions may be carried through without a war.

In all the above-mentioned cases, the impact of the military component of the correlation of forces is not confined to the outbreak of a domestic and/or an anti-colonial war, but also affects the early termination of such war, if it has not been prevented.

(2)   As regards interstate wars, which are now likely in the Third World, the outbreak of these also depends partly on how the prospective belligerents assess the correlation of military forces, and the support which they expect from outside. Such wars are terminated in many instances by political pressure from outside and/or the threat of a military intervention — for instance, by one of the superpowers. Although the superpowers both wish to prevent a change in the corre-

lation of world forces, they may be reluctant to intervene with their full strength because of the expected reaction by the other superpower. The Arab-Israeli wars provide an example.

(3) Finally, we may consider a war between the two antagonistic camps which, in the Soviet view, has been avoided only because the correlation of world forces, and primarily of its military component, has become increasingly advantageous to socialism.

It has been argued by Soviet analysts that in the 1950s, in spite of the American superiority in nuclear weapons, the overwhelming superiority of socialist states in conventional forces in Europe prevented the outbreak of a general war there. In the 1960s the growing nuclear potential of the Soviet Union was the factor preventing a nuclear war, and the direct and indirect support given to socialist forces in the Third World (in Korea and Vietnam) decisively contributed to the termination of the wars there and discouraged the United States from further open military interventions and from continuing these wars — which, in the Soviet view, were waged in opposition to social and national liberation revolutions. In the late 1960s and early 1970s, after the Soviet Union had gained a strategic parity with the United States, the *global* correlation of military forces, which also included the theatre nuclear and conventional forces, and the growing Soviet potentialities of projecting military power far from the Soviet boundaries, was said greatly to diminish the possibility that the great imperialist powers might start a war.

Thus, in the Soviet view, owing to the change in the correlation of military forces to the Soviet advantage, its impact has been considerably extended from wartime to peacetime. The general result of the change is to make wars less likely.

Changes in theory

These developments have been reflected in several changes in the Marxist-Leninist theory of war and revolution.

(1) A war between the systems is considered to be both undesirable and avoidable;

(2) Wars between particular developed countries have also been declared to be both undesirable and avoidable. This view underlies the theory and programme of peaceful coexistence;

(3) Armed violence in a domestic revolution — i.e., a revolutionary war — which was previously regarded as an indispensable means of seizing and then defending the state authority has begun to be presented as not inevitable.

(4) National liberation struggles are seen as leading to national independence without necessarily proceeding through the stage of anti-

colonial war. The defence of the newly independent countries against neo-colonialism can also be effected without an armed conflict, at least in some countries.

In sum, the entire theory of the inevitability of war — both intrastate and international — has been in certain important respects renounced; the gradual but decisive change in the correlation of forces to the advantage of the Soviet Union, and consequently of 'world socialism' is said to be the main reason for the renunciation.

Moreover, changes in the correlation of military forces, and particularly the USSR's attainment of strategic parity has also affected — to various degrees, however, — the *causes* of war of particular levels.

Soviet theory distinguishes between three levels of these causes: (1) the deep roots of each war, consisting in the existence of class antagonistic societies which generate war; (2) the basic contradictions inherent in each specific socio-economic formation (structure) which give rise to the particular types of war (as, for instance, the civil war between the bourgeoisie and the proletariat); and (3) the direct causes of the individual instances of war. Apart from these causes, individual *conditions* existing before the outbreak of particular instances of war may accelerate or retard their outbreak (or even prevent it), and they also affect the individual shape of war.

The basic root of wars, in the form of the existence of class antagonistic societies, remains unchanged. The sociopolitical structural causes characteristic of our epoch have begun to be greatly limited by the changes in the correlation of world forces. Nevertheless, they remain the potential causes of potential wars. The direct causes and the immediate conditons affecting the outbreak of individual instances of war have grown in importance. The global strategic parity and the regional and local balances of military forces greatly affect them. Because of these effects an intersystemic war has become improbable, as also any major war between the great powers and any local wars which may escalate to an all-out war. On the other hand, wars by proxy and local interstate wars have under favourable regional and local conditions become more probable.

The consequences of the global correlation of military forces as well as the impacts of the regional and domestic correlations on the likelihood of various types of war, have not yet been stated in the form of laws or principles as it has been in relation to the impact of the correlation of military forces on the course and outcome of war (see Chapter 10). (Admittedly, *détente* has been called 'the law of our times', but this is a highly general and abstract expression and an attempt to stress its importance rather than ascribing to it an actual scientific law-like status.) However, if the impact of the correlation of military forces in both the domestic and the international settings on the course of social development increases further, as the Soviet leaders and researchers predict, a further evolution in the theoretical apparatus connected with this category may be expected.

Impact is not automatic

As with other manifestations of the impact of the correlation of political forces or their military component, it has been pointed out that no correlation operates automatically, either in particular countries or internationally, to prevent war.[4] The outbreak, or the prevention, of any war depends on both objective and subjective factors, primarily, however, on the *material power* of the forces pushing for, or resisting war and on their skilful action based on an appropriate strategy. The rough strategic parity between the antagonistic camps and the existence of thermonuclear weapons, for instance, do not automatically prevent war. Potent forces are acting to escalate the arms race and this increases the danger of the outbreak of a total war; in capitalist countries a struggle is proceeding between the more and the less belligerent strata; and local wars may escalate into an all-out war. A general conclusion drawn by Soviet politicians and writers is that, in relation to each *type* of war and each likely *instance* of war, the socialist states and their allies need a permanent and consistent *political strategy* in order to maintain the *détente* and frustrate the plans of the warmongers.

Strategic parity and arms control

As mentioned above, the Soviets consider that it was only the establishment of strategic parity which made possible negotiations on arms control that had any chances of success. The maintenance of this parity has become the precondition of any agreement and any measure concerning arms control. Moreover, from being a *condition* for the reduction of armaments or averting the threat of war or the escalation of war, strategic parity has gradually become a tacit *goal* in the discussions on arms control. Since the ultimate aim of any measure concerning arms control is to diminish the danger of the outbreak of war, and strategic parity has been by Soviet theory and practice recognised as the main condition of preventing a major war between the great powers, indeed the establishment of measures to strengthen strategic parity has become the Soviet main concern in the arms control negotiations.

The Western critics of the Soviet position in these negotiations consider that the Soviet Union is not satisfied with strategic parity and consistently attempts to paralyse or weaken the American military effort and gradually to gain a global military advantage in various important respects. Therefore the Soviet representatives in the negotiations are accused of trying to include in the set of agreed limitations measures which slow down the technological development in the United States and particularly the design and production of new types of weapons systems; at the same time these measures should leave the Soviet Union a free hand in the vast areas remaining outside the technology discussed in arms control negotiations.

Comments on strategic parity

Parity may be transitory

For various reasons, theorists on both sides say that strategic parity and its impact on the maintenance of peace are transitory. Although officially both sides state that the 'balance of terror' is stable, and that with the growing nuclear arsenals there is no possibility of avoiding complete destruction if a nuclear 'exchange' will take place, they admit that a technological breakthrough is possible. Therefore *a casu ad casum* both adversaries state that there must be no further development of the nuclear potential.

However, each of the superpowers maintains that its own strategic superiority would be an even better guarantee against nuclear war than the existing parity. At the same time each accuses the other of striving for a superiority so great that it would be disastrous to the prospects of peace. Several Western politicians and the military leaders state that since the Soviet Union sees war as an instrument in the permanent class struggle which, if it occurs, must be won — even under nuclear conditions — the strategic parity cannot last for ever. It is also implied in Soviet writings, the critics say, that the laws of history operating to the advantage of socialism will in some indefinite future bring about a socialist superiority in all respects, including the military one. This also speaks against the eternal stability of strategic parity.

Likewise, the Soviet Union condemns the American policy as aiming at achieving a strategic superiority. In Brezhnev's words the very concept of superiority 'makes no sense now when there exist the huge arsenals of accumulated nuclear weapons and the means of their delivery'.[5]

Therefore both the Western and the Soviet politicians, military leaders and writers, assert — but for contrary reasons — that it is premature to view strategic parity as a guarantee of military stability and overall security. Both parity and stability express dynamic values which may change in the course of the rivalry between the opposing camps. They have no finite physical dimensions and must be permanently fought for. Parity and stability are now based on technical considerations, and they are related to the highest levels of military technology.

They do not cover the whole spectrum of military capabilities and do not constitute a combination of political and techno-military factors. An extreme view is that without the resolution of basic political conflicts — the prospects of which are very small — neither parity nor stable security can be ensured. They cannot be ensured until one side aims at preserving, the other at basically changing the world status quo.

During the 1970s, both adversaries used the proposition of the transitory character of strategic parity to justify their military efforts. During the early 1980s the Americans rarely asserted that the Soviet Union had achieved superiority, especially in Europe, while the Soviet politicians and military leaders constantly argued that the United States aimed to achieve global military superiority.

However, the Soviets also repeatedly stated that in spite of the American efforts, parity *could not be scrubbed*,[6] which in a sense contradicted their previous view of parity.

Georgi Arbatov's reasoning here is typical:

> Parity does not maintain itself like some kind of self-regulating system which is insensitive to destabilizing factors — i.e., new armaments programs. The guarantee of a stable strategic balance, which has taken shape over the past decades, lies primarily in the fact that it is far more difficult for one side to break this balance in its favour to any significant effect, than it is for the other side to hinder these attempts.[7]

He explains this relatively stable character of the parity by the following facts: (1) At the present levels of nuclear missile potentials, a further build-up of strategic factors in a quantitative respect will experience the law of diminishing returns; (2) The present detection systems and the combat readiness of the Soviet Union's strategic nuclear weapons — both of which continue to be improved and perfected — reduces to minimum the influence of the surprise factor and makes a pre-emptive missile strike purposeless; (3) No ABM system can reliably defend the extensive American territory against a retaliatory nuclear missile strike; (4) Rapid and comparatively cheap measures can have no perceptible effect upon the nuclear parity; the major military programmes which are capable of exerting this kind of influence require vast outlays and long periods of time to be implemented; (5) The Soviet Union now has the same means to be set against new US strategic weapons and has every potential to prevent the United States from changing the strategic balance in any respect, even in a situation of an unlimited arms race.[8]

The Western researchers make two contrary assessments of the USSR's chances of gaining a strategic superiority. In one the Soviets are given a good chance to achieve it. Many Western researchers argue that the Soviet military philosophy aims essentially to fight and win any war, including a nuclear one, and therefore to achieve a nuclear and global superiority. The Soviet military build-up in the past 15 years exhibits this tendency as well as some success in pursuing the aim. Here the arguments reinforce each other: the Soviets aim at a nuclear superiority because they want to win a war, and they may win a war because they are on the way to achieving strategic superiority.[9]

The other assessment is quite different: the Soviet leaders are said to fear the loss of the strategic parity which they have gained. They feel that they will be unable to prevent the erosion of certain advantages in the correlation of strategic forces as the American military build-up bears fruit in the later 1980s. In other words, the key aim of the USSR's military build-up in the last 15 years would in the late 1980s be lost and the Soviets would not be able to exploit these strategic advantages for political gains. Therefore in the nearest future they may try to exploit those advantages for the attainment of political and military-strategic goals.[10]

Inconsistencies in Soviet views

There seem to be several inconsistencies in the Soviet reasoning also. (1) On the one hand, the Soviet leaders assert that there is enough nuclear armament on both sides to destroy the whole world and therefore no side would dare to start a war. This is, in fact, a statement about the existence of a parity of deterrence. On the other hand, they insist on a 'balance of imbalances' or a symmetry of asymmetries: if one side enjoys a preponderance in one kind of weapons, this *must* be balanced by the superiority of the opponent in another kind of weapon. In the Soviet view, there does exist such a 'balance': the advantages of one side in certain strategic systems are counterbalanced by the advantages of the other side in others. The SALT II treaty is said to make the strategic parity more complete by fixing equal ceilings not only for all the strategic means of delivery but also for the components of these: missiles with multiple warheads and heavy bombers carrying long-range cruise missiles; and also by determining the important identical limits for a possible qualitative development of the means of delivery.

However, if, as the Soviet authors state, all these developments and agreements on liquidating the 'asymmetries' are *above* the level that suffices for mutual destruction, if all this concerns the 'over-kill capability' — i.e., if all the possible asymmetries cannot endanger the 'deterrence parity' — why the fear of any new asymmetry?

On the one hand, Soviet writers assert that 'taking into account the vast nuclear stockpiles already accumulated, military superiority is not only superfluous, but also pointless'.[11] A protagonist can achieve strategic superiority only for a short time, since the side that is lagging behind will — in the minimum time — restore the balance.[12] On the other hand, they assert that the United States aims at achieving a nuclear superiority, and this would be very dangerous. 'Dangerous' and 'pointless' are incompatible epithets, however.

(3) On the one hand, they assert that technological developments and the competition in these cannot be a cause of war. Soviet theory maintains that it is policy that causes wars. On the other hand, they reiterate that the arms race may lead to wars, although neither side desires war.

(4) They say, on the one hand, that military parity means stability, but, on the other, that the Soviet Union has the right and the duty to help change the status quo by means of armed violence. The United States cannot 'compel the Soviet Union to abandon its policy of supporting the progressive social changes that are being rapidly implemented in the vast areas of the developing countries'.[13] Admittedly, the USSR's acquisition of new allies in the Third World and new strategic positions there does not directly change the balance of military forces between the superpowers, but it does so indirectly since the change in spheres of influence *means* a change in that balance. In the Soviet view, however, such a change in the military balance does not endanger stability.

(Its seems, however, that some Western scholars over-emphasise the Soviet politicians' and researchers' approach to the concept of strategic parity as a tactical and transitory condition. Likewise they over-emphasise Soviet efforts to gain as much as they can beyond parity and the Soviet belief in the value of very numerous forces. Soviet military doctrine places a heavy premium on an abundance of manpower, they say — and, indeed, on possessing as large a margin of military advantages as may be feasible. They aim, in brief, at a military superiority.[14] This seems to be exaggerated also for the fact that the enormous costs of the strategic arms race must limit the Soviet efforts and must also affect their views concerning the value of a capacity for over kill.)

(5) Strategic parity is said by the Soviet leaders to have been achieved in the struggle against the United States which has always tried to maintain its superiority in order openly to use it against the Soviet Union. The question is: Why did the Americans not exploit their superiority while they still had it?

Sometimes the answer is that the United States did not dare to do this because the correlation of world forces was to their disadvantage. In such a case, however, the achievement of strategic parity cannot be presented as a basic shift in the correlation of world forces which made it impossible for the United States to decide to start a war.

(6) Moreover, the relationship between strategic parity and the correlation of world forces becomes unclear when Soviet politicians and military researchers simultaneously state two dependences: First, changes in the correlation of military forces are said to be a *result* of changes in the correlation of world forces in all respects: sociopolitical, economic, technological and others. On the other hand, the achievement of parity is said to be the *cause* of the decisive change in the correlation of world forces.

(7) There are inconsistencies in explaining why it was at the end of the 1970s and the beginning of the 1980s that the United States made a radical shift in military policy and began to aim at achieving a military superiority. In this situation:

(a) Either no explanation is given (or else the United States is said to show an ongoing and permanent tendency to strive for superiority, which would mean that no shift had, in fact, occurred);

(b) Or it is said that the Americans suddenly realised that parity was unfavourable to them since, with parity, they would lose in all the other fields of rivalry;

(c) Or it is said that the Americans began to prepare for winning a future all-out war;

(d) Or it is said that the Americans decided to try to exert political-military pressure on the Soviet Union without having to resort to war.

(e) Finally, the change is explained by the governmental take-over by the bellicose right. However, it is often asserted that both of the American political parties conduct essentially the same aggressive anti-Soviet policy.

In sum, the reasons for the alleged American tendency to strive for strategic superiority just in the early 1980s are unclear. On the one hand, an all-out war between the superpowers is excluded. On the other hand, the United States is accused of deploying anti-Soviet strategic nuclear weapons in Europe, which can only mean preparations for war. However, corresponding deployment by the Soviet Union of strategic nuclear weapons aimed at Western Europe is explained as a measure taken to establish a balance of power and, therefore to strengthen peace.

Likewise, the American research on the space-based ABM-system is called a preparation for an aggressive war, while the Soviet research on ABM defence has not been mentioned at all.

Similarities and differences

(1) The approaches of the main adversaries contain similar tenets. Both believe that strategic parity will *deter* the other side from an all-out nuclear war. Both seem to regard it as a parity of risks and terror rather than of strictly measurable strategic forces. While *not* believing in an *essential change* in this parity i.e., in its transformation into the superiority of one side — they attempt to improve the relation in certain aspects — in some weapon systems or some kinds of conceivable operations. Both sides regard strategic parity as a process and not as a permanent and unchanging relation, and they will continue the arms race in order to maintain the global equilibrium and to gain partial advantages.

(2) The differences consist — or at least, have consisted — in the very concept of parity. While the USA saw parity as being based on mutually vulnerable societies and survivable offensive forces, the USSR rejected such a principle as incompatible with its political and military philosophy because (a) the survival of Soviet society cannot be admitted to depend on the policy of the adversary and (b) war cannot be regarded as leading inevitably to the destruction of Soviet society and the reversal of the main trend of social history.

(3) The Soviet Union stresses the differences between strategic parity and military parity and it consistently views the former as a *means* of achieving a global military superiority.

Strategic parity and the correlation of military forces

Strategic parity is only a part of the correlation of military forces, and the latter must be viewed as a part of the global correlation of forces. Therefore, in the Soviet view, military parity is subject to the same laws and tendencies as social development as a whole.

Thus the correlation of military forces constitutes a comparison of *trends* rather than of given magnitudes which, moreover, are to a considerable extent incommensurable (see Chapter 12). Neither the political rivalry of the two opposing camps nor the technological development can be arrested and, in the Soviet view, this would not even be desirable. The laws of historical development are giving world socialism increasing advantages in all the spheres of rivalry, including the military one. Even if the situation of strategic parity continues for a long time, the global military superiority will be on the socialist side of the equation and it will bring a succession of political victories. Strategic parity means stability only in relation to certain types of war, while other types are still possible and even desirable.

The disappearance of war as a social phenomenon is not connected with any kind of military parity since war is rooted in the contradictions of the class-antagonistic society. Therefore various types of war may gradually become less frequent because of the growing military superiority of the socialist camp, yet the roots of war can disappear only with the disappearance of capitalism.

Impact on American military policy

Impact of the correlation of military forces on the American military doctrine and force posture

The basic assumption of Soviet military theory is that the American military doctrine is determined by the interests and global policy of the American rulers. In addition, it reflects the regularities and tendencies of the general military strategic orientation of international imperialism, led by the United States.[15]

However, in the Soviet view the correlation of world forces and especially its military component, which is continuously changing in favour of socialism, has been the main cause of the successive changes made in the American military doctrine, and particularly in its strategic concepts and force posture.[16] The other motivating factors have been: the development of military technology, the growth of the domestic social troubles, and faults in the American foreign and military policies.[17]

At the same time, however, Soviet writers assert that the American military doctrine is also affected by the assumption made by the representatives of the Pentagon and the military-industrial complex that the emergence of strategic equality between the superpowers with all the political consequences of it is a temporary phenomenon and that America should attempt to regain her superiority in strategic armaments as a whole, at least in the important qualitative indices. This is required, they say, to regain the lost positions.[18]

In the Soviet view, these two assertions concern two coexisting — and competing — tendencies in the American military policy, which caused deviations and sudden changes in the military doctrine. However, these changes have not affected the political basis and the essential aggressiveness of the American concept of military strategy. It was the techno-strategic rather than the political part of the doctrine which was changing under the pressure of the rivalry and of the change in the correlation of the military forces of the superpowers. In consequence of this disparity of the two component parts of the American doctrine — which, however, cannot be viewed separately — the concepts of military strategy were also being changed, but in a half-hearted and inconsistent manner.

Soviet military analysts distinguish between four or even five basic variants — which correspond to successive phases — of the American doctrinal strategy.[19]

1   In the initial post-war period, which was characterised by America's monopoly of nuclear weapons, and then its considerable superiority in this field, the declared strategy of nuclear deterrence disguised, in the Soviet view, the factual strategy of nuclear blackmail and military pressure which aimed at 'rolling back' Communism. If the military pressure did not succeed, a preventive war would be waged.[20]

Although the global balance of military power might have been seen as favouring the United States, the Soviets considered that their overwhelming superiority in ground forces in Europe and their capability for invading Western Europe constituted an effective counterweight to the strategic air power of the United States. The Soviet Union deterred America from initiating a war, thereby also invalidating the strategy of nuclear blackmail. This finally compelled America to reconsider its doctrinal strategy and force posture concerning the direct confrontation with the Soviet Union. The policy of the containment of Communism in the Third World, and especially the attempts to 'roll it back' also failed; the Korean war illustrated these facts. This also compelled the United States to reconsider its strategy and force posture.

2   The American strategy developed in the early 1950s into the concept of 'massive retaliation', which, in the Soviet view, continued to support the policy of preventing sociopolitical changes in the world, including the collapse of the colonial system.

This strategy assumed that the United States would be invulnerable to any nuclear strike by the Soviet Union; in contrast, by preparing for and threatening to make a pre-emptive nuclear strike, the United States might compel the Soviet Union to grant political concessions in Europe and in the Third World.

However, the Soviet Union with its continuing conventional superiority, continued to be capable of seizing Western Europe, and after 1957 the development of the Soviet ICBM began to undermine the basis of the doctrine of massive retaliation by rendering the American territory vulnerable to a Soviet nuclear retaliatory strike.

3   Thus by the end of the 1950s, according to Soviet writers, the United States was being forced to revise its concepts based on 'massive retaliation' and to adopt a new military doctrine embodying a new strategy, that of 'flexible response'. Although the new concept also assumed that the United States could deal with the Soviet Union 'from a position of strength', the change was primarily caused by the growth in the Soviet nuclear missile potential and consisted in replacing American strategy of a unilateral nuclear war by a strategy of 'nuclear exchange'.[21] Thus the first-strike strategy was replaced by a second-strike one.

The strategy of 'flexible response' was described by its authors as representing an attempt to avoid being forced to fight solely a general nuclear war and to broaden the range of options to include, for instance, the capability to wage a number of limited wars in several variants both against the main adversary (i.e., the Soviet Union) and against protagonists in the Third World. In other words, the loss of superiority in strategic nuclear weapons led to attempts to construct various concepts of strategy of limited wars and counter-guerilla wars.

While the United States saw the development of its capability to fight limited wars basically as a means of enhancing the credibility of deterrence against the global expansion of Communism, the Soviet Union regarded this development as marking a shift of emphasis in the choice of military means for the continuing aggressive policy of the imperialists. This policy was said to be still aiming at preventing socio-political changes that might be disadvantageous to America and to the capitalist system as a whole. Moreover, like massive retaliation, it was said to aim at 'rolling back' Communism.

Soviet writers also asserted that the United States was acting as if its strategy of flexible response would ultimately lead to a total war against the socialist countries. Limited conventional wars would serve the preparation of conditions for such a war, and limited nuclear wars — which could not and would not be kept limited — were regarded as an initial phase of such a war. Both in the Soviet propaganda and in the factual assessment limited wars were viewed as a means by which America could combat and suppress national liberation movements, without risking a Soviet intervention. The broad build-up of conventional and nuclear capabilities along the entire spectrum of force posture was said to provide confirmation of this view. The nuclear build-up served both the preparation for a direct use of strategic forces and the provision of a nuclear umbrella for the waging of local aggressions which were disguised as the answers to the direct or indirect expansion of Soviet power. All these developments were said to be ultimately caused by qualitative changes in the balance of military forces in favour of the Soviet Union.

However, once again the further growth of the Soviet military forces, and especially of their strategic nuclear arsenal, contributed to the final failure of the strategy of flexible response. In its 'total nuclear war' component, the growing Soviet arsenal of ballistic missiles ensured a capacity to survive an American counterforce strike and delivering a crushing counter-blow. This, in the Soviet view, invalidated the Pentagon's plans to fight a total nuclear war which would start with a pre-emptive counterforce attack. The Americans were compelled to abandon any ideas of launching such an attack and prepare instead for an 'escalation concept' of armed conflict, which perhaps could be stopped before it developed into an all-out war.

In local tests of strength, the Soviet Union intervened in Hungary and then in Czechoslovakia, avoiding any Western response; and it actively supported national liberation struggles and the newly established anti-imperialist regimes in the Third World. In contrast, the main American effort in this field of confrontation, in Vietnam, yielded no decisive results.

Thus in the view of Soviet military writers then and now, it was because the Soviets were approaching a state of strategic parity *vis-à-vis* the United States, which they attained at the end of the 1960s, that the Pentagon had to gradually modify its doctrine and force posture.
4 In the early 1970s, the Pentagon introduced the concept of a strategy of 'realistic deterrence', based on the idea of 'strategic sufficiency' and 'strategic stability'.

The American nuclear potential of a 'sufficient' size would serve primarily to prevent strategic nuclear war between the United States and the Soviet Union. Locally, the burden of deterrence and war preparation would be shared with the allies, and in some cases (counter-insurgency warfare) the United States would provide only logistical support.

Throughout that decade, further modifications were introduced because of the consolidation of the rough equality in the strategic nuclear forces of the two superpowers and also because of other developments: for instance, the declining home support for military policy (especially as the Vietnam war dragged on), and the emergence of new centres of power, particularly in Western Europe and Japan, which had several interests rivalling, if not opposing, those of the United States.[22] Soviet scholars asserted that mainly because of the development of a strategic parity with the Soviet Union, for the first time the need to revise even certain political aspects of the doctrine was recognised, particularly as regards the political instrumentality of military force.
(1) Significant constraints in the open use of military force were admitted, as well as the need to work out a range of its covert uses.
(2) It was recognised that America had no capabilities to resolve by its own efforts *all* the problems connected with the defence of the world status quo and it must share the military tasks with its allies.
(3) A better use of non-military resources and a sharing of costs with the allies were also included in the new assessment and new policy.

As regards the concepts of military strategy of the 1970s,[16] these were revised according to the types of war which American military force should have prevented, or to the types of war for which America should prepare, if deterrence failed: (1) a strategic nuclear war against the Soviet Union in two variants: a general (i.e., unlimited) war, and a war limited to selective strikes, mainly against military targets; (2) a nuclear war in a war theatre outside the United States — war in Europe, between the NATO forces and the WTO forces with the use of so-called tactical nuclear weapons was here a case in point; (3) a conventional war in a war theatre; (4) a local war. In the first type of war, the American forces would be the sole participants; in the second, both the nuclear and the conventional forces of the United States and its allies would be engaged; in the third, only the conventional forces of both the US and its allies would participate; and in a local war the main forces would be provided by the allies, while America would give logistical support and also intervene militarily, if necessary.

In the Soviet view, in all these types of war the following principles of the use of American military force were adopted: (1) the 'realistic approach', meaning the preparation and use of forces maximally corresponding to the military tasks and the political conditions for their use; (2) the 'selective' use of military force; (3) the use of military force to the full extent foreseen for the given type of war from the beginning of hostilities, without a risky and unrealistic programme for the gradual escalation of the level of military operations.

In comparison with the previous period America's possibilities of using military force again the main opponent, the socialist camp, were more limited and this resulted in the establishment of a more limited general concept of America's military planning. This was reflected in the transition from the formula of the 'two and a half wars' adopted in the 1960s (i.e., two great conventional wars, in Europe and Asia, and one small war in another region which American forces might wage *simultaneously*) to that of the 1970s consisting in preparing for 'one and a half wars' (i.e., one big conventional war together with the allies either in Europe or in Asia, and one small war in another region). The change concerned in the first place policy *vis-à-vis* the Third World countries: the plans for open use of military force in such countries were significantly reduced.

Thus the strategic parity established had one further consequence, in the view of some Soviet writers. It caused the introduction by the United States of *indirect strategy,* which uses the method of exerting economic, political and ideological pressures on the socialist states and attempting to disrupt their alliance. While Western theorists and politicians often try to present the 'indirect strategy' as an *alternative* to a strategy of the use of military force for deterrence or for war, in fact it is only a *complement* to military strategy, according to the Soviet writers. Indirect strategy is a part of the overall imperialist strategy which aims to weaken the socialist adversary and to prepare conditions for a more direct offensive in the future. At any moment, indirect strategy can be transformed into its apparent opposite, a military aggression.[24]

However, in the Soviet view, in spite of the American retreat from a higher level of military commitment abroad, the most significant elements of the continuity between this and the previous American doctrine were preserved: the United States did not abandon its aim of regaining a military advantage over the Soviet Union, or at least some one-sided advantages. It did not stop the arms race, and the concept of strategic 'sufficiency' — i.e., of possessing a sufficient arsenal of nuclear missile weapons — was so general that it could be used to justify a further military build-up. The Americans did not abandon the nuclear war strategy, or the concept of winning local limited wars.

Thus, although the United States had to adapt its strategic doctrine to the growing strategic nuclear power of the Soviet Union, it maintained the basic aims of its global anti-Communist policy.

Certain modifications in the American doctrinal strategy, which were announced in 1974 by the Defense Secretary James Schlesinger and were known as the Limited Nuclear Options (LNO) strategy, were quoted by Soviet politicians and analysts in support of the above-mentioned assessments. The main element in the proposed new strategic posture — which was the creation of a capability for a wide range of options, including that for precision attacks on both soft and hard targets — was criticised by the Soviets as an indication that the United States revert from deterrence to a nuclear war-fighting strategy to revive the concept of the first use of nuclear weapons. Such a development would be ineffective and dangerous, said the critics, since the United States would derive no unilateral advantages from a lowering of the nuclear threshold, and even limited strategic strikes against military targets in the Soviet Union would set off an uncontrolled escalation to total nuclear war.

The adoption of such a strategy would be highly destabilising, it was held. The strategy was discussed in 1974—6 but was not then adopted in its entirety. However some parts of it, such as an increase in targeting flexibility and accuracy, were incorporated in the American doctrinal strategy and strategic planning in the 1980s.

5 By the end of the 1970s, Soviet writers maintained, a new modification of the doctrinal bases of American military policy began, again mainly as the result of a further change in the correlation of world forces in favour of socialism.[25] It was then announced in July 1980 in the form of Presidential Directive 59. The new doctrinal strategy placed more emphasis on targeting military objectives on the Soviet territory: missile silos, command posts, and the Soviet warmaking capacity in general.

This modification called 'countervailing strategy' was asserted by the Soviet leaders as aiming at stopping the decline of the *relative* capabilities of the American forces and at activating the use of military force as a means of foreign policy.[26] The 'global responsibility' of the American military force — i.e., a readiness to use them everywhere — was replacing the selective use of them which had been advocated in the early 1970s. The declarations of readiness to fight two great wars

— a strategic nuclear war and a war in Europe — and three variants of a limited war in the Third World (some of them even against countries supported by the socialist camp) was replacing the previous concept of 'one and a half wars'. A policy declaration was made concerning a further build-up and modernisation of the strategic nuclear forces, an increase and modernisation of the US military forces in Europe and of the development of forces prepared for intervention in the Third World. More emphasis was placed on cooperation with the European allies in the military field, and China began to be regarded as a potential ally. In the Soviet view, the main aim of this programme was to annul the strategic parity with the Soviet Union by a significant increase in the strategic nuclear forces and the establishment of new concepts for their use.

One such concept involved the carrying out of *selective and highly accurate strikes* against the Soviet Union. This was regarded as a further step towards a nuclear fighting doctrine and as the abandonment of the pure deterrent and retaliatory posture. Another new concept was that of *extended deterrence.* In the Soviet view, the Americans, under the cover of regaining the capability to deter the Soviet Union from attacking their European allies, would try to regain the capability to strike at the Soviet Union locally, primarily in Europe. Thus the final variant of the United States doctrinal strategy would mean a return to its initial aggressive and offensive interpretation which prevailed in the late 1940s.

A military build-up has accompanied these changes.[27] The programme of modernising the strategic forces includes building the strategic B-1 and Stealth bombers, the MX and Midgetman ICBMs, strategic air-based and submarine-based cruise missiles, and expanding the fleet of aircraft carriers, each of which carries 40 nuclear-capable planes. It also includes an almost complete reorganisation on a new technical basis of the system of command and control, communication and intelligence that would be used in a nuclear war. A special role is assigned to the gigantic programme for a space-based ABM system called the 'Strategic Defence Initiative'.[28]

In the Soviet view, the entire post-war development of the American force posture testifies to the fact that the declared variants of military doctrine have always functioned as a disguise for the factual strategies. It was the first strike and not the second 'retaliatory strike' for which the American armed forces have always been preparing. It was a mixed counterforce/counter-city strategy and not merely a counter-city one. Three categories of targets have always been included in the planning: (1) strategic forces; (2) command, control and communication systems; and (3) cities and industrial centres.

The official concepts of 'strategic sufficiency', 'mutual assured destruction' and the like camouflaged the real strategies.[29] The changing balance of military forces between the two superpowers was used to justify a *continuous* qualitative and quantitative *build-up* of the American nuclear potential for the purpose of a massive strike on the Soviet Union.

To sum up, since the early 1980s, the Soviet criticisms of developments in the American military doctrine and force posture have included the following points:

(1)   In spite of the Soviet assertions that strategic parity cannot be annulled, the Americans are increasingly accused of trying to regain a strategic superiority.

(2)   According to Soviet researchers, this drive is connected with the Pentagon's increasing emphasis on the possibility of winning a nuclear war. One of the means for achieving victory is to ensure that, even after the first exchange of counterforce nuclear strikes, the United States would have enough strategic potential left to threaten the Soviet cities with destruction and thus impose advantageous political conditions.

(3)   The American interpretation given to the declared Soviet strategy of deterrence has been changing. When this strategy was introduced it was based on the conviction that the United States had an overwhelming superiority in nuclear weapons and this, in the Soviet view, meant intimidation (the Russian term *ustrashenie* or *zapugivanie*) or 'nuclear blackmail'. During most of the 1970s this concept was replaced by 'mutual deterrence', but since the early 1980s the Americans have been attempting to restore the original sense of the strategy of deterrence. Since unilateral deterrence — i.e., intimidation — can cause the Soviet Union to make concessions only if America has a strategic superiority, efforts are naturally made to achieve such an advantageous relation of forces.

(4)   It is now being stated more often that the United States is planning to change the balance of forces not only by building up its entire range of armaments but also by creating an effective anti-ballistic defence. The Soviet critics consider that, since the early 1960s, and parallel to the build-up of the arsenal of offensive strategic nuclear weapons, the Americans have speeded up their efforts to establish an anti-nuclear defence. The concept of the space-deployed anti-ballistic strategic defence has become the main object of Soviet criticism.

(5)   In connection with American accusations that the USSR is trying to regain a strategic superiority, some Soviet experts contend that comprehensive strategic parity was achieved *during* the 1970s, and not in the very beginning of that decade. Thus a semi-official publication reads in 1982 that 'a rough equilibrium in quality and quantity of the strategic nuclear arms of the two powers was established by the mid-1970s'; similarly, Trofimenko writes in 1985: 'During the 1960s and much of the 1970s there was no real parity in the strategic arsenals of the USSR and the USA... Thus in these conditions the abstract and

theoretical ideas of American writers concerning SALT served as a verbal screen for the American superiority.'[30] These are perhaps casual comments, since the established view has been that strategic parity was achieved in the early 1970s. However, they are characteristic of the efforts to show that it was not the Soviet Union which during the 1970s attempted to achieve superiority but the United States which decided at the end of that decade to regain it.

As we see, paradoxically enough, in the Soviet view, it was because of the evolution of the correlation of military forces unfavourable to America that the US military doctrine was forced constantly to *extend* the missions of armed forces, to include ever newer types of war for which they were preparing: first it was a global atomic war, then a tactical nuclear war, in the beginning of the 1960s a missile thermonuclear war, then a major conventional and a counter-guerilla war, and so on. However, this extension was always presented by the American leaders as the acquisition of a new kind of effective deterrence ability against a succession of new dangers rather than an increase in their capabilities of waging new types of war.

Moreover, the alleged growth of 'Communist threat', presented as the inevitable result of the worsening of the global military balance, was used to justify the periodical acceleration of the arms race for which the socialist countries were held responsible.

The impact of the global correlation of military forces on the NATO doctrinal concepts and force posture has not been considered here. Although this impact is much discussed in Soviet writings — at least as much as the development of the US military doctrine — [31] it has always been regarded as a corollary of the impact of the correlation on the American concept, which is said to determine the NATO doctrine and force posture.

Factual impacts

It seems that the Soviet writers exaggerate the allegedly determining influence of the correlation of military forces in general and the USSR's achievement of strategic parity in particular on the American concepts of military strategy.

Admittedly, the correlation of military forces is among the principal factors affecting the doctrine — and particularly the strategic doctrine — of both the potential adversaries. It may also in peacetime considerably affect the gain or the loss of political and strategic positions in the regions of interests and conflicts, as well as the outcome of international crises. The outcome of the Cuban crisis, for instance, was greatly affected by the American superiority in military forces on the spot at that time. In a case with a contrary regional correlation and thus also outcome, Afghanistan was occupied by the Soviet Union.

The impact of the military balance, particularly the strategic one, must therefore always be taken into account in relation to both the peacetime rivalry and a hypothetical war. However, the military balance makes two kinds of impact: (1) the impact of the constant and comprehensive Soviet *military build-up* both in the nuclear and the conventional components of the Soviet armed forces on the American basic strategic decisions and the changes in the American force posture; (2) the impact of the *strategic parity* achieved by the Soviet Union in the 1970s on the American strategic decisions.

The former impact is obvious and law-like, as it must be when the military force of the main adversary increases both continuously and rapidly; the latter, however, is much more elusive. (Before briefly discussing these problems, one should note that in relation to American concepts the term 'strategic doctrine', as used in this context by Soviet writers, must be given a special interpretation. The American strategic doctrine has never constituted a single, coherent and integrated set of ideas, values and beliefs, with clearly defined basic strategic goals closely related to political doctrine. Instead it has been an agglomeration of strategic concepts, publicly declared terms and propositions with which decisions concerning acquisition, deployment and employment policy have been debated and justified. Among the latter, the sets of targets established as the objectives of nuclear strikes had a prominent place. These concepts constituted two different kinds of ideas. One was based on the traditional principles of military action, which aimed at defeating the enemy forces, denying him his objectives and destroying his will and ability to wage war: this is often called 'the war-winning philosophy'. The other group of ideas was connected with the new phenomenon of the nuclear missile age — deterrence — and its purpose was to threaten the enemy with unacceptable destruction.)

In the first post-war years, when the Americans possessed atomic weapons and the Soviet Union was superior in conventional forces, the rather unclear American concept of a war against the Soviet Union was based on the idea of a large atomic air offensive against the Soviet homeland, hitting those cities which contained the heart of the enemy's war machine and thereby defeating him. Thus it was a concept of destroying in the shortest possible time the enemy's will and ability to continue the war, before he could use his conventional forces to make substantial territorial gains. In addition to the air attack, the ground and naval forces of the United States and its allies could carry out offensive and defensive operations to resist Soviet advances.

After the Soviet Union became an atomic power — which occurred earlier than the American experts expected — the United States had to change its concept concerning air attacks. The Soviet nuclear installations as well as the Soviet armed forces and their lines of logistic support were added to the list of targets; this was expected to prevent a Soviet nuclear air offensive against Western Europe and to slow down or stop the Red Army's advance into Europe. In other words, war could be decided as before by a single massive attack in which however, not one kind of targets but an 'optimum mix' of three main categories of targets would be hit: cities and industrial facilities; transportation lines whose destruction would slow the movement of the Red Army; and long-range air forces. The initial phase of war would be decisive and the hostilities might quickly end.[32] A variant scenario foresaw a simultaneous strike at the entire Soviet target system. Both concepts depended on having *invulnerable second-strike forces* available.[33]

Throughout the 1960s, Soviet nuclear power was acquiring the capability of inflicting enormous destruction on American territory and the military balance was changing towards *mutual deterrence,* but the *political* essence of the American doctrine, in the Soviet view, remained the same. The strategic doctrine however, underwent changes. This was the period when the concept of massive retaliation was replaced by doctrine of flexible response. The accompanying concepts were 'counter-force', 'damage limitation' and 'assured destruction'. The first of these meant that, in the event of a nuclear war, the destruction of the enemy's military force, rather than of his civilian population, was the principal military objective. It implied that America would make a pre-emptive strike against Soviet nuclear forces in retaliation for their attack on Western Europe. 'Damage limitation' meant a capability to reduce the weight of the enemy attack by both offensive and defensive measures. 'Assured destruction' meant the capability to destroy the enemy as a viable society, even after his well planned and executed surprise attack. All these concepts meant that war *could not be won* by a single massive attack (indeed, it could not be won at all) and the aim became to prevent war, to avoid the inevitability of a massive 'nuclear exchange' and to limit the disastrous consequences of such a war. In the view of the Soviet political and military leaders, these doctrinal changes were a direct consequence of the Soviet military build-up. It may be added that the changes seemingly meant not only a more cautious approach to the possibility of fighting a nuclear war and winning a sort of 'victory' but the evolution of the American strategic doctrine away from nuclear war-fighting concepts and towards a pure doctrine of deterrence. In any case, in the Soviet view, all these changes constituted a *forced response* to the deteriorating correlation of military forces.

In the late 1960s and early 1970s the third change in the correlation of military forces began to be more apparent: as the Soviet strategic offensive arsenal grew and became less vulnerable the capabilities of the American forces *vis-à-vis* the Soviet nuclear strategic forces declined. A massive American counter-force attack could no longer produce its full effect of destroying the bulk of the enemy's nuclear forces.

It became necessary again to re-examine both the American strategic doctrine and America's force posture, but was *this* re-examination so *radical* as the Soviet assertion about the 'fourth shift in the correlation of world forces' implied?

As regards strategic concepts, the impossibility of significantly limiting the damage to American territory in a nuclear war by a massive counterforce attack impelled the Americans to seek new ways of preventing an unlimited escalation. As a result, the concept of selective response options — i.e., of smaller and more precisely focused counterforce attacks — was formulated in January 1974 by Secretary of Defense James Schlesinger.[34] Limited nuclear options would (1) in general, facilitate the control of escalation, (2) terminate the war before cities were hit, (3) deter lesser Soviet attacks (e.g., on one or two US cities or on a handful of military installations), (4) salvage NATO's strategy by supporting theatre forces and increasing the flexibility of the existing strategic nuclear war plans. The control of the process of escalation was expected to limit the damage to the United States and its allies. Thereby the strategy of deterrence was also strengthened to cover a wider spectrum of military challenges.

In the following years this concept was refined to include the threat of striking nuclear blows in order to prevent or retard the enemy's military, political and economic recovery from a 'nuclear exchange'.[35]

However, with all these refinements, the need to retain the capability of targeting the *bulk* of the enemy's strategic nuclear potential continued to be stressed, since this would be the basic military action if escalation could not be controlled.[36]

Up to the end of the 1970s, *the general aim of the American doctrine*, which was to prevent a war against the Soviet Union and the Warsaw Treaty Organisation, was preserved and the aim of an eventual war was defined as the *defence* of the United States and Western Europe, as well as such a *punishment* of the enemy as would prevent his recovery from a nuclear war. Nor was *this strategy* revised in any essential way. As previously, the emphasis was placed on the preparation for a controlled escalation of military operations — if necessary, through the use of limited nuclear strikes — in order to terminate the war under acceptable conditions at the lowest level of conflict possible. If the war were to escalate to the level of a strategic unlimited exchange, the United States would seek to destroy the Soviet military, political and economic assets so as to prevent or retard the Soviet Union's recovery after the war, and to limit correspondingly motivated Soviet attacks on the United States.

Finally, let us examine the changes in the American *force posture*. If these were to constitute a direct answer to the Soviet military build-up, they should have corresponded to (1) the parity allegedly achieved by the Soviet Union in the early 1970s, and (2) the further increase in Soviet offensive and defensive capabilities. In fact, they did not correspond to these developments.

There were primarily two significant changes in the correlation of military forces which were regarded as meaning the achievement of strategic parity. The first was the USSR's attainment of a rough equality in offensive nuclear missiles which continued to grow throughout the 1970s. The United States decided *not* to match this build-up by adding to its own missiles but instead to work for a common ceiling on the total number of long-range delivery systems.

The second change was the increase in the amount of death and destruction which the Soviet Union could inflict on the United States. In the early 1970s, the amount was much nearer the amount of death and destruction which the United States could inflict on the Soviet Union and it grew throughout the 1970s. Once again, the United States decided *not* to match this important element in the correlation of military forces and, at the end of the 1970s, the Soviets were in a position, at least in a first strike, to inflict on the US an amount of damage similar to, or greater than that which the US, in its second strike, could inflict on the Soviet Union (100—140 million against 100—120 million). It was by failing to deploy the defensive systems, rather than by failing to maintain some ratio or margin in the offensive forces, that the United States lost its opportunity to maintain a nuclear superiority, in the view of a Western analyst.[37] The only almost parallel development concerned the production and deployment of multiple independently-targetable re-entry vehicles (MIRVs), which the United States began to deploy in 1970—1 and the Soviet Union in 1975—8.

To sum up, while there was never any doubt that the Soviet military build-up had a great influence on the American strategic doctrine and force posture, the developments in these in the 1970s following the USSR's attainment of strategic parity seem to have been less important than the Soviet military thinkers asserted.

The increasing American military build-up since the late 1970s seems to have further weakened the power of the Soviet assertions concerning the determining impact of the military parity. The decisions to implement this build-up were taken because of the deterioration in the military balance, as the American political and military leaders saw it, and the directions of effort were chosen with a view to the Soviet force posture. Soviet politicians and analysts had previously asserted that the United States was *adapting* its doctrinal strategy and force posture to the strategic parity. In the early 1980s, however, it had been held that America was accelerating a policy of *upsetting* the military strategic equilibrium and, in particular, the strategic nuclear parity. While the previous policy was largely *responsive,* the present one represents a *challenge,* since it means taking a series of initiatives in the arms race and threatens to outpace the Soviet Union in several important

302

respects.

· This change in the nature of the American strategic concepts and military build-up influences the Soviet arguments. The Soviet politicians and military analysts seem to have understood that their new gains with regard to the military balance constitute a two-edged sword which has been used by the Americans to justify their own accelerating build-up. The Soviets have stopped writing about the successful constraining effect of military parity and instead accuse the Americans of trying even harder to achieve a strategic superiority which they will use to implement their increasingly aggressive policies.

Comments

(1)   In general, it may be said that the American military doctrine and force posture was developing in the framework of the country's overall political doctrine and political strategy and under the impact of several factors, which weighed far more heavily than the growth and diversification of the Soviet military posture. Priority was given to efforts to maintain America's leading role in the Western world both in competition with the traditional powers and in sharp rivalry with the Communist states and the national liberation movements. Second only to this came the techno-military revolution which necessitated a radical reassessment of all the traditional doctrinal concepts and force postures. The unprecedented role of nuclear weapons brought the concept of deterrence into the political and military theory and practice. Economic developments and the enormously increasing costs of weapons and armed forces necessitated an ever keener scrutiny of military policy from the cost effectiveness angle. The first permanent politico-military alliance in history uniting the principal European powers required an interaction of the American and the allied military doctrines and force postures. The situation was complicated by the steadily growing political and economic potential of the allies and their increasing requirements for allied cooperation which would replace the American domination. Thus a number of factors affected the developments in America's military doctrine and force posture, and in its foreign and military policy.

(2)   On the basis of the above-mentioned developments in the balance of military power between the superpowers and their respective alliances one may conclude that this balance has affected the American theory and policy in two contradictory ways. On the one hand it has placed considerable restraints on the freedom of American foreign policy and military action, and on the achievement of political goals, both in Europe, *vis-à-vis* the socialist camp, and in the Third World, where the United States has attempted to counteract the collapse of

the colonial system. On the other hand, it has motivated a response from the Americans, who have made a corresponding military effort along the whole spectrum of military capabilities. The utilisation by the Soviet Union of its supposedly advantageous balance of military power for the military support of friendly governments, either directly or through proxies (Cuba, the German Democratic Republic and others) has produced a 'boomerang effect' in the form of an extension of the functions and corresponding capabilities of the United States armed forces, including the creation of the forces of rapid deployment.

A paradoxical juxtaposition of two ideas in the Soviet reasoning on this subject may be noted: (a) the leaders behind the American strategic doctrine and force posture were said to have been forced by the deteriorating correlation of military forces between the superpowers to abandon their plans to win a war of aggression; (b) for the same reasons, they were said to have accelerated the search for new ways to use military force in order to arrest the further deterioration in their political and military situation.

(3) The proposition concerning the constraining effect of the balance of military power on the American doctrine, force posture and military action was used to justify a continuous build-up of Soviet military power with no clearly defined upper limits, especially since the United States was said to be striving to *regain* a military superiority.

It was also used to justify the above-mentioned increase in Soviet military activity in the Third World which was based on the expectation that the Americans would not react.

(4) There were several apparent inconsistencies in the Soviet policy and propaganda line concerning the effects of the advantageous balance of power.

On the one hand, it was asserted that the strategic parity could not be liquidated, on the other, that the United States attempted to upset it, and was thus creating a dangerous situation.[38]

On the one hand, the idea that there could be no victor in a nuclear war was said to be universally accepted. On the other hand, the Americans were said to be preparing for a victorious nuclear war.

It was often stated that a nuclear limited war must inevitably escalate into a total nuclear war; however, the Americans were said to be preparing for the former.

On the one hand, the basic proposition was that a change in the balance of military power to the advantage of the Soviet Union decisively affected the American military doctrine and force posture; on the other it was denied that there was any 'boomerang effect': the increase in the American arsenal was said to reflect a policy of aggression rather than a desire to respond and match the increase in the Soviet arsenal.

Thus, for instance, the deployment of the American cruise missiles and Pershing-II missiles was said to be motivated by the desire to modernise those forces which might make a first nuclear strike against the USSR; this was a traditional line in the American military doctrine. 'Thus from the outset the USA was contemplating not a response to a hypothetical danger allegedly arising from the modernization of Soviet missiles (of which the numbers and the yield were even reduced in the process) but the deployment in Europe of first-strike weapons targeted on the USSR'.[39]

(5) Some of these inconsistencies are only apparent, however. The pattern of all the Soviet criticisms of the American military policy has been as follows:

(i) The United States has some hostile intent (for instance to attain military superiority or the capability for first nuclear strike and victory in nuclear war, to build a space-based ABM system, etc.), which reveals its aggressive ideology and policy.

(ii) The implementation of this purpose is, however, universally recognised as impossible.[40]

(iii) Nevertheless, the inevitable failure of the enterprise in question is not an automatic process but results from an inevitable counteraction by the Soviet Union.

(iv) This means that each such enterprise stimulates the arms race, which is both enormously costly and dangerous. In the final account, there can be no guarantee that the enormous military potential would not be used at some time.

It is implied in this reasoning that the Americans hope that in some way, in some respects, to some degree, and for some economic and technological reasons, the undertaking would not be adequately and promptly matched by the Soviet Union and thus it would have chances for success. This hope is dismissed as unrealistic, however.

(6) These inconsistencies culminated in a 'package' of contradictory statements concerning a more general phenomenon — namely, the revival of the Cold War in the early 1980s. In the Soviet view, a military parity still existed — the Soviet advantage in the global balance of power still existed and was even growing — yet *détente* which had previously been said to result from these military developments, was disappearing. While not renouncing this proposition, the Soviet politicians and analysts began to find more explanations for the deterioration in the climate — namely, the aggressive nature of American policy, the activities of the most militaristic and conservative forces in the American political and military establishment, the pressure of the military-industrial complexes in the United States and Western Europe, the influence of those military circles which had always aimed at nuclear blackmail and at the possession of a capability for a first disabling strike, for a victory in nuclear war and so on. The explanation was sought both in extra-military factors and in the assertion that military power was still the basic means of foreign policy in the United States.

These efforts to explain the American military doctrine and force posture by referring to the entire complex of political, ideological, economic and military factors represented a step in the right direction and accorded with the Marxist-Leninist methodology. However, they pointed up the one-sidedness of the previous explanations, in which the impact of the balance of military power was apparently exaggerated.

(7) Summing up, one might say that, instead of attempting to explain both of these contrary developments — *détente* and the later deterioration of international climate — by referring to the arms race and the changes in the balance of military power (*détente* explained by the changes favourable to the Soviet Union, and the Cold War by the American military build-up), the Soviet analysis would try to explain the ups and downs in the arms race with reference to general developments and a complex of political, ideological, economic and military processes. Such an argument would accord with Marxist-Leninist ideology.

Notes

1   L.I. Brezhnev, *Leninskim kursom*, vol. 7, Moscow 1979, p. 312. Cf. A.G. Arbatov, 'Strategicheskii paritet i politika administratsii Kartera', *SShA: Ekonomika, Politika, Ideologiya*, 1980:11, pp. 30 ff.

2   Cf. Geiling, 1982, p. 10.

3   Arbatov, 1980; Bykov, Razmerov, Tomashevskii, 1981.

4   Cf. Denisov, 1975. He criticises the so-called technological determinism, which automatically connects the likelihood of the occurrence of wars with the technical development. Similar ideas were often analysed and criticised by Y. Rybkin, for instance in his book on the causes of war (1979).

5   Brezhnev, 1979, p. 312.

6   Cf. Ogarkov, 1984, (*K.V.S.*, 1984:11); Slobodenko, 1984. Ogarkov writes: 'To attempt to break the established military equilibrium and to seek military superiority over the Soviet Union and the Warsaw Pact Countries is an undertaking no less futile than for the aggressor to nurture hopes of a victory in nuclear war' (ibid.). Slobodenko asserts: '... the deployment of US missiles in Europe considerably upsets the global strategic balance in favour of the United States and gives it a great advantage in delivering a first nuclear strike. The USSR is not going to accept the situation as it is ... the appropriate Soviet armaments will be deployed with due account for this circumstance in ocean areas

and seas. These Soviet armaments will be qualitatively sufficient to thwart the threat posed to the USSR and its allies by the American missiles emplaced in Europe' (ibid., p. 88). Cf. a semi-official publication *Otkuda iskhodit ugroza miru* which repeatedly and firmly stated that military equilibrium could not be broken (1982, pp. 65), 78 a.o.).

7   Arbatov, 1984.
8   Ibid.
9   Douglas, Hoeber, 1979, pp. 55 ff.
10 Ibid.
11 Semeiko, 1980, p. 121.
12 Arbatov, 1984.
13 Ibid., p. 124.
14 E.g. Benjamin Lambeth, 'How to Think About Soviet Military Doctrine' in *Soviet Strategy*, 1981, the section entitled 'Numbers matter', pp. 114—17.
15 Zamkovoi, Filatov, 1981, pp. 307—8. Cf. Ogarkov, 1985.
16 Zamkovoi, Filatov, 1981, pp. 307—8.
17 Soviet writers also call this set of ideas 'military strategic concepts'. In the American literature the most frequently used term is 'strategic doctrine'. But the terms 'strategy' or 'strategic concepts' are also used.
18 Trofimenko, 1976, 1977; Simonyan, 1976 a,b,c; *SShA: voenno-strategicheskie kontseptsii*, 1980; *Mezhdunarodnye konflikty sovremennosti*, 1983, pp. 200 ff. Khalosha, 1982. One of the main themes in Ogarkov, 1985. In various writings two other causes are also pointed out: radical shifts in the correlation of world forces and the development of the means of armed struggle (Simonyan, 1976).
19 Trofimenko, 1985, pp. 4 ff.
20 Ibid., p. 4.
21 *SShA: voenno-strategicheskie kontseptsii*, 1980, p. 7.
22 Cf. Trofimenko, 1985, pp. 4 ff.
23 Ibid., p. 4.
24 Zamkovoi, Filatov, 1981, pp. 284—301 ('Strategiya nepryamykh deistvii').
25 *SShA: voenno-strategicheskie kontseptsii*; cf. Vorontsov, 1976, p. 194; Trofimenko, 1985, pp. 5—6.
26 *SShA: voenno-strategicheskie kontseptsii*, pp. 54—5.
27 Katasonov, 1983; Trofimenko, 1985.
28 *Zvezdnye Voihy, Illyuzii i Opasnosti*, 1985, cf. Gorbachev, 1986.
29 The main theme in Trofimenko, 1985.
30 *Otkuda iskhodit ugroza miru*, 1982, p. 64; Trofimenko, 1985, p. 12.
31 Ibid., pp. 58—60; Trofimenko, 1985, pp. 5—6.

32   *SShA: voenno-strategicheskie kontseptsii,* pp. 51 ff. Trofimenko, 1985, pp. 6 ff.

33   *SShA: voenno-strategicheskie kontseptsii,* Ch. II.3: 'Voennaya doktrina SShA na poroge 80 godov', pp. 61–76; Trofimenko, 1985, pp. 9–15.

34   Trofimenko, 1985, p. 7.

35   Ibid., one of the main themes.

36   Cf. Khalosha, 1960, 1975, 1982; 'Voenno-blokovaya politika imperializma: istoriya i sovremennost', 1980; Akopov, Sukharkov, 1969; Petrov, 1962; *Armii stran NATO,* 1974; Simonyan, 1976; *SShA i NATO: istochniki voennoi ugrozy,* 1979 .

37   These ideas were expressed in the late 1950s in the Single Integrated Operational Plan (SIOP) for the conduct of nuclear war, prepared by the Joint Target Planning Staff. Cf. Secretary of Defense Robert S. McNamara, *Fiscal Year 1964 to 1968. Defense Program and Defense Budget for Fiscal Year 1964,* Washington: GPO, 30 January 1963, p. 30.

38   Arbatov, 1980; Trofimenko, 1985. Brezhnev was quoted for saying that the very concept of superiority is senseless, in the face of the existence of already accumulated nuclear weapons and the means of their deployment (*Leninskim Kursom,* vol. 7, Moscow 1979, p. 312 in Arbatov, 1980).

39   Vasilenkov, 1985, pp. 80–1.

40   For instance, Ogarkov writes: 'The point is that, with the quantity and quality of nuclear missile weapons now achieved it is simply impossible for an aggressor totally to destroy the opposite side's similar weapons in a single strike. And an immediate, crushing reponse, using even the limited quantity of nuclear weapons remaining to the defending side – a response making it impossible for the aggressor subsequently to wage war or to conduct any serious operations – becomes inevitable under present conditions'.

12 Measuring the correlation

Soviet analysis

Approach

In the Soviet non-classified literature the comparison of military forces was traditionally made without a conceptual analysis. The *concept* of the key items to be included in the assessment, and the *methods* of measuring and comparing them, were generally not discussed.

However, the growing interest among Soviet politicians, military leaders and analysts in the correlation of military forces could not leave unaffected the difficult methodological question of how to measure the forces being compared. Three ideas, it seems, underlie their approach.

First, the value of military force — and consequently the assessment of the correlation of military forces which constitute an instrument of class states — cannot be taken out of the *social context* — the respective socio-economic and political systems. These are said to affect the present adversaries in different ways and to create favourable conditions for the socialist armed forces which profit from the superiority of the socialist system.

Second, in measuring the correlation the focus must be on the capability for an *open action:* on the comparison of the combined quantitative/qualitative characteristics of the armed forces confronting each other in combat or under the conditions of an impending combat. The determining impact of *strategy* on the military value of the correlation — and especially on the manner and the degree in which the latter changes during the combat — is stressed. The correlation of military forces is regarded as a highly *dynamic* value.

Third, after achieving a formal recognition of the strategic parity of the two superpowers, and while continuing to increase their capabilities, Soviet politicians and military analysts also began to work with certain global qualitative and quantitative characteristics of the strategic forces under comparison which were related to both the prevention of war and the waging of war should it break out. They did this for several purposes: to confirm the parity, to refute allegations of the Soviet Union's striving for superiority, to be able to accuse the United States of such a policy and to justify the Soviet position in arms control negotiations.

This analysis has led to the Soviet concentration on three kinds of comparisons:

(1) A general comparison of military forces as a component of the correlation of world forces, both of which are presented as evidencing a global tendency in social development.

(2) A comparison of the strategic nuclear forces of the superpowers or alliances in a static form based on numbers and purely military characteristics;

(3) A highly dynamic comparison of forces in hypothetical military operations; each of the protagonists aims at changing the military correlation to his advantage.

In the Soviet view the first kind of comparison has great value as an instrument of global policy, particularly as a means of political propaganda. The second kind of comparison is a means of influencing the military policy opinion in other states as well as negotiations about arms control. The third is a prescriptive idea of military doctrine, a guideline in the strategic part of military policy.

None of these three kinds *per se* can serve as a basis for assessing the Soviet methodology of measuring the correlation of military forces. General conclusions may be drawn from an analysis of developments in the Soviet military posture and in the Soviet position in arms control negotiations and from the occasional criticisms by Soviet politicians and writers of Western military policy (such as their criticism of the new types of American weapons under development and in production, of changes in the American and NATO military doctrine and of NATO plans for modernising its force posture) as well as from individual articles on methodological problems.

Premises for assessment

(1) Correlation between United States and Soviet Union   The basis of the official Soviet assessment of the correlation of the strategic forces

of the superpowers is that their structures are asymmetrical. Their different compositions and different degrees and kinds of development partly reflect differences in the geographical and strategic positions of the two powers in question, and differences in military doctrines and policies as well as in the development of military technology.[1] The asymmetry is perhaps also rooted in their different military history and experiences.

Thus, for instance, in the early 1980s land-based ballistic missiles accounted for 70 per cent of the USSR's strategic potential as regards the numbers of warheads. About 80 per cent of the total American strategic potential, on the other hand, consisted of ballistic missiles installed in submarines and heavy bombers. According to the Soviet Minister of Defence, Marshal Ustinov, at the end of July 1983 the US possessed 13 aircraft carriers with 120 nuclear-capable aircraft, cruising outside Soviet waters, while the Soviet Union had no aircraft carriers.[2]

The second premise uses as a criterion of comparison the number of nuclear payload launchers — namely, ballistic missile launchers plus strategic (heavy) bombers, taking into account that some launchers are multi-warhead carriers. Soviet politicians, military leaders and analysts sharply criticise the American 'over-emphasis', as they call it, on Soviet superiority in land-based missiles and the alleged vulnerability of this component of the American nuclear 'triad'. The warheads of this type constitute only 24 per cent of the American arsenal, they say, and they are fully compensated by the American superiority in other components of the 'triad'.[3]

Third, in the Soviet view, the comparison should include all American carriers which can hit the territory of the Soviet Union from West European territories. Thus the new intermediate (medium)-range ballistic missiles and cruise missiles which the United States has stationed in Western Europe since the end of 1983 must be included.

Fourth, in comparisons of strategic forces and judgements about their 'equality', particular importance should be attached to 'those systems which are most effective in destroying the defensive warning system, command posts, and staffs and their communications but which lack reliable communications with headquarters — and therefore are more likely to operate without authorisation — and which require special operational procedures that can ease tensions'. According to these indexes, the most destabilising weapons are the ballistic missiles in submarines, heavy bombers, long-range cruise missiles and, perhaps, the *Pershing - 2* missiles deployed in forward positions.[4]

(2) Correlation between NATO and Warsaw Treaty forces   The criteria for assessing the correlation between the superpowers are also, of course, relevant to the comparison of the forces of the two military blocs. These may be divided into nuclear and conventional ones.

As regards the medium-range armaments in Europe — which are sometimes called 'theatre nuclear weapons' — up till 1983 the Soviet leaders asserted that there existed an approximate balance of carriers: each side had about 1000 of them. However, in an important index, such as the number of nuclear charges which can be discharged in a single launching, NATO was said to have a 50 per cent superiority.[5] The Soviet side asserted that the criterion for this comparison was simple. Soviet medium-range missiles and bombers opposed — and should be compared numerically with — the following weaponry: American nuclear-equipped planes stationed at bases in West European countries, with planes carrying nuclear weapons, US aircraft carriers in European waters, British and French land-based and sea-based medium range ballistic missiles and bombers of corresponding types, which constitute the so-called 'Forward Based Systems'. Such weapons have a range from 1000 to 4500 kilometers and can reach targets on USSR territory up to the Urals.[6]

As regards the balance of non-strategic nuclear forces, one item to be compared consists of battlefield nuclear weapons which are mainly artillery-fired atomic projectiles and short-range rockets. There is said to exist an approximate parity in such nuclear forces.

The comparison of conventional forces is a more complex matter, the Soviet leaders say. The asymmetry here is considerable and it is very difficult to compare the forces system by system or unit by unit. The NATO armed forces are superior to the Warsaw Treaty in overall numerical strength and in the number of combat-ready divisions and anti-tank weapons but somewhat inferior in the number of tactical aviation aircraft. The blocs are about equal as regards the number of artillery and armoured items. In the Soviet assessment, on the whole, there exists an approximate balance of conventional forces and equipment.

Methodological premises

The few methodological premises which have been discussed in Soviet writings may be summarised as follows.
(1) The evaluation of the correlation of forces in combat can only be partial and approximate and made only in relation to concrete types of military actions. As regards nuclear forces, the assessment cannot be restricted to the capability of performing strategic nuclear strikes, (which is a frequent approach in Western comparisons). All the main types of military actions must be considered, including a combination of strategic nuclear strikes and major operations in the theatres of military operations.
(2) The correlation of military forces is a *function of time.* It may be defined as 'the relationship of the combat capabilities of groups of the

armed forces of the sides participating in combat actions *at the given moment*[7] (italics added).

In the calculations on the strategic, the operational and the tactical scales, the initial data can serve only as one of the premises, since they will change rapidly; indeed, the numerical characteristics of the forces in combat constitute the most dynamic variable because of the quick changes in the combat situation.[8]

(3) The correlations of military forces — both the initial one and that which changes in the course of combat actions — depend on the expediency of the plan of operation and its timely realisation. In particular, they depend on whether the plan succeeds in correctly establishing the principal operational directions at the decisive junctures of an operation and thus in creating a favourable correlation of forces in these directions.

(4) As regards operations entailing the use of strategic nuclear weapons, their effectiveness also depends (a) on whether the plan succeeds in choosing the best variant of the first nuclear strike, which would correspond to the expected value of the initial correlation of forces; (b) on whether the plan succeeds in predicting the correlation of forces after the strike in order to plan further operations; (c) on whether the plan succeeds in a rational distribution of nuclear weapons against the active and passive targets;[9] in the Soviet view, the general premise is that maximum efforts must be directed against the former — i.e., against the nuclear weapons of the enemy — as well as against the various supporting systems, especially the control systems.[10]

(5) The success of any strategy and any plan for a concrete operation depends on a correct evaluation of the correlation of forces before, during and after the operation which, in turn, assumes a correct forecast of the changes.

A protagonist should see to it that his plan not only predicts but also *ensures* the most advantageous correlation of forces in his own favour after the strike is delivered.

(6) The assessment of the quality of the armed forces — their organisation, the abilities of their commanders, their training and combat readiness — is of primary importance.

(7) All these estimates also require a correct choice and correct assessment of the principal qualitative and quantitative parameters of the following aspects of military force:

(a) the quantity and quality — and, in particular, the destructive quality — of the weapons; (b) their vulnerability — at launching, during flight, or movement on land and on sea; (c) the quality of the control systems; (d) the quality of the reconnaissance system; (e) radio-electronic equipment — in particular, that used for counter-measures against enemy actions; (f) all types of support of military operations; (g) all types of active and passive defences.

(8)   As regards nuclear forces, some specific indices must be included, namely:

(a)   the distribution of nuclear weapons among the various branches of armed forces; (b) the techno-tactical characteristics of the carriers of nuclear weapons; (c) protection and mobility of the nuclear weapons; (d) the probability of overcoming the enemy defences and destroying the active targets.

Also of special importance are those indices which are common to the correlation of all the military forces, such as the initial correlation of nuclear forces, the effectiveness of the anti-air defences of the nuclear forces, the combat readiness (especially of the carriers of nuclear weapons), the control system, and the plan for nuclear strikes.

As to some numerical indices connected with the above-mentioned parameters, the correlation of military forces mainly means the relationship of the total area of the destruction that can be inflicted upon the same type of target and its approximate proportion to the relationship of the amount of TNT equivalents available. As to the distribution of nuclear weapons among the various branches of the armed forces, the coefficient of their distribution should be proportionate to the probability that a given type of carrier can overcome the enemy defences and destroy the given targets.

To these considerations, it should be perhaps added that several parameters which are presented in the Soviet literature as purely techno-military are, in fact, connected with the political characteristics of military operations. For instance, the combat readiness of nuclear carriers, which is said to be determined by the interval of time from the moment the launching signal is received to the moment when the carrier leaves the launcher, must be set in a broader framework. The interval in fact depends on — and must be measured from — the moment when the *political* decision to strike is taken: this gives the signal to launch the carrier. Again, the chances of destroying the enemy's control system depend on the quality of the system itself — which, in turn, goes far beyond a purely military control to include a broader system of *political* control — and so on. The broader framework includes, however, hardly measurable, indeed intangible values, which may render the entire calculation and the assessment of the correlation of military force even more difficult.

Finally, two implications of the correlation of military force considerations must be mentioned. These are connected with the above-mentioned methods in which a protagonist may establish a favourable correlation before and during the military operations and, in particular, with the methods of preparing an operational plan of which the primary aim would be to make the correlation of military force *increasingly favourable* to his own forces.

One method is connected with the temptation to *pre-empt* in order

314

to gain superiority at the very beginning of hostilities. The other method is to *destroy the enemy's command, control and communications system* — the *'brain'* of the armed forces — and thus to disrupt his war plans.

Difficulties in measuring the military correlation

Agenda

The apparently modest Soviet effort to develop a methodology of measuring the correlation of military forces — which would probably be smaller than the effects of the factual effort presented in classified literature — may be contrasted with the abundant Western literature on the subject. However, as further analyses are made constantly, difficulties seem to arise, as the Western politicians and military students themselves admit. Various approaches and individual proposals have been devised to overcome these difficulties.

The scarcity of such efforts in Soviet non-classified military literature does not mean, naturally, that the Soviet leaders do not recognise these difficulties. On many occasions they make comments concerning the asymmetry of forces and stress the necessity to take into account the non-measurable qualities. Thus the difficulties analysed in the West seemingly also relate to the Soviet methodology and practice.

At first glance, it seems easier to make a comparison of military forces than, for instance, a comparison of the 'world forces', since for several practical purposes there appears to be no need to consider the impact of economic factors, of the techno-scientific potential, the geopolitical position of the country or the national character. An apparent reflection of this apparent simplicity was that both SALT I and SALT II were largely based on a comparison of the numbers and statical values of military hardware such as radius or the destructive power of particular strategic weapon systems. Many of the discussions for or against these agreements — the former accomplished, the latter attempted — operated with such indicators.

Admittedly, without numbers and static indicators the arms control negotiations and agreements would have been impossible. However, it is also obvious that the *difficulties* in measuring the real value of individual weapon systems and combat units — and, in this perspective, of the global military force, (even confined to its so-called strategic component), and the *different ways* of measuring and assessing these values — contributed to the meagre results of the hitherto waged negotiations.

The difficulties in measuring military strength naturally have constituted only a part of the difficulties of achieving an agreement in the negotiations. Different political philosophies including the philosophy of the role and the uses of military force, and especially all the different policies of the participants, were obviously the determining obstacle. As we have stressed in this study, the military potentialities of a state cannot be considered separately from its political doctrine, political intentions, military missions and strategy.

The very rough assessment of the material strength of military force in mathematical data is, of course, necessary as a background to negotiations, but up to now it seems to have produced more confusion than factual evidence.

In this study, the difficulties in measuring military strength, and therefore of comparing military potentialities, may be considered separately only *for analytical reasons* from the entirety of the political difficulties of achieving an agreement on arms control.

The difficulties in comparing the military forces of two or more states begin in the initial phase when one tries to measure and assess an individual military force. It is far from sufficient to make an inventory of the troops and armaments and of all the data concerning the quantitative and qualitative characteristics of these. Several intangible values of crucial importance usually remain uncalculated and are not included: command, control and communications capabilities, training and morale and the cultural and structural societal variables.

If, despite these difficulties, an absolute value *sui generis* of the military force in question is obtained, the next step would be no less complex: it would be an assessment of the ability of the military force to take action. This involves the relation of the military force to its *missions* and to the *adversary's capabilities.* For instance, the possession of a number of medium-range missiles powerful enough to destroy some undefended cities but not to destroy his well-protected military objectives may not contribute to deterrence in any significant degree. The capability to perform a single military task or mission is, of course, a part of the capability to implement a strategy in its entirety. Only an assessment of the complex of all capabilities to perform the set of missions within the framework of a prepared strategy can serve as a basis for the evaluation of a military force and for the comparison of it with other military forces.

Then, however, there arise new difficulties connected with the *procedure of comparison* itself. Many of these are common to both the evaluation of a single military force and the comparison of several such forces.

Let us now examine some of the difficulties connected with (1) the methods of measuring military force and comparing two or more military forces; (2) the subjective approaches to the measuring procedure and (3) the factors to be taken into account in assessing the real value of military force, such as its multi-level structure, the multi-level structure of the correlation of military forces and the strategy of the intended use of military force.

Method

1   *Analytical apparatus*   The basic concepts used in comparisons of military forces are far from being agreed on. What is meant by the correlation of military forces, it may be asked? What are the contents of the basic terms used, for instance strategic forces?

To begin with the key concept of the correlation (or comparison or balance) of forces, it seems that the main comparison subjects are: (1) the balance between the United States and the Soviet Union which is based mainly but not exclusively on the comparison of their strategic nuclear forces; (2) the multi-level balance between the NATO forces and the WTO forces in Europe; (3) the regional balances in vital areas of the Third World.

The correlation of forces may also be interpreted as an aggregate or combination of all these correlations; while there may be a rough equality in the global balance, some of the components may be to the advantage of one side.[11] However, it is difficult to *generalise* concerning *all* these particular instances.

Then comes the difficulty of categorising the forces in the comparison. The global forces under comparison consist of components, thus the global correlation of military forces consists of component correlations. In a multi-level comparison the simplest set would include strategic nuclear forces, theatre nuclear forces (or tactical nuclear forces) and conventional forces.

However: (1) there are no generally agreed definitions which unambiguously distinguish between strategic nuclear and tactical nuclear forces; (2) even if such were agreed on, it would be difficult to include particular systems in a definite category of weapons or military units, since they may be used in different categories of missions depending on the type of war, place, phase of war and so on; (3) what one side may consider strategic the other may consider tactical.

A striking example of the latter difference is that the American command regards its forces in Europe as tactical forces or as a part of general purpose forces; the USSR consider them to be strategic forces. While the United States distinguishes between strategic nuclear forces, theatre nuclear forces in Europe and conventional forces assigned to NATO, the latter two elements in America's 'triad' in NATO are regarded by the Soviet Union as strategic forces. There are two reasons for this, Soviet analysts say:

First, these forces can directly attack the European territory of the Soviet Union. Second, in any war in Europe all elements in the Soviet armed forces would directly contribute to a unified strategic plan; NATO forces, it is believed, would act in a corresponding manner.[12]

The SS-20 missiles, on the other hand, are regarded by the Western European states as strategic weapons, since they can hit all the important targets in those states, while the Soviet leaders contend that they are not strategic, since they cannot reach the United States. To put it another way, what in an all-out war is tactical for the United States in its nuclear exchange with the Soviet Union, is strategic for the European NATO-members.[13]

Moreover, the same forces and weapons may in one strategy, or in one war scenario, play a strategic role but in others a tactical one. This depends on their deployment (which affects their radius of action) and their mission — i.e., expected utilisation in a first or a retaliatory attack.[14]

Apart from all these ambiguities, in view of the enormous destruction and the danger of immediate escalation, in any nuclear war the distinction would be blurred between (1) strategic weapons considered as a means of breaking the war will of the enemy side by destroying its principal administrative, industrial and military centres and large cities (with or without the simultaneous destruction of its armed forces) and (2) tactical weapons which may be used to attain particular military objectives by destroying or neutralising wholly or partly the enemy's armed forces.

With regard to the Eurostrategic theatre of military operations this blurring has become so obvious that one writer proposes to call all the nuclear forces which might participate in a war in Europe 'the nuclear forces in and for Europe' (*Die Nuklearkräfte in und für Europa*).[15] A feature common to these forces is that they can hit targets in Europe. At the same time such terminology might provide a basis for *comparing* the nuclear forces of the two alliances.[16]

The discussion about the NATO decision in December 1979 concerning the modernisation of NATO's theatre nuclear weapons (TNW) (the replacement of *Pershing I* by 108 launching platforms for *Pershing II* plus 464 GLCM — Ground-Launched Cruise Missiles) revealed some of these difficulties. It was partly about (1) the definition of TNW and (2) which of the TNWs should be included in the forces that were being compared with the respective Soviet forces.

There are many answers to the first question. The most frequent is that it is difficult to establish the upper and lower limits to the range of nuclear weapons if they are to be called 'middle-range'. Even more difficult is to establish limits for the description of some nuclear weapons as 'the European theatre nuclear weapons'. Besides, it may be asked whether these weapons should be called 'tactical' or 'Eurostrategic'. On the one hand, *Pershing II* would have the capability of reaching targets deep in Soviet territory. On the other, the SS-20 already has a Eurostrategic radius in relation to Western Europe, and even Soviet tactical nuclear weapons, formally assigned the task of near-combat but possessing a radius of 700 km, can be used 'Euro-strategically' if deployed near the frontier between the two Germanys.

The second question receives different answers from various quarters, but most different from the officials representing the opposing camps. In their calculations, the Soviet leaders regard as NATO's theatre nuclear weapons the American aircraft F-111, FB-11, F-4, A-6 and A-7 stationed in West Germany, in the United Kingdom and on American aircraft carriers in the Mediterranean, then also the British and French nuclear weapons (the British 64 Submarine-Launched Ballistic Missiles on four Submarines, and the 48-year-old Vulcan Bombers; the French 90 SLBM on five Submarines, the 18 MRBM in Haute-Provence and 33 strategic Mirage-4-Bombers). The result is 986 Western nuclear carriers *vis-à-vis* 975 Soviet ones.

In NATO's argument only some of the above-mentioned Western items of nuclear armament should be included in the comparison. Moreover, the focus is on the techno-military characteristics of the systems in the comparison: while NATO's weapons of this kind are said to be ageing, the Soviet side has introduced *new* systems (Surface-to-Surface Missiles SS-20) with greater accuracy, mobility and range than the previous ones (and also with multiple warheads) and with generally greater capability (Backfire-Bombers).

SS-20 with its 5000 km range covering all of Western Europe including the supply lines in the Atlantic and the Middle East, represents quite a new category of weapons. Moreover, 880 middle-range aircraft of three types prepared for offensive purposes can carry atomic bombs, and missiles with a range of 3700 km carried by submarines in the Baltic Sea have nuclear warheads. In effect, the Soviet side according to these NATO officials is superior in TNW in both the quantitative and qualitative respects.[17]

Another question is: *What part* of the forces at a certain level should be included in the assessment and the comparison? Total inventories or only items in operational units? Are stockpiles to be included or ignored? Are old bombers or missiles or tanks to be included? Missiles in storage without launchers? Only ICBMs and bombers on alert, and submarines at sea?

In the most comprehensive approach, the analyst would assess all the above-mentioned components, which naturally would generate the need — and the very difficult task — of making a correct assessment of the hierarchy of these components and their relative value and importance in the global correlation — their interaction, mutually complementary roles, and so on.

The assessment depends, of course, on the scenario of war. It depends, for instance, on whether the forces are to be used for a surprise attack or a retaliation. Some parts of the national forces are never used in war.

It also depends on the state of *combat readiness* of both of the forces in the comparison and on how the forces are divided from this point of view. Some analysts, for instance, divide the Soviet forces into three strategic echelons: (1) The first is manned at full strength (90 per cent day-to-day) ready to fight within a few hours, or less; (2) The second is manned at 20 per cent overall and 50 per cent for officers and key personnel, completely equipped; (3) The third is essentially unmanned, except for key command elements.[18] Apparently, the first echelon mentioned above should be included in the comparison of forces designated for an initial combat. However, for an assessment of a *correlation* of military forces based on such a categorisation of Soviet forces, a similar division of the American (and more generally of the NATO) forces should be made.

2   *Data base*   Here two difficulties arise. First, the analyst may not have complete information about the global capabilities of his own country and not much information about the capabilities of his potential adversary. Second, since the bodies of information obtained from different sources differ greatly from one another the calculations made on such base by individual researchers vary even more.[19]

The data released by, or leaked from, intelligence agencies tend to exaggerate both the knowledge of these capabilities and the adversary's military potential.[20]

The former is due partly to the fact that the agencies in question tend to exaggerate their own performance, the latter is connected with the mechanism of military policy: those who order and obtain the information and then channel it to the analysts — i.e., the military and civilian bureaucracies — usually desire high estimates of the threat (and of indicators of the enemy military force, such as kill-probabilities, rates of fire, combat readiness, systems' reliability, mobilisation potentialities, build-up rates, munition stocks, etc.) in order to justify the maintenance of high force levels, new weapons and defence research.

Therefore, a careful verification of the different sources of information is needed, but this cannot always be obtained.

3   *Indicators*   One of the main difficulties in any comparison of forces concerns the choice of the indicators of weapon systems. Some writers distinguish between the so-called static and dynamic indicators. In one approach these terms relate to the way in which the assessment of the correlation is made: at a given point of time (usually before the beginning of military operations) or after a particular phase of fighting (for instance, after the first nuclear strike, or after the retaliatory nuclear strike). In another approach, static indicators mean numbers

of forces and weapons, while dynamic indicators relate to their qualities which manifest themselves in the actions of combined forces and weapons.

It seems that the following development of the methods of measuring the military balance may be observed: from *static* indicators such as the number of forces or warheads or the payload in megatons to *more dynamic* measures, such as the invulnerability of the means and forces and qualitative criteria, such as the organisational capabilities of the commanders, the technique of choosing targets and the capability of changing them instantly.[21] This development also points to a much greater than before inclusion of the *quality of military units* and of the level of their *military art* as extremely important indicators of the military value of armed forces.

Most frequently used is the combined quantitative-qualitative criterion. Among the principal quantitative — and at the same time static — indicators are the numbers of warheads, megatons, throw-weight (+ payload and yield) and, hard-target kill capabilities.[22] Some call them the 'standard static indicators'.[23] Among the qualitative indicators (sometimes equated with the dynamic ones) are reliability, treliability, penetration probabilities, survivability (or survival probability), accuracy, mobility, deployment, as well as serviceability, reload capability, sortie rates and electronic countermeasures. Some of these criteria are especially important at the Euro-strategic level — for instance, those concerning reliability and/or accuracy. Survivability and all the indicators concerning maximal combat readiness — the ability to enter the combat with the minimal delay — are of great importance on the battlefield. In the view of the authors of an analysis of the nuclear balance in Europe, the following qualitative attributes of the opposing nuclear weapons systems ought to be considered: ranges of the weapons systems; the accuracy of the weapons; the nuclear yield and destructive potential carried by them; their refire (or 'reload') capabilities; their vulnerability to attack (survivability); and their ability to penetrate enemy defences.[24]

Both the quantitative and the qualitative indicators manifest themselves differently (1) in different *types of military operations* (and, more generally, in different war scenarios) depending, for instance, on whether the forces are used to make a first strike or a retaliatory strike; and (2) with regard to different *targets*. Under conditions of rough equality and the possibility of a devastating two-sided nuclear exchange, factors such as command, control communication systems and endurance are important. The global force posture and the structure of armed forces, including the relation between nuclear forces and conventional forces also become very important. All these factors defy straightforward assessment.

4   *Comparison of weapon systems*   There is also the difficulty of comparing the weapon systems. Static quantitative force comparisons do not reflect qualitative differences, particularly those connected with training, combat readiness, morale and other critical aspects of military capability.

Most of the static force comparisons concern similar types of equipment. Yet, anti-tank weapons do not fight anti-tank weapons, bombers do not fight bombers, ballistic missile submarines do not fight other such submarines, and so on. Besides, 'heavy bombers' do not mean the same in the American and the Soviet terminologies; missiles, divisions and ships may constitute larger and smaller items in the same class, and these should not count for the same. Dual purpose systems introduce additional difficulties. Even more difficult is the comparison of classes of weapons: how many bombers equal, or compensate for, how many ballistic missiles?

A further difficulty concerns comparisons of systems which belong to the same class but have many different indicators and consequently different degrees of effectiveness. The systems used by the adversaries may in some respects be superior but in others inferior to one another.[25] The same concerns manpower: one cannot foresee which indicators will be most important on the battlefield — outstanding initiative or an instinctive obedience to orders? Technological training or toughness?

Approach

1   *Reasons for subjective approaches*   The above-mentioned specific and very subjective interest of the governmental 'consumers' of information represent only one aspect of a more general danger: the subjective approach of those who *use* the information for an *analysis and a policy* that is based on their political, military and economic interests and aims. The analysts have their own view of the world, their prejudices, their biases and they also fight to promote some kind of policy — for instance, either to improve the defence capabilities of their country or to prevent the danger of war by bringing about a general reduction of armaments, or both. The political and military leaders not only have their view of the world but they pursue policies that serve definite interests. They may aim at increasing their armaments — either their global volume or the weapons assigned to particular armed services or arms or to particular armament systems. They may, on the contrary, use the information and evaluation made on its basis for arms control proposals; they may use it in political arguments — internal or in the alliance — and in interstate negotiations.

The reasons for differences in assessments may be unconscious, and a lack of professional knowledge in the face of the abundance of highly technical indicators may also contribute.

Be this as it may, the methodology used to assess the condition of military forces — both of one's own country and the probable adversary — is as a rule subjective. Not only the numbers may be and are manipulated in very different ways [26] but also the choice of the indicators for comparison, especially the qualitative ones, is usually made advisedly and depends on subjective preferences.[27]

To put it another way, any assessment of the correlation of military forces by policy-makers is necessarily subjective since:

(1) It is a part of the assessment of the global politico-military situation which underlies military policy (security policy) which, in turn, is an important part of state policy;

(2) It is made *in order* to provide a basis for taking political decisions about security, which depend on the established political doctrine and long-range policy;

(3) It may be used to achieve some *immediate* political advantages. One of the protagonists may claim to possess superiority in order to put military pressure on the allies of the main adversary or to 'make an impression' on third parties. On the other hand, he may say that his adversary has a superiority in order to justify his own military build-up or to influence public opinion in other countries to slow down their military programmes. In arms control negotiations such an approach is common practice, particularly concerning individual kinds of weapons.

Finally, for a number of reasons — but primarily for purposes of the negotiations on arms control or arms reduction — one side may claim that it has ground for establishing parity at a certain level (although it believes that it has a superiority) to counteract the adversary's claim to have to improve his unfavourable balance by modernising or increasing his forces up to the level in question. For instance, each time the NATO leaders talked of the need for more conventional armaments in the Western Alliance, the Soviet Union asserted that there already existed a balance of conventional strength in Europe. (However, in the beginning of the 1970s, the Soviet leaders admitted, and even emphasised, the Soviet superiority in conventional forces as a factor which, in their view, promoted the establishment of a *global balance* and of peace in Europe. They assumed that the socialist states were the champions of peace and that their superiority in any kind of forces was good for peace.)

NATO's decision in 1979 concerning the modernisation and expansion of their 'intermediate nuclear forces' was countered by the Soviet argument that the existing balance of power would then be destroyed and peace endangered.

Differences in the assessment of the correlation of forces are also possible in a particular country; they arise from the partisan interests of the armed services or various groups in the military establishment and the armaments industry. The civilian leaders in the Pentagon, for instance, said, with regard to the concept of mutual assured destruction, that in Europe conventional parity existed or could easily be established, and that a prolonged defensive campaign was possible there. They asserted that NATO's assessment of the inferiority of its own military balance in Europe was wrong since it failed to take into account qualitative indicators, such as the superiority of Western weapon-systems, the higher standard of training, logistics and other parameters in NATO. At the same time the United States armed services and the American NATO representatives considered, like the Europeans, that NATO had a conventional inferiority and demanded an increase in the credibility of America's nuclear answer to any military operations initiated in Europe. In these circles, any mention made on the possibility of fighting a conventional war in Europe was regarded as weakening the element of nuclear deterrence.

2   *Impact of alliances*   Uncertainties also arise because we have to look at the correlation of military forces — whether it be global, or between the United States and the Soviet Union, or between NATO and WTO — through the prisms of the respective alliances.

Will America fulfil its obligations to its NATO allies in a war, if this means the total destruction of its territory? (In such a case, America's strategic nuclear forces should be included in the comparison of forces.) Will all the Western allies fulfil their obligations and continue to stand up to the Soviet threat? (In such a case their forces should be included in both the nuclear and conventional components.) Can the Soviet Union rely on its allies? Will not some of the Soviet forces be occupied in holding down the satellite countries? How will the allies of the superpowers behave in a situation that threatens war?

These and other questions must be answered by any analysis of the correlation of the military forces of the two adversaries in the Euro-strategic framework.

The assessments of the correlation of military forces made by the main adversaries — the superpowers — may have the aim of influencing their allies. The United States has often alleged that NATO is inferior in conventional weapons in order to encourage the organisation to increase its efforts concerning these as well as the tactical nuclear weapons. The Soviet Union has said that WTO is superior in both of the main categories of weapons thanks naturally to the Soviet contribution — but for quite different reasons: it wished, *inter alia*, to strengthen its dominance in the Warsaw Treaty Organisation. However, the United States judged this matter differently.

As mentioned above, some circles in the Pentagon considered that Western Europe could successfully defend itself with conventional weapons for a long time and that an immediate escalation to a general nuclear war was not inevitable. For instance, at the beginning of the 1970s, some Pentagon publications argued that there existed a conventional parity in Europe and that NATO could defend itself near the Eastern frontier relatively long without resorting to nuclear weapons.

At the same time, the West Germans considered that the prospects for a successful defence were very dim. The European members of NATO maintained that the Alliance was inferior in conventional weapons in order to strengthen America's nuclear engagement and its readiness to deter in a credible way with its nuclear potential.

Strategies and missions

1   *Dependence on strategies*   The comparison of the value of the particular components of armed forces and of the systems of weapons highly depends on the place which is assigned to them in the adversaries' strategies — i.e., on how much of them will be used in the particular phases of war and for what kinds of operations.

These expected uses differ greatly in each kind of war. Concerning, for instance, a war based on counterforce strikes, the American doctrine seems to assume the possibility — while refuting officially — of a limited war and the flexible use of forces in this. The Soviet strategists exclude the possibility of such a war. The Americans assume that the military operations may be protracted, and some negotiations may begin at a certain point in the operations, or during a lull in them, while the Soviet leadership conceive of nuclear war as a very brief nuclear exchange. The two sides differ, naturally, in their predictions of who will finally win.

More generally, it may be said that, while NATO's strategy is oriented towards nuclear deterrence and conventional defence, the Soviet leaders expect to deter the 'warmongers' by planning for and acquiring the capacity to carry out offensive operations on all levels. These different assumptions represent various attitudes towards the introduction of different amounts and kinds of forces in the initial phase and therefore it becomes unrealistic to compare the forces in a scenario which would include the common assumptions in both doctrines.

In other words, the different emphasis in the various strategies is reflected in the differing emphasis in military preparations and in the development of particular systems of arms and weapons and in difficulties in the comparison of forces which would be fighting one another. To take the simplest example, while the WTO strategy requires numerous and well-equipped tank forces, NATO needs strong anti-tank defences. However, it is hard to compare the strengths of tank forces and

325

anti-tank weapons.

2 *Scenarios of war: a help or a hindrance in comparing forces?* Quantitative/qualitative assessments of the correlation of military forces are usually complemented by — or made in a framework of — scenarios for their conceivable utilisation. Scenarios, however, are highly hypothetical: they depend on the political doctrines and strategies which a protagonist (1) ascribes to his adversary and (2) describes as his own.

For instance, the Western officials, military men and writers assume that a nuclear war can begin only as the result of a Soviet conventional or all-out nuclear attack (or some intermediate alternatives). On the other hand, the Soviet officials, military men and writers maintain that such a war can result only from an escalation of a local 'imperialist aggression' or from an all-out attack by NATO forces. These voluntary assumptions entail quite different scenarios, at least in their initial phases. So must also be the assessment of how effective would be one's own and the adversary's military forces — i.e., what value will acquire the correlation of forces *in action.*

One of the reasons for this diversity of views is that war scenarios themselves, and particularly those concerning military operations entailing the use of nuclear weapons, are necessarily highly hypothetical and have several variants. Even if confined to the initial period of a nuclear war, the strategy would depend on the motives and aims of the belligerents at that time, on the assessment of the contemporary situation, and the potentialities for action, the risks which it has been decided to take, the decisions on the scope of operations, and so on. The further course of operations would depend on the same factors plus the outcome of the initial actions and their impact on the politico-military situation. The need to take account of the motives, decisions and actions of the partners in the coalition is an additional complicating factor.

One should also remember that many of the theoretical qualitative/quantitative parameters of the sophisticated nuclear and conventional weapons may, under combat conditions, differ from those that were expected. The behaviour and the performance of the troops may also differ from those expected.

It is probably easier to predict the options which may be *excluded* than those which may be *expected.* Excluding a surprise attack, the risk to the initiator of military operations — the attacker — may be greater than the risk to the defender. For all these reasons, it is difficult to compare the 'options' open to an aggressor and those available to the defender.

The primary difficulty is the non-predictability (and in a sense the 'non-measurability') of the adversary's political intentions. It is not by chance that the opposing camps, when they construct war scenarios, ascribe aggressive intentions to the adversary and connect his entire

326

military capabilities with the most far-reaching goals. In other words, they construct war scenarios for 'the worst case'.

But even other scenarios may be highly hypothetical and hardly used to any exact calculations. Western political and military leaders and researchers, for instance, sometimes assume that in an intersystemic war the Soviet command may prefer a variant of massive conventional operations in Europe leading to the rapid conquest of vast territories. This, according to the calculations ascribed to the Soviet leaders, would diminish the danger that NATO might use its tactical nuclear weapons and also destroy a large proportion of them, paralyse the movement of reinforcements across the Atlantic (by occupying the coastal territories), give the Soviet navy more freedom of action, and so on. Following these successes, the Soviets would be able to exploit the productive potential of Western Europe for both the continuing war and for the post-war economic recovery. This might obviate possible 'troubles' in Eastern Europe. Western analysts point out several 'items of evidence' of preparations for *such* offensive operations: the Soviet strategy focusing on the principle of the offensive at all levels — from the strategic to the tactical one; the deployment in the Eastern and Central Europe of forces assigned to such operations, such as large armoured and mechanised units.[28]

However, despite all these speculations and 'items of evidence', even such a scenario for a case less serious than 'the worst one' is regarded by other politicians, the military leaders and writers as hardly probable, taking account of the Soviet Union's real fear of unleashing an all-out war which, in spite of all possible gains in the initial phase in Europe, could only end with enormous destruction on Soviet territory.

3   *Missions and options*   The above-mentioned difficulties in measuring and comparing the military forces of states (or coalitions of states) means that various proposals, as the ulimate criterion, emphasise the *dependence of the assessment on the functions and missions of the armed forces.*

The analysis in terms of the missions which a military force must accomplish while making possible a better assessment of one's *own* capabilities related to missions nevertheless remains dependent on the assessment of those capabilities of the adversary which also concern missions. However, both the capabilities and the missions of the adversary are largely hypothetical.

The emphasis placed on the capability of performing definite missions led to the assertion that the strategic parity — and consequently the stability — might mean an equivalence (balance) of capabilities for a spectrum of missions and the possession of alternative *options* of military action. Such 'options' mean here the capability to use an appropriate military force in a certain scenario. Such a 'balanced performance capability'[29] would require an appropriate correlation of the forces of the adversaries, it is said.

If each option based on an attack were countered by an effective defence, or if each aggression were connected with an incalculable risk, one might speak of a *military balance* between the adversaries. Likewise, if each of the adversaries had the same number of 'promising' options connected with his initiation of the war, one might then speak of a *balance of options.*

The evaluation of the probable success of an 'option' or of 'missions' is based on a comparison of forces and thus the element of a quantitative/qualitative comparison is here preserved. This evaluation is, however, related to concrete scenarios of military operations and to the forces which are expected to be directly engaged in them. Therefore it is not necessary that the forces of the adversaries be globally and statically equal.[30]

If a belligerent has more options — i.e., more possibilities — for initiating an action which cannot be resisted, the correlation of military forces may be considered to be to his advantage.

It seems that the comparison of options, which is not free from all the difficulties connected with the comparison of the quantitative/qualitative indices of armed forces — since in the final account these must form one of the bases of the assessment — introduces another difficulty: the need to consider the *intentions* of both sides. Only politically realistic 'options' should be included in the assessment: those, which correspond to the political ideology of the given country, to its long-range policy and concrete politico-military developments. Certainly, this is a risky analytical enterprise. One can only agree with Stratmann who discussed in detail the difficulties connected with the assessment of military options.[31] However, other writers assert that, since *after* the making of such a political analysis the number of options which may be called realistic is significantly reduced, such a procedure means a 'reduction in the complexity' of the comparison of forces.[32]

Again, such an approach does not do away with all the difficulties connected with the comparison of the quantitative/qualitative indices of armed forces, since in the final account it must take them into account. This approach is perhaps more difficult, because it must also assess the 'options' open to the enemy; but it permits a more speculative analysis, and this always can obviate the need to make exact calculations.

The 'options' approach does not exclude the idea that each side should possess a capability to inflict unacceptable damage on the adversary: this would contribute to the prevention of war.[33] Both principles allow for being inferior in some forces, since it is not the exact parity which determines security.

328

1   *From two to four levels*   As mentioned before, the correlation of forces between the two opposing camps may be regarded as a multi-level balance. In the early 1950s it constituted a two-level correlation: the comparison of strategic nuclear forces, which gave a clear superiority to the United States, and that of tactical conventional forces, which gave an overwhelming superiority to the Soviet Union. Subsequently, the tactical nuclear level was added, which was in the West regarded as giving an initial American superiority. As the superiority in strategic nuclear weapons diminished, the increase in the Western arsenal of tactical nuclear weapons and forces both in numbers and in sophistication was believed to be compensating their continuing inferiority in the conventional component.

In the 1970s, the three-level correlation underwent further changes. The Soviet Union increased its tactical nuclear potential and created an arsenal of intermediate-range ballistic missiles, the SS-20s, which in a surprise attack could destroy important targets in Western Europe, including most of NATO's tactical nuclear weapons. A pre-emptive attack at this level might radically diminish the whole combat capability of NATO. Thereby a fourth level − that of intermediate-range nuclear weapons (or Euro-strategic weapons) − was added to the analysis of the correlation. NATO's decision of 1979 aimed at creating a parity or an equilibrium at this level. The Western side asserts that there now exists an imbalance of power at this level as well as at the conventional one. Therefore the *global* correlation of military forces between the opposing camps is said to favour the WTO.

Here the difficulties in measuring the correlation of military forces are seen clearly. Contrary to the above-mentioned assessment, many other writers, especially those representing various schools of peace research, contend that there is *no imbalance of power* in Europe; the comparison of military forces cannot be reduced to a comparison of the amounts of weapons, even if their qualitative characteristics are included; there is no need for *all* the levels of military forces to be equal: the strategic parity and the strategy of NATO ensure deterrence. Consequently there is no need to increase NATO's military potential. Let us consider the arguments in these two approaches.

2   *Mechanism of the balance*   (a) The differences in views begin with the assessment of the *functions* of the particular levels of the military structure of the opposing camps. At one extreme are those who regard conventional forces as merely the mechanism for unleashing nuclear escalation. In this approach, tactical nuclear forces form an escalatory link between the conventional and the strategic nuclear forces.

Consequently, strategic parity is considered sufficient to deter against any initiation of war: it ensures the 'parity of deterrence'. A corollary is that the correlation of conventional forces has no significance, since if a war breaks out in Europe, it would very soon become nuclear. A parity of nuclear deterrence renders superfluous any regional equilibrium of both conventional and tactical nuclear forces and, indeed, also the equilibrium of military forces of the superpowers other than their strategic nuclear forces.

At the other extreme are those who assert that precisely if there exists a strategic parity, only forces which can participate *in combat* should be included in the comparison. In one variant, tactical nuclear forces should also be taken into account with regard to their probable direct engagement on the battlefield. In another variant, however, the use of them can be only to the disadvantage of NATO and the comparison of forces should be confined to the conventional forces of the opposing alliances. Since the latter is clearly to the advantage of the WTO, the danger of a conventional aggression is said to have become very great.

(b) As a corollary of this controversy one may consider the differences in assessments of the strategy — and particularly the *mechanism of escalation* — from one level to another. At the one extreme are those who assert that, according to NATO's doctrine of flexible response, if WTO makes a conventional attack, a rapid nuclear excalation will be highly probable although not automatic. Flexible response, in the NATO version, is connected with the principle of 'incalculable' or 'uncertain' risk: this does not seem to mean a response strictly corresponding to the aggression (for instance, a conventional response to a conventional attack) but a response which the enemy cannot predict, and which creates an incalculable risk. This may mean, for instance, a semi-automatic nuclear counter-attack and retaliation, even in response to a conventional action. The conclusion is that NATO possesses all the means necessary to deter and to wage a war, if deterrence fails. In this sense, the forces of both camps are equal.

At the other extreme are those who assert that NATO *cannot use this strategy at all*. If WTO begins an offensive by conventional means and uses nuclear forces at all levels only as a *counter-deterrent* to a nuclear escalation, NATO will not be able to effect such an escalation. The method of flexible response can be used only when the user is superior in nuclear weapons, starting from the tactical level, — but NATO no longer possesses such a superiority.

(c) These general differences in assessing the contribution of the particular levels of the multi-level correlation of military forces should be considered in conjunction with the differences in the particular scenarios of a hypothetical war.

This was discussed above, but a further problem may here be mentioned. Western scenarios generally are based on the assumption that the Soviet Union strikes first, using either nuclear weapons at various levels or conventional mass armies, or both. Therefore many Western military writers also tend to compare the effectiveness of attack against that of defence. Here the disparity of views is also significant. At the one extreme are those military analysts who, roughly speaking, consider that defence requires smaller forces than attack: this is the orthodox principle of military art. On the other are those who assert that under the conditions of modern war — particularly in Europe where there is a relatively small depth of territory to defend and where the attacking enemy may very rapidly concentrate forces in one or a few directions to make a breakthrough — it is the defensive forces which must be superior in numbers, in mobility and several other indicators, if they are to hold the line.

Adverse impact on arms control

Two preconditions are necessary for any arms control measure, but especially for one concerning arms reduction:
(1)   a will among all the parties concerned to reduce military force and to cooperate in this measure;
(2)   similar assessments of the correlation of forces at the time of the establishment of an arms control measure and similar assessments of subsequent changes in that correlation. This is quite natural, since while the reductions of tension and of costs are usually among the political and economic aims of all the parties concerned, the preservation of the hitherto existing balance of power under which no war between the two opposing camps has occurred, and even a strengthening of it, has been regarded as the security aim. However, if the military forces are to be reduced, the method of measuring the reduction and comparing the two sides in the equation of military forces, and of measuring the reduction and the status of the forces after the reduction, become crucial.

In all kinds of negotiations different approaches were taken to these matters, and as a result, little agreement was reached. The situation was particularly difficult in the field of nuclear armaments, where there was a multitude of indicators and any accord depended on the strategies adopted and the scenarios to which the measurement of nuclear forces had to be related.

It might seem that the negotiations between the two opposing alliances in Europe on arms control in the conventional field would be facilitated by the simpler methods used to measure conventional armament and forces, and the changes in these. However, it was constant disagreement concerning the assessment of the correlation of the conventional forces since the beginning of the negotiations, in 1973, and the assessment of the changes expected if reductions were agreed led to the failure of the negotiations.

The West assessed the correlation of conventional forces as being unfavourable to NATO and aimed at achieving a *balanced mutual reduction* in the sense that, after such a reduction, the conventional forces in the two alliances would be roughly equal. (Hence the negotiations were said to concern 'Mutual Balanced Force Reductions' — MBFR.).

The Soviet Union discussed the correlation of conventional forces with regard to the influence hitherto exerted by it on the course of European affairs rather than with regard to an exact measurement of the forces themselves. Since the hitherto existing balance of conventional forces favoured the preservation of peace, it was considered that this should be taken as evidence of a kind of equilibrium. They called the subject of the negotiations the Mutual Reduction of Forces and Armaments and Associated Measures in Central Europe — MURFAAMCE. Any reduction should be symmetrical — it might consist, for instance, of up to 15 per cent of all the forces on each side. In particular, while the West proposed to make the most substantial reductions in land forces — in which, it was considered, the WTO had advantage — the Soviet Union insisted that the West should make proportional reductions in all kinds of conventional forces. The two different approaches to the negotiations were also reflected in other disagreements of this kind.

However, the main obstacles to any agreement arose from the divergent assessments (1) of the *existing forces,* in which the kinds of armament and units compared, the quality of weapons and the training of armed forces, their combat readiness and other criteria played far greater roles than the numbers of troops, (2) of the *strategies* adopted and the *perception* of them by the adversaries — and of their contents and the possibilities of implementing them.

Comments

The Soviet approach to measuring the correlation of the military forces of a state (or coalition of states) assumes that any assessment must include the characteristics of the socio-economic system and the policy of the state, together with its military policy. The need to go beyond the comparison of strictly military forces to include political and strategic parameters is also increasingly stressed in various Western approaches.

However, in the two approaches which we have compared, the methodology of such a comprehensive measurement has not been worked out — indeed it has not yet gone beyond the formulation of a few general principles. Soviet military and civilian students of military force and armaments are extremely reluctant to propose any methods of assessing the correlation of military forces. In unclassified publications, Soviet writers discuss a few principles to be applied in military operations with the aim or ensuring an advantageous change in the correlation of forces, but they pay much less attention to the measurement of such a change. However, Western writers who have produced much on this subject, while maintaining that the quantitative/qualitative statical characteristics of weapons and forces are of limited value in making a global assessment of a military force, often consider such a characteristic when discussing specific concepts of measurement.[34]

In seeking a methodology for the comparison of military forces, one may draw a few general conclusions from this analysis and criticism.

(1) No assessment of the correlation of military forces, even for peacetime, can be made without taking into account the military art expected to be applied — the strategy, operational art and tactics. The factual effectiveness of military force depends on several initial strategic decisions, such as the choice of a method of carrying out military operations, including that of the first targets to hit, the military objectives to pursue and the timing of the first operations. These choices may have a greater effect on the course and outcome of operations than the theoretical efficiency and the peacetime calculations.

(2) Apart from the impact of strategy, those indicators must be valued most which change least. It may be asked whether for these reasons such intangible values as endurance, training, command, control and communication systems, the logistical system and others which depend on the character of the socio-economic system and the level of cultural (including economic) development should not have more weight in the calculation of the correlation of military forces than they had in the previous analyses.

This is part of a broader problem. The military correlation itself, the state of parity or inequality, stability or instability connected with such an assessment, cannot be measured only in terms of military forces. It must be considered in close relation to the sociopolitical system and the peculiarities of the decision-making process — i.e., to the characteristics of the system of making executing decisions concerning war and the strategy of war.

(3) The introduction of the assessment of the political and military doctrines and strategies into the assessment of the correlation of military forces renders the methodology of a military assessment even more difficult. For a given protagonist, the divergent political characteristics of his own and his adversary's activities greatly complicate any *common* (or at least *similar*) global assessment of military forces and therefore also the prediction of the course and outcome of a hypothetical war.

The difficulties may be somewhat reduced by assuming that no war should occur or be expected since it *must* be prevented. The existing correlation of military forces may be examined merely with regard to the question of *whether it ensures the mutual destruction of the belligerents independently of the scenario of a hypothetical war.* With such an assumption the assessment may be made in magnitude of order rather than of numbers, which is a much easier procedure than any comparison of armaments and forces.

Notes

1   Arbatov, 1980:11, p. 34. Cf. The interview with General N. Petrov, in *Pravda*, 22 June 1983. Cf.*Otkuda iskhodit ugroza miru*, 1982.

2   Marshal Ustinov's answers to the questions of a TASS correspondent, *APN-Pravda*, 31 July 1983.

3   Arbatov, 1980, pp. 34–5.

4   Interview with Petrov (Note 1).

5   Answers of USSR Defence Minister, Marshal of the Soviet Union, Dmitri Ustinov, to the questions of TASS correspondent, in *APN-Pravda*, 17 December 1982.

6   In the view of the Soviet leaders, the American missiles deployed since the end of 1983 upset this balance.

7   Anureyev, 1967 (Note 42 in Chapter 10).

8   L. Semeyko, comment to Anureyev, in *Voennaya Mysl'*, 1968:8, in *Foreign Policy Digest* Nr. 0019/70, 30 March 1970.

9   Active targets constitute primarily those nuclear means and the most important arrangements which ensure an effective use of nuclear weapons. Passive targets include the military-economic and administrative-political centres, and also other targets which are not directly involved in the use of nuclear weapons (Anureyev, 1967).

10   Semeyko observes that correlation of forces should include the optimal variants of destruction of merely the enemy nuclear means, and not include all important targets 'in general', which do not directly use nuclear weapons (referred to by Anureyev as 'passive targets'). The measurement and calculation of the influence of the destruction of passive targets on the use of nuclear weapons available at the start of a war can hardly be accomplished with the aid of mathematical methods (1968).

11   For instance, the balance of 'distance and capability' decisively favours the Soviet Union in the Persian Gulf because the con-

tiguity of the Soviet Union and its large medium-range air lift capability gives it a clear advantage over the remote United States (Martin, 1981, p. 12).

12 Cf. Fritz Ermath, 'Contrasts in American and Soviet Strategic Thought' in *Soviet Military Thinking*, 1981, pp. 59—61.

13 Cf. *Das Kontrollierte Chaos: Die Krise der Abrüstung*, Suhrkamp Vg., Frankfurt, 1980, Ch. II.2.

14 For instance, *Pershing* missiles with their range 100-1000 km may be used for several missions. Cf. Lutz, 1981, p. 65.

15 Ibid., Part II.

16 Cf. Arbatov, 1980, p. 37 ('medium range nuclear means'); Bykov, 1981. (He writes that during many years 'a parity has been established in the medium-range means... about 1000 carriers on each side' — p. 27). Perhaps to avoid at least some of the difficulties connected with classifying a weapons system as either 'strategic' or 'tactical', in both American and Soviet political and military publications the term 'intermediate-range nuclear weapons' or carriers is now being used. From the viewpoint of the Western alliance, this had the additional advantage of avoiding the expressions 'theatre nuclear forces' (or weapons) which is associated with the concept of fighting a nuclear war limited to Europe — a highly unpopular idea in European public opinion, and producing an anti-NATO effect in public debate on these weapons.

17 Cf. West German White Paper on Security, 1983. Here a difference was even pointed out between 'longer-range intermediate nuclear systems', 'shorter-range intermediate nuclear systems' and 'short-range nuclear systems'.

18 Douglas, Hoeber, pp. 58 ff.

19 Cf. Lutz, 1981, pp. 61—2.

20 Cf. Anthony H. Cordesman, Preface to *Imbalance of Power*, 1978, p. xxix.

21 Robert Kennedy, 'Das Messen des strategischen Gleichgewichts', in *Die USA und die strategische Gleichgewicht*, 1980, p. 31.

22 These problems were discussed, among others, by Thomas A. Brown, in 'Number Mysticism, Rationality, and the Strategic Balance', *Orbis*, Fall 1977, pp. 479—97; cf. id. 'U.S. and Soviet Strategic Force Levels: Problems of Assessment and Measurement', *The Annals of the American Political Science Association, 1981 (457)*, pp. 18—27.

23 Ibid. The equivalent megatons, linear kill potential, strategic nuclear delivery vehicles equivalent weapons and lethality may also be included.

24 Cotter, Hansen, McConnell, 1983, p. 2.

25 For instance, the Soviet T-62 tanks are regarded by Western experts as superior to the US M-60 in the following indicators: size (smaller), width (less), weight (lighter). In other respects

(sights, turning spans) they are inferior.

Paul H. Nitze describes three approaches, in which some quantitative indices such as the number of strategic nuclear delivery vehicles, the number of warheads, global megatonnage, equivalent megatonnage, equivalent weapons, or throw weight can be used for measuring the balance: 'These approaches focus on: (1) the pertinent strategic military resources possessed by each side before, or in the absence of, a strike by the other side; (2) the pertinent resources remaining to the United States after an initial strike by the Soviet Union primarily directed at reducing the American retaliatory potential; and (3) the pertinent resources remaining to each side after an exchange in which the Soviet Union first attacks American forces and the United States responds by reducing the greatest useful extent Soviet strategic forces not used in the initial attack' ('The Global Military Balance', in *The Soviet Threat: Myths and Realities,* Praeger, New York 1970, p. 7). Characteristic of this reasoning is the absence of any qualitative parameters and influencing factors.

26 Cf. Carola Bielfeldt, Gert Krell, Stephan Tiedtke, 'Aufrüstung durch Rüstungsvergleiche. Europäische Sicherheit: ein Rechenstück?', in Carola Bielfeldt u.a., *Frieden in Europa? Zur Koexistenz von Rustüng und Entspannung,* Reinbek 1973, pp. 10 ff.; Dieter S. Lutz, 'Besitzt die Sowjetunion in der konventionellen Rüstung eine militärische Uberlegenheit?', *IFSH — Forschunsberichte,* 9/1979, Lutz, 1981, pp. 59 ff. Cf. Andreas von Bülov, 'Problematik des Kräftevergleiche zwischen NATO und Warschauer Pakts', *Soldat und Technik,* 1979:6, p. 289; Cf. Stratmann, 1981, pp. 45 ff.

28 Cf. Gert Krell, 'Abschreckung und Kriegführung in der Nuklearstrategie der USA und der Sowjetunion', in *Kernwaffen und Rüstungskontrolle,* 1984, pp. 214—15 ('Die Strategie der offensiven Verteidigung in Europa').

29 Lutz, 1981, p. 61.

30 Cf. Lutz, 1981; Krell, 1984.

31 Cf. Stratmann, 1981 V: A.II.

32 Lutz, 1981, Ch. 2.4.: 'Plädoyer für Komplexitätsreduzierung durch Szenarioanalysen' (pp. 68—72).

33 Dieter Lutz, 'How much is enough? Wieviel an Vernichtung (skapazität) ist genug? Ein Worst-Case-Szenario gegen West Europa', *IFSH-Diskussionsbeiträge,* 17/1980, p. 9. Cf. Lutz, 1981, 1.1 (pp. 17—19) and 2.1 (pp. 60—1). Stratmann, 1976, pp. 31—2.

34 The analyses prepared by a West German researcher provide examples of this procedure: he makes an excellent analysis of several shortcomings of the quantitative/qualitative assessment of weapons and forces and of the data on which it is based. However,

afterwards he gives an extremely detailed assessment of the same kind and bases his own proposals on it (Lutz, 1981). Cf. Wolf Graf von Baudissin, 'Arms Reduction in Europe' in Baudissin, Dieter S. Lutz, 'Kooperative Rüstungssteuerung in Theorie und Wirklichkeit', *IFSH - Forschunsberichte* 6/1978. Cf. Lutz, 1981.

13 Comments

Correlation of world forces

(1) As a paradigmatic concept, the correlation of world forces stand and falls together with the Marxist-Leninist philosophy, sociology and theory of international relations. Moreover, it must be taken together with the assessment of the tendencies in the development of intra-societal and international relations which Marxism-Leninism regards as stable. These tendencies may be summarised in three propositions:

The world revolutionary process is under way; the struggle for social and national emancipation is gaining momentum; and the general crisis of capitalism is worsening.

(2) The world is filled with social and national transformations which can be called just and progressive — although these terms are sometimes out of favour with political scientists.

A definite tendency towards social and national liberation is connected with the growth of social and national awareness among peoples and the working masses. This awareness has many roots, including particularly the general development of material and spiritual culture. One can therefore speak of a general correlation between the forces of progress on the one hand and the forces of reaction on the other, although these are hardly possible to measure and assess. One may also suggest another expression, and speak of a correlation of power between the forces that fight for national and social liberation and, by induction, those that try to hinder it.

However, the relationship of these forces to what is termed in the

339

Marxist-Leninist theory the two antagonistic camps remains to be tested and demonstrated. It also remains to be demonstrated that the world correlation decisively influences the innumerable fights for national and social liberation which are waged in so many countries and between social forces of many kinds.

(3) The concept of the correlation of world forces aims at justifying the status of the Soviet Union as one of the two leading world powers which, with its military posture, can back a widening range of interests. It also justifies Soviet policy in general and its policy in the particular regions; it supports the policy of a permanent military build-up; it confirms the Soviet leadership of the socialist camp; and it tries to buttress the bargaining position of the Soviet Union in negotiations concerning arms control and the global and regional balances of power.

(4) Thus the different aspects and components of this correlation are emphasised in its application to various issues.

With regard to the superpower status, the most general concept of world-wide camps is used and the importance of its intangible values is stressed. In the bilateral negotiations with the United States on the global balance of power and arms control, the correlation of military power between the superpowers is the principal subject. When the Soviet military presence in Eastern and Central Europe and the regional balance of power are discussed, the joint military power of the Warsaw Treaty constitutes one side in the correlation.

And finally, as regards the leading role of the Soviet Union in the socialist bloc, the interstate relation of forces in the camp which primarily includes the economic and military potentials form the terminological and conceptual points of reference.

(5) The two camps constituting the opposite sides of the world correlation, are very heterogeneous and this makes comparison difficult. Soviet politicians and analysts are quick to point out the heterogeneity of the so-called imperialist (or bourgeois) camp, but they do not admit the same concerning the socialist camp. Although they distinguish between the position and policy of the so-called imperialist bourgeoisie in the highly developed Western states and those of the 'national bourgeoisie' in the newly independent countries of Asia and Africa, and though they point out that the latter are torn by serious conflicts, they do not hesitate to describe them as components of a single 'world bourgeoisie'. Likewise, the differences in national interests between the socialist states are not allowed to spoil the picture of them as brotherly nations, nor are the differences in tactics and strategic aims between the Soviet Union and the West European Communist parties allowed to throw doubt on the overall solidarity of the socialist international army.

The choice of allies does not lessen the heterogeneity of the two camps. The Western powers see some socialist states, including

Yugoslavia and Romania, as their allies and expect the activities of China in the socialist system to be disruptive. On the other hand, the Soviet Union and its bloc support various anti-Communist regimes (in Libya, Syria, etc.) as political allies which may strengthen the strategic position of the socialist system in relation to its adversary.

(6) The concept of the correlation of world forces is based on the principal ideological assumptions, on the view of the general development of world events and on an intuitive calculation of intangible values. It concerns the global potentialities of the opposing camps, expressed in general terms rather than the measurable and measured forces.

The assessment is also elusive since the supposed value of any correlation of social forces is a very dynamic one. It is constantly reproduced and thus it must be re-assessed. It indicates the direction of the development rather than the state of the correlation at the moment. It deals with the *possibilities* which may be exploited by rational action rather than with facts based on a calculation. It is more a correlation of *tendencies* than of *magnitudes.*

Thus the assessment of the correlation depends on the importance attached to its particular components and on the qualitative assessment of them — as well as of the direction of their development, all of which are differently evaluated in different ideologies and in different perspectives. The ways in which the alignment of forces in a certain country affects the outcome of class struggle are viewed differently by the opposing social forces; the same is true of the correlation of inter-state and inter-coalition forces in a certain region. For instance, the ways in which a supposed balance of military forces in Europe affects the future of the continent and the outcome of particular conflicts are differently perceived in the two rival camps — *inter alia,* because of the differences in expectations as regards the evolutions of the non-military elements in the European alignment of forces. Likewise, the emergence of a new independent country in the Third World and its internal developments may arouse different expectations in the two camps.

Thus what the Marxist-Leninists in the USSR are expressing are qualitative judgements about the correlation of world forces based on the assumption that socialism is superior in all respects to capitalism. The correlation is said to be 'favourable', the military power of the socialist states is in several respects 'superior' — these or similar expressions do not indicate the *degree* of the superiority and consequently of the influence exerted on world events. How favourable? How much superior? This cannot be established or tested or proved.

What makes the assessment of the correlation of forces — as the Marxist-Leninists see it — a calculation based on intuition rather than a measurable magnitude (even roughly approximated) is that most of its components are hardly quantifiable.

Even if one considers only the military component, every method of measuring it falls seriously short of exactitude, and for several reasons. Apart from the main difficulty — the asymmetries between the force structures — and from the necessity to equate dissimilar units, there is always a lack of accurate estimation of what both sides really have at their disposal, what its value is, the state of development and design, which is not without significance when we are to assess such a relative magnitude.

As regards the non-military components, the role of which is said to be constantly increasing, the comparison becomes even more elusive. 'Forces' included in the assessment represent the aggregate national power — made up of political, economic, techno-scientific, and strictly military and spiritual components which, according to Soviet teaching, are rooted in, and based on, *the character and quality of the socio-economic and political system.* These, to a much greater degree than the military components, are intangible values. As regards the coalition of states (or 'system' — socialist or capitalist) as a whole, the sum of these powers is even less measurable.

To complete the picture, as a result of the dynamic character of the correlation, it is even more difficult to assess its value, not only at a given moment but during a period of time which would be needed for the attainment of some far-reaching political and military aims. However, just the assessment during a longer period is the most important one since it indicates the *tendency* of the regional, and in the broad framework, the world's development.

(7)   The concept of the correlation of world forces may serve only as a very general theoretical, and perhaps also methodological, guideline to the assessment of the tendency in the development of the world situation. The concept may also be of some use in the analysis of the state power of individual countries, and of the sides in particular conflicts. It cannot become a fully effective scientific tool, since it has too many lacunae. Some of these are indicated below.

(a)   It seems that, for the benefit of the analysis of the value and the effectiveness of the *power of an individual state,* the assessment of the contemporary conditions of the correlation of *world forces* should be combined with those of the *regional* correlation, taking into account the place of the state in an *alliance* (or its relation to alliances), and the correlation of forces between the state in question and its potential *local adversaries.* The conditions of the contemporary international *political situation* are not without significance either. Soviet scholars, however, have not presented more detailed ideas on regional and local balances of power, on the alignment of forces within alliances (especially the socialist alliance), or on the interaction of those 'levels' of power alignment, or correlation of forces, in certain typical situations.

(b)   The Soviet concept has not dealt in any detail either with the mechanism of the impact of the correlation of world forces, or all other 'levels' of the alignment of correlation of forces, on *individual conflicts,* whether armed or unarmed, their outbreak, course and outcome. Soviet scholars usually confine the presentation to a general statement that the world correlation exercises a determining influence on all political developments.

(c)   One more kind of correlation should be included in the discussion of the impact of the world 'level' of correlation of forces: *the intrasocietal correlation of forces.* In contrast with the correlations of world forces, in which military power is the main element on both sides, this one basically consists of asymmetric elements. A specific alignment may only be temporary, emerging and existing during a crisis. Popular masses may here play a determining role, paralysing the action of the armed forces (Iran, 1978–9). The internal forces do not operate in a vacuum; they, too, are affected by the world and regional correlations of forces which may act on behalf of, or against, an intervention from outside; however, it is very often difficult to forecast *how* the internal development will be affected by external factors.

(8)   In sum, the interaction of numerous factors is a principal reason why it is extremely difficult to tell in advance how the correlation of world forces will affect a concrete conflict. The correlation may deter both of the main antagonists from intervening, or only one of them, while the other can exploit a regional, or local, or internal correlation, favourable to him, in order to give direct or indirect aid to one of the antagonists. These problems, however, are not conceptualised in the Marxist-Leninist theory.

Apparently, no common *generalisations* can be made about the *military component* on the particular levels of the correlation of forces. It certainly constitutes a very essential component of the world correlation; it deters the main antagonists from a major war and from intervention in local conflicts, both interstate and internal. These always represent a struggle for power: power including military force plays a determining role in the resolution of national and social conflicts. Thus all such developments must depend on the concrete regional and local alignment of power.

However, the lower the level of conflict, the more diversified is the picture: the role of the military component of power moves between two extremes — at times it determines the outcome by itself, at other times it is overshadowed by the non-military forms of the sociopolitical struggle.

Although the concept of the correlation of forces may serve as one of the guidelines to the analysis of conflicts and developments on all levels of internal and international relations, any analysis must take into account all the concrete circumstances. Generalisations and predictions made on the basis of an assumed 'favourable correlation of forces' are hardly to be applied to individual conflicts. They may be applied only to the most general course of world development — and sometimes hardly even that.

Military correlation

(1) It seems that no objective measurement and proof of the actual correlation of military forces and, in particular, of its main component, strategic nuclear forces, can be provided. Among several reasons for this, two are worth mentioning:

(a) Because of the asymmetry of forces and weapons no comparison of numbers and qualities can be exact.

(b) Because the forces and weapons do not provide exact indices of combat power, they must be assessed in the framework of military doctrines, and in terms of the particular strategies and combat readiness, and the abilities of both the political and military leaderships to use them.

(2) Even if a fully objective evaluation of the state of the correlation of military forces were possible, it would not be of decisive political value since the main impact on the relations between states is exerted by the *perception* of the correlation by the adversaries, the allies and the neutrals.

Moreover, the self-perception by a state of its own power allows for an active foreign policy. The Soviet leaders regard the military force of the USSR as superior to that of any potential adversary and particularly in intangible values of a sociopolitical and moral nature. They also assert that there exists a strategic parity between the superpowers and opposing blocs and use America's admission of this not only in negotiations but generally in their politics and propaganda.

(3) Soviet politicians and writers accuse their Western counterparts of a preoccupation with the military component of the correlation of world forces. This preoccupation is said to underlie Western countries' efforts to regain their previous military superiority. The same accusations are made by Western politicians and writers in relation to Soviet policy. However, both sides are inconsistent when they accuse the adversary of shifting the emphasis in its assessment of the correlation of world forces away from the military component and trying to achieve a global superiority in the political, economic and ideological components.

(4) The Soviet side seems to have the following reasons for emphasising the importance of the correlation of military forces:

(a) Such an emphasis justifies their great military effort, which is said to aim at countering the adversaries' military build-up.

(b)   It justifies the Soviet position in negotiations on arms control and helps to prevent or at least slow down the development and acquisition of new weapons by the adversaries — i.e., the United States and its NATO allies.

(c)   It justifies the USSR's claim to lead the combined forces of the socialist camp.

(d)   It justifies the open and covert uses of Soviet military force in interventions in other countries; these are explained by, *inter alia,* the need to preserve the present correlation of world forces.

(e)   The emphasis on the correlation also plays a large propagandist role; it emphasises the Soviet military strength, its parity with the United States, its importance for maintaining the status of a world power entitled to co-decide on all world affairs and events, and particularly international conflicts. Moreover, it is said to testify to the superiority of the socialist socio-economic and political system, with its great record of achievements in a short time.

(f)   It enables the Soviets to criticise any American military build-up as an aggressive action designed to destroy the military parity and stability — i.e., the stability of security.

(g)   Finally, the actual professional comparison of military forces, which is much more realistic than in non-classified writings, plays a very important role in the elaboration of military doctrine — especially of strategy — and in preparations of the military posture for the use of armed forces in both peacetime and war.

Bibliography

Books

Adomeit, Hannes, *Soviet Risk-Taking and Crisis Behaviour: From Confrontation to Coexistence?*, Adelphi Papers, No. 101, IISS, London, 1973.

Adomeit, Hannes, *Die Sowjetmacht in internationalen Krisen und Konflikten*, Nomos, Baden-Baden, 1983.

Afheldt, Horst, *Verteidigung und Frieden*, Carl Hanser Vg., Munich and Wien, 1976.

Akopov, G.M.I.A., Sukhar'hov, *Imperialisticheskie bloki: realnost' i perspektivy*, Moscow, 1969.

Apalin, G., Mityayev, U., *Militarism in Peking's Policies*, Progress Publishers, Moscow, 1980.

Arbatov, Georgi, *The War of Ideas in Contemporary International Relations: The Imperialist Doctrine, Methods and Organisation of Foreign Political Propaganda*, Progress Publishers, Moscow, 1973.

Arbatov, Georgi, *Cold War or Detente, The Soviet Viewpoint*, Zed Books, London, 1983.

Arms Control and Defense Postures in the 1980s, Richard Burt, (ed.), Westview Press, Boulder, Colorado, 1981.

Arms Control and Military Force, C. Bertram, (ed.), Gower, Farnborough, 1980.

Baranovsky, V.G., *Politicheskaya Integratsiya v Zapadnoi Evrope*, Nauka, Moscow, 1983.

Barraclough, Geoffrey, *An Introduction to Contemporary History*,

Penguin, Baltimore, Maryland, 1968.

The Basics of Marxist-Leninist Theory, Progress Publishers, Moscow, 1982.

Bialer, Severyn, *Stalin's Successors: Leadership, Stability, and Change in the Soviet Union,* Cambridge University Press, Cambridge and London, 1980.

Bikkenin, N.B., *Sotsialisticheskaya ideologiya,* Politizdat, Moscow, 1978.

Bogdanov, R.G., *SShA: Voennaya Mashina i Politika,* Izd. 'Nauka', Moscow, 1983.

Brutents, K., *A Historical View of Neocolonialism,* Novosti Press Agency Publishing House, Moscow, 1972.

Brutents, K., *Osvobodivshiesya strany v 70-e gody,* Politizdat, Moscow, 1979.

Bull, Hedley, *The Anarchical Society: A Study of Order in World Politics,* Macmillan, London and Basingstoke, 1977.

Bunkina, M.K., *Tsentry mirovogo imperializma: itogi razvitiya i rastanovka sil,* Mysl, Moscow, 1970.

Bykov, O., V. Razmerov, D. Tomashevsky, *The Priorities of Soviet Foreign Policy Today,* Progress Publishers, Moscow, 1981.

Challenges to America: US Foreign Policy in the 1980s, C.W. Kegley, Jr, P.C. McGowan, (eds), Sage, New York, 1979.

Change in the International System, Ole R. Holsti, Randolph M. Siverson, Alexander L. George, (eds), Westview Press, Boulder, Colorado, 1980.

Civil-Military Relations in Communist Systems, Dale R. Herspring, Ivan Volgyes, (eds), Westview, Boulder, Colorado, 1978.

Cline, Ray S., *World Power Assessment 1977,* Westview Press, Boulder, Colorado, 1977.

Collins, John M., *US — Soviet Military Balance: Concepts and Capabilities 1960—1980,* McGraw Hill, 1980.

Cotter, Donald R., James H. Hansen, Kirk McConnell, *The Nuclear 'Balance' in Europe: Status, Trends, Implications,* USSI Report 83—1, United States.

Dahrendorf, Ralph, *Essays in the Theory of Society,* Stanford University Press, Stanford, 1968.

Defense Policy Formation: Towards Comparative Analysis, James H. Roherty, (ed.), Carolina Academic Press, Durham, North Carolina, 1980.

Denisov, V.V., *Sotsiologiya nasiliya,* Izd. Politcheskoi Literatury, Moscow, 1975.

Diplomatiya razvivayushchikhsya stran, Izd. 'Mezhdunarodnye Otnosheniya', Moscow, 1976.

Doktrina 'natsionalnoi bezopasnosti' v globalnoi strategii SShA, Izd. 'Mezhdunarodnye Otnosheniya', Moscow, 1980.

Dolgopolov, E.I., *Natsionalno-osvoboditelnye voiny na sovremennom Etape,* Voenizdat, Moscow, 1977.

Dougherty, James E., R.L. Pfaltzgraff, Jr., *Contending Theories of International Relations,* Lippincott, Philadelphia, New York and Toronto, 1971.

Douglass, Joseph D., Amoretta M. Hoeber, *Soviet Strategy for Nuclear War,* Hoover International Studies, Stanford 1979.

Dziak, John J., *Soviet Perceptions of Military Doctrine and Military Power: The Interaction of Theory and Practice,* Crane, Russak and Co, New York, 1981.

Ellis, John, *Armies in Revolution,* Oxford University Press, New York, 1974.

Erickson, John, *Soviet Military Power,* The Royal United Service Institute, London, 1971.

Faramazyan, R.A., *SShA: Militarizm i Ekonomika,* Izd. 'Mysl', Moscow, 1970.

Filosofiya i voennaya istoriya, Izd. 'Nauka', Moscow, 1979.

Filosofskoe nasledie V.I. Lenina i problemy sovremennoi voiny, A.S. Milovidov, V.G. Kozlov, (eds), Voenizdat, Moscow, 1972.

Finer, S.E. *The Man on the Horseback: The Role of the Military in Politics,* Penguin, Harmondsworth, 1976.

Force in Modern Societies: Its Place in International Politics, Adelphi Papers No. 102, IISS, London, 1973.

Force in Modern Societies: The Military Profession, Adelphi Papers No. 103, IISS, London, 1973

Frankel, Joseph, *International Politics: Conflict and Harmony,* Penguin, Harmondsworth, 1969, 1973.

Freiheit ohne Krieg?, Dümmler, (ed), Clausewitz-Gesellschaft, Bonn, 1980.

The Fundamentals of Marxist-Leninist Philosophy, Progress Publishers, Moscow, 1982.

Fundamentals of Political Science, Textbook for primary political education, Progress Publishers, Moscow, 1979.

The Future of Soviet Military Power, Lawrence L. Whetton (ed.), Macdonald and Jane's, London, 1976.

George, Alexander, Richard Smoke, *Deterrence in American Foreign Policy: Theory and Practice,* Columbia University Press, New York, 1974.

Global Problems of Our Age, N.N. Inozemtsev, (ed.), Progress Publishers, Moscow, 1984.

Golub, P., *The Bolsheviks and the Armed Forces in Three Revolutions,* Progress Publishers, Moscow, 1979.

Gooch, John, *Armies in Europe,* Routledge and Kegan Paul, London, 1980.

Gorbachev, Mikhail, *Political Report of the CPSU Central Committee to the 27th Congress of the Communist Party of the Soviet Union,* Novosti Press Agency, Moscow, 1986.

Gorshkov, S.G., *Morskaya moshch gosudarstv,* Voenizdat, Moscow, 1976.

Gray, Colin S., *The Soviet-American Arms Race,* Saxon House, Farnborough, 1976.

Grechko, A.A., *Vooruzhennye Sily SSSR,* Voenizdat, Moscow, 1974, 1st ed., 1975, 2nd ed., (changed title: *Vooruzhennye Sily Sovetskogo Gosudarstva).*

Grewe, Wilhelm G., *Spiel der Kräfte in der Weltpolitik. Theorie und Praxis der internationalen Beziehungen,* Ullstein, Frankfurt, Berlin and Vienna, 1981.

Gromyko, A., *Leninskim Kursom Mira,* Izbrannye stat'i i rechi, Politizdat, Moscow, 1984.

Ideino-politicheskaya sushchnost' maoizma, Izd. 'Nauka', Moscow, 1977.

Inozemtsev, N.N., *Contemporary Capitalism: New Developments and Contradictions,* Progress Publishers, Moscow, 1974.

Inozemtsev, N.N., *Leninskii kurs mezhdunarodnoi politiki KPSS,* Izd. 'Mysl', Moscow, 1978.

Insurgency in the Modern World, Bard E. O'Neill, William R. Heaton, Donald J. Alberts, (eds), Westview Press, Boulder, Colorado, 1980.

International Perceptions of the Superpower Military Balance, Donald C. Daniel, (ed.), Praeger, New York, 1978.

Istoricheskii materializm i sotsialnaya filosofiya sovremennoi burzhuazii, Akademiya Nauk SSSR, Institut Filosofii, Izd. Sotsialno-Ekonomicheskoi Literatury, Moscow, 1960.

Ivanova, I.M., *Mirnoe sosushchestvovanie i krizis vneshnepoliticheskoi ideologii imperializma SShA.,* Izd. 'Mezhdunarodnye Otnosheniya', Moscow, 1965.

Jacobsen, C.G., *Soviet Strategy — Soviet Foreign Policy,* R. Maclehose and Co., The University Press, Glasgow, 1974, 2nd ed.

Janowitz, Morris, *Military Confrontation. Essays in the Institutional Analysis of War and Peace,* SAGE London, 1975.

Janowitz, Morris, *Military Institutions and Coercion in the Developing Nations,* The University of Chicago Press, Chicago and London, 1977.

Kahan, Jerome H., *Security in the Nuclear Age. Developing US Strategic Arms Policy,* The Brooking Institution, Washington, 1975.

Kaiser, K., Schwartz, H., *America and Western Europe: Problems and Prospects,* Lexington Books, Lexington, Mass., 1979.

Kapitsa, M.S., *KNR:Dva desyatiletiya — dve politiki,* Izd. Politicheskoi Literatury, Moscow 1969.

Kaplan, Morton A., *System and Process in International Politics,* Wiley, New York, 1957.

Katz, M.M., *The Third World in Soviet Military Thought,* Croom Helm,

London, 1982.

Kernwaffen und Rüstungskontrolle, Hans Günter Brand, (ed.), Westdeutscher Vg., Opladen,1984.

Kiessling, G., *Krieg und Frieden in unserer Zeit*, Militärverlag der DDR, Berlin, 1977.

Khalosha, B.M., *NATO i atom*, Voenizdat, Moscow, 1975.

Khalosha, B.M., *Voenno-Politicheskie Soyuzy Imperializma*, Osnovnye osobennosti i tendentsii razvitiya v 70kh — nachale 80 kh godov, Izd. 'Nauka', Moscow, 1982.

Kharin, Yu. A., *Fundamentals of Dialectics*, Progress Publishers, Moscow, 1981.

Klimov, I., *Armiya i politika*, Voenizdat, Moscow, 1981.

Knorr, Klaus, *On the Uses of Military Power in the Nuclear Age*, Princeton University Press, Princeton, 1966.

Knorr, Klaus, *Military Power and Potential*, Heath, Lexington, Mass., 1970.

Knorr, Klaus, *The Power of Nations*, Basic Books, New York, 1975.

Kokoshin, A.A., *SShA v sisteme mezhdunarodnykh otnoshenii 80kh godov*, Izd. 'Mezhdunarodnye otnosheniya', Moscow, 1984.

Konstantinov, F.V. *et al.*, *Kritika teoreticheskikh kontseptsii Mao Tsze-duna*, Izd. 'Mysl', Moscow, 1970.

Kontinuität und Wandel in den Ost-West Beziehungen, Boris Meissner, Axel Seeberg, (eds), Markus Vg., Cologne, 1984.

Kooperative Rüstungssteuerung — Sicherheitspolitik und Strategische Stabilität, Wolf Graf v. Baudissin, Dieter S. Lutz, (eds), Nomos, Baden-Baden, 1981.

Kortunov, V.V., *Kommunizm i antikommunizm pered litsom sovremennosti*, Izd. Politicheskoi Literatury, Moscow, 1978.

Kosolapov, N.A., *Sotsialnaya psikhologiya i mezhdunarodnye otnosheniya*, Izd. 'Nauka', Moscow, 1983.

Krasin, Yu., *The Contemporary Revolutionary Protsess, Theoretical Essays*, Progress Publishers, Moscow, 1985.

Krell, Gert, Dieter S. Lutz, *Nuklearrüstung im Ost-West-Konflikt — Potentiale, Doktrinen, Rüstungssteuerung*, Nomos, Baden-Baden, 1980.

Kritika sovremennoi burzhuaznoi politekonomii, Akademiya Nauk SSSR, Institut Mirovoi Ekonomiki i Mezhdunarodnykh Otnoshenii, Izd. 'Nauka', Moscow, 1977.

Kubalkova, V., A.A., Cruickshank, *Marxism-Leninism and Theory of International Relations*, Routledge and Kegan Paul, London, Boston and Henley, 1980.

Kubalkova, V., A.A., Cruickshank, *International Inequality*, Croom Helm, London, 1981.

Kurs marksistsko-leninskoi filosofii, E.A. Khomenko, M.I. Yasyukov (eds), Voenizdat, Moscow, 1974, 2nd ed.

Kuz'min, G.M., *Voenno-promyshlennye kontserny*, Voenizdat,

Moscow, 1974.

Kuz'min, V.V., *Kitai v strategii amerikanskogo imperializma,* Izd. 'Mezhdunarodnye Otnosheniya', Moscow, 1978.

Lange, Peer, *Zur politischen Nutzung militärischer Macht,* Der sowjetische Denkansatz, Berichte des Bundesinstituts für östwissenschaftliche und internationale Studien, Cologne, 1978.

Lebedev, N.I., *Novyi etap mezhdunarodnykh otnoshenii,* Izd. 'Mezhdunarodnye Otnosheniya', Moscow, 1976. (English translation: N.I. Lebedev, *A New Stage in International Relations,* Pergamon Press, Oxford, 1978.

Lebedev, Nikolai, *The USSR in World Politics,* Progress Publishers, Moscow, 1982.

Lenin, V.I., *Imperialism, The Highest Stage of Capitalism,* International Publishers, New York, 1939.

Leninism and the World Revolutionary Working-Class Movement, Progress Publishers, Moscow, 1976.

Leninskaya teoriya imperializma i sovremennost', Izd. 'Mysl', Moscow, 1977.

Leninskaya teoriya sotsialisticheskoi revolutsii i sovremennost', Izd. 'Mysl', Moscow, 1980.

Leninskaya vneshnyaya politika i razvitie mezhdunarodnykh otnoshenii, V.V. Alexandrov, (ed.), Izd. 'Mezhdunarodnye otnosheniya', Moscow, 1983.

Lider, Julian, *On the Nature of War,* Saxon House, Farnborough 1977, reprint, 1979.

Lider, Julian, *The Political and Military Laws of War: An Analysis of Marxist-Leninist Concepts,* Saxon House, Farnborough, 1979.

Lider, Julian, *Military Force: An Analysis of Marxist-Leninist Concepts,* Gower, Farnborough, 1981.

Lider, Julian, *Military Theory: Concept, Structure, Problems,* Gower, Aldershot, 1983.

Lider, Julian, *British Military Thought After World War II,* Gower, Aldershot, 1985.

Liska, George, *Quest for Equilibrium, America and the Balance of Power on Land and Sea,* Johns Hopkins University Press, Baltimore and London, 1977.

Little, Richard, *External Involvements in Civil Wars,* Martin Robertson, London, 1975.

Lockwood, Jonathan Samuel, *The Soviet View of US Strategic Doctrine,* Transaction Books, New Brunswick and London, 1983.

Löwe, Bernd P., *Klassenkampf oder sozialer Konflikt? Zu den Gleichgewichts-und Konflikttheorien der bürgerlichen Soziologie,* Verlag Marxistische Blätter, Frankfurt, 1973.

Luttwak, Edward N., *Strategic Power: Military Capabilities and Political Utility,* The Washington Papers 38, Sage, Beverly Hills and

London, 1976.

Luttwak, Edward N., *Strategy and Politics: Collected Essays,* Transaction Books, New Brunswick, New Jersey, 1980.

Luttwak, Edward, *The Grand Strategy of the Soviet Union,* Weidenfeld and Nicolson, London, 1983.

Lutz, Dieter S., *Das militärische Kräfteverhältnis im Bereich der euronuklearen Waffensysteme,* IFSH-Forschungsberichte 12, Frankfurt, 1979.

Lutz, Dieter, S., *Weltkrieg wider Willen?,* Rowohlt, Reinbek b. Hamburg, 1981.

Mamontov, V., *Disarmament — the Command of the Times,* Progress Publishers, Moscow, 1979.

Maoizm: Voennaya teoriya i praktika, Institut Voennoi Istorii Ministerstva Oborony SSSR, Voenizdat, Moscow, 1978.

Marksistsko-leninskaya filosofiya i metodologicheskie problemy voennoi teorii i praktiki, Voenizdat, Moscow, 1982.

Marksistsko-leninskoe uchenie o voine i armii, D.A. Volkogonov, (ed.), Voenizdat, Moscow, 1984.

Marxism-Leninism on War and Army, Progress Publishers, Moscow, 1972.

Marwick, Arthur, *War and Social Change in the Twentieth Century,* Macmillan, London and Basingstoke, 1974.

McNamara, Robert S., *The Essence of Security,* Harper and Row, New York, 1968.

Melnikov, Yu. M., *Vneshnepolitisheskie doktriny SShA,* Moscow, 1970.

Metodologicheskie problemy zashchity mira i sovremennost', Izd. 'Nauka', Moscow, 1979.

Mezhdunarodnye konflikty, V.V. Zhurkin, Y.M. Primakov, (eds), Izd. 'Mezhdunarodnye Otnosheniya', Moscow, 1972.

Mezhdunarodnye konflikty sovremennosti, Akademiya Nauk SSSR, Izd. 'Nauka', Moscow, 1983.

Militarism in Developing Countries, K. Fidel, (ed.), Transaction Books, New Brunswick, New Jersey, 1975.

Militarizm v ideologii i praktike maoizma, Y.L. Ivanov, (ed.), Voenizdat, Moscow, 1976.

The Military and Security in the Third World: Domestic and International Impacts, Sheldon W. Simon, (ed.), Westview Press, Boulder, Colorado, 1978.

Militärische Optionen in Ost und West, Europa-Union-Vg., Bonn, 1979.

Millar, T.B., *The East-West Strategic Balance,* Allen and Unwin, London, 1981.

Mirovoi revolutsionnyi protsess i sovremennost', Akademiya Nauk SSSR, Institut Mezhdunarodnoi Ekonomiki i Mezhdunarodnykh Otnoshenii, Izd. 'Nauka', Moscow, 1980.

Mirovoi sotsializm i problemy razvivayushchikhsya stran, V.D.

Shchetinin, (ed.), Izd. 'Mezhdunarodnye Otnosheniya', Moscow, 1979.

Mirskii, G.I., *Armiya i politika v stranakh Azii i Afriki*, Izd. 'Nauka', Moscow, 1970.

Mirskii, G.I., *Tretii mir': obshchestvo, vlast', armiya*, Izd. 'Nauka', Moscow, 1976.

Mitchell, R. Judson, *Ideology of A Superpower: Contemporary Soviet Doctrine on International Relations*, Hoover Institution Press, Stanford, California, 1982.

Moskvichev, L.N., *Teoriya 'deideologizatsii': illuzii i deistvitelnost'*, Izd. 'Mysl', Moscow, 1971.

Moskvin, L., *The Working Class and Its Allies*, Progress Publishers, Moscow, 1980.

Müller, Wolfgang, Oelschlägel, Rudolf, *Streitkräfte im Klassenkampf unserer Zeit*, Militärverlag der DDR, Berlin, 1972.

Nadel, S.N., *Contemporary Capitalism and the Middle Classes*, Progress Publishers, Moscow, 1982.

National Security in the 1980s: From Weakness to Strength, W. Scott Thompson, (ed.), Institute for Contemporary Studies, San Francisco, 1980.

NATO's Strategic Options. Arms Control and Defence, David S. Yost, (ed.), Pergamon Press, New York, 1981.

Nauchno-Tekhnicheskii Progress i Revolutsiya v Voennom Dele, Voenizdat, Moscow, 1973.

Nauchnyi kommunizm, Izd. Politicheskoi Literatury, Moscow, 1973, 2nd ed.

New Dynamics in National Strategy: The Paradox of Power, Maxwell D. Taylor, (ed.), Crowell, New York, 1975.

Newman, William J., *The Balance of Power in the Interwar Years, 1919—1939*, Random House, New York, 1968.

Nitze, Paul H., James E. Dougherty, Francis X. Kane, *The Fateful Ends and Shades of SALT: Past... Present... And Yet to Come?*, Crane, Russak and Co., New York, 1975.

Ogarkov, N.V., *Istoriya uchit bditelnosti*, Voenizdat, Moscow, 1985.

Osgood, Robert E., *Containment, Soviet Behavior, and Grand Strategy*, Institute of International Studies, University of California, Berkeley, 1981.

Otkuda iskhodit ugroza miru?, Voenizdat, Moscow, 1982.

Padeldorf, Norman J., George A. Lincoln, Lee D. Olvey, *The Dynamics of International Politics*, Macmillan, Collier, New York and London, 1976.

Payne, Keith B., *Nuclear Deterrence in US-Soviet Relations*, Westview Press, Boulder, Colorado, 1982.

Peace and Disarmament, Academic Studies, N.N. Inozemtsev, (ed.), Progress Publishers, Moscow, 1982.

Pekin: kursom provokatsii i ekspansii, A.L. Narochnitskii, G.F. Kim (eds), Politizdat, Moscow, 1979.

Perlmutter, Amos, *The Military and Politics in Modern Times,* Yale University Press, New Haven, 1977.

Petrovskii, V.F., *Doktrina natsionalnoi bezopasnosti v globalnoi strategii SShA,* Izd. 'Mezhdunarodnye Otnosheniya', Moscow, 1980.

Philosophy in the USSR: Problems of Historical Materialism, Progress Publishers, Moscow, 1981.

The Political Implications of Soviet Military Power, L. Whetten, (ed.), Crane, Russak and Co., New York, 1977.

Political-Military Systems: Comparative Perspective, Catherine McArdle Kelleher, (ed.), Sage, Beverly Hills and London, 1974.

Politicheskaya ekonomiya sovremennogo monopoliticheskogo kapitalizma, 2 vols, 'Mysl', Moscow, 1970.

Popov, M.V., *Sushchnost' zakonov vooruzhennoi bor'by,* Voenizdat, Moscow, 1964.

Problems of Contemporary Militarism, Asbjorn Eide, Marek Thee, (eds), Croom Helm, London, 1980.

Problemy sotsialno-ekonomicheskikh formatsii, Istoriko-tipologicheskie issledovaniya, Moscow, 1975.

Problemy voiny i mira, Kritika sovremennykh burzhuaznykh sotsialno-filosofskikh kontseptsii, Izd. 'Mysl', Moscow 1967. *Problems of War and Peace,* Progress Publishers, Moscow, 1972.

Prokop'ev, N.P., *O voine i armii,* Voenizdat, Moscow, 1965.

Prospects of Soviet Power in the 1980s, Part I and II, Adelphi Papers, IISS, London, Summer 1979.

Protsess formirovaniya i osushchestvleniya vneshnei politiki kapitalisticheskikh gosudarstv, V.I. Gantman, (ed.), Izd. 'Nauka', Moscow, 1981.

Rapoport, Anatol, *Conflict in Man-Made Environment,* Penguin, Harmondsworth, 1974.

Rau, Günther, *et.al., Gerechte und ungerechte Kriege,* Deutscher Militärverlag, Berlin, 1970.

Razryadka mezhdunarodnoi napryazhennosti i ideologicheskaya bor'ba, Akademiya Nauk SSSR, Izd. 'Nauka', Moscow, 1981.

Razvitoi sotsializm, Politizdat, Moscow, 1978.

Rüstungskontrolle und Sicherheit in Europa, Erhard Forndran, Paul J. Friedrich, (eds), Europa Union Vg., Bonn, 1979.

Rybkin, Y.I., *Voina i politika v sovremennuyu epokhu,* Voenizdat, Moscow, 1973.

Rybkin, Y.I., *Kritika burzhuaznykh uchenii o prichinakh i roli voin v istorii,* Filosofsko-istoricheskii ocherk, Izd. 'Nauka', Moscow, 1979.

Savkin, V.Y., *Osnovnye printsipy operativnogo iskusstva i taktiki,* Voenizdat, Moscow, 1972.

Schmidt, Helmut, *Strategie des Gleichgewichts,* Seewald Vg., Stuttgart and Degerloch, 1969. (English translation, *The Balance of Power*, William Kimber, London, 1971.

Scott, Harriet Fast, William F. Scott, *The Armed Forces of the USSR*, Westview Press, Boulder, Colorado, 1979.

Seleznev, I.A., *Voina i ideologicheskaya bor'ba*, Voenizdat, Moscow, 1964, 2nd ed., 1974.

Seleznev, M.A., *Marksistsko-leninskaya teoriya sotsialnoi revolutsii*, Izd. 'Mysl', Moscow, 1982.

Serebryannikov, V.V., *Osnovy marksistsko-leninskogo ucheniya o voine i armii*, Voenizdat, Moscow, 1982.

Shakhnazarov, G. Kh., *Agressivnye bloki — ugroza miru*, Voenizdat, Moscow, 1957.

Shakhnazarov, G., *The Destiny of the World: The Socialist Shape of Things to Come*, Progress Publishers, Moscow, 1979.

Shakhnazarov, Georgi, *Futurology Fiasco: A Critical Study of Non-Marxist Concepts of How Society Develops*, Progress Publishers, Moscow, 1982.

Shakhnazarov, Georgi, *The Coming World Order*, Progress Publishers, Moscow, 1984.

Shavrov, I.Y., (ed.), *Lokalnye voiny, istoriya i sovremennost*, Voenizdat. Moscow, 1981.

Sheidina, I.L., *Nevoennye faktory sily vo vneshnei politike SShA*, 'Nauka', Moscow, 1984.

Shelyag, V.V., *Mir i voina*, Izd. 'Mysl', Moscow, 1978.

Simonyan, R.G., *Voennye bloki imperializma*, Voenizdat, Moscow, 1976.

Skirdo, M.P., *Narod, armiya, polkovodets*, Voenizdat, Moscow, 1970.

Sotsializm i natsii, Materialy mezhdunarodnoi konferentsii 'Razvitie i internatsionalnoe sotrudnichestvo sotsialisticheskikh natsii', 'Mysl', Moscow, 1975.

Sotsiologicheskie problemy mezhdunarodnykh otnoshenii, Izd. 'Nauka', Moscow, 1970.

The Soviet Asset: Military Power in the Competition over Europe, Uwe Nerlich, (ed.), Bellinger Publishing Co., Cambridge, Mass., 1983.

The Soviet Impact on World Politics, Kurt London (ed.), Hawthorn Books, New York, 1974.

Soviet Military Power, Department of Defense USA, US Government Printing Office, Washington, 1982.

Soviet Strategy, John Baylis, Gerald Segal, (eds), Croom Helm, London, 1981.

The Soviet Threat: Myths and Realities, Grayson Kirk, Nils H. Wessell, (eds), Praeger, New York, 1978.

The Soviet Union in World Politics, Kurt London, (ed.), Westview Press, Boulder, Colorado, 1980.

Sovremennaya epokha i mirovoi revolutsionnyi protsess, A.M. Kovalev, (ed.), Izd. Moskovskogo Universiteta, Moscow, 1970.

Sovremennye burzhuaznye teorii mezhdunarodnykh otnoshenii, Kriticheskii analiz, Izd. 'Nauka', Moscow, 1976.

Spirkin, Alexander, *Dialectical Materialism,* Progress Publishers, Moscow, 1983.

SShA: Voenno-strategicheskie kontseptsii, R.G. Bogdanov, M.A. Milshtein, L.S. Semeiko, (eds), Akademiya Nauk SSSR, Institut Soedinennykh Shtatov i Kanady, Izd. 'Nauka', Moscow, 1980.

SSSR i strany Afriki, Izd. 'Nauka', Moscow, 1977.

Starushenko G.B., *Sotsialisticheskaya orientatsiya v razvivayush-chikhsya stranakh,* Izd. Politcheskoi Literatury, Moscow, 1977.

Stoessinger, John G., *The Might of Nations,* Random House, New York, 1965.

Strategiya imperializma i bor'ba SSSR za mir i razoruzhenie, Akademiya Nauk SSSR, Izd. 'Nauka', Moscow, 1974.

Strategic Thought in the Nuclear Age, Hossein Amirsadeghi, (gen. ed.)., Laurence Martin, (ed.), Heinemann, London, 1979.

Strategies, Alliances and Military Power: Changing Roles, US Army War College, Sijthoff, Leyden, 1977.

Strategiya imperializma i bor'ba SSSR za mir i razoruzhenie, Izd. 'Nauka', Moscow, 1974.

Stratmann, K. Peter, *NATO-Strategie in der Krise? Militärische Optionen von NATO und Warschauer Pakt in Mitteleuropa,* Nomos, Baden-Baden, 1981.

The Struggle of the USSR for Peace and Security, USSR Academy of Science, Ed. Board, 'Social Sciences Today', Moscow, 1984.

Timorin, A.A. *Armiya i sotsialisticheskoe obshchestvo,* Voenizdat, Moscow, 1972.

Tomashevskii, D.G., *Leninskie idei i sovremennye mezhdunarodnye otnosheniya,* Izd. Politcheskoi Literatury, Moscow, 1971, *Lenin's Ideas and Modern International Relations,* Progress Publishers, Moscow, 1974.

Triska, Jan F., Finley, David D., *Soviet Foreign Policy,* Macmillan, New York, 1968.

Trofimenko, G.A., *Strategiya globalnoi voiny,* Izd. 'Mezhdunarodnye otnosheniya', Moscow, 1968.

Trofimenko, G.A., *SShA: politika, voina, ideologiya,* 'Mysl', Moscow, 1976.

Tyushkevich, S.A., *Filosofiya i voennaya teoriya,* Voenizdat, Moscow, 1975.

Die USA und das strategische Gleichgewicht, Bernard und Graefe, Munich, 1980.

USA, Westeuropa, Japan — imperialistische Zentren der Rivalität, IPW — Forschungshefte, Berlin (East), 1976.

Vakhryshev, Vasily, *Neocolonialism: Methods and Manoeuvres,*

Progress Publishers, Moscow, 1973.

Voennaya sila i mezhdunarodnye otnosheniya, Akademiya Nauk SSSR, Institut Mirovoi Ekonomiki i Mezhdunarodnykh Otnoshenii, Izd. 'Mezhdunarodnye Otnosheniya', Moscow, 1972.

Voina, Istoriya, Ideologiya, V.S. Makhalov, A.V. Veshentsev, (eds.), Izd. Politcheskoi Literatury, Moscow, 1974.

Voina i Armiya, Filosofsko-sotsiologicheskii ocherk, D.A. Volkogonov, A.C. Milovidov, S.A. Tyushkevich, (eds.), Voenizdat, Moscow, 1977.

Vooruzhennaya bor'ba narodov Afriki za svobodu i nezavisimost', Izd. 'Nauka', Moscow, 1974.

Vooruzhennye sily kapitalisticheskikh gosudarstv, Voenizdat, Moscow, 1974.

Waltz, Kenneth N., *Man, the State and War: A Theoretical Analysis*, Columbia University Press, New York and London, 1959.

Waltz, Kenneth N., *The Spread of Nuclear Weapons: More May Be Better*, Adelphi Papers no. 171, IISS, London, 1981.

Warner, Edward L., III, *The Military in Contemporary Soviet Politics. An Institutional Analysis*, Praeger, New York and London, 1977.

Wiatr, Jerzy, J., *Marksistowska teoria rozwoju spolecznego*, KiW, Warsaw, 1973.

Yepishev, A.A., *Ideologicheskaya bor'ba po voennym voprosam*, Voenizdat, Moscow, 1974.

Yermolenko, D.V., *Sotsiologiya i problemy mezhdunarodnykh otnoshenii*, Izd. 'Mezhdunarodnye Otnosheniya', Moscow, 1977.

Yurkovets, I., *The Philosophy of Dialectical Materialism*, Progress Publishers, Moscow, 1984.

Zakharov, M.V., *O nauchnom podkhode k rukovodstvu voiskami*, Voenizdat, Moscow, 1967.

Zamkovoi, V.I., Filatov, M.N., *Filosofiya Agressii*, Izd. 'Kazakhstan', Alma-Ata, 1981.

Zamkovoi, V.I., Semeiko, L.S., *Problemy voiny i mira v sovremennoi ideologicheskoi bor'be*, Izd. 'Znanie', Moscow, 1978.

Zarodov, K., *Leninism and Today's Problems of the Transition to Socialism*, Progress Publishers, Moscow, 1983.

Zhurkin, V.V., *SShA i mezhdunarodno-politicheskie krizisy*, Izd. 'Nauka', Moscow, 1975.

Zimmermann, William, *Soviet Perspectives on International Relations*, Princeton University Press, Princeton, 1979.

Zueba, K.P., *Vopreki dukhu vremeni. Nekotorye problemy teorii i praktiki mezhdunarodnykh otnoshenii v rabotakh Raimonda Arona*, Izd. 'Nauka', Moscow, 1979.

Zum Charakter internationaler Konflikte, Studien aus West-und Osteuropa, Wilfried von Bredow (ed.), Pahl-Rugenstein, Cologne, 1973.

'Zvezdnye Voiny', Illyuzii i Opasnost', Voenizdat, Moscow, 1985.

Articles

Abbreviations of periodicals

IA — International Affairs (Moscow)
KVS — Kommunist Vooruzhennykh Sil
MEMO — Mirovaya Ekonomika i Mezhdunarodnye Otnosheniya
MZh — Mezhdunarodnaya Zhizn'
SMR — Soviet Military Review
SShA — SShA — Ekonomika, Politika, Ideologiya.
VIZh — Voenno-Istoricheskii Zhurnal

Albert, Bernard S., 'The Strategic Competition with the USSR — What is it and how are we doing?', *Comparative Strategy*, 1979:3.
Alexeyev, I., G. Apalin, 'A Soviet Assessment of China', *Coexistence*, vol. 15.
Alford, Jonathan, 'The East-West Balance: A Position of Unstable Equilibrium', The Round Table, *The Commonwealth Journal of International Affairs*, January 1980.
Apel, Hans, 'Grundsätze einer Strategie des Gleichgewichts in unserer Zeit', *Bulletin des Presse- und Informationsamtes der Bundesregierung*, 15 April 1980.
Arbatov, G., 'O sovetsko-amerikanskikh otnosheniyakh', *Kommunist*, 1973:3.
Arbatov, A.G., 'Strategicheskii Paritet i Politika Administratsii Kartera', *SShA*, 1980:11.
'Armiya', in *Sovetskaya Voennaya Entsiklopediya*, vol. 1, 1976.
Aron, Raymond, 'Staaten, Bündnisse und Konflikte', in *Freiheit ohne Krieg?*, 1980.
Askin, G.K., ' "Pluralisticheskaya demokratsiya" ili vsevlastie monopolisticheskoi elity', *SShA*, 1983:4.
Aspaturian, Vernon V., *et al.*, 'The Military-Industrial Complex USSR/USA', *Journal of International Affairs* (Special issue), 1972:1.
Aspaturian, Vernon V., 'Soviet Global Power and the Correlation of Forces', *Problems of Communism*, May-June 1980.
Azovtsev, N., S. Gusarevich, 'Leninskie idei o edinom voennom lagere', *VIZh*, 1975:4.
Babich, Y., 'Strategiya politicheskogo avantyurizma', *KVS*, 1980:24.
Bagdasarov, S., 'Krushenie kolonialnoi sistemy kolonializma', *KVS*, 1975:15.
Ball, Desmond, 'The Future of Strategic Balance', in *Strategy and Defence*, Australian Essays, Desmond Ball, (ed.), Allen and Unwin, Sydney, London and Boston 1982.

Barnett, Roger W., 'Trans-Salt: Soviet Strategic Doctrine', *Orbis*, Summer 1975.

Belyi, P., 'V tiskakh neprimirimykh protivorechii', *KVS*, 1977:13.

Bennecke, Jürgen, 'Gleichgewicht. Eine Überlegung zum Jahresbeginn', *Europäische Wehrkunde*, 1981:1.

Bienen, Henry, 'African Military as Foreign Policy Actors', *International Security*, Fall 1980.

Bienen, Henry, 'Civil-Military Relations in the Third World', *International Political Science Review*, 1981:3.

Bogdanov, Radomir, Lev Semeiko, 'Soviet Military Might: A Soviet View', *Fortune*, 26 February 1979.

Bogdanov, R.G., 'Paritet ili "ustrashenie"?', *SShA*, 1984:10.

Bondarenko, V., 'Sovetskaya nauka i ukreplenie oborony strany', *KVS*, 1974:18.

Bondarenko, W., 'Das militärisch-wissenschaftliche Potential — Wesen und Hauptmerkmale', *Militärwesen*, 1982:3.

Bratishchev, I., 'Sovremennaya voina i ludskie resursy', *KVS*, 1971:22.

Brown, Harold, 'The Objective of US Strategic Forces' (Address by US Secretary of Defence), *Survival*, November/December 1980.

Brown, Thomas A., 'US and Soviet Strategic Force Levels: Problems of Assessment and Measurement', *The Annals of the American Academy of Political and Social Sciences*, September 1981.

Bull, Hedley, 'The Balance of Power and International Order', in *The Theory and Practice of International Relations*, Fred A. Somermann, David S. McLellan, William C. Olson, (eds), Prentice Hall, Englewood Cliffs, New Jersey 1979, 5th ed.

Burlatskii, F.M., 'Filosofiya mira', *Voprosy Filosofii*, 1982:12.

Burt, Richard, 'Reassessing the Strategic Balance', *International Security*, Summer 1980.

Butenko, A.P., 'Protivorechiya razvitiya sotsializma kak obshchestvennogo stroya', *Voprosy Filosofii*, 1982:10.

Bykov, O., 'Zakreplenie ravnovesiya ili stavka na prevoskhodstvo?', *MEMO*, 1981:11.

Bykov, O., 'Any Alternative to Military Equilibrium?', in *Peace and Disarmament*, N.N. Inozemtsev, (ed), 1982.

'Chairman Mao's Theory of the Differentiation of the Three Worlds is a Major Contribution to Marxism-Leninism', *Peking Review*, 4 November 1977, no. 45.

Charisius, A., 'Militärisches Gleichgewicht — Ausgangspunkt für militärische Entspannung', *Militärwesen*, 1981:3.

Charne, Leo, 'Ideology and the balance of power', *Annals of the American Academy of Political and Social Sciences*, March 1979.

Chevrov, Nikolai, 'Twisting Figures to Conceal the Truth', Comments on the Pentagon's provocative booklet 'Soviet Military Power', *APN*, 19 October 1981.

'Concerning the Dialectics of Categories'. The results of the work of an international Study Group, *World Marxist Review*, 1981:11.

Davis, K., Moore, W.B., 'Some Principles of Stratification', *American Sociological Review*, 1945:2.

Däniker, Gustav, 'Stabilisierung und Destabilisierung des strategischen Gleichgewichts seit 1945', *Europäische Wehrkunde*, 1981:5.

Deane, Michael J., 'The Soviet Assessment of the "Correlation of World Forces": Implications for American Foreign Policy', *Orbis*, Fall 1976.

Deane, Michael J., 'Soviet Perceptions of the Military Factor in the "Correlation of World Forces" ', in *International Perceptions of the Superpower Military Balance*, Donald C. Daniel, (ed.), 1978.

Dmitriev, A.P., 'Znaniya o voine i mire kak element mirovozzreniya', *Voprosy Filosofii*, 1978:5.

Dolgopolov, Y., 'Molodye armii i sotsialnyi progress', *KVS*, 1976:21.

Dolgopolov, Y., 'Vazhnyi politicheskii faktor: O roli armii v razvivayushchikhsya stranakh', *Krasnaya Zvezda*, 21 April 1978.

Dolgopolov, Y., 'Army and Social Progress', *SMR*, 1979:2.

Dornan, James E., 'US Strategic Concepts, SALT, and the Soviet Threat: A Primer', *Comparative Strategy*, 1979:3.

Ehrentreich, D., 'Zur Bedeutung und Methodik der Erläuterung des internationalen Kräfteverhältnisses', *Militärwesen*, 1980:5.

Ellsworth, Robert, 'Military Force and Political Influence in an Age of Peace', *The Atlantic Community*, 1976:2.

Ermath, Fritz, 'Contrasts in American and Soviet Strategic Thought', *International Security*, Fall 1979.

Federov, Yu, 'Globalnye problemy sovremennosti i razoruzhenie', *MEMO*, 1979:1.

Fedoseyev, P.N., 'Nekotorye metodologicheskie voprosy obshchestvennykh nauk', *Voprosy Filosofii*, 1979:11.

Fedoseyev, Piotr, 'The Dialectics of Social Life', *World Marxist Review*, 1981:9.

Filuyov, A., 'In the Labyrinth of Numbers', *IA*, 1974:7.

Foster, Richard B., 'From Assured Destruction to Assured Survival', *Comparative Strategy*, 1980:1.

Fyodorov, V., 'Non-Use of Force, a Fundamental Principle of International Relations', *IA*, 1985:2.

Galkin, A., 'Sotsialnaya struktura v traktovke burzhuaznoi obshchestvennoi nauki', *MEMO*, 1982:4.

Gantman, V., 'Class Nature of Present-Day International Relations', *IA*, 1969:9.

Gareyev, M., 'Military Science as an Important Factor of Defence Potential', *SMR*, 1976:12.

Garthoff, Raymond L., 'Mutual Deterrence and Strategic Arms Limitation in Soviet Policy', *International Security*, Summer 1978.

Garthoff, Raymond L., 'Soviet Views on the Interrelation of Diplomacy and Military Strategy', *Political Science Quarterly*, Fall 1979.

Gasteyger, C., 'Soviet Global Strategy', *NATO Review*, October 1977.

Geiling, K., 'Zur Bedeutung des militärischen Faktors in der Entwicklung des internationalen Kräfteverhältnisses', *Militärwesen*, 1982:3.

Glazunov, N., 'Strategicheskie kontseptsii i razvitie vooruzhennykh sil Severoatlanticheskogo soyuza', *VIZh*, 1978:11.

Gouré, Daniel, McCormick, Gordon H., 'Soviet Strategic Defence: The Neglected Dimension of the US-Soviet Balance', *Orbis*, Spring 1980.

Gray, Colin S., 'Soviet American strategic competition: Instruments, Doctrines and Purposes', in *Nuclear Strategy and Nuclear Security*, Robert J. Pranger, Roger P. Labrie, (eds), American Enterprise Institute, Washington, 1977.

Gray, Colin S., 'The strategic forces triad: End of the road?', *Foreign Affairs*, July 1978.

Gray, Colin S., 'Strategic Forces and SALT: A Question of Strategy', *Comparative Strategy*, 1980:2.

Gray, Colin S., 'Strategic Stability Reconsidered', *Daedalus*, Fall 1980.

Grewe, Wilhelm G., 'Machtvergleiche in der Weltpolitik. Kräfterelationen und Modelle der Konfliktvermeidung', *Merkur*, May 1980.

Grewe, Wilhelm G., 'Krafteverhältnis und Strategien der Supermächte im heutigen System der Weltpolitik', in *Kontinuitat und Wandel in den Ost-West Beziehungen*, Boris Meissner, Axel Seeberg, (eds), 1984.

Groll, D., 'Die Rolle der Streitkräfte in der nationalen Befreiungsbewegung', (Konsultation), *Militärwesen*, 1977:1.

Groll, K., K. Gleisberg, 'Zum wachsenden internationalen Einfluss sozialistischer Militärpolitik', *Militärwesen*, 1978:3.

Gromyko, A.A., 'V.I. Lenin i vneshnyaya politika Sovetskogo Gosudarstva', in *Za mir, razoruzhenie i bezopasnost' narodov*, Letopis' vneshnei politiki SSSR, Izd. Politicheskoi Literatury, Moscow, 1983.

'Andrei Gromyko Interviewed by Political Analysts', *IA*, 1985:2.

Hoffman, Heinz, 'Streitkräfte in unserer Zeit', *Einheit*, 1976:3.

Hoffman, Stanley, 'Weighing the Balance of Power, *Foreign Affairs*, July 1972.

Hoffman, Stanley, 'Notes on the Elusiveness of Modern Power', *International Journal*, Spring 1975.

Hoffman, Stanley, 'New Variations on Old Themes', *International Security*, Summer 1979.

Holloway, David, 'Military Power and Political Purpose in Soviet Policy', *Daedalus*, Fall 1980.

Howard, Michael, 'The Forgotten Dimensions of Strategy', *Foreign Affairs*, Summer 1979.

Howard, Michael, 'Social Change and the Defense of the West', in

NATO: The Next Thirty Years, Kenneth A. Myers, (ed.), Westview Press, Boulder, Colorado, 1979, 1980.

Husband, William B., 'Soviet Perceptions of US "Position-of-Strength" Diplomacy in the 1970s', *World Politics*, July 1979.

Inozemtsev, N.N. 'O kharaktere protivorechii v nashu epokhu', *Problemy mira i sotsializma*, 1973:9.

Inozemtsev, N.N., 'O novom etape v razvitii mezhdunarodnykh otnoshenii', *Kommunist*, 1973:13.

Inozemtsev, N.N., 'Sotsializm i globalnye problemy sovremennosti', *Pravda*, January 1979 ('Socialism and today's global problems', *Socialism — theory and practice*, 1979:4).

Inozemtsev, N.N., 'Nauchno-tekhnicheskaya revolutsiya i uglublenie ekonomicheskikh i sotsialno-politicheskikh protivorechii kapitalizma na sovremennom etap, *MEMO*, 1979:7.

'The International and the National in the Working Class Movement'. A survey of proceedings at the international theoretical conference, *World Marxist Review*, 1981:8, 9 and 10.

Iovchuk, S., V. Andreyev, 'Socialist Community: 40 years of Peaceful Construction and Fraternal Cooperation', *IA*, 1985:6.

Jacobsen, C.G., 'Soviet strategic objectives for the 1980's, *The World Today*, April 1979.

Jahn, Egbert, 'The Role of the Armament Complex in Soviet Society (Is There a Soviet Military-Industrial Complex?)', *Journal of Peace Research*, 1975:3.

Janowitz, Morris, 'Towards a Redefinition of Military Strategy in International Relations', *World Politics*, July 1974.

Jervis, Robert, 'Why Nuclear Superiority Doesn't Matter', *Political Science Quarterly*, Winter 1979—80.

Kaltefleiter, Werner, 'The Resource War: The Need for a Western Strategy', *Comparative Strategy*, 1983:1.

Kapchenko, N., 'Scientific Principles of Soviet Foreign Policy', *IA*, 1977:10.

Kapchenko, N., 'The Problem of Preserving Peace and the Ideological Struggle', *IA*, 1983:7.

Kapchenko, N., 'Marxist-Leninist Methodology of Analyzing International Relations and Foreign Policy', *IA*, 1984:7.

Karabanov, N.V., 'K voprosu o marksistsko-leninskoi teorii mira', *Nauchnyi Kommunizm*, 1978:2.

Karenin, A.A., 'Teoriya "balansa sil" ', *Voprosy istorii*, 1975:2.

Kashlev, Y., Kolosov, Y., 'Psychological Warfare — A Weapon of Reaction', *IA*, 1983:10.

Kashlev, Y., 'Ideological and Propaganda Subversion Against Socialist Countries — A Weapon of Imperialism', *IA*, 1984:1.

Katasonov, Y.N., 'Voenno-politcheskaya strategiya SShA na rubezhe 70-80kh godov', *SShA*, 1980:2.

Katasonov, Y., 'Military and Political Strategy of the USA Today', *IA*, 1983:11.

'Kategorii voennoi nauki', in *Sovetskaya Voennaya Entsiklopediya*, vol. 4, pp. 121—22.

Keil, S., 'Zur Rolle der Gewalt in gegenwärtigen Kampf um die Sicherung des Friedens', *Militärwesen*, 1979:8.

Khalipov, V., 'Sovremennyi mirovoi revolutsionnyi protsess: kharakter i zakonomernosti', *KVS*, 1974:3.

Khalipov, V., 'Sovremennaya epokha i ee osnovnoe protivorechie', *KVS*, 1975:9.

Khibrikov, N., 'Krushenie kolonialnoi sistemy imperializma. Osvobodivshiesya strany Azii, Afriki i Latinskoi Ameriki', *KVS*, 1978:6.

Khmara, N., 'Nekotorye osobennosti grazhdanskikh voin v sovremennuyu epokhu', *KVS*, 1974:16.

Khokke, E., G. Kissling, V. Sheler, 'Voina i mir kak filosofskaya problema sovremennosti', in *Metodologicheskie problemy zashchity mira i sovremennost*, 1979.

Khrushchev, N.S., 'Za novye pobedy mirovogo kommunisticheskogo dvizheniya', *Kommunist*, 1960:1.

Kiessling, Gottfried, Wolfgang Scheler, 'Friedenskampf und politisch-moralische Wertung des Krieges', *Deutsche Zeitschrift für Philosophie* (DDR), 1976:1.

Kim, G., 'Sotsializm i sovremennye natsionalno-osvoboditelnye revolutsii', *MZh*, 1977:7.

Kim, G., 'Ideological Struggle Concerning the Newly-Free States' Road of Development', *IA*, 1984:1.

Kirshin, Y.Y., 'Mirovaya politika: sushchnost', osnovnye cherty i tendentsii' *Voprosy Filosofii*, 1982:12.

Klopper, I., 'Kampfkraft und Kräfteverhältnis im Luftkampf der Gegenwart', *Militärwesen*, 1982:3.

Knorr, Klaus, 'On the International Uses of Military Force in the Contemporary World', *Orbis*, Spring 1977.

Kodachenko, A., 'Newly-free countries: a strategy of independent development?', *IA*, 1984:2.

Kokoshin, A.A., 'Diskussii po tsentralnym voprosam voennoi politiki SShA', *SShA*, 1985:2.

Kondratkov, T., 'Problema klassifikatsii voin i ee otrazhenie v ideologicheskoi bor'be, *KVS*, 1974:11.

Kondratkov, T., 'Moralno-politicheskii potentsial voennoi moshchi Sovetskogo gosudarstva', *VIZh*, 1982:3.

Konoplev, V., Kovalev, V., 'O roli vooruzhennykh sil v sovremennom obshchestve', *KVS*, 1971:4.

Konstantinov, F.B., 'Razum i bezumie v sovremennom mire', *Voprosy Filosofii*, 1980:4.

Korotkov, V., 'New Factors in International Relations and Bourgeois Politology', *IA*, 1977:9.

Kortunov, V., 'The Leninist Policy of Peaceful Coexistence and Class Struggle', *IA*, 1979:5.

Kortunov, V., 'War and Politics in the Nuclear Age', *IA*, 1981:6.

Kortunov, V., 'The Ideology of Peace Versus the Ideology of War', *IA*, 1983:11.

Kovalev, A.A. 'Eskalatsiya razryadki i deeskalatsiya konfliktov', *SShA*, 1979:4.

Kovalsky, N., 'Religious Forces Against War Threat', *IA*, 1983:7.

Kölsch, Hans, 'Fragen des Kräfteverhältnisses im Kampf der Arbeiterklasse', *Deutsche Zeitschrift für Philosophie*, 1976:2.

Krehbiel, Carl C., 'Military Asymmetries in the Soviet-American Strategic Balance', *RUSI*, June 1980.

Krell, Gert, 'Die Entwicklung des Sicherheitsbegriffs', *Beiträge zur Konfliktforschung*, 1980:3.

Kuczynski, Janusz, 'Philosophische Aspekte von Krieg und Frieden', *Deutsche Zeitschrift für Philosophie* (DDR), 1976:12.

Kulish, V.M., 'Detente, International Relations and Military Might', *Co-existence*, 1977:2.

Kulish, V., 'Socialist International Relations: Substance and Development Trends', *IA*, 1983:7.

Kuz'min, E., ' "Politicheskii pluralism" — maskirovka vlasti monopoli', *MEMO*, 1983:11.

Lambeth, Benjamin S., 'The Political Potential of Soviet Equivalence', *International Security*, Fall 1979.

Lebedev, N., 'The Dialectics of the Development of International Relations', *IA*, 1980:9.

Lebedev, A., S. Gribanov, 'Lenin's Concept of Peaceful Coexistence, and Present-Day World', *IA*, 1984:5.

Lebow, Richard Ned, 'Misconceptions in American Strategic Assessment', *Political Science Quarterly*, Summer 1982.

Legvold, Robert, 'The Nature of Soviet Power', *Foreign Affairs*, October, 1977.

Legvold, Robert, 'Strategic "Doctrine" and SALT: Soviet and American Views', *Survival*, January/February 1979.

Lehman, Christopher M., Hughes, Peter C., ' *"Equivalence" and SALT II'*, *Orbis*, Winter 1977.

'Lokalnye voiny i ikh mesto v globalnoistrategii imperializma', Shabrov, I., (ed), I-II, *VIZh*, 1975:3-4.

Lukava, G., 'Sovetskaya voennaya nauka i boevaya gotovnost', *KVS*, 1984:2.

Lukava, G., 'Voennoe ravnovesie i bezopasnost'narodov', *KVS*, 1984:23.

Mackintosh, Malcolm, 'The East-West Military Balance and Soviet

Defence Policy', *Brassey's Annual,* 1972.

Maier, L., 'Dialektik der Anpassung: Zu einigen neuen Problemen der Imperialismus-Analyse', *Einheit,* 1972:4.

'Marksistsko-leninskoe uchenie o voine i armii', in *Sovetskaya Voennaya Entsiklopediya,* Moscow, 1978, vol. 5.

Martin, Alexander, 'Kriterien des internationalen Kräfteverhältnisses', *Deutsche Aussenpolitik,* 1975:11.

Martin, Alexander, 'Wirkungen und Dynamik des internationalen Kräfteverhältnisses zwischen Sozialismus und Imperialismus', *Deutsche Aussenpolitik,* 1977:7.

Martin, Lawrence, 'The Role of Military Force in the Nuclear Age', in *Strategic Thought in the Nuclear Age,* Hossein Amirsadeghi, (gen. ed.), 1979.

Matveyev, V., 'The Inadmissability of Nuclear War — The Imperative of the Times', *IA,* 1983:7.

Matveyev, V., 'Ideology of Aggression: the Essence of Washington's Diplomacy', *IA,* 1984:1.

Mazing, V.A., S.K. Oznobishchev, 'Pentagon: kurs na dostizhenie voennogo prevoskhodstva', *SShA,* 1983:7.

McLucas, John L, 'Betrachtungen zum strategischen Kräfteverhältnis', *Wehrkunde,* 1974:3.

McNamara, Robert, 'The Declining Strength of the Soviets', *Guardian,* 9 August, 1982.

Melnikov, Y., 'Rol' armii v osvobodivshikhsya stranakh Afriki', *VIZh,* 1982:6.

Menshikov, S., 'Militarism and World Politics Today', *IA,* 1984:2.

Menshikov, S., 'Interconnection of Politics and Economics in World Relations Today', *IA,* 1984:11.

Michl, A., 'Sozialistische Militärmacht und der Kampf um militärische Entspannung', *Militärwesen,* 1976:12.

Migolatyev, A., 'Progress mezhdunarodnykh otnoshenii i protivniki razryadki', *KVS,* 1975:21.

Migolatyev, A., 'Reaktsionnyi kharakter sovremennykh burzhuaznykh teorii voiny i mira', *KVS,* 1978:6.

Mikhailov, A., 'Maoistskie "doctriny" voiny, mira i revolutsii', *KVS,* 1980:22.

Mikhailov, V., Yu. Khudyakov, 'Imperialisticheskie armii i voennye bloki', *KVS,* 1975:16.

Milovidov, A.S., Y.A. Zhdanov, 'Sotsialno-filosofskie problemy Woiny i mira', *Voprosy filosofii,* 1980:10.

Milshtein, M., 'Amerikanskie voennye doktriny: preemstvennost' i modifikatsii', *MEMO,* 1971:8.

Mirskii, G.I., 'Rol' armii v sotsialnom razvitii Azii i Afriki', *Voprosy Filosofii,* 1979:3.

Mirsky, Georgy I., 'The Role of the Army in the Sociopolitical Development of Asian and African Countries', *International Political Science Review*, 1981:3.

Morozov, Y., 'Klassovyi kharakter sovetskoi vneshnei politiki', *KVS*, 1975:19.

Morozov, V., S. Tyushkevich, 'O sisteme zakonov voennoi nauki i printsipov voennogo iskusstva', *Voennaya Mysl'*, 1967:3.

Müller, W., 'Zur Verfälschung der Rolle der Streitkräfte im Klassengesellschaft durch bürgerliche Ideologen', *Militärwesen*, 1977:5.

'National Security Policy for the 1980s', *The Annals of the American Academy of Political and Social Sciences*, Robert L. Pfaltzgraff, (Special Editor), September 1981.

Nekrasov, V., 'Realities of Modern Europe and "Atlanticism" ', *IA*, 1984:5.

Nezhinsky, L., 'An Alliance for World Peace and Security (On the 30th Anniversary of the Warsaw Treaty Organization)', *IA*, 1985:6.

Nikitin, N., 'Evolution of US Military Doctrine and Strategic Concepts After World War II', *VIZh*, 1977:4.

Nitze, Paul, 'Assuring Strategic Stability in an Era of Détente', *Foreign Affairs*, January 1976.

Obminsky, E., 'Proponents and Opponents of Restructuring International Economic Relations', *IA*, 1984:7.

Ogarkov, N., 'Voennaya nauka i zashchita sotsialisticheskogo otechestva', *Kommunist*, 1978:7.

Ogarkov, N., 'Na strazhe mirnogo truda', *Kommunist*, 1981:10.

Osadczuk-Korab, Bogdan Alexander, 'Das sowjetische Konzept des internationalen Kräfteverhältnisses', in *Kontinuität und Wandel in den Ost-West Beziehungen*, 1984.

Parsons, T., 'A Revised Analytical Approach to the Theory of Social Stratification', in *Essays in Sociological Theory*, Glencoe, 1964.

Petersen, Phillip, 'American Perception of Soviet Military Power', *Parameters*, January-April 1978.

Petrovski, V.F., 'Silovoi faktor v globalnoi strategii SShA', *SShA*, 1979:5.

Petrovsky, V., 'Disarmament and the Political and Ideological Struggle', *IA*, 1984:1.

Petrovskii, V.F., 'Strategicheskoe ravnovesie − neobkhodimoe uslovie bezopasnogo mira, *SShA*, 1985:7.

Pfaltzgraff, Robert L., 'Soviet Military Strategy and Force Level's in *The Soviet Union in World Politics*, Kurt London, (ed.), 1980.

Pfaltzgraff, Robert L., 'The Superpower Relationship and US National Security Policy in the 1980s', *The Annals of the American Academy of Political and Social Sciences*, 1981.

Platonov, A., 'Military Balance and Peace', *IA*, 1982:2.

Platonov, A., 'Peace and Security of States', *IA*, 1984:7.

Platonov, A., 'Militarization of Outer Space — A Threat to Mankind', *IA*, 1985:2.

Plekhov, A., 'Armiya v politicheskoi sisteme razvitogo sotsializma', *KVS*, 1982:17.

Pletnikov, Yu. K., 'Social Relations', in *Philosophy in the USSR*, 1981.

Puchkovsky, M., 'Anticommunism — Imperialism's Weapon in the Struggle Against Peace and Progress', *IA*, 1983:4.

Punanov, I., 'Neravnomernost' razvitiya kapitalizma - istochnik protivorechii v agressivnykh voennykh blokakh', *KVS*, 1963:12.

Ra'anan, Uri, 'Soviet Strategic Doctrine and the Soviet-American Global Contest', *The Annals of the American Academy of Political and Social Sciences*, 1981.

Razin, V.I., 'The Political Organization of Society', in *Philosophy in the USSR*, 1981.

Reynolds, P.A., 'The Balance of Power: New Wine in an Old Bottle', *Political Studies*, 1975:2, 3.

Rodin, V., 'Nekotorye voprosy proiskhozhdeniya i razvitiya voennykh soyuzov, *VIZh*, 1975:2.

Rumyantsev, N., 'Agressivnye voenno-politicheskie bloki imperialisticheskikh gosudarstv', *KVS*, 1984:2.

Rybakov, O., Y. Shiryayev, 'New Frontiers of Socialist Economic Integration', *IA*, 1984:9.

Rybkin, Y., 'Sotsiologicheskii analiz istorii voin: osnovnye kategorii', *Voprosy Istorii KPSS*, 1973:1.

Rybkin, Y., 'Pravda o voine — oruzhie mira', *KVS*, 1977:10.

Rybkin, Y., 'XXV s'ezd KPSS i osvoboditelnye voiny sovremennoi epokhi', *VIZh*, 1978:11.

Rybkin, Y., 'Armiya v politicheskoi sisteme razvitogo sotsializma', *VIZh*, 1982:2.

Rybkin, Y., 'Modern International Relations in the Light of the Marxist-Leninist Theory on War and Peace', *IA*, 1983:5.

Rybkin, Y., S. Kortunov, 'Military Parity as a Factor of Security', *IA*, 1982:8.

Rybkin, Y., S. Kortunov, I. Tyulin, 'Anatomiya odnogo burzhuaznogo mifa', *MEMO*, 1982:8.

Rybkin, Y., A. Migolatyev, 'The Ideology of Present-Day Militarism', *IA*, 1974:7.

Ryzhkov, N., 'New Stage in Cooperation Between Fraternal Parties and States', *IA*, 1984:9.

Sanakoyev, Sh., 'Foreign Policy of Socialism: Sources and Theory', *IA*, 1975:5.

Sanakoyev, Sh., 'The Alignment of World Forces: How to Prevent Nuclear War?', *IA*, 1983:4.

Sanakoyev, Sh., 'Historical Optimism of the Policy and Ideology of Peace', *IA*, 1984:1.

Sapozhnikov, Boris G., 'National and Social Functions of the Armed Forces in the Class Society in the Orient'. A report on the XI International Political Science Association World Congress, Moscow, 1979.

Sarkesian, Sam C., 'A Political Perspective on Military Power in Developing Areas', in *The Military and Security in the Third World*, Sheldon W. Simon, (ed.), 1978.

Sawjalow, I., 'Der Verteidigungscharakter der sowjetischen Militärdoktrin', *Militärwesen*, 1981:9.

Schilling, Walter, 'Die sowjetische Einschätzung der internationalen Machtverteilung', *Europäische Wehrkunde*, 1979:9.

Schilling, Warner R., 'US Strategic Nuclear Concepts in the 1970s: The Search for Sufficiently Equivalent Countervailing Parity', *International Security*, Fall 1981.

Schmidt, 'Militärstrategische Gleichgewicht, politische und militärische Entspannung', *IPW Berichte*, October 1980.

Schönherr, S., 'Das ökonomische Potential — Grundlage für die militärische Stärke des Sozialismus', *Militärwesen*, 1980:12.

Semeiko, Lev, 'SALT-2 Treaty: Priority of Political Aspects and Parity of Strategic Interests', *Current Research on Peace and Violence*, 1980:2.

Semenov, V.S., 'Problema protivorechii v usloviyakh sotsializma', I-II, *Voprosy Filosofii*, 1982:7, 9.

Semin, V., 'Voenno-politicheskii oboronitelnyi soyuz stran sotsializma i boevoe sodruzhestvo ikh vooruzhennykh sil kak ob'ekt issledovaniya', *VIZh*, 1982:7.

Semyonov, V.S., 'The Ensemble of Social Structures and the Social Structure of Society', in *Philosophy in the USSR*, 1981.

Semyonov, Yu. I., 'Socio-Economic Formations in the Historical Process', in *Philosophy in the USSR*, 1981.

Serebryannikov, V.V., 'K voprosu o roli armii v zhizni obshchestva (Kritika sovremennykh burzhuaznykh kontseptsii)', *Voprosy Filosofii*, 1982:12.

Sergiyev, A., 'Leninism on the Correlation of Forces as a Factor of International Relations', *IA*, 1975:5.

Shakhnazarov, G., 'O sootnoshenii sil v mire', *Kommunist*, 1974:3.

Shakhnazarov, G., 'Deistvennye faktory mezhdunarodnykh otnoshenii', *MZh*, 1977:1.

Shakhnazarov, G., 'O nekotorykh kontseptsiyakh mira i mirovogo poryadka', *MEMO*, 1980:11.

Shishkin, G., 'Nuclear War Propaganda in the USA and Washington's Imperial Ambitions', *IA*, 1984:1.

Shmelev, N.P., 'Marksizm o yedinstve vsemirnogo khozyaystva. Retrospektsiya i sovremennost', *SShA*, 1983:12.

Sidelnikov, I., 'Komu i dla chego nuzhno voennoe prevoskhodstvo?',

Krasnaya Zvezda, 15 January 1980 (German translation, 'Wem und wozu dient militärische Überlegenheit?', *Militärwesen*, 1980:4).

Simonyan, R., 'Kontseptsiya "strategicheskoi dostatochnosti" ', *Krasnaya Zvezda*, 24 August 1976.

Simonyan, R., 'Voiny glazami Pentagona', *Krasnaya Zvezda*, 27 May 1976.

Simonyan, R. 'Kontseptsiya "vybora tselei" ', *Krasnaya Zvezda*, 18 September 1976.

Skrylnik, A., 'Ideology and War', *SMR*, 1976:7.

Slobodenko, A., 'The Strategy of Nuclear Adventurism', *IA*, 1981:1.

Slobodenko, A., 'Soviet Military Threat Myth: Attempts to Tip the Military Strategic Balance', *IA*, 1984:1.

Smolyan, G.L., 'Printsipy issledovaniya konflikta', *Voprosy Filosofii*, 1968:8.

'The Soviet View of East-West Correlation of Forces'. Seminar by Prof. Michael Voslensky, minutes by N. Friedman, Hudson Institute, New York, 24 February 1976.

Sredin, G.V., 'Marxist-Leninist Doctrine on War and Army', *SMR*, 1978:1.

Sredin, G.V., 'Leninskoe uchenie o mire, voine, armii i sovremennost', *Voprosy Filosofii*, 1980:4.

'Strategiya voennaya', in *Sovetskaya Voennaya Entsiklopediya*, vol. 7, Moscow, 1979.

Stratmann, K. Peter, 'Probleme der Bewertung der militärischen Optionen der NATO und des Warschauer Pakts in Europa', in *Rüstungskontrolle und Sicherheit in Europa*, Erhard Forndran, Paul J. Friedrich, (eds.), 1979.

Stratmann, K. Peter, 'Das "eurostrategische" Kräfteverhältnis', *Europa-Archiv*, 1981:13.

Subarev, W., 'Die Entwicklung der Theorie der Verteidigung des Sozialismus', *Militärwesen*, 1976:9.

Sumbatyan, Y., 'Armii politicheskoi sistemy natsionalnoi demokratsii', *Narody Azii i Afriki*, 1964:4.

Sumbatyan, Y., 'The Army in the Developing Countries', *SMR*, 1975:8.

Sumbatyan, Y., 'Mirovoi revolutsionnyi protsess, ego cherty i dvizhushchie sily', *KVS*, 1976:21.

Sumbatyan, Y., 'Sotsialism i natsionalno-osvoboditelnoe dvizhenie', *Krasnaya Zvezda*, 25 August, 1977.

Tabunov, N., 'Ideinoe protivoborstvo dvukh sistem', *KVS*, 1980:6.

Thee, Marek, 'The Deterrence Myth and Historical Analysis', *Bulletin of Peace Proposals*, 1979:1.

Timofeev, T.T., 'Realizatsiya Programmy mira i nekotorye voprosy ideologicheskoi bor'by', *Voprosy Filosofii*, 1976:1.

Timorin, A., 'Vooruzhennye sily zrelogo sotsialisticheskogo obshchestva: osobennosti i osnovnye tendentsii razvitiya', *KVS*,

1975:20.

Timorin, A., 'V.I.ˉ Lenin, KPSS o sotsialnoi prirode i istoricheskom naznachenii Sovetskikh Vooruzhennykh Sil', *VIZh*, 1980:6.

Tolkunov, L., 'Ideological Struggle and Peaceful Coexistence Today', *IA*, 1984:1.

Tolkunov, L., 'Detente Can and Must Be Restored', *IA*, 1985:2.

Tomilin, Y., 'Curbing the Arms Race: The Road to Peace and Progress', *IA*, 1984:2.

Topornin, A., 'The Balance of Power Doctrine and Washington', *SShA*, 1970:11.

Trofimenko, G., 'From Confrontation to Coexistence', *IA*, 1975:10.

Trofimenko, G.A., 'Strategicheskie metaniya Vashingtona', *SShA: Ekonomika, Politika, Ideologiya*, 1980:12.

Trofimenko, G.A., 'Voennaya strategiya SShA — orudie agressivnoi politiki', *SShA*, 1985:1.

Trofimenko, Henry, 'The "Theology" of Strategy', *Orbis*, Fall 1977.

Trofimenko, Henry A., 'Counterforce: Illusion of a Panacea', *IS*, Spring 1981.

Troitsky, I., 'Socialist-Oriented Countries: The National Question', *IA*, 1977:4.

Tyagunenko, V., 'Mirovoi sotsializm i natsionalno-osvoboditelnye revolutsii', *Kommunist*, 1973:8.

Tyulin, I., 'Ob odnoi iz burzhuaznykh "teorii" mezhdunarodnykh otnoshenii', *MEMO*, 1977:8.

Tyushkevich, S., 'Balance of Forces in Armed Struggle', *SMR*, 1968:4.

Tyushkevich, S., 'Sootnoshenie sil v mire i faktory predotvrashcheniya voiny', *KVS*, 1974:10.

Tyushkevich, S., 'Istochniki voin — mnimye i deistvitelnye', *KVS*, 1979:15.

Tyushkevich, S., 'Leninskaya politika mira i mify antikommunizma', *KVS*, 1981:13.

Ustinov, Dmitri, 'Answers of USSR Defence Minister, Marshal of the Soviet Union, Dmitri Ustinov, to Questions of TASS correspondent'. *Pra-APN*, 7 December 1982.

Vasilenkov, E., 'European Security — A Major Prerequisite for World Peace', *IA*, 1985:2.

Vidyasova, L., 'Militant Anticommunism: the Basis of Washington's Reckless Course', *IA*, 1984:1.

'Voennaya nauka', in *Sovetskaya Voennaya Entsiklopediya*, Moscow, 1976, vol. 2.

'Voina', in *Sovetskaya Voennaya Entsiklopediya*, Moscow, 1976, vol.2.

Volkogonov, D.A. 'Militarizm i vneshnyaya politika imperializma', *Voprosy Filosofii*, 1974:10.

Volkogonov, D.A., 'Nesostoyatelnost' burzhuznykh kontseptsii prichin voin', *Voennyi Vestnik*, 1976:3.

Volkogonov, D., 'Ideologicheskaya bor'ba v usloviyakh razryadki', *KVS*, 1977:3.

Volkogonov, D.A., 'Klassovaya bor'ba i sovremennost', *KVS*, 1979:4.

Volkogonov, D., Arbatov, G.A., 'On Some New Tendencies in the Development of American Military-Strategic Concepts', *SShA*, 1976:4.

Vorob'ev, K., 'Armiya i sotsialnyi progress', *Krasnaya Zvezda*, 6 September 1979.

Voslensky, Michael, 'The Correlation of Forces: The Soviet View'. Paper presented for Peace Science Society, Conference in Zurich, 1975.

Waltz, Kenneth N., 'The Stability of a Bipolar World', *Daedalus*, Summer 1974.

Welch, Claude E., 'Civil-Military Relations: Perspectives for the Third World', *Armed Forces and Society*, Winter 1985.

Weltman, John J., 'On the Obscolescence of War', *International Studies Quarterly*, December 1974.

Wessell, Nils H., 'Soviet Views of Multipolarity and the Emerging Balance of Power', *Orbis*, Winter 1979.

Wettig, Gerhard, 'Abschreckungstheorie und Gleichgewichtskonzept', *Information für die Truppe*, 1979:11.

Wimmer, Ernst, 'The Middle Strata and Its Revolutionary Movement', *World Marxist Review*, 1979:11.

Wohlstetter, Albert, 'Is There a Strategic Arms Race?', *Foreign Policy*, 1974:15.

Wohlstetter, Albert, 'Rivals, but no "Race" ', *Foreign Policy*, 1974:16.

Yagodovsky, L., I. Chelyshev, 'Formation of the World Socialist System', in *The Struggle of USSR for Peace and Security*, 1984.

Yasyukov, M., 'Obshchestvennyi progress i voennoe nasilie', *KVS*, 1973:12.

Yeremin, Yu. Ye., 'Democracy and Classes', in *Philosophy in the USSR*, 1981.

Zaitsev, A., 'Sovetskoe sotsialisticheskoe gosudarstvo — glavnoe orudie postroeniya kommunizma i zashchity ot imperialisticheskoi agressii', *KVS*, 1976:24.

Zhilin, P., 'Voennaya istoriya i sovremennost, *VIZh*, 1975:5.

Zhilin, P., Y. Rybkin, 'Militarism and Contemporary International Relations', *IA*, 1973:10.

Zhurkin, V.V., 'Strategiya yadernoi agressii', *SShA*, 1984:9.

Zhukov, Y., I. Melnikov, 'An Imperative: Actions Capable of Making a Durable Peace — Reality', *IA*, 1984:7.

Ziborov, G., 'Ideological Sabotage — An Instrument of Imperialist Policies', *IA*, 1984:4.

Name index

Subject index

187, 277, 283, 305, 306; d. as 'the law of our times' 282
Deterrence 232, 239, 251, 287, 289, 293, 297, 298, 299, 301, 325; 'deterrence parity' 237, 330; extended d. 296; mutual d. 297, 300
Development through evolution theories *48—50*
Disarmament 100, 251, 276

EEC (European Economic Community) 174
EFTA (European Free Trade Association) 174
'Economic determinism' 23
Equilibrium theories of social system *45—8*
Ethiopia 182, 278
Europe 146, 149, 220, 244, 276, 285, 288, 294, 300, 303, 317, 318, 323, 325, 331; Central E. 170, 327, 332, 340; Eastern E. 39, 103, 207, 208, 244, 327, 340; Southern E. 126
Eurostrategic Nuclear Balance 275

Far East 126, 234, 244
February Revolution in Russia 103, 110
Force posture (military posture) 321; American *290—306*; Soviet 303, 310
'Forces of social renovation' 154, 155
Formation (structure), socio-economic 12, 13, 22, 31, 39—42, 50, 55, 64, 65, 66, 74—5, 82, 107, 116, 123, 128, 142, 148, 150; primitive 83; slave-owning 39; feudal 39; capitalist 39; socialist (communist) 39, 50; transitory 40
France 100, 105, 172, 180

General purpose forces 238, 275
Germany 41, 218; West Germany 91, 100, 171, 180, 319; German Democratic Republic 304, 319
Greece 100, 104

'Hegemony of the proletariat' 93—4
Helsinki Agreement 278
Hungary 135, 293

Ideology 16, 18, 22, 28, 29, 42, 52, 69, 100, 124, 128, 132, 147, 151, 157, *159—63*, 166, 210, 218, 221, 235, 305; ideological struggle 42, 65, *159—63*
Incalculable (uncertain) risk, principle of 330
Indian Peninsula 126
Indicators of weapons systems *320—21*, 331
'Industria' 47
Inevitability of war, theory of 144, 186, 282; of world war 210
Intelligentsia 26, 96, 97, *99-101*, 107, 111, 129
Interests, social 82—6; national 82—6, 105, 131, 133—4, 136—7, 164, 187; international 133—4, 164; class 187
Intermediate (middle) social strata 86, 89, 91, 94, 95, *96—101*, 102, 107, 111, 114; 'single middle class' 97, 98
Internal mechanism in world socialism *159—65;* in world capitalism *165—70*
International ('world') classes 5, 85, 86, 132, 146, 211; international bourgeoisie 38, 85, 129, 141, 147, 149, 177, 208, 340; international work-

ing class 123, 129, 132, 141, 147, 149, 165, 177, 205, 208

International conflicts *179—81*, 219, 236, 343

International division of labour 187

International revolutionary (communist, workers') movement 131, 133, 137, 147, 148, 150, 151, 154, 164, 165, 166, 176, 201, 205, 219

Internationalism, proletarian *131—7*, 143, *164—5*; 'socialist' 132

Iran 343; Iranian revolution 182

Islamic countries 145

Italy 100

Japan 36, 41, 91, 100, 125, 148, 163, 171, 173, 174, 180, 200, 201, 216, 220, 234, 293

Kenya 208

Laos 234

Latin America 108, 155, 182, 200, 205, 215, 220

Laws, dialectical 10, 11, 12, 13, 43, 63, 151, 152

Laws, social: general sociological (laws of social development, of history) 13, 20, 31, 34, 41, 42, 43, 44, 45, 46, 48, 49, 67, 76, 93, 135, 152, 163, 166, 168, 178, 188, 214, 220, 284, 289; law of the necessary correspondence of the relations of production to the forces of production 128, 134; 'law of peaceful coexistence' 186; law of the uneven economic and political development of capitalist countries 31, 87, 96, 115, *170—71*, 211

Laws of war and warfare: 251—

2, *255—67*; general laws of war *256—63*; basic law of war 261—3; general laws of warfare 256, *263—7*, 268

League of Nations 202

Libya 341

MBFR (Mutual Balance Force Reductions) 332

MURFAAMCE (Mutual Reduction of Forces and Armaments and Associated Measures 332

Maoism 207, 208

Mass media 68, 162, 201

Mediterranean 126

Mexico 100

Middle East 126, 234, 319

Militarism 103, 160, 161; military regimes 104

Military art 234, 247, 266, 268, 321, 331, 333

Military doctrine 333, 345; American *290—306*, 310; Soviet 310

Military-industrial complex 290, 305

Military policy 6, 313; American *290—306*, Soviet 310

Military potential 29, 246, *248—9*, 257, 258, 259, 260, 316

Military power 127, 146, 153, 158, 159, 200, 216, 217, 220, 243, 245, 246, 247, 249, 251, 258, 260, 291, 304, 305, 341

Military theory 250, 256, 257, 268, 290, 303

Mongolia 167

Multipolarity of power 126, 216, 218, 221

NATO, Western Alliance 126, 146, 153, 173, 174, 180, 187, 219, 234, 239, 244, 251, 274, 276, 293, 298, 301, 310, 311, 312, 317, 318, 319, 320, 323,

Protection of environment 145, 164
Psychological warfare *160–63*

Racism 160
Red Army 300
Reformist ideology 93
Reforms, social, democratic 51, 96
Restructuring of international relations 172, 179, *183–4*
Revolution 17, 18, 21, 22, 32, 33, 35, 36, 38, 40, 41, 42, 48, 50, 51, 52, 53, 82, 83, 88, 90, 91, 92, 94, 102, 107, 115, 131, 134, 135, 136, 137, 142, 170, 171, 172, 179, 162, 183, 202, 281; anti-colonial 155, 202; national 172, 179, 182, 281; scientific-technical 25, 51, 166, 167, 186, 303; world revolution 32–6, 141, 205
Revolution of 1905 in Russia 110, 111
Revolutionary movement 21, 34
'Rolling back' Communism, policy of 291, 292
Romania 341
Russia 30, 116, 170

SALT (Strategic Arms Limitation Talks) 184, 185; SALT I 315; SALT II 286, 315
Sahara 108
Scandinavia 126
Social development 9, 11, 13, 14, 40–2, 43–5; mechanisms 45–55; d. through class struggle 48–50; d. through revolution versus d. through evolution 50–53; the resolution of the basic conflict versus ubiquity of conflicts 53–5
Social democrats, soc. dem. movement 50, 51, 91, 147, 149, 201
Social liberation struggle 16
Social systems, analysis of *42–55*
South Yemen 277
Soviet Union 15, 17, 37, 38, 69, 70, 125, 135, 142, 143, 149, 150, 151, 152, 153, 154, 155, 156, 161, 162, 167, 168, 169, 177, 178, 182, 183, 184, 185, 200, 205, 206, 207, 208, 209, 212, 213, 214, 216, 219, 220, 235, 237, 239, 244, 274–306, 310, 311, 317, 318, 323, 324, 327, 329, 331, 332, 340, 341, 345
Soviets of Workers' and Soldiers' Deputies 111
Spain 104, 105
Status quo, international world 35, 46, 49, 151, 202, 220, 285, 287; in Europe 278; domestic 46, 49, 85, 113, 202
Strategic defence forces 275
Strategic Defence Initiative 296, 297
Strategy: of assured destruction 300; of mutual assured destruction (MAD) 296; counterforce 300; mixed counterforce /countercity 296; flexible response 239, 292, 330; massive retaliation 291–2; Limited Nuclear Options 295, 301; realistic deterrence 293, 294; indirect 294
Stratification of society, theories of 112
Structural functionalism *46–8*
'Subjective-idealistic' approach 44
Superiority 237, 284, 289, 298, 323, 329, 330, 344; military 185, 214, 236, 261, 274–5, 276–7, 284, 285, 287, 288,